TIME WITHOUT WORK

TIME
WITHOUT
WORK

People who are not working tell their stories
How they feel • What they do • How they survive

WALLI F. LEFF
MARILYN G. HAFT

SOUTH END PRESS
BOSTON

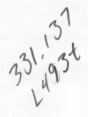

The quotation on page 144 from *Look Homeward, Angel* by Thomas Wolfe is used with the permission of Charles Scribner's Sons copyright © 1929; renewed 1957 by Edward C. Aswell, Administrator, C.T.A. and/or Fred W. Wolfe.

Verses from the last stanza of "Nevertheless" are reprinted by permission of Macmillan Company from *Collected Poems* by Marianne Moore copyright © 1984 and renewed 1972 by Marianne Moore.

The quotation on page 189 is from *Escape From Freedom* by Erich Fromm reprinted by permission of Holt, Rinehart and Winston, Publishers copyright © 1944 and 1969 by Erich Fromm.

Verses from Le Testament by François Villon are from *The Complete Works of François Villon*, translated by Anthony Bonner, published by David McKay Company, 1960.

Library of Congress No: 83-061477
ISBN 0-89608-185-0 paper
ISBN 0-89608-186-9 cloth
Cover design by Gerald A. Lynas

South End Press 302 Columbus Ave Boston MA 02116

*For our families and
our family of friends*

CONTENTS

FINDING ONESELF

KNOWING ONESELF

PART III
by Walli F. Leff

ACKNOWLEDGMENTS

One bitter, cold winter evening a man we had never met, but whom an acquaintance recommended we contact when we hit Chicago, arranged for three people who weren't working to come to his apartment so that we could interview them. He gave us each a private room to talk in and disappeared. After we had finished, he sat us down in the kitchen and loaded our plates with a delicious chicken dinner, then insisted we top it off with dessert.

Frank Nash believed in what we were trying to do and was eager to do everything he possibly could to help the book along. Later, in the freezing night, we were still warm within, glowing from his generous hospitality and genuine contribution.

Every step of the way, other kind, helpful and competent people contributed to this book and made our experience in creating it rewarding, gratifying and fun.

The love, patience, wise counsel and support of Sam Leff, Peter L. Delaunay, Lillian Feder and Marilyn J. Appleberg gave us the wherewithal to make it through the months and months of labor that this project entailed. Not even Damon and Pythias had greater faith and loyalty than they.

Without the involved and concerned interest of OmShanti Parnes and her fast fingers at the typewriter, the months would have numbered many more. She translated mumbles into clear speech and made sense of nonsense with good humor that dissolved tension into laughter.

Jane Adams and David Hood gave invaluable advice and encouragement from the book's inception to its completion. Danny Schechter made it possible for us to realize the fruits of our labor.

Barry Samuels, Jane Shapiro and Judy Padrone showed how creative people can be when they are not preoccupied by jobs. In many ways they were models of inspiration.

Helen Kolsky, Jay Levin, Betty Lee, Roger Hanson, Claire Peterson, Jennifer James, Bob Royer, Steve "Rufus" Feld, Henry and Virginia Wiener, Sherman Goldman and Obie Benz led us to dozens of people to interview. But their support did not end there—they made sure that wherever we happened to be, we were secured by shelter, food, transportation and good friendship.

Fred Johnson and Abe Rodriguez and the Goddard Riverside Community Center, New York City; Charlotte Brody and the Carolina Brown Lung Association and Sy Kahn and the Amalgamated Clothing and Textile Workers Union (ACTWU), Roanoke Rapids, North Carolina; Frances Katz and Social Services on the Beach, Miami Beach; Inez Addy and Violet Cameron and the Jefferson County Committee for Economic Opportunity, Birmingham, Alabama; Terry Moore and Fran Hernandez and the AFL-CIO Omaha Central Labor Union, and Larry Weewell, Personnel Director for the City of Omaha; Ron Chisholm and the TREME Community Center of New Orleans; George Nishinaka and Special Services for Groups, Kerry Doi and Wanda Chang and the Pacific Asian Consortium in Employment (PACE), and Tommy Chung and the Asian American Drug Abuse Program (AADAP), Los Angeles; and Santiago Soto and Giovanni Romero and Santa Fe Jobs for Progress (SER), Santa Fe, New Mexico, pinpointed scores of people whom they knew had interesting stories to tell. In many cases they set aside whole working days and their own office space so that we could meet and interview these people whose needs they serve. Without the interested, responsible support of these community organization leaders, we would have had a real struggle on our hands trying to make contact with the broad scope of people we wanted to cover.

There is no way to describe the openness and cooperation of the nearly 150 men and women who opened their doors and their lives to us. That they shared their private joys and sorrows, doubts and confidences, misery, delight and other secrets, is a tribute to the generosity of the human spirit and a valuable gift to us all. We are very grateful.

PART I

THE MYTH OF A NATION AT WORK

Time without work—dreaded and longed for, sometimes simultaneously—certainly one of the least discussed, most poorly understood experiences we can have.

What do people do when they have time without work? How do they feel about themselves and their lives? How do they make ends meet? What is it like not to work in this society where occupation is such a vital part of identity?

Curious about these questions at a time when unemployment was rising dramatically and the only information about not working was in statistical abstracts, Marilyn and I conceived of the idea of doing a book in which people would tell their own stories, in their words, of what it is like not to work. The more people knew about an experience, the better equipped they would be for dealing with it, we reasoned.

Our interest was more than casual, as we were both about to have time without work ourselves. It was not to be our first such experience. During the sixties and early seventies, before we knew each other, we had been among the tens of thousands of people actively questioning the meaning of work in a changing society. Neither one of us believed that submission to a stifling, deadening routine was an acceptable trade-off for·

financial independence and the right to call ourselves by an impressive-sounding title. We went looking for situations that would be stimulating, that could contribute something to other people, and which would permit us to express ourselves creatively.

Following our natural bent, we spent time abroad exploring foreign cultures and time in our own land experimenting with alternative culture. We became involved in political and community organization and the anti-war movement. Through the diverse people we met and the unique events in which we played a part, we became very different from the women our early lives would have molded us into.

But we also had been well-educated for professions—I was a psychologist, Marilyn a lawyer—and although we had criticisms of many of the traditional practices of our respective fields, we were interested in the fundamental issues they dealt with. So we spent some time working, too. Marilyn practiced tax law and joined the staff of the ACLU. I taught at universities and did social psychological research. We amassed working credentials.

Finding ourselves on the verge of not working once again, we could see that things had changed radically from the way they had been the last time either of us had had time without work. The counter-culture of the sixties that, critical of society's institutions, had introduced awareness of widespread inequities and abuses into young people's consciousness, had spread; a mass movement had developed. People of all ages were seeking both to redress social wrongs and to control their own lives by taking steps that had previously been the province of artists and the practice of adventurers, not the way of the "solid citizen." The "good wife and mother" who served as ever-present chief cook and bottlewasher, housemaid, baby-sitter, and chauffeur, the "good husband and father" who had provided status and was a stalwart breadwinner—the "loyal, dependable mainstream"—were suddenly eager to renounce these roles they felt trapped in.

An unusual spell of economic affluence and a more generous policy toward social programs, together with the encouraging social mood, supported the unprecedented numbers of people who were making sweeping changes in their lives and in

4

society. Professionals and business people were junking suits, ties and two martini lunches and turning their backs on the rat race; blue collar workers were thumbing their noses at oppressive foremen and nitpicking managers and walking off the job. Whether seeking authenticity and self-fulfillment or dedicated to making a real social contribution, they were abandoning their dreams of promotions that would never come or that, disappointingly, would not tint their days rosy if they did come. Still others felt this desire to bring about change in their lives, but, for economic or emotional reasons, finally chose not to act on the impulse to make a dramatic break with the way they had been living. But in recognizing the need, they too were part of a new cultural spirit. In this mass process of self-exploration, people were not merely challenging the mythic pre-eminence of the work ethic as a basic American value, they were hacking away at its very foundations.

Then the economy shifted. As the recessionary spiral mounted, the security of affluent times slipped away. The decisions by corporate managers to replace workers with robots, computers and other forms of automation were making a discernible dent in U.S. employment practices. Economic competition from Japan and western Europe hit U.S. industry hard. Weaknesses in the economy rooted in the post-World War II emphasis on investment in the military and, especially, in the policies of the Vietnam War came home to roost. And the opportunity to realize substantially higher profits through taking advantage of the cheap cost of labor in underdeveloped countries sent manufacturers scurrying to relocate their operations abroad.

Everywhere we looked, we were struck by the fact that growing numbers of people did not hold jobs. It seemed to us that two highly contrasted national trends—a personal "taking stock" operation that was engaging millions, and unemployment brought about by drastic economic transformations and shifts in industrial policy—had come together.

Clearly, what we were observing was going to be having radical social implications, because in this society people are expected to work and make money. Work is such a rock-bottom basic that occupation or labor skills have become our principal source of identity. Indeed, one of the things that most intrigued us was that many of the unemployed people we were coming across seemed much more concerned about being in a state of incomplete identity because they were not working than about the difficulty they were having in paying the rent or putting food on the table.

But hardly anybody was talking about what it was like not to work. We never heard people express their feelings, emotions and worries or describe what they did with their time. It was striking that people would volunteer many facts, even intimate facts, about themselves—whether they were married, single or divorced, how far they had gone in school, their struggle in losing weight and how terrible it made them feel—but when it came to admitting they were not working, they could be as evasive as a professional diplomat. And to say they were not working was clearly an admission; not working was considered cause for shame. People who had extenuating circumstances for being unemployed and were not personally responsible for their condition made sure you knew about it.

How revealing it was that the very fact of not working and any description of what the experience was like were so closely concealed. The reason, we soon began to see, resulted from the prevailing social belief that "everybody" works. According to that notion there are, of course, certain exceptions. Some people, such as mothers of small children, the retired, and the physically or emotionally disabled occupy a special role that exempts them from being expected to hold a job (though, contrary to stereotyped expectations, many of these people do, indeed, work for wages). Then there are a small number of people on welfare who by all accounts are "deserving." But, all in all, the belief has it that the number of people not working represents only a small proportion of the population.

It is fascinating, though, that when you stand back and look at the facts, this notion that "everybody" works is more a myth than a true reflection of labor statistics. Millions of people do not work. The Bureau of Census projections for 1980[1]

---

[1] *Social Indicators, 1979.* A report of the Office of Federal Statistical Policy and Standards and the Bureau of the Census, U.S. Dept. of Commerce. Issues December 1977, pp. 321-398.

broke down a population of 167,659,000 people 16 years of age and older into 103,761,000 workers and 63,898,000 nonworkers. By these figures only 62 percent of the population was projected to be working in 1980, a rate scarcely different from 1975's count of 61 percent. The work force was expected to remain 60 percent male and 40 percent female.

Even removing the 3,007,000 men and women 65 years of age and older from these calculations—although 12 percent of them, too, were expected to be workers—does not render a picture of a nation at work where all eligible people dutifully go off to the factory bench, office desk or cash register when the alarm clock rings. The 100,754,000 workers remaining are but 70 percent of all people aged 16 to 64.

Not only is the labor force much smaller than is commonly believed, but the unemployment rates are undisputedly conservative estimates of the real population parameters. Many underemployed people who work just part-time or sporadically choose to call themselves workers out of pride, so they are included as workers in the statistics. However, they may work no more than do people who report themselves as out of a job and are classified as unemployed, but manage to pick up a few odd hours' work here and there.

Moreover, the government's 1976 projections did not predict the economic disaster that actually befell us. In July 1980, only 96,996,000 people were employed, according to the Bureau of Labor Statistics—6,765,000 fewer than had been forecast. Industry payroll employment dropped by 240,000 people and the unemployment rate rose back up to 7.8 percent.[2]

In December 1982, unemployment stood at 10.8 percent, the highest level since World War II brought an end to the Great Depression. In the one month period between November and December the number of people without jobs increased by 436,000 to 11,987,000. The number of people working declined by 61,000. The decline was across the board, with the greatest

[2]"U.S. Jobless Rate Remains Steady for Third Month," *New York Times,* 2 August 1980.

7

loss of jobs occurring in the automobile and steel industries and in the manufacturing of machinery. Analysts could see no evidence that the job market would be improving.[3]

Not only were people being laid off, but businesses, both large and small, were going under at an alarming rate. For the first fourteen weeks of 1982 Dun and Bradstreet reported a failure rate of 83 per 10,000 businesses, the highest figure since 1933, when, during the Depression, 100 of every 10,000 businesses failed. And these figures did not include the companies that closed after paying off their creditors, only those that failed owing money. The failure rate was expected to worsen.[4]

The statistics officially show that nowhere near as many people work in this society as most people ever begin to imagine. But actually, even fewer people work than the figures indicate, for the method of assessment used to compile these statistics systematically underestimates the number of people not working, by the government's own admission. To be counted as unemployed, a person must have made specific efforts to find a job in the four weeks before the interview. People who have given up jobseeking do not figure at all in the data reported; they are not considered part of the labor force.

In 1976 a government survey counted 911,000 people who were not working and not looking for a job, but who said they would like to have a job "now."[5] It named these people "discouraged workers." In the third quarter of 1981 the Bureau of Labor Statistics reported that discouraged workers had increased to 1.1 million, of whom 65 percent were women, 32 percent were black, Asian-American and Native American.[6]

But these figures are a gross underestimate of the real number of people discouraged from jobseeking. The Bureau of Labor Statistics interviewer is instructed to count a person as

[3]"U.S. Jobless Rate Climbs to 10.8%, A Postwar Record," *New York Times,* 4 December 1982.
[4]"Even Gloomier Failure Rate Predicted," *The Tennessean,* 19 April 1982.
[5]Report of the Office of Federal Statistical Policy and Standards, *op. cit.,* p. 383.
[6]"Eight Percent, Or Maybe Twelve," *Dollars & Sense,* January 1982, pp. 14, 15.

discouraged only when no other reason for not working is given. So a person who could not find a job and went back to school or stayed home with a family is not considered discouraged, but is said to be not working because of other responsibilities, even when he or she would prefer to work. According to the Brookings Institute, only 15 percent of unemployed people who have stopped looking for work are classified as discouraged, although 46 percent of them said they wanted a job.[7]

The numbers of people not working are underestimated for other reasons as well. For one thing, their somewhat greater geographical instability makes them hard to locate, so they are not proportionately represented in the samples interviewed. Economic hardships force many discouraged workers to move in with friends or relatives, for example. Then, some people who are seeking work and are willing to relocate are on the road or in transient housing, so as far as interviewing goes they are phantoms—wholly inaccessible. Finally, the government simply has no category that accounts for the substantial number of people who admit that they do not want to work; they still remain uncounted.

The myth that working is universal rings hollow as a kettledrum, then. And like all untruths, it takes a toll. It is costly for a society to be misinformed about its real nature. Our powerful work ethic has conferred a moral obligation on working, causing us to scorn or patronize those who do not work. Joined with the myth that everybody works, it has inhibited people from sharing what it is like not to work, so the experience remains a private one. Not working, despite its prevalence, is thus viewed as a personal aberration, rather than as the failure of our institutions, and implicitly people believe it is cause for shame.

That this experience is hidden as though it were a personal weakness is most unfortunate. The glaring dishonesty of sweeping such a massive public reality under the carpet is decidedly unhealthy for the society as a whole and for the

---

[7]*Ibid.*, p. 14.

individuals who comprise it. The more information people have about the obstacles they are apt to encounter when they are not working, the opportunities that might await them, and the feelings they are likely to be having, the better. People who are armed with knowledge and aware that they are not the only ones to go through what they are enduring have a far better chance of withstanding the formidable stresses they face and of doing something positive with their time.

For the impact of unemployment can be devastating and what minimal support our society had recently been offering for surviving it has been severely diminished. The budget cuts President Reagan succeeded in having Congress adopt have reduced food stamps and health benefits, virtually eliminated the special benefits for workers in industries such as steel, automobile, and shoes, who lost their jobs because of imports, and reduced the amount and duration of workers' compensation benefits.[8] And as the unemployment rate was rising to record highs, the Reagan Administration cut funds by as much as 50 percent for the state employment agencies that administer unemployment insurance, find jobs for workers in businesses that need employees, and collect the data that describe what is happening in the nation's job markets.[9]

Contrary to the explanations the Administration has given for its reductions, the drastic cuts in social and economic programs were not designed to reduce costs or balance the budget. Rather, the budget set forth shows that the monies previously spent on social programs have been shifted to military applications.

Cutting social programs has had the direct effect of transferring our tax wealth to corporations that profit from producing missiles, tanks and other military matériel and services at a time when vast numbers of citizens have very serious questions about the U.S.'s growing militarism. The cuts have

---

[8]"Aid Programs Shrinking As Jobless Rate Climbs," *New York Times,* 13 January 1982.
[9]"As Jobless Rate Rises, Reagan Cuts Funds for State Employment Agencies," *New York Times,* 19 December 1981.

also had indirect effects. The unemployed have become more desperate, so they are more likely to accept exploitative, no-future jobs at low wages. Working people have become fearful of losing their jobs, so they accept reductions in salaries and benefits and tolerate poor working conditions. Thus, the shifts in government spending whacked millions of people, both working and unemployed, with a double whammy: measurable reductions in their buying power and incalculable damage to their morale and well-being.

Making the burden of unemployment even harder, many people who have lost their jobs do not avail themselves of even those services that do exist. In studying the layoffs of 34,000 workers from the Hartford, Connecticut aircraft industry, which suffered economic disaster less than three years after its 1968 boom of 87,000 employed, Brandeis Univerity sociologist Paula Rayman found that very few of those out of work made use of public agencies: only five percent were getting Aid to Families with Dependent Children, ten percent food stamps. It was not that they were so well prepared in advance for losing their jobs that they had no need of help. Seventy-five percent had received only one week's notice that they would be out of work; 92 percent had four weeks or less.

According to Rayman, the people laid off themselves expressed the psychology of "blaming the victim." Her sample, 54 percent of whom were Catholics with Eastern European backgrounds, felt they were personally responsible for their own unemployment, so would not use public funds. Instead, they went to family and friends for help.[10]

On a nationwide basis, a comprehensive study commissioned by the U.S. Congress revealed that over a forty year period, unemployment, inflation, and changes in income had all had an impact on social trends and health, but that unemployment played the most profound role of all.[11]

---

[10]"Mental Health and Unemployment," Workshop at the Annual Meeting, American Orthopsychiatric Association, New York City, 30 March 1981.

[11]Brenner, M. Harvey, "Estimating the Social Costs of National Economic Policy," Study for the Congressional Joint Economic Committee. Baltimore: John Hopkins University, 1976.

The report documented that from 1970 to 1975 more than 1500 suicides and more than 1700 murders were related to the 1.4 percent rise in unemployment. Over 26,000 deaths from cardiovascular and kidney disease, 870 deaths from cirrhosis of the liver, and more than 51,000 deaths from all causes were traceable to unemployment, as well. And the rise in not working was found to be associated with more than 7600 state prison and over 5500 state mental hospital admissions. These figures represented 5.7 percent of all the nation's suicides, 8.0 percent of the homicides, 2.7 percent of the total number of deaths, 5.6 percent of imprisonments, and 4.7 percent of the mental hospital admissions. The findings are very significant, yet they are only a signal of what is in the offing from the even greater unemployment that has followed the study's report.

This overall correlation of health and crime rates with unemployment figures is supported by in-depth research on the unemployed. In a study of employees of two plants that shut down permanently, Susan Gore of the University of Michigan's Institute for Social Research found that men who had relatively little support for their situation from their wives, friends, and relatives, and who did not feel they had many opportunities for being sociable, had more health symptoms and days of illness, higher cholesterol levels, seemed to have more ulcer activity, made a poorer economic recovery, and showed more depression and self-blame than men with adequate social support.[12]

A study carried out by the University of Michigan's Institute of Labor and Industrial Relations revealed that the relatives of unemployed people, in particular, the wife and children of men who are laid off, are often the main emotional victims of unemployment. Said research director, Louis Ferman, "We now feel the relationship between unemployment

---

[12]Gore Susan, "The Influence of Social Support and Related Variables in Ameliorating the Consequences of Job Loss." Prepared for the Manpower Administration, U.S. Dept. of Labor, Ann Arbor, Michigan: Institute for Social Research, University of Michigan, 1973.

and physiological or psychological stress is so strong that every pink slip should carry a Surgeon General's warning that it may be hazardous to your health."[13]

Different social groups suffer the impact of not working in different ways. Some white collar workers and professionals, whose lifestyle depends on job security and whose identity is inexorably defined by their occupations, may have extremely painful emotional reactions, much as Hans Habe decribed a doctor stripped of his right to practice medicine in his novel, *The Mission.*

> The status he had possessed, the work he had accomplished, the fame that had crowned him—these were not like clothes one could take off and yet remain the man one was; they were like the skin that one cannot take off without bleeding to death.[14]

In general, white collar workers tend to react to losing their jobs with intense anxiety and depression. "I think for the first time there is real fear among these people, who have always perceived of themselves as untouchable because of seniority or position of adequacy," said Sandra Lyness, a psychiatrist who has treated many automobile executives in the Detroit area. Feeling out of control, realizing the corporation is not going to protect them, the executives begin suffering what Lyness and her colleague, Walter Ambinder, call an "imposter syndrome"—believing they are less talented than their positions indicate. Lyness and Ambinder also found that the executives displayed the physical and mental problems of men ten or fifteen years older.[15]

As immunity from job loss which has been a prime characteristic of bureaucracies, its disappearance is, perhaps, what makes the cutbacks so hard for white collar workers to bear. "The air controllers thought they were indispensable," said

---

[13]"Recession is Linked to Far-Reaching Psychological Harm," *New York Times,* 6 April 1982.

[14]Habe, Hans, *The Mission.* New York: Coward-McCann, 1966, p. 41.

[15]"Once-Unflappable Auto Executives Show Stress Symptoms," *New York Times,* 18 January 1982.

Arthur B. Shostak, labor and workplace specialist at Drexel University. "Now we have 11,500 air controllers permanently traumatized by the demonstration of their dispensability. I regard that as a harbinger of what lies ahead for many white collar workers."[16]

Senior citizens suffer especially urgent problems. CBS reported that increasing alcoholism and loneliness, the highest suicide rate in the country for men over sixty-four, and a high poverty rate, which in Iowa alone meant that more than one quarter of retired citizens were living below the poverty level, were just some of the difficulties older people experience in what passes for "the golden years."[17] Even the American Medical Association has voiced concern about retired people, stating that the sudden cessation of productive work and earning power often leads to physical and emotional deterioration and premature death."[18]

It is a sad reflection of the racism in our society, but predictable as fireworks on the Fourth of July, that when the job market becomes tight, blacks and other minorities are rapidly dealt a walloping punishment. The November 1982 unemployment rate for blacks was a staggering 20.2 percent, nearly twice the nationwide figure of 10.8 percent. Then there is the harrowing situation of black youth, whose unemployment rate in April 1983 was still an unbelievable 49 percent.[19] A four-part series published by the *New York Times* when the rate was hovering at 40 percent outlined the situation in detail.[20] Summarizing the problem, former NAACP Labor Director Herbert Hill said, "It is evident that a permanent

---

[16]"Recession and Spreading Layoffs Hitting the White Collar Worker," *New York Times,* 12 January 1982.

[17]"The Retirement Revolution," aired 26 July 1977.

[18]"Retirement A Harsh Reward for Many Americans," *New York Times,* 18 July 1977.

[19]"Jobless Rate Dips to 10.2%; State Figure Drops Sharply," *Los Angeles Times,* 8 May 1983.

[20]Herbers, John, Johnson, Thomas A., Flint, Jerry, and Reinhold, Robert, "Young, Black and Unemployed," *New York Times,* 11-14 March 1979.

black underclass has developed, that virtually an entire second generation of ghetto youth will never enter the labor force. This means that a large part of the young black urban population will remain in a condition of hopelessness and despair and that the social and psychological costs in wasted lives continues a major tragedy in American life."

That jobs are avidly sought by young blacks is evidenced by the massive turnout of applicants who besiege employment offices whenever openings are available. With jobs a rarity, however, a way to survive must be found somehow. Picking up stints of day labor and working occasionally off the books are common, but while the informal economy of the ghetto provides a convenient financial stopgap, it produces no careers and, moreover, can subject young people to a series of humiliating experiences that spell no good for their growth and self-esteem.

The stunning paucity of jobs available to ghetto adolescents is a national disgrace and, in the many instances where racist discrimination is the cause, one more pattern of civil rights violation, as well. Job opportunities in the inner city are a critical need. Because the public schools fail so miserably to prepare black youth for participating in the larger American society, these teenagers are understandably likely to drop out of school and go into the streets, where opportunities for engaging in crime of all sorts abound. According to the *Times* series, Patrick V. Murphy, president of the Police Foundation, found that crime rates were often 50 to 100 times higher in urban areas of high unemployment than in other parts of the cities. And Alex Swan, Texas Southern University sociologist and criminal justice authority, estimated that 48 percent of hard-core unemployed black youths could be expected to commit what he termed the "survival crimes"—robbery, mugging, petty theft, dealing in stolen goods and working in the numbers racket.

Expedient as survival crime may look in moments of crisis and need, it is often the beginning of a downward spiral for those who adopt it, however. Not only does it harden the heart and produce cynicism, but getting caught and having a prison record is a near guarantee of future unemployability. The opportunity to work for decent pay and under respectable

15

working conditions would give ghetto youth a chance to break out of the cycle of poverty and crime that racism has bred and gain valuable job experience; it would be a way of resisting the pressures on them to survive by hurting other people and getting into serious trouble themselves.

Another far-reaching and ominous result of unemployment in the ghetto is the effect it has had on the nation at large—the fear that the increase in crime has created in society. This fear of being the victim of black violence and crime, though objectively irrational, has created a vicious resurgence of white racism that has already been manifested by intensified Ku Klux Klan activity. The same *New York Times* series referred to the work of Charles B. Silberman, director of the Study of Law and Justice, in noting that while the most likely victim of a violent assault in any city is a young, black, poorly educated male, more than half the people living in large cities—black and white—are afraid to go out at night. And according to the Figgie Report, 40 percent of a nation-wide sample of Americans are "highly fearful they will be murdered, raped, robbed or assaulted, although the actual incidence of murder is .009 percent of the population; rape, about .06 percent; robbery about .19 percent and assault .26 percent."[21] History has amply shown the inhumane behavior that can result from distorted and untruthful views of what a people is like. The desperation and fear bred by economic crisis are an inflammatory contribution to an already dangerous situation.

The final result is that, all too often, those who are not working are held responsible for the profuse and dangerous problems that follow in unemployment's wake. We can look for the explanation for this widespread practice of blaming the victim in the fact that our economy is oriented toward profit rather than human well-being.

For the high U.S. unemployment rate is a matter of policy; it is not the "natural" outcome of some regrettable but unavoidable limit to our economy. There is more than enough work to

---

[21]"Living in the Shadow of Fear," *New York Times News of the Week in Review,* 21 September 1980.

be done—building housing, rebuilding our decayed inner cities, roads, and bridges, preserving our landmarks, raising our literacy standard, caring for the neglected needs of senior citizens, delivering basic health care to all our communities, cleaning our water and our air, ridding the land of toxic wastes—the list could go on and on—to provide jobs for all who want them.

Resources for financing these essential services indeed exist. They are just not being made available to meet these needs because our economy is structured to maximize profit and it is more profitable to supply military demands. For this reason, vital social functions remain undone and large numbers of people are kept out of work.

Given this economic policy, heaping blame for the ills associated with not working upon none other than the policy's victims—people who are struggling to live without adequate income, productive activity and a work identity—is unjustifiable. It is cruel—truly an undeserved punishment.

The research on unemployment is sobering and serious. Of course, none of the findings detracts from the equally well-documented fact that working, too, can make people sick, violent and quite, quite mad. But they do make it easier to see that because this society views not working as a negative life condition and provides only grudging and spare support to those who do not work, some special knowledge is required if people are to resist the loneliness, disease, depression, poverty, suicide, crime, fear and mental illness that not working can provoke. For indeed, people do resist. While no one can be immune from feeling the pressures that result from the central role working plays in this society, some people do make the most of their experience not working.

We had heard some people tell what it was like to spend time without work and were fascinated by the unusual tales and uncommonly rich feelings they expressed. We saw that the experience had the power to provoke both emotional devastation and extraordinary growth and strength. Though basically the experience of not working is kept in the closet, concealed as though it were a bald spot to be covered by a hairpiece, we found that when people did talk about it they had such fresh and unique things to say, it was a real revelation. So

17

to rescue not working from its public disguise as an abstraction of labor statistics, we decided to collect stories that would illustrate some of its breadth and depth.

We had two aims for the book. Since it was clear that, more and more, people will be spending time without work, either for occasional or extended periods, we wanted the book to serve as a guide to the experience—to be, in effect, a psychological roadmap to not working. Knowing how others have fared could help people who were themselves going to spend time without work to make wiser decisions, we believed. They might find it easier to deal with the challenge to their identity and their emotional life through seeing how others in the same position had managed. By plotting the terrain, by describing the creativity and personal dominion that may be opened up, by sketching out the pitfalls, risks, and opportunities, the effects on relationships, identity and emotional well-being, the book, we saw, could serve not only as a documentary of a part of American life of which the personal essence has been virtually ignored, but also, for many readers, as a guidebook to their own future.

To demystify the clichés and superficial beliefs about what it is like not to work in a society where working is such an overridingly important value was our other purpose. Little is known about the interior quality and dimensions of the experience of not working. We wanted to express this hitherto unorganized and inarticulate aspect of American life as clearly as we could. We agreed that our aim could be achieved most directly and effectively by presenting a variety of stories tapping the experiences of a large number of people. And we agreed that the stories should be told in the people's own words.

Oscar Lewis had pioneered this method in his presentation of the lives of five members of one family in *The Children of Sánchez*. His technique successfully showed not only the vivid contrasts between the separate individuals, but also permitted the reader to see the underlying identity that linked all five people together. Then Studs Terkel artfully developed the method to recapture what the Depression was like in *Hard Times*, to portray Chicago and its people in *Division Street*, and to disclose how people felt about what they did to gain their livelihood in *Working*. The work of both Lewis and Terkel served as models of conceptual clarity on which we gratefully drew for fashioning our own storytelling model.

To find the people whose stories we would present, we forewent conducting a rigorous scientific study based on a random, representative sample. Aside from the sampling problems that would have arisen from the difficulties inherent in defining and locating the population that does not work, we simply had no resources available for such an undertaking. In addition, for literary reasons, we wanted to be free to select people who had rich and unusual stories; we wanted this initial probe into undeveloped, unexplored territory to pique interest and to read well. The in-depth material we would gain could then inspire and inform hypotheses to be tested in scientific studies.

We set out on the road with our tape recorders and, following up contacts made through professional colleagues, social service and legal organizations, friends and relatives, interviewed 145 men and women, aged nineteen to eighty-five, in New York City; Washington, D.C.; Boston; small Massachusetts towns; Roanoke Rapids, North Carolina and environs; Miami Beach; Birmingham, Alabama; Nashville; Chicago; Omaha; Seattle; Santa Fe and small New Mexican towns; New Orleans; San Francisco; Los Angeles; and small California communities.

Though we had a detailed interview protocol of standardized questions to provide a baseline of relevant information, we also encouraged people to speak freely and at length about the events and feelings that were important to them. In effect, we combined direct examination and a clinical interviewing approach with the method anthropologists use for their ethnographic studies—obtaining detailed, intensive accounts from well-informed local residents.

For purposes of collecting interviews we defined not working as "not employed for pay," despite the fact that we were personally of the opinion that very often people considered not to be working do, in fact, work very hard. But we wanted to explore the concept of work—discuss what it means and how it is changing—and we also wanted to share a mutual frame of reference with our readers. So, to provide both a document of the times and a jumping-off place for a discussion of what work actually is or could be, we used the conventional meaning of not working.

To be included in the book, a person had to be "not working" at the time of the interview. Some people who described themselves as not working occasionally did some work for pay, we learned—either to put bread on the table, or, in some circumstances, to assure a comfortable and even a rather luxurious life. But as long as they were not working at the time of the interview, we accepted these self-judgments of people whose energy and consciousness were directed toward other interests and retained the interviews. However, we did not interview people who told us they were holding jobs, even if they had just gone through years of not working. The immediacy and the salience of the experience of not working would be gone, we believed, replaced by a very different consciousness.

The only exception we were prepared to make was for artists. We felt an excellent case could be made that what artists do is the quintessence of work, and that another excellent case could be made that no matter how hard artists may toil, because what they do is art, it is not work at all. Because of the special perspective artists had to offer on working, we decided that as long as people found their identity in being artists, we would interview them regardless of whether they were paid for their art or whether, to survive, they might be working at a job that had nothing to do with their art.

To protect the baring of the soul, the people we interviewed were guaranteed anonymity. Our purpose was to encourage full and honest self-expression about any subject—emotional, political, sexual, social, economic—and of any feeling—anger, sadness, vindictiveness, resentment, depression, elation, contentment, triumph, self-satisfaction, well-being—and we knew that many people might be reluctant to express themselves publicly. There were also bound to be some people who did one or another illegal act to survive who would never assent to telling their stories under their true names.

Some people requested that their real names be published, but most chose to have their identities concealed and many asked to have other information disguised. This protection helped create an atmosphere conducive to open communication. As we hoped, a good many of the people we interviewed were remarkably forthcoming, amazing even themselves at the connections they were making and the insights they were having.

What finally resulted were intimate descriptions of how people spend time without work—the hard times they endure and their lack of resources for dealing with them, the ingenuity and strength they can summon for coping with their situations. Together the stories present a rich and complex portrayal of what the experience of not working is like. They show not only people who are plagued with anguish and doubts, but also people enriched from their discovery that time without work can lead to a new integrity—a sense of self independent of job identity.

THE WORK ETHIC'S CHECKERED PAST

Forming identity through occupation or profession is as much a product of industrial society as wall-to-wall carpeting and rush hour traffic jams. And just as they have accepted nylon broadloom and gas-fuming, slow-moving lines of cars as part of daily life, people caught up in the routines of modern life have also taken work-based identity for granted. "What do you do?" we are asked when we meet somebody new. We have been confronted with one or another form of that question since childhood, when we were expected to have a ready answer to the question, "What do you want to be when you grow up?" But work-based identity is not a universal part of the human condition, nor has it ever been.

In the more traditional societies from which American immigrants came, kinship and other factors related to family descent, such as religion and place of origin, were the chief determinants of identity. With the anonymity of urban and suburban life, our geographical mobility, and the fragmentation of our families, traditional life may seem like ancient history, but actually, contemporary America is closer to it than many people realize. For although our grandparents and, in many cases, our parents, may have left their ancestral villages and cities behind, they brought their tradition-based values with them.

At great personal sacrifice, they sent money home, paid the passage over for relatives who wanted to come to America, housed the new family members when they arrived, and devoted their energy and resources to assuring that their children had an education and a trade. It is a real irony that these people, whose personal honor and integrity were founded upon living by and for family-based identity, helped hasten the emergence of occupation-based identity through their dedication to having their children live better than they did. If "my son, the doctor" has become a cliché depicting the intensity of their effort and drive, it is nonetheless an accurate shorthand. For it demonstrates succinctly how immigrants to this undeveloped land, rich in resources and free of a feudal past, interpreted the best use they could make of the opportunities that lay before them.

With the enactment of civil rights, affirmative action, and equal opportunity laws after long and bitter battles, blacks, Latins, Native Americans, Asian Americans and women also began gaining access to the positions of higher challenge and pay that the sons of industrial age immigrants clambered into so eagerly. The legal breakthroughs held out a possibility that our society would move even more swiftly away from its roots in descent-based identity and traditional role structure to equal opportunity for all. But sadly enough, the legal promise has not been fulfilled. The economic crisis has further impeded the already uphill and difficult course of progress; deliberate efforts to roll back gains through legislative actions and judicial judgments have placed new obstacles along the path. Affirmative action rulings have been maddeningly irksome to enforce.

Interestingly, however, this new attention placed on work through the struggle for equal opportunity has had the unexpected twist of bringing about widespread recognition that, for the most part, the jobs to which women and minority group members are seeking equal access are far from inherently gratifying; in some cases they are enough to kill you.

For the past generation, social scientists, government planners, management representatives of some industries, and above all workers—not to mention people who are not working—have been wrestling with how work can be recast and its scope expanded so that it can fulfill the individual and collective needs of those who actually perform it. To do this, it has been necessary to examine what we mean by work, and this process has broadened our understanding of what work can be.

In his comprehensive analysis of the psychological meaning of work, psychologist Walter Neff defines work as a human, instrumental, self-preservative and alternative activity. Its purpose, he finds, is to preserve and maintain life, its objective to alter the environment in a planned way in order to make self-preservation more certain and efficient.[1] Defined that way, work is obviously something that goes on in all human societies to keep the societies going. But it does not have the same meaning to all people. It has not been structured or rewarded in the same way in all societies, nor has it been valued the same way at all moments in history.

Neff observes that in certain hunting and gathering tribes, where providing for the community's needs is so all-pervasive and continuous a task that everyone must participate, work as "a distinctive sphere of behavior" different from non-work probably has no meaning. Under these conditions work is as fundamental a part of life as breathing, something that is nearly always going on in one or another form. If people are busy making a tool or otherwise occupied with something that contributes to daily life even when they are merely sitting around a fire, work can be considered a "natural" activity that cannot be separated from leisure, feels Neff.

The Mbuti pygmies who live in the Ituri Forest are a living example of a people in whose culture work is integrated as one facet of an organic whole.[2] Food is plentiful in the forest. The pygmies hunt game as it is needed and also gather nuts, fruits, and vegetables to round out their daily food needs. Their forest villages are impermanent; they last about a month then spontaneously break up when the people decide to find a new

---

[1] Neff, Walter, *Work and Human Behavior*. Chicago: Aldine, 1968.
[2] Turnbull, Colin, *Wayward Servants*. Garden City, New York: Natural History Press, 1965.

site where hunting is better or to seek some luxuries in the non-pygmy villages at the edge of the forest, for a change. The work involved in building a new village does not take much time. A band can build a new camp in a matter of hours.

Since the pygmies do not live in an environment of scarcity, they do not need to devote every waking moment to working for their survival. They have time for music, for celebration, for dancing. Finding, distributing, and preparing food, making and repairing tools, building new huts and maintaining the village, watching over and teaching the children are integrated into the rest of life. The pygmies do not set aside these things that we would call work from the activities we would consider leisure.

The easy, organic fusion of work into all of life is true also among the Tikopia, a Polynesian people studied by Raymond Firth. In her discussion of Firth's study, Dorothy Lee drew a comparison between the Tikopia's way of working and our own fragmented view of work.[3] The key value among the Tikopia is *arofa*, or the social warmth of people who live closely together. The Tikopia's work is carried out in a manner which enhances closeness, both physically and symbolically. If a Tikopia man needs to do work alone, he tries to take a child with him. Every member of the extended family household participates in preparing a meal; the focus is on joking and storytelling, not on efficiency. Guests of honor at celebrations will even give up that role, in which they must stand apart from the preparations, and assume another role they can claim on the basis of their kinship, in order to join in the work—working when they could be exempt from it in order to be more socially involved.

The conception of work in the western world is strikingly different. The spread of agriculture had introduced toil—work that is more severe and tiring, work that involves more struggle. People who toil must have rest in order to recuperate physically and spiritually, and the sabbath, a day on which no work can be done, came into being. With agriculture there was

---

[3]Lee, Dorothy, *Freedom and Culture*. Fort Lee, N.J.: Prentice Hall, 1959, pp. 27-38.

surplus, and a regular free day was economically possible. Rest was such a critical need that the ancient Hebrews codified the sabbath as a commandment, and a separation between work and leisure was thereby institutionalized.

According to Neff, by the fifth century B.C. a negative attitude toward work had taken form in the civilized world. The ideal life for the Classical Greeks entailed having slaves and non-citizens perform all labor, thereby freeing male citizens to spend their time in the *agora* discussing philosophy and politics. Woman's "place" was already in the home. Work carried the opprobrium of being considered servile and somewhat degrading. This attitude prevailed in Europe until after the Protestant Reformation. Then, in the sixteenth and seventeenth centuries, as feudalism died and capitalism was born, the Protestant Ethic, which considered work ennobling and a path to salvation, took hold. The growing numbers of merchants and craftspeople who did not own land and command the labor of serfs to support them, but had achieved their status through their own labor, had every reason not to consider work a disgrace. Peasants and laborers, who had no vested interest in elevating work to the level of moral injunction, were swept along with the new order: their lot was to work or starve.

With the rapid spread of capitalism, the idea that work was a virtue struck friendly ground among enthusiasts of the early factory systems that were eager to exhort the greatest effort from workers. It met an especially fertile reception in the United States because of this country's vast territories, extreme labor scarcity, special interest in commerce and manufacturing, and predominantly anti-aristocratic attitude. Manufacturers in the pre-industrial United States were joined by respected statesmen such as John Adams and Benjamin Franklin in touting the work ethic. These leaders were convinced that cultivating enthusiasm for work was the only way to promote the development of industry, which they considered both healthy and essential for the new nation, though significantly, they failed to recognize that this veneration of work was also an effective rationalization for sweatshops, even for chain gangs. America's Horatio Alger belief that you could start at the bottom and work your way up caught hold and held sway. With such formidable powers behind it and with the genuine opportunities that did exist, the work ethic became an official American myth.

As a myth, the work ethic has had enthusiastic adherents and willing believers for over two centuries. A key component of our culture, it has had a strong influence upon the definition of our national character, to be sure. People know that to win social respect, they are expected to work. While the idle may be envied, Neff notes that they are also derogated.[4] If poor, they are regarded with contempt for not wanting to work; if rich, they are tolerated, but not respected.

Supported by the economic and political powers of the industrialized world, the myth of the work ethic has effectively corralled enormous amounts of human energy. Its power was epitomized with supreme—and unbearable—irony for all of time in the slogan "Arbeit Macht Frei," (Work Brings Freedom), wrought in metal over Auschwitz's gate: the sight of that bold lie reportedly inspired the belief and hope in new arrivals to the death camp that with a stint of honest labor they would once again be free.

But myth the work ethic is. And like the myth that everyone works except for a small number of people officially accounted for every month in the unemployment rate, this myth is no accurate mirror of reality, either. Nor, in fact, has it ever been. Since the United States began industrializing at the end of the eighteenth century, most jobs have made a fragmented business of work, separating it from the other activities of a person's life.

Such work can be characterized as *alienated labor,* a term originated by Karl Marx. This basic concept regarding the nature of jobs under industrialization includes four elements: 1) Workers see the product of their labor as outside themselves, therefore alien and not of their own nature. 2) Because the very activity of working becomes merely a means for satisfying other needs, rather than the expression of their essential nature, workers become alienated from themselves. 3) As a species, human beings are denied the possibility of fully developing their unique, transcendent capability, conscious-

---

[4]Neff, *op. cit.,* p. 68.

ness, and reduced to a struggle for physical existence. 4) As a direct consequence of being alienated from the product of their labor, the activity of working, and the essential nature of their species, people are alienated from one another.[5]

The concept of alienated labor also comprises the notions of: *powerlessness*—lack of control over policy, employment conditions, or work process; *meaninglessness*—lack of knowledge about the purpose of work or about how one's own work fits into the whole process; *isolation*—not being part of a group of peers or regulated by their norms; and *self-estrangement*—failure to consider one's own work as self-expressive or as a central interest in life, and feeling depersonalized detachment at work.[6] These concepts were later extended into a psychological framework by Erich Fromm;[7] they have been used by many sociologists.

Alienated labor is a far cry from work that is self-managed and integrated into the whole of life. By no means is it a "natural" activity. To do it requires a strong incentive, a strong fear of the consequences of refusing to do it, or the resigned belief that to risk doing something economically less secure is not worth the trying.

The work ethic touched the vast majority of the U.S. population as this country grew, for most of the people drawn here in search of a new life sought jobs as soon as they arrived and immediately became part of the industrial work force. Their numbers were impressive; in 1880 more than three quarters of the people in half a dozen of this country's major cities were immigrants or the children of immigrants. But as Herbert Gutman showed in his excellent essay,[8] some highlights of which are summarized in the following discussion, no

[5]Marx, Karl, "Economical and Philosophical Manuscripts," in E. Fromm, *Marx's Concept of Man*. New York: Ungar, 1961. pp. 93-109.
[6]Argyle, Michael, *The Social Psychology of Work*. Harmondsworth, England: Penguin, 1972.
[7]Fromm, Erich, *The Sane Society*. New York: Holt, Rinehart, and Winston, 1955.
[8]Gutman, Herbert, *Work, Culture, and Society in Industrializing America*. New York: Alfred A. Knopf, 1976, pp. 3-78.

sooner did these newcomers begin working than tensions arose, for their traditional ways conflicted with the work demands of industry.

Among Slavic immigrants in Pennsylvania mines and mills, for example, absenteeism ran high. A Polish wedding lasted three to five days. Greek Orthodox and Roman Catholic workers in the same workplace celebrated different holy days and many of them, so employers were always short of staff. With more than eighty festivals a year in the Greek Church, and with the Slavs observing each of their many saints' days by taking a holiday, employers' irritation ran high.

Orthodox Jews could not work on Saturdays or Jewish holidays. In order to observe their religious obligations, the most strictly religious tended to work for one another, thereby minimizing the degree to which they would be assimilating into the larger community. Jews who did work in the factories had to secure the right to observe the holidays without jeopardizing their jobs. Time off was more easily won for regularly occurring holidays than for occasional events, such as the ritual of circumcising newborn sons. Traditionally, circumcision occurred on the eighth day after birth and was followed by a joyous celebration. Under the six day work week in the factory system, circumcisions had to be postponed until Sunday. Everybody knew that Sunday was not the right day for the celebration; joy over the happy occasion was mingled with mourning over the conditions that prevented Jews from following their custom. The event became "one for secret sadness rather than rejoicing."[9]

Workers' traditions of communality and conviviality died hard, however. Independent artisans were accustomed to their own working style, where periods of intense labor often alternated with spells of idleness. New York City cigarmakers had a newspaper read to them while they worked, as did former fishermen and farmers turned shoemakers in Lynn, Massachusetts. The cobblers also took ample time out for festivals, fairs, games, excursions and drinking. Coopers traditionally spent Saturday drinking beer and playing poker

[9]*Ibid.,* p. 23.

in the workroom until they received their pay. The night on the town that followed inevitably stretched over into Sunday, so on Monday the coopers were not in any shape to work. With no production to speak of going on until Tuesday, the real number of working days in their six day work week numbered four.

Many of the workers who had left their native lands or their rural American homes and were forming this country's industrial force were not standing over their machines daily because they were particularly imbued with the work ethic and viewed labor as their means to personal salvation. Rather, they saw industrial work as a temporary, expedient way to make enough money to improve the life they had previously known and were planning to return to with the money they were saving.

Young, rural New England women who worked in the Lowell cotton mills, for instance, became depressed and anxious removed from nature. They managed to work the day through only because they did not expect to remain in the factory for long. Most of the South and East European peasants working in the Pittsburgh steelmills had immigrated with the idea of putting away enough money to buy farmland at home; indeed, from 1908 to 1910 forty-four actually left for every hundred that arrived. The time they did put in at the mills took a terrible toll, however; during the years 1907 to 1910 alone, accidents reached the shocking rate of 25 percent of workers injured or killed.

Not only were workers physically abused by the conditions they were forced to work under, but the cultures they were intent on preserving were affected as well. The pressures and erosion exerted by the industrial process radically changed the way in which people lived. For, intent on increasing productivity and minimizing their costs, manufacturers imposed rules, many of which were outrageous infringements of personal rights and which callously disregarded cultural traditions.

In a Massachusetts firm, for instance, workers who were unwilling to attend church were required to stay indoors to "improve their time" by reading, writing or performing other valuable activities. Mill owners forbade drinking and gambling and justified the twelve hour day and the six day week as keeping workers from "vicious amusements."

The first lesson of a pre-World War I brochure prepared by International Harvester Co. to teach English to its Polish workers illustrates the typical position management took toward the workers:

> I hear the whistle. I must hurry.
> I hear the five minute whistle.
> It is time to go into the shop.
> I take my check from the gate board and hang it on the department board.
> I change my clothes and get ready for work.
> The starting whistle blows.
> I eat my lunch.
> It is forbidden to eat until then.
> The whistle blows at five minutes of starting time.
> I get ready to go to work.
> I work until the whistle blows to quit.
> I leave my place nice and clean.
> I put all my clothes in the locker.
> I must go home.[10]

An 1888 document headed "NOTICE! TIME IS MONEY!" included the following in its rules for a New Hampshire factory: "There are conveniences for washing, but it must be done outside of working hours and not at our expense."[11] In comparing the 1971 work rules for General Motors to their historical predecessors, Gutman finds them no less authoritarian, stringent and rigid.[12] Historically the rules formed an intrinsic part of the developing capitalist structure; they cannot be dismissed as merely an occasional aberration of a few malevolent, particularly nasty entrepreneurs.

Some employers fined workers for drunkenness and other transgressions. Some rewarded workers for compliance. Of course, employers fired workers for all kinds of infractions, as direct punishment or to instill fear for their own job security in other employees. And to assure a relatively compliant and available workforce, the industrialists went about eliminating the other means of making a living that did not involve

---

[10]*Ibid.*, p. 6.
[11]*Ibid.*, p. 7.
[12]*Ibid.*, pp. 6, 7.

working for wages. The most effective measure they took was to squeeze out small property holders so that disenchanted workers could not opt to earn their keep on the land. Thus, a pool of unemployed people who would compete for jobs and for the "right" to perform exploitative, alienated labor was created.

But despite the forces against them, many workers found quitting their jobs as easy to do as employers found firing them. Within a month after one Nantucket silk mill opened, for example, the women and children who had been clamoring for jobs left, unwilling to conform to the manufacturer's demands. The plant shut down soon after.

Even a regular salary, held out before people like a carrot dangled before a donkey, was not a foolproof enticement to join and remain in the industrial labor force. Once alienated labor was experienced, it clearly did not take so easily.

TOWARD A NATURAL WAY
OF WORKING

In recent times, the non-compulsive attitude toward work that has characterized so much of human history has, if anything, become even more typical and pervasive. The case of the Lordstown auto workers was so widely discussed, people often forgot it was far from unusual for its time. But, in fact, during the late sixties and early seventies discontent in the labor force was common. Widespread disaffection from a society that would fight an unjust war in Vietnam while letting crises of violence, racism and poverty fester at home had severely weakened the moorings of the work ethic as a national creed. Thousands of dropouts—from high schools, industry, the professions and from marriage and family—unplugged themselves from the slots into which they had been unwittingly dropped to go searching for a more fulfilling way to live and express themselves.

But American society had few mechanisms that could accommodate this quest for independently wrought identity. Its assets were committed to military and industrial expansion, its most powerful institutions pledged to traditional values. The forces that held sway were not inclined to encourage a self-actualization movement that would seriously threaten many of the premises sustaining their domination.

Nor were they willing to allocate resources for building the kinds of community necessary to nurture the independent growth on which such a movement was based. Not surprisingly, even the most disaffected eventually found it difficult to sustain a personal identity that did not depend on occupation. Little by little people began drifting back to work in order to gain a firmer grip on their sense of themselves.

Re-entering the mainstream did not mean going back to pick up a life previously abandoned as alien and unfulfilling, however. In the course of self-discovery many people had had unusual experiences and tapped previously unknown skills. It was only natural for them to want to develop these talents and perspectives, so in school or self-taught, they studied new trades and professions, thus beginning the trend toward multiple careers. In choosing to join the work force they were not embracing the work ethic. Rather, they were seeking to express themselves productively through non-alienated labor.

Then, in the mid-seventies, the U.S. economy plunged into crisis. In the new era of high technology, Japan and Western Europe gained the competitive edge on the most attractive, advanced products dominating the world marketplace. Money grew tight, inflation ballooned, the unemployment rate soared. The energy crunch made bad matters worse.

Alarmed, U.S. industry saw the ascendancy it had been enjoying for thirty years vanish. Hurriedly, plants began transferring their production abroad to take advantage of cheaper foreign labor. New computer technology and self-service systems transformed domestic businesses into ghostly operations manned by a few lonely technicians, clerks and security guards. The job squeeze intensified.

As the last crumbs of the affluent era's free lunch were swept away, a sober urgency about working replaced the sanguine sense of exploration that had characterized the previous ten years. Suddenly automation was no longer some remote futuristic abstraction; it was real, it was current, and it was swallowing up jobs. U.S. business was demonstrating to workers that their services were not going to be courted, even if the economy were to pick up.

And, indeed, except in those rare industries suffering from a shortage of qualified workers, such as the electronic chip manufacturers in California's Silicon Valley, workers have been anything but courted. Wages do not keep pace with inflation, cutbacks in the work force mean a heavier workload for those able to hold on to their jobs, and the gestures toward humanizing the workplace won in the seventies such as day care centers, are no longer even on the agenda in worker-management negotiations. In search of higher profits, corporations act by executive fiat to cut labor costs by transferring production abroad or to states where anti-union forces prevail, even if it means shutting down a factory that operates at a profit and putting a thousand or more members of a community out of work, as happened in the scandalous closing of the General Electric metal steam iron plant in Ontario, California in 1982.[1]

In general, conditions in the labor market are far from conducive to building an attachment to work and working. Nor is it only in factories that disaffection is a problem. Morale in the huge government labor force, for example, has hit rock bottom. In its budget-cutting zealotry the Reagan Administration's "reduction in force," or RIF, made secretaries, file clerks and photocopy staff of high-salaried specialists who have devoted years to the civil service. A "riffed" worker with seniority can bump an employee without veteran status and remain in the lower grade job, without loss of pay, for two years. To a $47,000 a year former public health advisor who finds himself typing letters in a job nine civil service grades below his old post, the morning alarm clock can scarcely be said to signal a challenging day at work.[2]

Workers in offices where advanced electronic computer and word processing units have been installed now experience the same monotony and stress that have long characterized speeded-up assembly lines, the same strictly monitored restrictions on socializing to keep productivity high. The work is so highly specialized that it utilizes few of the all-around skills

---

[1]Pennick, Adrian, "At GE, Profits Are Their Most Important Product: Runaway Plants," *L.A. Weekly*, 19-25 February, 1982.

[2]"Reagan RIF Effect Puts Bosses in Typing Pools," *New York Times*, 7 April 1982.

workers can provide; it is so fragmented, it denies workers the chance to assume responsibility and respond to challenge. In certain industries such as the insurance business, which operates on a massive scale, these jobs also preclude the possibility of feeling any pride that might be associated with mastering even the limited tasks required. Just as in *Through the Looking Glass* Alice had to run faster and faster to keep in the same place, workers in automated offices find that when they reach the productivity level that had been specified for them, a new, faster level of acceptable performance is automatically set. The machine is programmed like some giant video game where the action speeds up when the player catches up.

As the vaunted boon to society it was heralded to be, automation is turning out a mixed bag. In factories, robots and their automated cousins have indeed eliminated many tedious drudge jobs that needlessly taxed workers' bodies and spirits and are far better done by machine. In offices, "user friendly" systems with advanced telecommunications capacities are freeing executives, who now have much more time to devote to creative work. But for the growing numbers of workers whose job it is to feed the software into these systems, working conditions are as alienating and dehumanizing in their own way as industrial conditions have ever been.

The dehumanized nature of the workplace is especially true of physical conditions, which all too often are downright unsafe. Most industries do not institute health and safety measures unless forced to do so through worker pressure and the law. Even when standards are enacted, nothing guarantees they will be enforced. The policy shift away from regulation, backed by drastic cutbacks in appropriations for inspection staff, has seriously interfered with the ability of federal and local agencies to oversee industry practices and enforce the law. Moreover, it is difficult for inspectors to enforce correction of violations when reform would cost a company more than it is willing to pay. Companies immediately set their lawyers to work appealing the case and pleading special circumstances. Years of entanglement with regulatory red tape and costly court action may go by, during which time the hazards in the workplace remain.

The control which business wields over labor is so entrenched and well-organized that not even union-represented workers—who amount to but a small minority of the work force—no more than 14 per cent to 18 per cent—can exercise much influence over working conditions. Entire industries, nuclear and chemical production prominent among them, have blatantly refused to bring factory conditions up to healthful standards demanded by unions or ordered by government. In the case of the textile plants in the south, management has even refused to recognize their employees' legally organized union bargaining agent, in contempt of court-ordered directives. With the economy so shattered, few unions now even include health and safety improvements in their demands, but have retreated to minimal bargaining positions. Some, in outright capitulation that marks a critical loss of power for the labor movement, have actually given up rights gained after bitter, hard negotiation in order to stave off further plant closings and layoffs.

The nature of work in the U.S. today is a far cry from the fertile ground that would nurture freedom, which Erich Fromm, in his classic analysis, *Escape From Freedom*, described as the state in which one "can relate himself spontaneously to the world in love and work, in the genuine expression of his emotional, sensuous and intellectual capacities; he can thus become one again with man, nature, and himself, without giving up the independence and integrity of his individual self."[3] Instead, labor practices lend support to Dorothy Lee's observation that the concept of freedom in America is a negative condition referring to the absence of requirement, of "have to," that free time is not something of inherent value, but is, rather, passive, empty hours to be compulsively filled with planned activities.[4]

If the best that is offered workers is paid alienated labor for which the pay does not keep pace with inflation, and, perhaps, disease or a painful death from on-the-job hazards, to boot—in effect, foreclosure on the possibility of attaining personal

---

[3]Fromm, Erich, *Escape From Freedom*. New York: Avon, 1969. p. 161.
[4]Lee, *op. cit.*, pp. 53-58.

freedom—it should come as no surprise that people would question why they should give their lives as sacrifice on the altar of a religion in which they have no faith. And it should come as no surprise that some should choose not to make the sacrifice. Considering how hard it can be to get along in this society without working, even rigid adherents to the work ethic might see that those who refuse to spend away their energy for the enrichment of a few strangers who control the workplace might be making their choice not from parasitical laziness, but from courageous, if off-beat, self-respect.

Still, despite the fact that contemporary labor practices are stacked against it, a view of life and self that values working, but in which the work ethic is still conspicuously absent, has come into its own. From their in-depth studies of modern worker attitudes, the polling and consulting firm Yankelovich, Skelly, and White report a definite shift away from the Protestant work ethic concept of self-denial to a new focus-on-self."[5] They have identified a new "work attitude"—fulfillment-seeking—held by about 20 per cent of the work force, mostly young and well-educated people, many of whom are professionals or managers. These fulfillment-seekers work for psychic rewards and require strong feedback about their performance. Emphasizing non-work activities in their lives, they demand excitement on the job and are easily bored.

For the most part, the self-absorbed psychology of these fulfillment-seekers is strikingly different from the activist concerns of those who preceded them by a half-generation. But, since they were shaped by the revolutionary sixties era in which they grew up, the fulfillment-seekers do share some vital attributes with those who, in effect, paved the way for them: they value their own worth and are intent on pursuing their own personal interests, regardless of whether they conform to mainstream expectations or not. After all, they are part of a unique generation about which the noted social critic, Murray Bookchin pointed out, "When cybernated and auto-

---

[5]"Finding Lost Work Ethic Becomes Important As Productivity Fails," *New York Daily News*, 11 June 1979.

matic machinery can reduce toil to the near vanishing point, nothing is more meaningless to young people than a lifetime of toil."[6]

It is as though the youth of this era had taken as a personal admonition the observation Paul Lafargue wrote some eighty-five years before.

> A strange delusion possesses the working classes of the nations where capitalist civilization holds its sway. This delusion drags in its train the individual and social woes which for two centuries have tortured sad humanity. This delusion is the love of work, the furious passion for work, pushed even to the exhaustion of the vital force of the individual and his progeny....And meanwhile, ...the class which in freeing itself will free humanity from servile toil and will make of the human animal a free being—the proletariat, betraying its instincts, despising its historic mission, has let itself be perverted by the dogma of work. Rude and terrible has been its punishment. All its individual and social woes are born of its passion for work.[7]

(Karl Marx's son-in-law, Lafargue must have brought some spicy controversy to family dinner table discussions.)

But this consciousness that rejects alienated labor and recognizes the possibility of freedom finds scant support, for our economic and social system gives it little room in which to move. It is not surprising to learn, then, that Yankelovich, Skelly, and White found another group, equal in size to the fulfillment-seekers, which they called the money-seekers—people who do not seek psychic job rewards, but strive for money in order to live an adventurous life outside the job. It is ironic and not a little frightening that the pressures that have produced the money-seekers' resignation, the deliberateness with which they view work as an instrumental act, and their alienation are exemplified by our contemporary way of leisure. As Fred Thompson points out in his introductory notes to

---

[6]Bookchin, Murray, *Post-Scarcity Anarchism*. San Francisco: Ramparts Press, 1971, p. 15.

[7]Lafargue, Paul, *The Right To Be Lazy*. Chicago: Charles Kerr, 1975. pp. 35, 38.

Lafargue's essay, leisure, like industry, has become "capital intensive."[8] Though work hours have been reduced, commuting has made less time available for play. Society offers planned activities for filling those reduced hours and those activities are expensive.

Many people, of course, do resist the lures that would hook them into putting ever more energy into working in order to gain more money to spend on leisure-time activities. Thompson is encouraged by the generation of young workers who want to humanize the job and have some fun on it, too, calling them "forerunners of a future in which work and leisure are indistinguishable, purposeful activities, ...freed from all taint of commodity culture because we work for the fun of it and get what we want for free."

His rather playful view is implicitly utopian, for it would make play of work. But making play of work is precisely the core of the issue. Over long years a transcendent view linking work and play has been taken for granted in at least one area—art. Our very language proclaims that the musician is playing, that the actor on stage is a player, regardless of how many weeks or years of thoughtful and disciplined, arduous effort may have been put into practice and rehearsal.

There is good reason to believe that the implicit connection between play and work that characterizes art could be made as readily for other human endeavors. If you look hard enough through contemporary psychological theory on play, for example, you find that the distinguishing feature of play is that it is intrinsically motivated; that is, play is undertaken only for reasons that are inherent in the activity itself.[9] If people "play" for any other reasons—for instance, to make money or win accolades—the activity can no longer be considered playful.

---

[8]*Ibid.,* III. About Labor and Leisure, pp. 31-32.
[9]Vandenberg, Brian, "Play and Development from an Ethological Perspective," *American Psychologist, 33* (8), August 1978, pp. 724-738.

With characteristic playful charm, the great piano virtuoso, Artur Rubinstein, validated this psychological theorizing quite clearly. "I don't feel that making art should be called work," he said, "Work is something disagreeable that you have to do. Don't tell Hurok," (Sol Hurok was for many years his impresario) he admonished one interviewer, "but I'd play the piano for nothing, I enjoy it that much."[10]

As a telling example of how play is transformed when it is done for money, consider professional sports. Most people are well aware that team owners and the mass media make immense profits from what is ostensibly recreation. Even avid fans envy or resent the awesomely huge salaries which, in recent years, the biggest stars whose ability they so admire have been able to negotiate through hard-nosed professional business agents. And for many spectators themselves, the games are not merely a passive form of leisure and a vicarious release. Gambling has turned sport into serious personal business.

Clearly, play may take on attributes that most people would associate with working. And similarly, work that challenges the spirit and enhances the skills of the person who performs it, so that he or she wants to do it—not just for the money, not just for the duty, but for the sake of doing it—is "suspiciously" like play.

Historian Theodore Roszak, originally known for his analysis of the "counter-culture," later wrote about work in a way that promotes this very view. Calling work a necessity as a "paramount means of self-discovery," he argued that "our personhood is realized in responsible work."[11]

Neff, too, feels that work can be sought, not as a means for fulfilling the work ethic, but for its own sake. In support of this position he offers the psychological theory of Robert W. White, who proposed that there is an unlearned, independent ego-energy for exploration and manipulation—an energy that

---

[10]*New York Times,* 21 December 1982.
[11]Roszak, Theodore, *Person/Planet.* Garden City, N.Y.: Anchor, 1978, p. 232.

41

permits a person to interact effectively with the environment—that he termed "effectance."[12] White further identified the feeling of pleasure that accompanies being active and having an influence on something as "efficacy."

You can see right off that White's definition rests upon the concepts of curiosity-investigation and curiosity-manipulation which are essential for adaptation and survival. These energetic activities, performed for their own sake with no reward, have been observed in every niche of animal life and found to be more common and more ingenious as you move up the phylogenetic scale.

You need not be a professional zoologist to recognize the truth of this biological observation. Anyone who has ever spent time with pets knows that nothing is immune from the thorough investigation of a puppy's keen nose and floppy paws, and that curiosity can consume a kitten, if it rarely actually kills a cat. Monkeys, farther along on the evolutionary scale, far surpass cats and dogs in exploration. But, observes Harry Harlow, whose studies of monkeys reared with wire or cloth surrogate mothers prompted new understanding of the importance of the social context in behavior, "The rhesus monkey is actually a very incurious and nonmanipulative animal compared with the anthropoid apes, which are, in turn, very incurious nonmanipulative animals compared with man."[13]

Humans, who have transformed their biological drives into psychological motives through the elaborate processes of culture, express at least part of their boundless curiosity and exploratory drive by the need for achievement, studied in depth by John Atkinson and David McClelland.[14] A highly focused and goal-oriented mechanism, the need for achievement is capable of channeling vast amounts of exploratory energy. In our society it is often coupled with the need for power, the net result of which is all too frequently destruc-

---

[12]Neff, *op. cit.*, pp. 146, 158.

[13]Harlow, Harry F. "Mice, Monkeys, Men, and Motives," *Psychological Review*, 1953, *60*. pp. 23-32.

[14]McClelland, D.C., Atkinson, J.W., Clark, R.A., and Lowell, E.L. *The Achievement Motive.* New York: Appleton-Century Crofts, 1953.

tive—of no social and of dubious personal value. But when it operates more independently, the need for achievement can fuel significant human accomplishments and foster a sense of worth and competence.

It should be intuitively evident that White has put his finger on a basic and essential force in human motivation. For who does not yearn to be effective? Daydreams teem with proud and daring personal accomplishments made noble through generous deeds. Asleep, we spend vast amounts of energy confronting emotions, conflicts, and aspirations and making creative connections between seemingly disparate events. Our conscious and unconscious fantasies reveal how wide is the gap between what we have and what we want, and so, say much about the shortcomings of the world we have inherited and, in our turn, created. More often than not, unfortunately, we dismiss as "mere fantasy" the figments of our unconscious mind that so tellingly attest to our drive for effectance, without bothering to cultivate the insights this fertile terrain produces, wasting a valuable human resource.

Not that our clever flashes of mind or embellished narratives bear much relationship to the jobs we may work at. In his classic analysis of ten thousand dreams, Calvin Hall found that for only one per cent were the settings described as office or factory. "Considering the amount of time that people spend in places of work, such as offices, factories and classrooms, these places appear with disproportionately low frequency in dreams," he observed, in what may be the most striking understatement in the whole of psychological literature.[15]

Despite its current failure in satisfying our need for effectance, work, as Neff observes, is certainly a prime candidate for fulfilling this goal. Many of the people we interviewed for this book felt this keenly. Said Gus,

> The reason I just loved that job so well was that they gave me a chance to learn and they also gave me a chance to put it to work—to experiment, to make some mistakes. The

---

[15]Hall, Calvin S., "What People Dream About," *Scientific American*, May 1951.

benefits were just tremendous. What I learned and what
they gained from it were out of this world....I loved it. I've
done my share of hard work, but it's given me some things
that I don't feel right about taking to the grave, so to speak.
I feel that I have an obligation to share what I have with
the people who need it. It isn't money; it's knowledge. And
I'd like to sell it. I think it would benefit the community—it
would benefit the country. Any place we start to improve
productivity it's got to be helpful.

And Martin, who was very happy not working, who felt no
guilt about it, no psychological requirement to work, and
looked upon his choice as a political act, was also fully capable
of describing the pleasure he had once had doing farmwork
with traditional tools. Indeed, he even waxed rhapsodic.

...the horse, the smell of the sweat of the horse, the smell of
your own sweat, and the smell of the hay—so much of what
we're robbed of in the city is the olfactory sense. You are out
there half naked and you have these extraordinarily long
poles, and at the end the prongs, and you learn to lift these
really immense quantities of hay. It's a technique, like
everything else. You put them on their huge wagon and the
horse takes the wagon to the barn, sweating like a pig. It is
beautiful! It is marvelous! Then, of course, you have to pitch
the hay into the hayloft, and at the end of the day it's
almost as though you had sex. You are exhausted, but it's
beautiful exhaustion...I can picture, in a perfect society,
people opting to do that and being supported to do that for a
while, as they would be supported to paint or to write
poetry. But the life of a real farmer is not like that at all.
This kind of work, as Marie Antoinette knew, is fun if you
don't have to do it, you see. It's what I call Petit Tria-
nonism.

In the face of it, then, work has obvious potential for
satisfying our need for effectance, as its very purpose is
productivity. But no matter how natural it may seem as an
arena, the limitations of most jobs as they are currently
structured mean that attempting to use work for achieving
this aim is essentially a losing battle.

That workers have been growing increasingly dissatisfied
as the scope of their jobs becomes more and more restricted is
borne out by national surveys. In a poll of employees of 159
companies taken annually by Opinion Research Corpora-

tion,[16] 32 percent of the clerical workers questioned said they were unhappy with their work, a rise from 24 percent eight years earlier. Thirty-eight percent of workers paid on an hourly basis said they disliked their jobs, compared to the 31 percent who disliked their work when the survey began. Of the 6500 managers, 91 percent said they were satisfied with their work, but since managers are only a small fraction of the employees compared to the 62,000 other workers, from an ecological point of view the picture of the workplace has a decidedly gloomy cast.

And discontent has spread among white collar workers. A study prepared by the University òf Michigan's Institute for Social Research for the U.S. Department of Labor reported a decline in job satisfaction at all education levels, with the biggest dip among college graduates. Many workers complained that their skills were underutilized on the job. For four key indicators—pay, job security, working hours, and on-the-job challenge—satisfaction ratings declined. The highest levels of job satisfaction were reported by the self-employed.[17]

The discontent has begun to have ramifications in industry, albeit in an extremely limited way. In February 1982 the Ford Motor Company and the United Auto Workers agreed to a new two year contract with a guaranteed income provision of 50 per cent to 75 per cent of their salaries for senior employees laid off from their jobs, a "lifetime employment" program protecting 80 per cent of the workers at two of the company's plants from layoffs, and profit-sharing for blue-collar workers.[18] After negotiations failed in January, General Motors agreed to a similar contract with the union in April.[19]

---

[16]"Job Discontent Found Rising Among Workers," *New York Times*, 13 August 1977.

[17]"U.S. Workers Growing More Dissatisfied With Most Aspects of Jobs, Study Shows," *Los Angeles Times*, 18 December 1978.

[18]"Ford Pact Backed by Union's Board," *New York Times*, 15 February 1982.

[19]"Auto Workers Narrowly Favor New G.M. Pact," *New York Times*, 10 April 1982.

The hard-won concessions addressed very few of the complaints noted in the report of the Institute for Social Research and were achieved at considerable cost to the workers—below-scale wages and benefits for new employees, deferred cost-of-living pay increases and elimination of the 3 percent annual pay increase and of six to nine paid days off. The agreements may be a start, but on balance they are far from a victory.

To find a way of stimulating profits and productivity, and, perhaps, as a sop to dissatisfied workers, U.S. businesses, particularly the ailing auto industry, are showing interest in the Japanese industrial system, which is far more productive than American methods have proven to be. However, a good part of the success of Japanese industry is due to the fact that their system is carefully structured to satisfy their traditional cultural values. Thus, workers have lifelong job security, but management exercises tight control over workers' lives on—and off—the job.

This trade-off may work in Japan, but it is simply not a part of our culture. It would be a serious mistake to think that the Japanese system could be duplicated with the same results in the west. While there is much to be learned from Japanese industry, perhaps the best lesson offered by their success is that we would do well to pay serious heed to our own values and cultural patterns in our effort to restructure work. America will need to create its own way out of job disatisfaction and lack of productivity.

One way or another, America certainly ought to be addressing itself to these and other problems of working and not working. Not only are people with jobs unhappy, but those who do not work are by no means having an easy time of it either. The economic problems that loom before any but the most fortunate of freelancers can be a major stopping block, the absence of social approval at crucial moments when some support is needed, a spiritual killer. So even though people who do not hold jobs may be spared the indignity of submitting to somebody else's exploitative terms, the isolation and financial hardships that may come with not working can make rough going of it.

Not working is no bed of roses. And until substantial transformations are made, people who cannot find work, people who walked away from work, people who are following their dream, people who gave up dreaming, people who retired, people who are just beginning—they and the other people who are not working all have to get by somehow. The way in which some of them manage to do so is revealed in the stories that follow.

With generous openness, the storytellers revealed their vast range of feelings about the experience—anxiety, self-doubts, anger, depression, envy—relief, delight, pride, joy, curiosity, freedom—hope. The lid of this Pandora's Box is easily tipped off. Isolation, the "non-occupational hazard" of not working, if you will, tends to magnify and distort the escaping contents, making them much harder to examine, shoo away, or recapture.

Though the psychological terrain these people were crossing was well-traveled, it is, at the same time, uncharted, left vague and mysterious, like other taboos. Not working activates strong needs and fundamental life values, and to make the experience even rougher, it excites all these things simultaneously. So this psychological terrain is fertile soil for contradictions. Indeed, readers may be surprised at how glaring the contradictions can be—wanting to work and wanting to stay free of work, luxuriating in free time and longing for structure, feeling happy to be free of materialism and feeling worried and angry that there may not be enough money to survive. In a single sitting, people who otherwise give every indication of being thoughtful, intelligent, and insightful may gainsay with conviction the feelings they have just fervently declared.

The contradictions probably say little about the storytellers' capacity for logical thought and more about the nature of not working in a society where work is the keystone of identity. The psychological forces the experience rouses can easily dominate logical views. Since ambivalence is the tried warhorse of psycho-logic, it is altogether realistic that we would find mutually contradictory feelings co-existing. In any event, the loss of logic is no real deprivation; there is valuable information to be discovered from mapping out the emotions associated with not working.

The people interviewed for the book were ordinary and extraordinary people who had the customary human array of adequacies, inadequacies, successes, failures, confidence, and doubts. We did not press them to relate their triumphs or reveal their daring; we simply asked them to describe how they came to be not working and what the experience was like for them. If many freely confided details of courage and creativity that could make them appear inspiring or heroic, many also freely confided weaknesses and shortcomings, so are vulnerable to being seen as unappealing.

Naturally, readers may find some of the people more attractive than others. However, the people who told their stories were not implicitly agreeing to enter a sweepstakes of heroism or to chance being written off as losers. They relied upon us to present their stories in the most accurate, non-judgmental context we could create and we tried to fulfull that trust. The trust now passes on to the readers.

Finally, we hope you will be aware that the choices people made about the tales they told and how they told them often had much more to do with personal needs for expression than with concern about how the story would eventually read. Storytelling is an art, and as generations of people have learned, some people are just more talented at spinning a yarn than are others.

To broaden the understanding of what it is like to have time without work, we have sought to bring you good stories, as artfully told as possible. But the art was also a means for moving closer to another goal. As Picasso said, "We all know that art is not truth. Art is a lie that makes us realize truth."

PART II

OUT OF WORK

THE NEWSPAPER FOLDED

Alan   Chicago, Illinois

The final edition of the Chicago Daily News was on prominent display at every newsstand—collectors' items for a city that would be losing an important part of itself after the last copy was gone. One of the immediate casualties of the paper's demise was Alan—a slight, dark-haired man in his mid-twenties—who had just lost his first job as a reporter and had been unemployed not quite ten hours and fifteen minutes. Agitated, glad to have company, he spun right into his story—pacing around the table when he was angry, cradling his head in his hands when the tears wouldn't stop, laughing delightedly at his own humor and irony.

I was at the *Daily News* for nearly four years. It was my first newspaper job out of journalism school. At the time I graduated the newspaper situation was so grim, recruiters didn't even come to my school, which was known to graduate the crème de la crème.

Then I got a call that the *Daily News* was hiring. Unfortunately it was not reporters, but copy clerks. They told me I was overqualified, but if I wanted the job, it was mine. I took it.

After a month I got pretty fed up because being a copy clerk is what I used to describe as being shit on feet. You did anything that had to be done—get cheeseburgers for the editor, xerox, pay people's utility bills, sharpen pencils *(laughs)*.

They said it couldn't be done, but I rose up there. The *Daily News* was the kind of place where if you showed you were capable, you would be able to do certain things. I got put on the night shift, which had a smaller staff. The City Editor had heard I was a journalism graduate, so he gave me some writing chores, the same thing you read about. I started writing obituaries, then I did rewrites for public relations handouts, and pretty soon I was helping out on police rewrite. In nine months I had quite a pile of clippings with my by-line on them.

A job opened up on the Action Line—you know, "Dear Action Line, I sent fifty dollars to Field's for yellow boots six years ago and they still haven't arrived. Please help me," and I got the job. It's a good training ground for a reporter because you get on the phone and yell at people and get a lot done. I was called an editorial assistant because they were too cheap to pay me as a reporter, but two years ago I was finally hired as a reporter.

And now the paper has folded. We'd been laboring for years at the *Daily News* with rumors that Marshall Field was going to fold the *News* and beef up the *Sun-Times*. Right before I went on vacation two months ago, I heard the newspaper was going to go down. I didn't want to be around when it happened, so the timing suited me just fine.

When I came back the TV critic said that the *News* had cancelled its big television advertising campaign. The next day people were clustering around in small groups in the City Room asking, "What do you know?" We had a real strong inkling, but the company would not confirm or deny anything.

And then about five to five that Friday afternoon our squeaky-voiced publisher, Marshall Field, mounted a credenza in the City Room and said, "It's been great to be on the winning side, but it's not great to be on the side when you're losing"—some crap. Because of the legalities he wouldn't even come out and say it. He said, "The Board of Directors of the *News* is contemplating the eventual closing on March 4. We're going to try to ease all your hardships." Blah blah blah blah. So that was it.

That weekend they contacted the people they didn't want to lose; there were no plans to contact the rest. There were about 149 editorial people let go and it will be several hundreds more with the truckers, printers, and machinists *(voice cracks, clears throat)*.

I had a glimmer of hope that I would be retained, but logically I figured I wasn't going to be because if they went by seniority there were a lot of folks who had been there a lot longer than me. But until you're given the word you always hope they'll need another mope to do obits or something. There was always the feeling that a miracle was going to happen, that some fairy godpublisher, if you will, would swoop down and say, "I'll buy the newspaper." Whether they admitted it or not, a lot of people had that hope. I know I had it, faint but persistent.

"There was always the feeling that a miracle was going to happen, that some fairy godpublisher, if you will, would swoop down and say, 'I'll buy the newspaper.'"

The criteria for deciding who stayed and who went were not released to us as we had requested, but I don't think they fired based on competence. There was no rationale; it was a Mad Hatter experience. The management people, who you didn't even know, were making the decisions. The ones that are really in shock are the people at the *Sun-Times* who were let go to make room for folks from the *News*. At least my paper is dead, so I don't feel rejected.

Still, it's like someone springs a trap door out from under you and you're flying in space, trying to grab onto something. Not only has a wonderful newspaper folded, but your whole life is sort of upset. Work is such a security blanket.

A kind of shock prevailed over the whole joint for the last month; some people stopped functioning altogether. There was black humor and guys were coming to work without shaving, wondering what the hell was the use, anyway.

Last week they gave a surprise party for a City Desk lady who had been there fifty years. She was like the eye of a hurricane; while everybody would be cursing and swearing, she was just as calm and nice as she could be, a wonderful person.

They had two cakes the size of a table and they had champagne. But while the editors were getting up to praise her, one of the other employees was pasting up a seating chart for people who were going over to the *Sun-Times*, some crap that says "You guys are through here." That's when I cried a little bit.

Yesterday it was like high school graduation time in the City Room. A year ago an anthology of *Daily News* writing came out and yesterday we were all passing around our little books and signing them. They had us pose for a group picture and I got on the shoulders of the biggest guy on the staff and was rocking back and forth up there. It was very unreal and I was still disbelieving.

"Still, it's like someone springs a trap door out from under you and you're flying in space, trying to grab onto something...Work is such a security blanket."

Last night was our big wake. I had had second thoughts about going to that party, but it was really nice. I thought people would talk about how they couldn't believe that that asshole, Marshall Field, would fold the paper, and about how they thought they would wind up, but they didn't; they talked about other things.

I didn't think that getting a job at another newspaper would be any too easy, but an instant job market has been created for us. Newspaper editors flew into town the day after the *Daily News* folding was announced and were interviewing people by the score. We really had a marvelous reputation. I sent out resumes to twenty-five or twenty-six places and got eight responses. Next week I have two job interviews.

But I don't want to jump into another job right away. I would like to take a vacation and lie down in the sun somewhere. This can be a wonderful opportunity to sit back and take stock of professional and personal goals. Those editors know we just went down the tubes; they must know the psychology of the thing. I'm too traumatized by this to think clearly and that's what I'm going to tell them. They must understand.

I can afford to hang out for a while. They're giving us severance pay—two weeks pay for every year you've been there—as provided by the union contract. And I think the company is going to throw in a couple extra weeks, just to show what a swell outfit it is. There is unemployment, plus I managed to salt away some money. I also have a couple of part-time things lined up.

But I don't think I could afford to live here indefinitely without a job. I can think of going South, someplace warm—Atlanta seems like an interesting place—or maybe the West, but there are right-wing publishers there.

The next newspaper I work on I want to be a star. Other people have said that to me, too. Just yesterday a guy my age, twenty-six and a half, was saying how he was tired of being on the mope list, excess baggage. We want to be considered indispensable. I'm thinking about a smaller operation, maybe in New England, where I could even run the show. Why not?—you get tired of taking orders from twelve people. I know guys who have done it out West and liked it a lot, but think that they lost their shirts.

I don't really want to move. I like it here, I have close school friends here and I live with a woman. We haven't even had a chance to talk about whether she would move with me. But now I have the realization that if I want to stay in the newspaper business it's going to involve moving.

It's very mysterious about why the newspaper folded. As Royko wrote, it would be one thing if we had turned into a rag, but with a few exceptions it was a dignified enterprise. The *Chicago Daily News* was a great newspaper. Last November we got so many scoops; it was making my head reel.

But still, our circulation dipped. The company wouldn't release the full sets of figures to back up its claim, and they're not legally obligated to do so. They said that people don't read evening papers—they watch TV instead, but I can't believe that because evening papers sell in other cities.

All week the way they were doing things has been just...They have a note in the final edition that the cartoonist whose work is on the front page will appear in the *Sun-Times*. I thought that people who would want to know would know. They could have left that stuff out of our last edition *(stifling tears).*

I really have a fondness for the *Daily News* people. I was not very close to many of them, but there was still a feeling of unity. The *Daily News* staff was wonderful people: a newspaper is like a living organism made up of all those people. I'm not going to be so unrealistic as to say that it was a perfect place because everybody bitched like crazy every day. It's like when a relative dies; you think of nothing but good.

All those feelings were going through my head till the very end. Still, I didn't think it was real until I went to the newsstand this morning and it said, "Final Edition—This Is It, Folks." There's a little bench by the El station and I just sat there and read the papers and tears were streaming down my face.

Alan found another job as a reporter in another city.

RARIN' TO GO

Julius Harris   West Hollywood, California

One block from the Sunset Strip, the light, airy apartment overlooking the pool could have been a set for a film about laid-back life in the California sunshine. Instead, the mood Julius evoked had the intensity of New York theater. In a deep, resonant voice, with commanding presence and a formidable display of emotions, he portrayed his frustration at not working so dramatically, it was easy to imagine that he would be a compelling performer.

Two months ago I played a cad in a show for "The Hardy Boys" television series, and that's about it at this particular point. For some reason or other I'm at a hiatus. You talk to agents, to casting people, and nothing is happening. All of a sudden you don't work anymore.

And I wonder why. After a while you begin to think, "What the hell is wrong with you?" You lose a little confidence. I can't explain what it is, but I think it's unfair. They pull people off the street to work when you've got actors sitting back here starving.

Back in the sixties I was part of the big, big upsurge of New York actors moving to Hollywood. I came out here because there was money that had to be made to take care of my two

57

kids and I knew I couldn't make it in New York. Sure, there's stage there, but how many plays are going on? I don't do musicals. So I came here with the hope of improvement in my work status. Black films were being made and I started moving up the ladder.

I did maybe ten films—*King Kong, Nothing But A Man, Live And Let Die, Islands In The Stream, Let's Do It Again.* There was a whole slew of black films and a lot of TV stuff. But I haven't been working like I should be working.

In my case being a black man nearly fifty-five may have something to do with it, plus I have a feeling that most of the casting people have typecast me in the heavy department because I'm a big man. As an actor I can play a lot of roles—I don't have to always be a preacher or a pimp or a thug or a pusher—but let's face it, how many things are being written for a guy like me unless he's a pimp or hustler or cop? Or some bum?

Hollywood has a very bad habit—dealing with glamour. I'm not a glamour boy, one of these flighty young boys that don't know his ass from a hole in the ground. I'm a man and my type of man hasn't really been shown on the black side yet, not even on TV. There have been isolated incidents, but it's not a steady diet as part of the American mainstream.

People here take advantage of talent and they don't use it. Individuals who could care less about your talent want to know how much you are worth in the box office. I feel like an amateur out here now. You go into a casting office and one of these guys says, "Well, Mr. Harris, we've heard of you. What have you done?" or "Would you mind reading for me?" Sometimes I read and sometimes I say no. You don't know what I've done—what are you doing in casting? What credits do you want?

I've got a following out here. I don't know how much of a box office attraction I am—I haven't been able to put a dollars and cents value on it—but when I'm walking on the street, people see me and say, "Hey, Jule, we just saw you in this or that. When you gonna do something else?"

I have to push and shove and get my own work. Not that my agents aren't any good—they're among the best—but there comes a point where they can't do anything for you; all they can do is submit.

But things may change. I'm talking to people now. There's a possible series and I am up for a couple of things, but I wish the hell I knew when they're going to happen.

It makes me feel angry—*angry*—but I ain't giving up—no, I'm not giving it up. I'm not going to sit back; I'm going to fight it every step of the way that I know how and let these people know who the hell I am. I am a professional actor who likes to work, who wants to work, and can do the job. Man, this is my profession. I'm not out here to be a Hollywood glamour boy and all of that bull—I'm out here to be an actor. I hope they can understand it.

I do get a little depressed. I don't get in that state of depression where people get to drinking heavy lines or get into drugs a heavy lot or some people jump off of the roof or drown themselves, but I do feel that, damn, I must have done something wrong, or somebody don't like me somewhere. I get disappointed when some things go down differently from what I have been told; I have been rejected for a few things after being informed that I was on it.

But after a while I get over it and say the hell with it. I always come up with some rationalization that I was better off not in the picture, which gets me over. I can't go crying over spilt milk. What's the old saying out in New York? If you miss one bus, there's always another one coming. And if I put myself in that bag of feeling that I'm no good, I'll wind up with a heart attack and ulcers, and I'm not ready to go yet. I figure I got another twenty years in this business.

Right now, though, I don't know where the next dollar's going to come from. I have a heavy case I have to deal with there, but slow but sure it comes together. When I have bills to pay and others coming in the mail, when the rent man is looking at me in the face, it kind of bothers me; still, I survive because I come out of the streets from a long line of survivors. One day you don't have a crust of bread, but the next day you have a whole loaf. One way or the other I get it together—I don't rob a bank yet. I thought about it a couple of times *(laughs)*—then I go and talk it out with my buddy.

Fortunately I've got a lot of friends in this town. Most of them are New Yorkers too. We sit and rap and do a few things together. I come on home, I read, I watch a lot of TV—I'm a heavy TV buff, I go to the movies. I'm not one of these tennis or golf players—I don't go running all over the place. Just leisurely go my way, keep my sanity together, and wait for the next day.

It's the only thing you can do. I mean, I love the business—don't want to do anything else, really. I can't go out and get me a nine to five any more. I could, but—what? What could I do? I haven't built up a thing for the lecture circuit: I don't believe in standing up in front of a bunch of people and talking a whole lot of nonsense just to be hearing myself talk.

I love to work—I love it. Working is one of the greatest highs I've ever had. When I played Idi Amin in the television film "Victory At Entebbe" I was high for two days.

Godfrey Cambridge, who was a good friend, was going to play that character and dropped dead, unfortunately. I got a call at ten o'clock the night that it happened and went in the next day. I had about fifty-two pages of dialogue and shot it all in one day. After we wrapped up the last scene and the director said, "Cut, print, that's it," the cast playing the part of the refugees applauded me, which is like my peers, man—it really turned me on. Helen Hayes kissed me. I was so exhilarated by bringing the character alive that I was high for days.

"I love to work—I love it. Working is one of the greatest highs I've ever had....Why should I not be working? I ain't dead."

When I come home from shooting I don't care how tired I am, I've accomplished something and I can look back at that scene and say, "Well, I've got that one in the can." Or if I go on stage, when the curtain comes down and the audience applauds, I feel good. It's like an artist painting a picture. All of a sudden you see it unfolded in front of you—"Uh huh, beautiful, thank you." And you go about your business to the next thing.

It's going to work—it's got to. Why should I not be working? I ain't dead. I'm in good health, I feel good, I've got my sanity. It's just a matter of time, that's all. I wish it would hurry up—it's kind of dragging a little bit there. I wish my future would come and catch up with my head. If anybody wants to know if I want to work, just put a script in front of me and say, "Let's do it." I'll make the character come alive.

Louis   Miami Beach, Florida
_____

*He retired from his guidebook publishing business at age
sixty-six. Two years later he had a heart attack and a
successful bypass operation, which left him feeling as energetic as a fifty year old. With his new-found energy and the
pressures of inflation, he tried to work again, but was incensed
to find that no one wants a man over sixty-five.*

*He sat upright at the edge of his chair as if poised to jump up
to work should the opportunity present itself.*

I'm dying to find something and now, nobody wants me. I
could really use some extra money now. My wife has a social
work job and I live on Social Security, but being self-employed
all of my life, I never paid enough Social Security because in
the old days you didn't have to pay. I lost twenty years with my
bypass operation two years ago, but no one wants my head; no
one wants my experience. It's a crime.

I never planned to retire. I just got a good opportunity to sell
my magazine and I did it. Then inflation hit me and I wanted
to unretire. I'd always had such a simple time finding a job, it
never entered my mind that I would have a problem. I thought
I'd take a year off and then get back into harness. But when
they say they don't want you after sixty-five, they don't want
you.

I don't want full-time work—I don't need it and I don't think
I could take it—but I could use my head all day long. I'm an
expert in figures. I'd be perfect in a supervisory capacity in
either insurance or advertising because I know them backwards. Insurance companies are desperate for people. They
are now paying two hundred dollars a week to send youngsters
to school, but they won't even talk to me. Chances are that I
know more about the business than the man doing the
interviewing and hiring because I spent twenty-five years in
it. But I don't want to get back in the insurance business. It's
changed too much since I left; it's a good business now for a
young man.

I've been looking in the papers. You can get three dollars an
hour on the telephone selling junk, but I don't want to do

anything like that, because you're robbing the people. I've been honest all my life and I don't want to change now.

Right now my greatest worry is financial. I never thought that would happen to me because it was always so easy for me to make more than a good living, but I didn't prepare and we're just about down to the last few dollars. Being an insurance man, I knew that Social Security was not the answer and it has been proven right. In fact, I don't know why the government doesn't junk Social Security right now. The young people are paying for me, which isn't fair, and I'm getting more expensive, even though I only get $170 a month. That's more than I'm entitled to because I only paid in for about five years. If I could sit down with young people, say, in their forties, and advise them about their futures, I would say IRA is a good preparation. They allow a man to pay in thirty, forty years and these men will amass a quarter of a million dollars by the time they're sixty-five. No question about it, your money doubles in ten years, quadruples in twenty years. They'll never get that from Social Security.

"Somebody's got to use my head for something besides putting a hat on it."

I feel funny about my wife being the breadwinner after all these years. It's funny—she went to work at the age of sixty-six when I retired. You spend forty-five years—you're the bread-winner, and three years she's the breadwinner. It's tough. Before that she only worked part-time, on and off, to get trousseaux for my daughters as they got married or things for the grandchildren. She never was pressed to earn money to eat.

My wife is in good shape except this job is too tough for her. She's too conscientious. If she'd work like other civil servants it would be fine, but last night, she worked on her paperwork at home until midnight. She's indispensable there. She'll be seventy next month and all the others are thirty and forty years old, but she's the only worker in the place. I want her to work part-time. She could do it and not lose any money because she'd still get her Social Security. I broke it down for her the other day. Working full-time she's getting just fifty dollars a month more, so she's actually working for Uncle Sam, not for herself.

I help my wife with her work. I pass the time helping her deliver food stamps and food to people who need it. I've done a lot of reading in the last four years, mostly just keeping up with current events, like *Newsweek, Time* Magazine, *Reader's Digest*. When I was working in advertising I read the sports pages and headlines and stuff like that, but I didn't really have time to delve into the world. I just can't sit all day with old men and talk—all they talk about is their grandchildren. I love my grandchildren too, but I can talk about other things besides grandchildren, for example, the stock market. I've got nothing in common with people my own age. I love sports—football and all that. I'm seventy years old with a mind of forty. All my friends are forty, forty-five, but my wife feels out of place with them so we're in real bad shape that way.

I can't see anything positive about not working. Maybe if I was financially solvent—they show you those pictures of the golden years where you play golf and all. I couldn't do that though. That would become monotonous—anything could become monotonous. See, I want to find a job and fire my wife because she can't make it anymore. Besides, I told you, I'm fifty years old and I feel just great, just fine. I'll find something. Somebody's got to use my head for something besides putting a hat on it.

Gus   A Town in the Midwest

A forty-nine year old executive with a briefcase, but without an office to be busy in, Gus seemed a bit surprised and more than a little chagrined that he had suddenly been cast adrift. With a warm smile and a firm handshake, he got right down to recounting the dilemma that was taxing his resources and ingenuity. Confident that eventually he would somehow be able to resolve his problem himself, he was nonetheless extremely grateful that finally there was somebody who wanted to listen and could understand.

I had been in a management position in manufacturing and I've been out of work just about two months. I worked for a manufacturing company that sold a piece of irrigation equipment for the farm industry. I had had a real nice promotion and was getting a fairly good salary for this area, and I did a real, real fine job. Saved the company a ton of money and did what I was supposed to do and more.

Things were going along pretty good until last year, when all of a sudden the price of grain went way, way down. The farmers were not able to get loans to buy equipment and they didn't even need our product with the rain they were getting.

Early this year the company had to do a lot of looking over of their situation. There were three reorganizations, and I participated in each one, even the last. My job was high enough in the organization so that I knew what was coming off—I'd helped plan what we were going to do. One night, seven weeks ago, I had a job when I left the office. The next day my boss presented the reorganization we had planned and was told he had to cut deeper—he had to cut a slice off the side of the organization instead of off the bottom, which meant some management positions. So my job was eliminated. It wasn't just me—there were a lot of other people. I was in pretty good company.

There are very, very few jobs available in this area that are similar to what I was doing. It looks as though it's going to be almost impossible, or at least very, very difficult, to find another job here at the level of the one I had. It may take a while.

It puts me on the horns of a dilemma because my desire is to stay in this particular city. I really like it here. It has all the things I need, and a year and a half ago, when things were good and I was making a good salary, I built my dream house. It's just exactly what I want. A particular piece of ground is unique—it can't be duplicated—and the particular piece of ground that I'm on right now is great. I don't mind traveling and I don't mind doing some things new, but I find it more important to have a nice place to relax in in the evening than I used to. Ten years ago I didn't care; now I care. So I suppose if somebody said, "Here's your ideal job, but it's in Casper, Wyoming," I don't know if I'd take it. I might take a less than ideal job in order to stay here.

Am I placing too high importance on staying? Maybe so. It's hard to know. But I really hate to part with the house.

I go to tell the story to an employment agency fellow and they say, "Boy, we can put you right to work. You've got everything we need. You can go to work in Cleveland or Detroit or Pittsburgh. You can go to St. Louis."

And I say, "No, I don't really think I want to do that."

"How about Chicago?"

And I say, "No, I lived in that part of the country—I'd rather live here."

"There is nothing here," they say. "You have to take a big cut in wages and start over at some other level."

And I have a problem with that. If I take a wage reduction and start low again, what will that look like in the future? I have to make a decision either to start low and worry about what it will look like, or move, which I really don't want to do. That's my dilemma.

I think I'm flexible. I'm not that rigid that I've got to be doing something exactly equivalent to what I had. The problem I'm running into is people asking how much I was getting. I tell them I was getting just under $35,000. Back East that's not a lot of money, but here it is, and they say they don't have anything for me. I ask what they do have and they want to know how low I would go. I don't know. I suppose I could take something like around $25,000, I would think, and still live the way I want to live, but they won't even give me a crack at some of those jobs because I'm overqualified—I'm too high-powered. They're afraid that if they hired me at a lower salary, I'd be looking for another job from Day One and I wouldn't be very permanent.

The kind of job I go into now is important for another reason, too. If I had to take just any job—if I had to go back, say, to being a line supervisor—I guess I'd have a problem feeling I was underutilized. I would also be awfully pissed about all the people I know who are younger and not so talented, not so experienced, who'd be making more. I guess I would be bitter—I don't know. And I may be faced with that. I don't know where

I'm going with that one yet. When I get there, I'll see how I handle it.

I'm still suffering a kind of disbelief that my job was eliminated because I really did produce—I did a super, super job. And I loved my job because they gave me a chance to experiment—make some mistakes and learn. What I learned and what they gained from it were just out of this world. For the first time in my life I had a job that I really, really enjoyed and which came close to fitting my ideals. It wasn't perfect, but it was closer than anything I could imagine. Not having that any longer has taken away a great deal of satisfaction.

It hurt my boss to have to part with me, but it was a matter where he had no choice. I think what he did was the right thing. The company was in a maintenance situation and didn't need growth. He had to figure out what was absolutely necessary to the organization and get that done with the very least amount of salary—that was all there was to it. It meant taking some chances on younger people. I would have done the same thing.

My boss probably cut me out for me as much as for himself. Out loose I'd at least have an opportunity to continue to grow, whereas there'd be no opportunity if I stayed. But I'd be lying if I said I was completely dispassionate, because without any question I think I did an outstanding job there. The words that my boss used in his letter of recommendation for me pretty much explain it: I'm on the move, on the upswing, even at this late hour in life. I am a good manager.

I'm still pissed—I can't say I'm not. To be told that the reason I was losing my job was because I make too much money, and in the same sentence be told I was worth more and I wasn't being paid what I ought to be getting was really something to hear. That's a hell of a note when you work hard to get there, then when you've got there, you can't stay there because you worked hard to get there.

I would be interested in starting my own business and if I could get a business going, hell, I'd sweep floors or anything. I'd be willing to take a part-time job, if it would help. With money to do it, it would be great to have a business, but I do not have the resources. My only resource would be the equity in the house, and I really don't want to part with that if I can help it. If I'm going to stay in this town, I'd like to stay right there. If

I'm going to have to sell the house, then I might as well move out of town.

One business I'm thinking about that I could start without capital would be consulting. I think I do have a lot to offer, and I know there's a need for what I have, so I am looking seriously at it. What I have isn't money; it's knowledge—knowledge on how to make businesses run better, how to get people to appreciate their jobs, how to get workers and managers to work together and generally improve the whole situation.

I discussed this with some consultants I've worked with, but they're not real keen about seeing any more competition in a business that isn't really all that great in this community. There's also a kind of fraternity of M.B.A.'s and P.h.D's. A bachelor's degree doesn't quite hack it. I am going to night school at the university trying to work on my master's and I kind of enjoy it, but it's going to take me a long time.

I was optimistic, but I'm not now. My job search has just not been that fruitful. I've had three interviews and that's not very much in six weeks.

I'm beginning to resent a little bit some of the people in hiring positions looking at my resume and telling me what I'm good at, making generalizations and saying, "Oh, well, this is your strong suit and there's nothing for you." I'm beginning to resent their shallowness, their not going into depth with the individual in front of them to find out who they're really talking with.

"If I thought it would help, I'd get plenty emotional, but who's going to listen? Who gives a damn?"

In my past I've probably been guilty of what I'm accusing them of now, so maybe I can identify and feel for what they're doing, but it doesn't make me feel any better about it. Generally speaking, management people hiring in personnel departments are not only insensitive but, I think, dumb, just dumb. It has caused me to think I'd like to have done some things differently when I was back there, made some different decisions.

I'm emotional, but I don't get all that emotional about my

circumstances, at least not yet. My salary continuation goes on for another four weeks. When it runs out, I probably should apply for State Unemployment Compensation, which is a pittance compared to what I made. I guess as I get closer to that time my emotions may become more noticeable.

I've been aware of some down days, but normally I'm pretty high-spirited and I feel pretty good. I'm being realistic, maybe. I'm not sure that getting all excited or all ticked-off would do any good. If I thought it would help, I'd get plenty emotional, but who's going to listen? Who gives a damn? My wife cares, but what good does that do? She's not in a position to do much about it.

What I'm going through now is lonely. There's no one else can feel what I feel. There's no one else can feel the disappointment from having lost a job because you did a good job. And there's no one else can feel the frustration from not being able to duplicate the job I lost. You can have some empathy—I can—for other people who've been there, but to really get inside, it's a lonely business.

The only thing to do is just work double hard and get out of it. When the company laid us off, it ran a little seminar for finding employment, which I thought was very good. It had to do with taking a look at what your strengths and weaknesses were, making a good appraisal of your own self and determining what you want to do. There are a couple of good books on the subject.

Maybe I'm licking my own wounds too much to be real objective. The trick is not to let yourself get wrapped up in your own moroseness, I guess.

Ron   New York, New York

"When will you come? I've never worked, you know," Ron had asked, eager for people to know his story. Tall and handsome, with a dazzling smile, he had spent the morning in his sunny, crowded little walk-up apartment anticipating the meeting impatiently. Being interviewed was a break he was looking

forward to as a relief from the daily monotony of no freelance photographic assignments and no money for diversion.

I don't seem to work a great deal, but this is natural for someone who has moved to a new city, is establishing contacts and creating a reputation for himself. I'm an American, thirty-two years old, but I spent all of the sixties and most of the seventies in Europe. I've only recently come to the States to live.

The only slaves I've done were working in a color processing lab for a year and a half, being a messenger for the *New York Times* for three days when I was seventeen, and working one day in a laundromat when I was eleven. But I've worked freelance and independently as a photographer for a considerable amount of time. I've done portraits, fashion, reportage, personalities—all kinds of things like that—and have been published in magazines in America, Australia and Europe.

I usually develop my own creative ideas which I try and sell, but I'll probably have to change my tune about that and become more malleable. Most art directors have their own hard and fast ideas about the way they want pictures, and if I want to work and make money, I can't hold out too long being absolutely independent and autonomous as a source of ideas.

People think my work is very good. Some people think it's probably too good to put in certain magazines because it is so unique in its content and form. It is more artistic than commercial and I shall have to become more commercial to start getting jobs.

Although it is hard to find work, I don't question my ability. I have a strong sense of my artistic integrity, though it can be a millstone around my neck too. If I weren't so sure of my own capabilities, then perhaps I would start to look around and take on a less elevated situation.

I don't mind not working. Well, I'll take that back; I do mind not working. It feels as if I'm not using my creative abilities to earn a living and to express myself. It is depressing, I get angry and I tend to sleep a lot. But ever since I've been living with Judy, I find it's not so hard to fill in time as it used to be. I don't go out for coffee in coffee shops quite so much and I have her here beside me to talk to and cuddle. Most times in the evening I'm happy to stay home. I'm most happy when she cooks a nice meal and we eat it together and watch TV, then hop into bed.

I'm supported by donations from my mother and by Judy's unemployment checks. I have gotten a few jobs which have brought me some money. I do not earn enough to make it from month to month. My mother pays my rent, so I have a pad. I have enough to eat and if I run out of Marlboros, I can run to the store and buy another package. I would like to be making more money so that I can go see my eight year old son in Europe more often, but until I start getting some more commercial jobs, that will have to wait.

I had a nervous breakdown six and a half years ago and it takes a long time to get out of it. I'm still getting out of it—ha ha—I still have about eight to go on the Rolling Stones' "Here Comes Your Nineteenth Nervous Breakdown." Actually, I just had kind of a mini-nervous breakdown last month. I had a pretty rough couple of weeks, but I pulled out of it. I'm in chemotherapy and that helps, then doing Transcendental Meditation helps to smooth out the edges. TM is an enormous channel of strength and peace and happiness for me.

"I worry a lot and I pray a lot too, especially that marvelous part in the Lord's Prayer where it says, 'Forgive us our debts as we forgive those who we are in debt to.'"

I worry a lot and I pray a lot too, especially that marvelous part in the Lord's Prayer where it says, "Forgive us our debts as we forgive those who we are in debt to."

I love working. I don't just like taking pictures for the sake of taking pictures; I like to take pictures with an end in mind. I would consider myself to be working if I were doing jobs freelance on a fairly regular basis, and that's what I intend to be doing. I just live every day in the hopes that it will come about quickly, that the phone will ring and I'll say, "Hello? Hello? Yes, I'll do it. Sure. Thank you."

Less than one year later Ron committed suicide.

"EXPERIENCE REQUIRED"

Billy   Omaha, Nebraska

His previous employer had given him a hard time and it had taken Billy a while to collect all his back pay. Now he waited, uncomplaining, in the union hall where a building construction training program was administered, hoping he would be lucky enough to be admitted to the next class. Nineteen years old, slight and fair, and on the shy side, he found it hard to elaborate all his feelings about not working, but he made it quite clear that he was intent on getting set in a useful trade that would bring in a reliable income.

I worked with a guy for about six months doing painting and general repairs, not real hard construction. I enjoyed working with my hands and building. But it's been three months since that job. I would have kept working, but he bounced a few payroll checks on me and there was a problem.

I just more or less quit on him. It's not right for him, bouncing a payroll check on me. Every time I went to cash it, there was no money in the bank. I just couldn't put up with that. I was out the money until it was settled through the County Attorney.

71

I tried for a few jobs, but it's all Experience Required, so I feel that if I get a chance to go to school and then to work, that's what I want to do. I thought of college, but I couldn't be a full-time student—even a part-time one. That's just too much studying, whereas I'd be more interested in a trade.

I have a chance to go into a trade school to learn building construction. While I'm doing that, they'll place me in a job, so it will really be a good thing if I can get in. It's just a matter of when the opening's going to be. I've been waiting to hear. She told me yesterday that I have a chance to get in starting next class. The kid before me dropped out of the waiting list and there's just one more position for someone to show up for.

I feel like I can do it; I just haven't had the opportunity. I never really had no real good experience because I'm just nineteen and trying to find out what I want to do. Going through the program I'm doing something with myself. I wouldn't want to sit and run a machine for the rest of my life. People who do that get paid a good wage—anyone can do it, I guess—but I want to learn something, put myself to use.

"I wouldn't want to sit and run a machine for the rest of my life. People who do that get paid a good wage— anyone can do it, I guess—but I want to learn something, put myself to use."

Since I haven't been working, I haven't been doing too much, really. I find things to do at home—work on my car or something. I don't just sit there and watch TV; I try to get out, keep motivated. I go out bowling or play basketball at the gym by the house, the Salvation Army Community thing. But mostly I've just been waiting to have her get hold of me and tell me that I can start the program.

I still live at home with my mother. It feels like I'm too dependent on my mother. I lost my dad a couple years ago and I couldn't leave her there, so I'm going to live at home for a while, but it's tough. I'd like to move out, but I can't do it unless I have a job.

I'm not too sure of myself. I get nervous not having a job. I think about it all the time. I don't feel like I'm doing anything useful like I want to. I get depressed sometimes, but I don't really let it get to me.

I've got bills to pay. I always meet them, though I'm slowly running out of money. I could go out and get a job as a dishwasher or something, but I'm not broke yet, so as long as I can, I'll hold out. When I go broke, if I absolutely cannot wait no longer for the training program, then I will have to go find something. I'm sure I can, but I think it might be worth the wait. I hope it will be, anyway.

My ma asks, "When are you going to get a job?" My sister comes over and says, "When are you going to get a job?" But I can deal with it. I just hope things go right for me. I just have to wait it out.

Michael   Brooklyn, New York

Trim, dark-haired Michael sat rocking his infant son in the sunny little kitchen. A professional gambler and graduate student in philosophy, he was accustomed to spending a lot of time at home. But his wife had left her job and he was feeling an urgent need to go to work in a "regular" job for the steady income and for his own sense of identity. All keyed up, he put the baby to bed and suggested we move into the living room, where there would be room for him to pace the foor. Talking seemed to calm him down. He ended up refreshed—pleased at having new perspectives to mull over.

It has been approximately two years since I've worked. It's a problem. I obviously have to work now. My wife has just had our second child and has quit her teaching job. We're not in a role-reversal situation and I have to start bringing in a steady income. Though Julie has worked steadily until this semester and I haven't, it was not the sort of thing where we agreed that she would be the breadwinner for a while and I would stay home. Julie was always working on the assumption that some day I would take over.

When we married, with Julie working I could devote myself to graduate school and hop around pretty freely from one job to another, if I wanted to. Julie had seniority and was making excellent money. Not only was it rather hard to turn your back on that money, but any job I might have found would not have approached her salary, so there wasn't much motivation for me to work. I have a Master's degree in philosophy and I'm minus my dissertation for a Ph.D. The fact that I was in school always gave us direction—at least a goal that I'd finish and then have some sort of nice job so it didn't look as if I were just a wanderer. I thought I would teach philosophy.

I also had many, many hobbies, and always imagined that eventually one of them would pan out in the sense of making money for me. But as time goes by I realize nothing's going to develop out of any of these things except for one—gambling. I know quite a bit about gambling and I consider myself a rather good poker player. Poker's a personal game. You can size up your opponents quickly. It's not as mathematical as many people believe. For the past six months, maybe a year, I've been playing quite a bit and doing OK. Over the summer things were going very well and we managed to accumulate a little money. However, for the last two months or so I haven't been playing very much, so there hasn't been a steady income. The few times I did play, I didn't win by much and I did lose a few times. Consequently our savings are diminishing.

Even while you're winning you tend to forget that eventually a loss will occur and you overspend. That's a problem. Also, it's not easy to find poker games. They run for a month or two months or three, and then they just die for no apparent reason. Between games there's just nothing to do. Another disadvantage is that it requires very long hours. It's not uncommon for me to sit down and play for twenty-four hours straight, which is really rough, especially on the family.

But I've also been looking for a job. Lately I've been concentrating in the area of computer programming. I've studied it and I've studied quite a bit of mathematics, so I have the technical background. I was rather good at it; in fact, I would write programs to test blackjack systems. I've just never done it professionally. I don't know how well I'd like writing programs for other people.

Computer programming is a strange area. I'd been told that only a few years ago a person who walked through a computer center too slowly would be snatched up and hired. I decided to move in that direction because of those rumors, but that's not the case any longer. In fact, the way things are today, there may be 300 other applicants for a trainee position, most of whom were computer science majors. And how do they decide who to hire?—they give them a test. I don't think this is true in any other area of comparable education. You would never give an engineer a test.

I do look for other kinds of jobs as well. I'm always looking for something. Initially I was advised that the best way to find employment was to put your best foot forward: If you're well educated, then say so. If you're very bright, tell them. I created resumes that attempted to convey those facts and I found that they weren't well received at all. On interviews I met with contradictory attitudes. There was a certain amount of esteem because I was an academic, but then they'd wonder why a person with my education would want to be a programmer. They would figure I must be desperate and would stay only until a position opened somewhere else, then leave. There was also the feeling that since I was an academic, I didn't know anything about the "real world."

I tried to resist the temptation to dilute my resume, but eventually I did it. Instead of indicating that I was a doctoral candidate in philosophy, I just eliminated graduate school altogether. Instead of listing the "nicer" jobs I've had, I eliminated them. I said, for example, that I worked as a bank teller for two years. It isn't true—I only did it for a few months—but it filled a time period. I said I drove a cab for four years, which isn't true. I did drive for a while but not that long. Instead of showing that I went to school full-time, I indicated I went part-time. The resume created the impression that I was a hard-working person with two children who worked during the day, went to school part-time, and wanted something better out of life. I looked like a person inching his way up slowly—struggling and fighting. The responses became more favorable, though I didn't actually get hired. Interviewers would invariably say, "Ah, you went through college the hard way." That was a plus—you could tell by the way it was said.

The problem, however, was that I had no experience in any area, and apparently in today's economy nobody can afford to train anyone. You have to come in knowing your job. I think I'm on the right track now. If something should appear, I'll take the job. It doesn't have to be a good job—I'll take basically any job. I'm thirty years old and I don't have much longer to accumulate some experience. At this point that's what I'm concerned with. It's my major stumbling block to making any progress.

"I'm not someone to miss an opportunity because of failure to lie. It's absurd. If somebody wants such and such a type person, it may take me a little while to discover what he wants, but I'm going to be that person."

I discovered something about tactics in the process, though, and that is to lie. I'm not someone to miss an opportunity because of failure to lie. It's absurd. If somebody wants such and such a type person, it may take me a little while to discover what he wants, but I'm going to be that person.

I think that not being able to say you are competent in some specific area takes its toll on you psychologically. It would be nice if I could say that I were, say, an engineer, a physician, or something like that. It's almost like classifying yourself. It's not to say that that's all you are, but that there's one area in which you are something of an expert. I really can't say that, and it bothers me.

I picked rather prestigious examples, but it could be even, say, a policeman or a fireman. But I'm not anything. I'm a thinker, a philosopher. At one time that sounded great because I thought I'd be working in that area, but now I'm not. And just to be a philosopher?—I don't know—what is that? That's not anything.

I used to think that the ideal life was something like the way the classical Greeks understood it—discussing politics in the marketplace during the day, perhaps exercising in the afternoon, coming back at night and philosophizing. Going to sleep and doing the same thing the next day. Then all of a sudden that ideal life didn't seem so attractive any more. I'm not sure why it doesn't.

When it starts to bother me, I feel depressed and I start to blame myself and condemn myself. I may become a little withdrawn. I can still laugh and do whatever else I do, but inside I feel different. Occasionally I suggest that I'm not so happy and this seems to surprise close friends. It seems to be happening more frequently now than in the past, but just how frequently is hard to say. When you're in a state of depression, it seems you've felt that way for a long time.

I was not raised in an environment in which other people's expectations would create this sort of guilt feeling. My immediate family—my mother, my father, brothers, and sister—have all lived pretty much the way I'm living right now, unfortunately. My father has made his living gambling all his life. I love my father in many ways, but I wouldn't like to be like him in all respects, and sometimes I'm afraid that I'm repeating the same sort of life he has led. That annoys me. What I'm most afraid of is that his type of life has possibly helped to create his character and that it will create the same type of character in me.

For example, I find myself occasionally lying. In general it's bad policy to lend money playing poker, and people have developed various techniques to prevent having to do it. Lying is one—putting money away and saying you don't have any. I was always very critical of that and now I find myself doing it.

My father is always asking to borrow money from me. Once in a while I'll say no. It's true he always pays—he doesn't owe me a single cent—but he likes to hold my money. He says, "What's the difference? When you need it, you ask me and I'll give it to you."

And it's true—that's just what happens—but I can't see why I should have to worry. Maybe something will come up where I'll need money and my father won't have it, so we'll have to go somewhere else and borrow money. That annoys me.

Lately I've been getting the jump on him, so to speak, borrowing money from him that I don't need. Since I have a little of his, he can't come to me because I owe him money. The most he could do is get back what I borrowed from him.

I don't like to do these things. I don't like to have to be devious, but I find that you can't compete unless you play by the same rules. You're at a disadvantage if you're straight. I think that I do a better job at being straight than most people, but nevertheless a certain amount of deviousness seems almost necessary. And I wonder whether I'm going to become that way permanently if I do it for a long period of time. Maybe this concern is contributing heavily to my desire for a job.

Working doesn't seem very attractive, but my concern about having some steady source of income is growing in importance. I worry that I won't be able to establish it and I also worry that I won't be able to finish my degree. Now why should I want to? It's not going to get me a job; it's not going to do anything for me at all. However, I did start and I want to finish. It worries me that it's fairly common for a person to find it hard to finish a degree once he's gotten away from it.

Not working sometimes feels good and sometimes feels very bad. Sometimes I am very happy with the freedom. I wake up pretty much when I like, I go to sleep when I like, I'm with my wife and my family most of the time. When I want to go out to play poker, I go. If I don't feel like going out on a particular night, I don't.

Right now I'm staying home a lot because of the kids. Our lives are particularly unstructured because of the baby getting up every two hours during the night. Julie has to sleep some time. If she can't get up with the baby at two or four a.m., I have to do it, but then I won't be able to get up at eight because I've been up at two and four. If I'm not here to help, Julie has to stay awake all night then all day, so when does she sleep? If I've been out playing poker for twenty-four hours straight, I have to sleep when I come home. It presents a problem.

Under more normal circumstances, without the baby keeping us up at nights, our lives are still rather unstructured, but not as bad as they are right now. On a typical day we'd wake up about eleven, assuming we got to sleep the night before. I'll go out and maybe stop at my mother's. My brothers will be there and we'll discuss our plans—we're always planning. Perhaps I'll spend a few hours in the library and get little things like stopping at the bank out of the way. And depending upon what evening it is, I'll start to plan who I have to meet to go to this place or that place to play. If I'm not playing poker, around ten-thirty or eleven o'clock comes another study period of about three hours.

Probably what I do most of the time when I'm not depressed is learn things, pretty much anything. I think I'm rather versatile, so I can go from philosophy into very technical chemistry or mathematics or gambling. Whenever something strikes my fancy, I can go right into it, and if I'm feeling good I can really enjoy it. Maybe I won't do anything for a week, but when I become interested in something, it's nothing for six hours to go by like six minutes. I'm sure that the person who works on a regular basis doesn't get any more work done than I do.

When I enter into something of my own volition, I'm a very hardworking person. In fact, every once in a while when I start to feel guilty about things, I remember that fact and it makes me feel much better.

I feel pretty productive—of what, I don't know. Character, I guess. I feel I'm always improving myself or trying. I don't think there's any more need for justifying that than there is for justifying sex. It's enjoyable, so you do it. I try to make my family happy, do whatever is necessary for the kids, and teach them. That's productive enough.

"I'd just be more comfortable if I could call myself something."

The only thing I might feel deprived of is a sense of security, perhaps. I'd just be more comfortable if I could call myself something. If I could say, "I'm a poker player," or "I am a philosopher," I would be happy, but I can't say these things because I'm not sure of where I'm moving.

What I would like would be to accumulate enough money so that I could put it to work for me, rather than work from nine to five each day. I think I would die if I had to work like that. I might be able to do it for short periods of time, but not for a long period and take orders.

I'm not very good at taking orders from people; that's very unpleasant. I always had trouble in school because I was in an inferior position and I didn't do very well in the service because of that. In fact, I've had trouble with it all through life. I'm certain it has contributed a great deal to my distaste for work.

Gamblers recognize that the life of a person who works from nine to five is better materially than their own in some respects, but I find that most of them have a certain degree of contempt for the average working person, and I share it to a certain extent. The feeling comes mostly from recognizing

---

"I've seen people kowtowing to their bosses so often that I've come to regard it as almost necessary to working."

---

that the nine to five situation is almost a form of slavery. I've seen people kowtowing to their bosses so often that I've come to regard it as almost necessary to working. I wonder how a person could humble him/herself before another person. I'm not the haughty type, but I don't humble myself either. The contempt I feel has its source, I'm sure, in seeing people give up their freedom and autonomy, losing their worth.

When I was teaching college, if I got involved in something I could cancel my classes for a week, then make them up the next week and no one gave me any trouble about it. The university may be the only place where you can live that kind of life. I expect that I wouldn't find that experience on a job and I expect a job to be an alienating experience, if only for the fact that I would be at someone's call and have to do what I'm told or at least, make a pretense of doing it. And that wouldn't make me happy.

I always thought I was something special—not in the sense of being better than anyone else—I don't think I've ever suffered from that delusion—but I always thought that I had ability and would do something wonderful. I haven't given up that hope yet. I'd be very, very unhappy if I thought that some day I would. Perhaps what frightens me most in trying to satisfy practical needs now is the feeling that in the course of satisfying them I'll sort of lose track of this other thing.

Joseph   Los Angeles, California

When twenty-seven year old Joseph came into the small office to talk after his bookkeeping class at the job-training program, the contrast between him and the students laughing and joking in the corridors was startling. Sober and beaten-looking, the dark, sweet-faced man was of the age of the "Now Generation," but looked as though he hadn't had a moment's fun in years. Still, he was not defeated. And though English was a struggle for him, he was determined to get his whole story out.

I'm from Egypt and I have a problem in Egypt. I felt discriminated. The people who are Moslem religion they get a job right away. We are Christian. So I had to leave the country and my sister invited me to come over here.

My sister is a doctor in New York. She's American citizen. And I think she lied when she said that everything is very easy over here. She brought me from Egypt, but there's no brother, sister give you money—nobody take care of others. I like somebody to clear the way for me.

I was in New York for three years, and I worked most of the time at construction work. I like construction work, but it's not my profession and they don't keep me for long. I have to go from one job to another job because I didn't have local experience. They ask many questions and after many interviews they reject me. I thought that maybe I got to go to another state to get better chance, so almost one year ago I come to Los Angeles.

In Los Angeles I tried to go to many interviews, to many jobs. I made test for the county, interviews for United Parcel Service, for Post Office. To all of them you need local experience. Wherever you go they just give application and say, "No, thank you," or "We'll call you," and I never heard nothing.

All I find was a part-time job as a security guard. Then I get this career program to learn to be a bookkeeper. This program has helped me because it pays me as a full-time CETA student. It's very hard to get through this program, but I know that when I get through they try to help and find a job.

Before I entered this program I go to school to improve my English, but I can't work and go same time to college. I didn't have chance to study. All the English I know is what I had to do for college in my country. But it is not too good and I need some practice.

I have a financial problem. I have to pay installment for the car and I have to pay my rent. I thought that maybe I can sell the car or give it back to the bank, but I'm afraid I cannot travel without the car. The school's too far and I have to go from one place to another for a job. I have to go here and there, and so I get my car back.

Before I got into the program I cannot control my financial problem. Sometimes I don't have enough money to feed myself. I told my wife to go back to Egypt until I can stand on my feet. She went over there and she stayed almost one year and a half. She just coming back last month., I'm looking for a future better now, but before I looked unhappy because I sent my wife back to Egypt for her father to support. It's hard for me to leave my wife to go back for money problem.

"If you have a good job, everybody would be your friend, but if you don't have a job, nobody helps you, even looks at you—that's true."

If you have a good job, everybody would be your friend, but if you don't have a job, nobody helps you, even look at you— that's true. I feel sometimes like going back to Egypt, but I feel disappointment to go back. Everybody look at me and say it's too bad to go back.

Almost most of my family they came down to New York, but they felt the same thing. They felt disappointed after they came and I think they going to go back. It's hard for everyone to find work, especially for the people that just came in. They arrive from overseas and they feel lost. They don't help them at unemployment office—they just tell them look at the board and you find something. It's like I did three years in New York. I didn't know what I'm doing.

I like to work. I like to work hard. I try to get job. I'm trying to save some money. Three years in New York I didn't save one penny. In America long time now I didn't improve my situation.

The don't want to give me full-time job. All they have is part-time job. They give for American people full-time job and the part-time job give for foreigner. They don't want to give time and a half for overtime for people, so they give full-time people Monday through Friday, forty hours, then they give another people chance and they hire many people just for part-time job.

It feel me bad to stay home because I'm young enough—I'm twenty-seven. Why I stay home—for what reason? I don't have any children. I can't get children now because my income is very low. I need to buy a home, to have kids and to have family. The situation I have now is very bad.

I didn't have somebody to clear the way for me, to show me how is this country, how is the custom, how is English, and how is the situation I come to. It takes me time to find by myself. Some people help if you ask—some, not all. There should be some organization to give information about this country—how to get through it—like these Asian people who run this program have. I took a long time for me to get around to find all the way by myself. My people don't have any organization.

I don't know if I'm going to get a job right away when I finish this program. They try hard to get jobs for all people, but they don't have jobs for all people. I don't know how long it will be—right away, a short time, a year. I still have hope. I think it is a bad period of time, looking better for the future.

LET GO

Roberta   Gaston, North Carolina

She was taut with tension and every so often the anger from having just been fired exploded through. Here was a well-organized, competent woman whose life had been firmly under control and now—this. A southern textile mill and a strong union member mix about as well as oil and water.

I'm upset because I lost my job! I probably could manage because my husband works and he makes good money, but that's not the point. We have bills and I have kids who are not my husband's. If I didn't have nobody but myself, it probably wouldn't make no difference whether I work or not, but I don't want to lose my job and be dependent on my husband.

I was going into my sixth year of working in the card room at the Rosemary mill, one of the J.P. Stevens plants. I had been out for almost two weeks with the flu and my supervisor was going to make me come in and work when I was running a temperature and taking penicillin. They hassled me the whole two weeks I was back, calling me in the office every day. Tuesday they had the checker on my job in the morning and in the afternoon both, when usually it's either one or the other.

The day before yesterday, after my morning break my overseer told me to come in the office. I thought maybe he

84

wanted to talk to me about how the job was running, but he said that I had been on my break for twenty-five minutes.

I told him I hadn't and that six of us had been sitting in there and he could ask them. He started yelling at me and I just yelled back at him. He told me as long as he'd be there I wasn't going to take a break, and I told him as long as he stayed there and as long as I worked, I was going to take a break.

He kept asking me if I was going to quit. I didn't tell him anything, so he threatened me, telling me if I yelled at him again just what he might do. Then he told me to get out. I got my coat and things and went to the union office. They told me to go back to work the next morning.

Yesterday, when I went back to work my supervisor came over and said, "I thought you quit." "Well, I didn't," I told him. He told me to go to the office and brought the job overseer in with him. He told me he wasn't explaining nothing—to get my coat, give him the dust mask and my locker key, and get out.

It was payday and I asked for my check, but he said he didn't have it. I left but I went back when the shift had changed and got my check. I left at eleven o'clock and they had another girl in there at one o'clock.

"I'm feeling really bad about this. It even made me sick in the stomach last night."

I don't know why they fired me and I can't understand why they been hassling me in the office every day for two weeks. They talked about my production and I'm running more than anybody that runs my job on either shift.

I went back to the union yesterday morning and talked to them. One of them said she called up the plant and they might call me to come back Monday. I hope the union will protect me. I'm pretty sure they will. They have protected a lot of them back up there. I know the plant tried to get rid of one boy who couldn't wear the dust mask and the union got the plant to transfer him to another job last Monday. He said he knows he wouldn't have gotten his job back if it hadn't been for the union.

I already applied today for a job at another mill. They start you off with the lowest pay, five dollars an hour, because it's the paper mill. It's a good mill to work for because they already have a good union, but they ain't been hiring women there, only men. But it really couldn't be no harder than in the card room—it couldn't.

I filed for unemployment today, but I'd rather be working than drawing unemployment. I was laid off once for three months and I drawn it and I just didn't ever like it. It's almost to me like somebody on welfare.

I'm feeling really bad about this. It even made me sick in the stomach last night. I got so angry with my supervisor I have even said that if I could catch him in the street, I'd probably shake him, though that would probably do no good.

I want my job back, but I have often thought about doing something else. I even asked several times for a transfer out of the department because I think it really damages. There's quite a lot of dirt and dust. The doctor from Durham told me that anybody who works in that department as much as five years is automatically brown lung. It has affected me a lot already, coughing and breathing.

This just might be a way to find someplace else to work. I said, "Well, I got married one time and I didn't make it and I was scared to try it again. But I tried it again and it was better. So maybe I'll try another job. Maybe it will be better." I just have this feeling that I'll get another job if I want. I've got that much hope. It might not be what I exactly want and not pay as much, but I'll get something. I'm not really worried because I have a Practical Nurse's license and I can get a job nursing, but working in the mill pays more money. But the way they treat you up there!

Still, I would love to go back to that same plant on another job in that department. I don't want to quit until the union gets the contract signed. I would stay there and work if I had a better job. I'm going to fight for it.

Danny   Los Angeles, California

His Spanish-style house had character and charm and Danny
had been spending a lot of time in it. If he ventured outside and
closed the door behind him, the pressure was very hard to bear.
In shock from being laid off from his "secure" civil service job,
he was at a loss about how to deal with his situation.

I was a title examiner for the County of Los Angeles for twelve
and a half years. And three months ago Proposition 13 came
along. They claimed it was the greatest revolution since the
American Revolution. I don't know if it is or not, but the
tremendous revenue created from property taxes was eliminated and budgets and personnel were to be cut.

I had approximately a six week span of speculation before
they announced the cuts and during that time some friends
approached me with a business proposition which sounded
exciting and would have been much more lucrative than
working at the County. I felt that since I'm thirty-nine, I've got
the wisdom of the ages—I'm going to be all right. I was saying,
"Jeez, I hope I get laid off. This is going to be a golden
opportunity and I'm going to make a killing. Oh, it's going to
be great."

I had not gotten along at the office very well and in twelve
and a half years I had never gotten a promotion. It was just a
general bad scene. I had grown a beard, I refused to wear a tie,
and I was Jewish, which I felt had a lot to do with it. I disliked
it very much and I tried sometimes to get out. I went to law
school at night, but without passing the bar. Law degrees in
California are a dime a dozen. I flunked the California Bar six
times, and after you get hit over the head that many times, you
feel it wasn't meant for you.

I thought my job would be safe with my seniority. At the
most I figured there would be a 10 percent cut, maybe one or
two bodies. Last month they called the senior title examiners
into the conference room and when they came out, four had
been demoted and had to take a $300 a month drop in pay.
Then they simply gave eight or ten of us an envelope. It was
about a 33 percent cut in staff, based on position and seniority.

My boss and my section head said, "Sorry this had to happen. It was beyond our control. You did a great, great job for us." This was bullshit because I was always at odds with them and we hated each other's guts, but I figured, why burn bridges behind me and said, "Oh, thank you. I enjoyed working for you."

I felt bad. I tried to rationalize it by saying, "I have a good job offer; I'm better off," but I felt angry and hurt and I didn't know what I was going to do.

I invited all the guys who were laid off over to the house for a beer bust and everybody sat around drinking and trying to be jovial. Some of the guys were mimicking a character from a television show who said, "I'm so confused. What am I going to do?" It was kind of sad. We all hated the title companies and nobody wanted to go back to them. It's a high pressure job and the pay is at the low end of the real estate field. But most of the guys had no alternative. We had the depression you get from having to go back to the shit you thought you had gotten away from.

"I thought I was secure with Civil Service—you know, you can't get those bums out with a crowbar."

I started doing things with the business venture right away. I looked for store locations, talked to rental agents, and had business meetings with my two prospective partners. But now the plan is down the drain and the realization has hit me: I don't have this great opportunity any more, I don't want to go back to the title companies, I am not a member of the bar. What am I going to do?

I feel very frightened. When I quit college in my senior year, I got my first job as a title searcher because the address was close to where I got off the bus. I put in for my second job, at the County, at my uncle's insistence. I've always taken the easy path. I'm basically a lazy guy—thirteen years I get up at a certain time, I go to work, I do the work in my sleep, I reach out and get my paycheck twice a month. I thought I was secure with Civil Service—you know, you can't get those bums out with a crowbar.

At unemployment Friday they said, "Oh, we've got a job for you." It paid about $200 less than I had been making and I thought that was a step back, but it was as legal assistant to the corporate secretary at Getty Oil and I had high hopes. I figured that if they liked me, I could always negotiate a higher wage.

There was no interview. I dressed casually, but not too casually, just in case they did want to talk to me, and went to deliver my resume.

The personnel officer told me they had decided to make an offer to someone else, but that she would still submit my resume. I asked her to call me either way. It has been three days and I haven't received a call back. I feel—aaach—here I am, my first time out and I'm rejected already.

I've been out of work for one month now, but I had a month's vacation pay built up so I haven't drastically altered my lifestyle. At the end of this month there will be no more vacation money, just $104 from unemployment, and I can feel that my anxiety about meeting my bills will so overwhelm me that I will get out there and do something quickly.

We've lived beyond our means—never saved a penny— always lived up to the hilt. The payments on the house are exorbitant, and the only way we made it was that my wife and I were both working full-time. But I'd always said I'd rather live good when I'm young and sit on the rocking chair on the porch when I'm old. I don't have any regrets that I didn't save some money. One of the other guys had tremendous sums of money and he was more depressed and upset than any of us.

If I had enough money to support my lifestyle, I wouldn't want to work. I would be what I consider a hustler—hang around the coffee shop with the time and flexibility to find out about an opportunity here, a quick buck there, a deal here. In my fantasies these things must exist out there, and if you hang around long enough you would meet people and fall into things.

I made this commitment to myself: I don't care about the money; I do not want to take another job I don't like. If I have to work for $800 a month, it will be in the job I like, maybe something like selling sporting goods. People say I would be a great salesman because I have the gift of gab, but I was always afraid I wouldn't sell anything and I never had the guts to try it.

Since I've been laid off I've gone into what is probably an escape mechanism. I don't stay in the house all the time or spend that much time goofing off, but one or two days I took a nap in the afternoon and I've always been an escapist into TV.

When the business deal dropped through I was really down in the dumps. I hold things in. I'm probably depressed today. I just try to shove it aside, but I do get a little more snappy with my family; I'm a little more on edge and I'm more short-tempered. I had a big fight with my mother-in-law—I felt she was calling me a dummy. What's funny though is that I had high blood pressure and this past month it has dropped back to normal.

I gamble for release. I'm almost a compulsive gambler, though I don't invest a lot of money into it, which is why I don't think I'm really compulsive.

"When they ask what I do at a party, I say, 'Nothing. I'm an eccentric millionaire.'"

In some social settings I must be feeling embarrassed about not working because I seem to joke about it. When they ask what I do at a party, I say, "Nothing. I'm an eccentric millionaire." In some respects not working is a loss to my identity, though it was not like calling yourself "Joe Blow the musician," because there was no identity tied up in the work I did: I was never proud to be a title examiner.

Right now I'm sort of a folk hero, one of the guys that got slapped by Proposition 13. I was asked to come on a radio talk show, but the guy is a real flake and he hasn't called me back. I would do it if he called. When the bill passed I said, "You're trying to cure a headache by cutting off your head." I felt Proposition 13 was a very poor legislative act and that the people were being shortsighted. I agree that there was a legitimate need for a property tax reform, however, and I don't think it's the people's fault. Any anger I feel is toward the stupid politicians in Sacramento, who had all the time in the world to act on the need, but goofed around, causing the voters to vote for something as stupid as Proposition 13.

Right now I don't feel optimistic. I've been on a downtread as time has gone on. I don't have another "thing" to do and I don't think I would retrain for a new profession. I've already approached middle age and my attitude is that I should be established by now. I have a law degree, I have what I call a decent intellect, I've shown by my work record that I can stick it out for twelve and a half years, and I don't think I should have to start taking welding courses now. I'll have to learn new procedures and techniques for any new job, but I couldn't go back to school and start all over again.

"Nobody is a complete zero—just the law of averages says that if you want something and go out and hustle, you'll get something...Now the question is, am I that lazy or will I go out and hustle?"

I know I can do something, and I know something will present itself if I actively seek it, so I'm going to draw on my own self-confidence to carry me through this next month. Nobody is a complete zero—just the law of averages says that if you want something and go out and hustle, you'll get something. You've got to believe in yourself. Now the question is, am I that lazy, or will I go out and hustle?

Four months later Danny took a job in a title company.

Lionel   Birmingham, Alabama

The lean, attractive man in his twenties holding his young daughter by the hand ambled over from the house next door where they had been visiting a relative. Lionel talked easily, enjoying the chance to tell his story to strangers. He was even able to joke about his impoverished situation and bleak prospects. But the way he suddenly interrupted himself to yell at his child for something one would have scarcely paid any heed to was a dead giveaway that he was under enormous tension.

Until nine months ago I was a lift truck operator, loading rail cars. I worked for that company for four years.

I had been involved in an accident and I had a doctor's slip to take back to work, but they didn't accept it and put it on the record as time off. But the main reason they terminated me was for leaving the plant without clocking out. It wasn't my intention, but when you work hard all night and it comes time for everybody to go home, you just rush out. When it happened once before I called back and told the man and he just wrote me out.

When they terminated me for good, it was for not clocking out on my lunch hour, but half of us that worked on night shift didn't clock out on our lunch hour. I feel he should have gave me a notice, saying if I did it again he'd fire me. But they was out to get me or didn't want me. I've never been terminated from no other job but that one.

I went down and filed for my pennies—unemployment—and I waited to hear from Montgomery. They sent me a denial, saying I was disqualified. I appealed it and they still denied it. I had $2900 coming to me to draw and they deducted $830 from that for the penalty.

The only way I can draw my unemployment is to earn $830, so I went looking for a job. Every time I hear somebody is hiring somewhere I go, and twice a week the unemployment office sends me on referrals. I went for a truckdriving job for a railroad and for a consumer warehouse. You name it—I went to every company in town.

My main job is going to be a truckdriver. That's all I wanted to be all my life. There's three of us in the family doing it— Dad's been driving twenty years, my uncle's been driving eighteen and my brother's been driving twelve. I've been driving three and I got the experience; I drove all types. I wanted to make it my career, but I ain't got no job.

The freeze is on and it's just one of them things. I'm not the only one out of work. Everywhere I go looking for a job there are people. Like this morning there was 250 people up there looking for work.

The plant superintendent told me he would hire me back, but it would be some time next year because they got a 150 now in the layoff. He told me hisself he don't remember when it's been like this. During the winter the milling companies run full speed because the grass is dry and the cows and dogs have got to eat, but around April all the grass gets green, people start grazing their cattle, and they ain't going to buy that high feed, so the mills cut back. They have to let the people with more seniority get in and that throws the youngest men in the streets. It's just one of them things.

The way I been getting by is catching the trucks and rail cars on their biggest days, Monday, Wednesdays, and Fridays and unloading them. I probably make about seventy-five or eighty dollars. But this ain't every day now, it's just when you catch one. And there's more than me out there. A lot of people depend on it like I do. It's cash and no receipt, so it doesn't add up for the $830 I need for unemployment.

"I watch television when it's playing, but it done conked out. Everything is conked out. Morning, noon, evening and the day is over. That's about it."

My wife doesn't work but my granddaddy and my father and my mother-in-law do. We've been making it somehow. I'm getting food stamps now. I never would have put in for them, but my mother was going to mail us some food stamps from down where she lives but I didn't want her to get messed up in no kind of way. I told her I'd just go on and apply for them up here so that's what I did. I been broke so long, I can't remember the last time I saw a dollar.

I stay around the house, doing what's to be did. Nothing to be did, really, so I might walk next door and probably go look for a job. I watch television when it's playing, but it done conked out. Everything is conked out. Morning, noon, evening and the day is over. That's about it.

I've never been the lazy type that liked to freeload off nobody. If I don't find me a job, I wouldn't take charity. Mama told me before I left home, "A piece of your own is better than a whole of somebody else's." If I'm staying in your house, I got to eat when you eat, or eat when you feed me, and I don't want it like that.

I'm twenty-six now and I got two kids to support and one more to come. I know my kids will be well fed. Mama's got greens, she's got a garden, she's got a lot of hogs and a lot of chickens, so if it boils down to we have to go back home, I won't feel bad. I'd do it in a minute because I never been the type to see my kids ask for something and I can't give it to them.

I'm jolly and laughing all the time, but I'm serious too. Now that I'm not working, I been distressed and under pressure. I take it out on the kids sometimes, but not too much. A lot of times, though, I'll be sitting around here, looking at my wife, looking at myself, and a lot of thoughts cross my mind.

So many times the days went by when I had no money and the kids needed things. I'm being honest. I wanted to crack somebody over the head and take stuff. But, hey, that's no good."

So many times the days went by when I had no money and the kids needed things. I'm being honest—I wanted to crack somebody over the head and take stuff. But, hey, that's no good. I don't want to spend my life behind bars for taking something. So it's just only for a second then you kind of get your mind together, you know. Mostly I carry the Lord with me. He say wherever there's a will there's a way. He might not be there when you want Him, but He be on time.

I'd like to work. I know the only way to make it is to work. Ain't nobody going to give you nothing. And since I've been out of work it ain't no fun. It's boring; really it is.

You might think this is jive, but believe me, if there was any way that I could get me some money or work somewhere, I would be out there. I don't like sitting around doing nothing. It's so many days I sit and look out that window at that pasture out there and wish I was working somewhere, even if it was back home in the fields.

Scott   Seattle, Washington

*Though his features were pleasant enough, it was Scott's
manner—the fact that he was accustomed to being looked
at—that drew people's attention to him. A former TV talk
show host, he settled himself on the couch, genial and smiling
as though it were he who was doing the welcoming. He began
sketching out facts with "journalistic objectivity," but his
experience in being out of work defied professional packaging
and little by little the pain he had been feeling started showing
through.*

Most of my adult career has been in broadcasting. My last job
was as host of a local evening talk show on NBC television in
Seattle for six months. It was the local Douglas-Merv Griffin-
Carson entertainment and interview type show. There was a
live studio audience and we did it five nights a week. It was
basically about Seattle and the people who work here, about
celebrities and authors who might be passing through—
anything to do with Seattle.

   In essence I was fired because the ratings fell. They would
not attribute the cause to me, and in fact they said, "We don't
think it's you," but some of the things they had to do to raise
the ratings were too expensive, so they said they had to let me
go.

   When I took the job I was pretty much a realist. In my
business, or any business, if you make a pretty good income
it's insecure and you pay for it with the risk of being fired, or
changed, or kicked upstairs or downstairs. They kept it a
pretty good secret and I had heard no talk whatsoever, but I
knew something was going to happen because I had seen the
ratings. I knew it wasn't my fault, but I knew I was going to be
the one.

   They were really good to me at the station. I got six weeks
notice. Some people get fired with no notice in this business,
and two weeks is considered kind of generous. You only work
fifteen week contracts which are renewable. I worked on a
thirteen week contract, and in order to fire me they had to let
me know by the ninth week, but they let me know on the

seventh week. Then they actually gave me three weeks which is kind of unusual, because in TV or radio, they usually escort you to the door.

But we had a very good relationship and still do. I had an awful lot of respect for them. From the day I was hired, they paid me well, they treated me like I was human, and I remember saying several times that if they fired me that day, I would have as much respect for them as the day I started. You never know if you really mean that or if you're only paying lip service until it happens. It happened, and I've had as much respect for them as I did the first day I was hired. I wouldn't trade that year and a half. I would do it all over again.

There was no way you could have known I had been fired until it came out in the papers. They told me they would announce it any way I wanted it announced, that I might want to say I had some business I wanted to explore. I thought about it that weekend and decided my ass has been fired and if I try to fool people, which I've never been able to do, they're going to see right through me. And maybe if somebody who was interested in me thought I had all these business interests, they would not approach me. So I decided to be honest about it. It has really paid off in the sense that I felt better about myself.

For a few days after the last show I'd get up in the morning like I had a place to go, shower and shave and put on coat and tie. Then I realized that I didn't have a lot of places to go, so I abandoned that and put on a tee shirt and Levis. For a couple of weeks I was just seeing people and having lunches, then I went back to Channel 5 for two weeks to fill in on their morning show. I haven't worked since then except for part-time, once-a-week gigs on Channel 5.

I'm out doing things and seeing people I know in the business, trying to keep myself somewhat visible. I do a television commercial now and then. I started taking tap dancing lessons. I figured there are three things that I'd like to learn to do in this time. One is tap dancing—you never know when you can use that, especially when you are on TV—another is juggling, and the other is singing. I haven't gotten to the juggling.

I don't do a heck of a lot else in my free time because of two decisions I made: one is to stay in Seattle, the other is to stay on the air—on TV—both of which really narrow my opportunities.

There are only three television stations in town and not all of them do a lot of things, so I'm really limited. I guess I worry somewhat about putting all my eggs in one basket. I guess I'm going to find out.

If I were in the mood, I could get a good paying job. There are a lot of TV jobs out there in America, but I don't want to leave Seattle. I came up here from California six years ago with the intention of going back there in two or three years, but I don't want to go back now. You've got the mountains, the water and the clean air, and you've got a city that is really coming into its own. It doesn't have the sophistication of San Francisco and it's not as cosmopolitan as New York City, but it still has its own things to be proud of and it's growing.

The decision to stay also has something to do with the fact that I'm recognized here. If you are recognized and your name is known, why leave all that to go to a strange city? If I really had to I would do it, but I want to walk into most restaurants and walk up and down the streets and have most people recognize me. How many billboards are you going to have to buy to do this in a strange city and what's it going to cost me? I really think I should make use of that.

On TV the recognition factor is very important because if no one recognizes you it means that no one is watching you. That sometimes really messed my mind up because you can't go anywhere without being recognized and that gets in the way when you want to go out to dinner and not be bothered. But I think I can handle it. I realize that I'm like anybody else and I can lose a job like anyone else. I've got a good handle on that but I still like being recognized.

You never think things can happen to you, whether it's a car accident or losing your job, but it does happen. I view this as a strengthening time, but I'll believe that more when I get a job. I will get a job; I just know I will. If I haven't anything towards summer, then I'll really sit down and figure out what to do. I've got to think positively. I have a fairly good reputation. It hasn't gotten me a job yet, but I do fairly good work.

Sometimes I wonder about my own success. I never had those doubts before and when I start feeling that way I try to look at the positive side of what has happened. For example, I have a lot of things going for me that an ordinary person doesn't have. I'm recognized; I get stroked an awful lot. When I go into a restaurant friends or even people who don't know me ask how they can help. I really think the identity thing is important.

On the negative side I worry about the failure. The feeling of failure is important, and the income, of course, is very important.

As of probably the middle of this month I will have gone through my savings. My wife has considered getting a job. I would never force her to, but I'm more than willing to let her. I think it will be good for her and probably good for me.

I don't know if I'm entitled to unemployment; I don't think so. I don't know if I'd collect it anyhow, but that's probably just ego. I'm just critical of it. If I could get someone else to stand in line for me... But I make enough money so I don't know if I'd qualify anyhow.

You know, the truth is that I don't miss doing that show. After it got dull, I never felt that it was right for me anyhow. When I was working with a woman on the morning show I got to screw off a hell of a lot more because she could maintain the direction and I could have a lot of fun without getting her insulted. She was a professional, she knew how to handle it, and we got along very well. Once I had my own show, I had nobody to play off of. You can't play at a guest's expense and you cannot be consistently funny. It's like stopping and starting a car.

"Somebody thinks you're a loser, so maybe you are."

If you look at it, Johnny Carson has got Ed McMahon and Doc Severinsen, and that's important—you need those crutches. Carson is very good, mind you, very good, and he did make it pretty much on his own in the beginning. But I did not have those crutches that I thought were important. Some nights would be just great, just dynamite, but it would be five or six nights before we had another really good one, and although the other nights were very passable, you have to be more consistent than that.

People don't like losers. They like people who are good at what they do and even though they may continue to say to me,

"You know, you're really good," deep down they know you were fired and you're out of work. Somebody thinks you're a loser, so maybe you are.

One thing I have noticed is that there is a tendency to always say you have a deal going. When people say, "How are you doing?" you answer, "Ah, things are fantastic. Over at Channel 7 they are really interested in me, and over at Channel 5 we've got two or three shows we're talking about. Things are really great." And it's all phony. And you have a tendency to make excuses for why you're not working yet.

I have caught myself doing both those things and now I'm to the point where people say, "Do you have anything going?" and I say, "No. No, I don't."

"One thing I have noticed is that there is a tendency to always have a deal going. When people say 'How are you doing?' you answer, 'Ah, things are fantastic'... And it's all phony."

I have absolutely nothing going right now. I have a nice relationship with Channel 5, but even if they do start a new show it usually doesn't start till September, so they're not going to hire me in March, if in fact they do hire me. And maybe they'll start a new show and I'm not the one they want to do it. There are a lot of possibilities and I'm trying to be as realistic as I can.

People often blame others—it's society's fault, or the other guy's fault. One thing I haven't done is blame anybody else. Maybe something I do caused this. The month before I was fired, nine days before Christmas, I moved into my new $100,000 home overlooking the lake. You always think it happens to somebody else.

Eventually Scott relocated in order to stay in television.

"THE WAY THEY TREAT YOU..."

Joe   Omaha, Nebraska

"Hey, how ya doin'," was Joe's greeting to every person who passed through the union office, where he had been spending hour after hour since leaving his plumber's job a month before. With a square chin and wide-set eyes that crinkled when he grinned, he was an outgoing, assertive man in his late forties. He was friendly but edgy. The pleasure he took in having companions about him and in being on top of all the union news was mixed with anxiety about the hard time he was having finding a new job.

I was a plumber at the university for seven years and me and my supervisor had a conflict. He wasn't filling the evaluations out—he was faking it so that it looked like I wasn't doing anything. For eighteen months I fought the guy and finally, thirty days ago, rather than blow up, I resigned.

He was going to get me fired the following week anyway, so I resigned just to get away from him. I liked working as a plumber and I didn't want to resign because I have a family, but I just couldn't take the pressure from him any more.

You very seldom run into this kind of supervisor. Ever since he came in three years ago he's caused all kinds of morale problems. This guy is—I don't know—he's a funny kind of guy.

He wouldn't tell you anything to your face; he'd tell everybody behind your back. Then when it came up time for your evaluation, he'd put things down that you didn't even know about.

I fought him a couple of times on it, but to file a grievance you've got to have written proof. Guys have got to sign their names and they just won't do it; they don't want to be involved. They talk support to your face, but they won't back you up; they're scared for their jobs. There's nothing anybody can do.

The day I resigned I was just about ready to knock him for a loop. Just before dinnertime I felt something was in the wind because a couple of guys had heard him talk and said something about it to me. After dinner I got a call to meet him at this place where I did a job. I knew something was up—they found everything wrong with it.

I was a little depressed that afternoon and finally I just said the heck with it. I went over to personnel and asked them how to go about resigning. The personnel director, he told me, "I knew that they were after you. I told you to watch it." "Yeah," I says, "but anything I did was wrong for him. He didn't care what it was or where it was or how I did it. I just couldn't satisfy him."

"It was just one of them things. He was after me and he never let up."

After I left, they had an outside man come to do the work over. He told them the job was all right, but they didn't seem to agree with that either. They made him tear everything out and put it in different.

It was just one of them things. He was after me and he never let up. And like that record says, "Take This Job and Shove It"—that's just about what I told them.

I resigned because to me it looked like I'd have a worse record if I didn't, but the way it's going here lately, I don't know. Maybe I should have let him get me fired. Looks to me like it's worse if you resign. They look at you like you committed a crime. When you tell them why you quit, they seem like they don't want to believe you. They say, "We'll give you a call," and then you might just as well forget it, because they'll never call you. I can't draw unemployment, and if I went to the Veterans and asked them to pay some bills for me, they wouldn't do it because I resigned. If I got fired, they'd pay everything.

I've been looking for work ever since I got off, but it's a slack season—pretty hard time. The last couple of months it's been rough and there's a heck of a lot of guys on the bench.

If I find something else to get into that I can learn real fast, I wouldn't mind doing it. I've done other work. I supervised men in the sewer maintenance division of the City of Omaha. The only reason I left that job was that they were after me for my union activities.

We were in negotiations and I brought up a couple of things that hit 'em right between the eyes and I said I would let it out to the press. I made a couple of mistakes and that's all it took. We all knew it was union activity that cost me my job, but we couldn't prove that that was behind it.

Being out of work is starting to worry me now. It makes things tough. I'm forty-seven years old, I've got five kids at home, and a daughter that's been married and divorced and a grandson I've got to take care of too. The family's not small. My wife's working, but what she makes is not too much. I've got a couple of kids who are working, but I can't take all their money. I've got this pension money coming back to me, so that will hold us for a little while. We're making ends meet right now, but come the next couple of weeks, I don't know.

I can get money but the idea of taking a bank loan...I can go down and get food stamps. I got them a couple of years ago when my wife wasn't working. I could go to the church and get the St. Vincent de Paul to help, but I haven't gone that far yet. I don't feel like doing it in a way, but it's there, and if I have to, then I'll do it. I've been trying to hold off.

I've got a car to keep up and a mortgage, but what's getting me down is that if something really happened, I got medical insurance only until the first of the month, then it's going to drop out. Then I ain't got no insurance if something happens to these kids.

Sometimes my spirits go up and other times they go real down, real fast. I'm getting a little depressed and probably getting a little irritable, I guess. Starting to holler at the kids again. My wife's been pretty good. Before I resigned I talked it over with her first and we haven't had any problems as of yet. But eventually it'll be getting on her, too.

When you're not on a schedule, you still wake up at a certain time. You know you can't go anyplace, so you lay there and you toss and turn and you finally get up, sit around and re-read the paper. It's pretty hard to relax. I've been fixing the house up and been doing small odds and ends, but when you run out of money to buy materials, you can't do that.

I don't stay at home too much. I stop in here at union headquarters and see if they've got something. I do like to go and play shuffleboard, and if the weather was better than it is I'd probably go play some baseball or basketball.

I just need to get a job. There is some work in the area; the idea is to get it. Some of them pay just the minimum wage. Maybe I could do that for a while, but I don't think I could go for that and support a family, not in this day and age.

I'm just hoping I might find something eventually. If I had it to do again, I probably would think a little bit more before I'd resign. I would make them fire me so I could draw and have some resources coming in to take care of things. Because if I could have went on unemployment, I'd have been all right.

Elena — San Gabriel Valley, California

She was simply disgusted with her record of going from one tedious, underpaid clerical job to another and had made the decision never to repeat what she had been through again. Thirty years old, with lustrous black hair and creamy soft skin, she had enrolled in college again, determined to acquire the credentials that she believed would secure her a comfortable, dignified future. In her sister's comfortable middle-class home, she detailed her history, looking for clues that would help her gain perspective on the past.

I've been fired five times and laid off twice. I've never quit a job. I once worked four years in a job I really hated as if I had to prove to myself that I was capable of staying in one place over time. I ended up laid off.

Once I was fired from a job and I couldn't go home with that image in mind, so I went for a cup of coffee and looked in the newspaper. I saw an opening advertised and ran right over and took the job, even though it meant a seventy dollar cut in pay. I lasted only four months before I got fired again.

I went into clerical work because the few summers I had spent helping my mom at a sewing factory while I was in high school were enough to let me know I didn't want to work in a factory. I've gone from one job to another because that is what you do to support yourself. I have never really had much job satisfaction and I hate the work. I hate being thought of as mindless, as a sterile human being with no opinions and without any kind of feelings as most people think you are in those positions.

I have found out that most clerical work is really very much like a factory—it is the factory of the 1960s and 1970s, but instead of sewing machines, we have adding machines and typewriters. The pay is almost impossible to live on, and when you talk about getting more money, they look at you as if you have a colossal amount of nerve. The worst thing is that no one really thinks you're worth very much, including yourself. One employer told me that clerks were a dime a dozen. That does wondrous things for your ego. And with that attitude that you're doing a mediocre job come restrictions.

In that job that I could not stand the thought of being fired from, we were not allowed to have coffee while we worked because they were afraid we would spill it. We were not allowed to have candy bars because they were afraid that if we left them in the desk, they would bring cockroaches. There were no telephone calls. Most of the women had children, but they had to use a public telephone outside the building on their lunch hour. Two women would walk up and down the aisles to make sure the other hundred women were working and not talking. They played the role of the heavy so that the two male supervisors could be joking and pleasant.

I would get outraged that we were not allowed to talk to each other, not given the respect that we could possibly carry on a conversation yet be responsible to the work. And I hated it more when the boss would come by and then it was OK to talk—to him. It was fine for him to sit on the desk and chit-chat and flirt with some of the younger women, but you couldn't turn around and talk to another woman yourself. I had various confrontations about these things, but it never occurred to me to quit.

One afternoon, when I was looking something up, I started talking to a woman standing next to me. We were very careful to be working while we talked, although that was ridiculous, because people automatically do stop working for a moment. Our supervisors were in two little glass offices where we could hear them chit-chat with each other about baseball, football, and who the hell they were dating that night. I knew they were staring at me because I was talking, and that just inflamed me more.

One supervisor came up and told me I could not talk while I worked. I said, "Why can't I stand here and talk while I work? I know you've been looking at me and have seen that I have been working all along, even though I have been carrying on a conversation. It's quite possible to do this."

"I'm telling you I do not want you to stand here and talk while you work," he said.

"Why?" I asked.

"I'm going to tell you one more time," he said, "You always give me an argument, and if you say one more word about this, I'm going to terminate you."

"They called me a bitch and I was terminated."

"Why?" I asked.

"You're fired," he said.

I went downstairs to personnel and asked if I could be fired for asking a question. The supervisor came down too, and the personnel officer said that it was clear the supervisor had given me a choice.

I asked, "But why? This is what I was asking. It's a question. I find it difficult to accept this kind of treatment."

They called me a bitch and I was terminated. The personnel

officer turned to my supervisor and said, "I can understand why you fired her."

I felt good, I really did. That is, one part of me felt really good, but the other part said, "Oh, my God, you're hopelessly unemployable. This is the third time you've been terminated."

I had just moved into an apartment and I was trying to go back to school. I needed a full-time job and I couldn't find very many swingshift jobs, so I started work on the graveyard shift in the emergency road service department of the Automobile Club.

I just couldn't hack it. What with going to class, trying to study, and also sleep during the day it was just impossible. I ended up dropping all but two of my classes and I was a nervous wreck. I was torn, because if I quit, who would pay my rent? But I wasn't achieving the purpose that I had started working that stupid job for, so I decided that I would quit.

The day I went to quit, I was fired. I had been warned that I couldn't be as much as two minutes late for work; they were very strict about being there at exactly 11:15. I understand they're a little more lenient now; the new person gets there at 11:30.

I moved in with my sister and a friend told me about a job with a chiropractor. I really wanted to go back to school, but it was a chance to get $800 a month, and that's pretty good for clerical work. I thought I could work just five months, then go to school in the summer.

Besides, I wanted to work. It's hard to deal with the stigma of being unemployed and with the idea that you might be unemployable. I think we're socialized to feel we have to have a job. I could have had unemployment through last fall, but it was really difficult for me to know that I was not contributing to my own independence. When you go to an unemployment office you feel that you're taking a hand-out. Not having any money coming in is like living off people or leeching.

So I took the job with the chiropractor. I was supposed to take care of the front office. Bank reconciliations had not been done for six months and things were awfully behind. It was going to take about two months to clean the place up so it would be workable.

The chiropractor wanted an office manager doing general office work and supervising the people working in the reception area. That was fine, but a day and a half after I started, there was no one in the reception area at all. Now I had never done any reception work and it wasn't what I was hired to do, but I pitched in.

Even in this kind of office there are shit positions. He did not like to send his gowns out, so whoever was working the receptionist's desk was expected to put the gowns and towels in the washing machine. I thought that, really, I was not going to be working as some kind of laundress, but I came to terms with that and rationalized it by saying he was going to pay me a lot of money to do his towels.

The more I got into the work, the more I realized that it was quite a position he was asking me to fill. I was getting farther and farther behind on office work because I was putting in eight hours as a receptionist and it was taking me a long time to become familiarized and proficient.

When I realized how much work was involved and what I was responsible for, I realized that the $800 he was paying me was really not very much at all. Besides I was privy to the fact that his accountant had told him to pay someone $1200 to do this work.

So I told him that I wanted higher pay. He said he was planning on giving me fifty dollars. I told him he could either give me $900 or terminate me then and I would work for a couple of weeks until he could get someone else. Or, if he wanted to go along with me, then in three months we would renegotiate a salary. He was affronted that I was asking for more money, but finally he said we would renegotiate in three months.

The next day he didn't even say hello to me, though he had made a point of saying, "Good morning, how are you? You're doing such a fine job." That night he was going for a few days vacation and barely said good-bye. I asked him to sign a few blank checks in case of emergency. He was really upset about that, but he did.

That night he called and said he'd gone through the desk and couldn't find the check he had signed. That struck me as kind of odd, but I told him I had locked it up because anyone could go through the desk. The next day the X-ray technician told me the chiropractor wanted him to have the check.

That really got me. I felt he was letting me know without mincing any words that he had no trust in me at all. He must have thought I was very stupid, because only a fool would cash such a check.

When he came back, I wanted to speak to him, but he avoided me all day long. I couldn't cope with his being so petty and decided to give him notice the next day. But my sister convinced me to take off a day and call in sick, instead.

At 6:30 that night the X-ray technician called and said they no longer needed my services. It turned out that they had hired my replacement the day before.

God, that made me mad. The chiropractor didn't even have the nerve to call me up himself and tell me I was canned.

I didn't think I would have any problem getting unemployment because as far as I could see I was fired without cause. I got one check and out of curiosity asked what grounds the chiropractor had given for terminating me. When they learned I had been terminated, they took the check back.

On top of everything, the chiropractor didn't want to give me my pay for more than half a month's work. When I finally got it, my pay raise was not included. That made me so angry I called up the Labor Board, who told me that with only a verbal agreement the employer only had to pay the amount of the last raise.

After everything was over, I was glad not to be working so I could go back to school. School really keeps me going. It builds up my morale and my ego. In the past, when I wasn't working I moped around a lot and felt useless, lethargic and very depressed. I had headaches and tension. Sleep was my escape; I had to force myself to get up. I was ashamed to call friends, afraid they would say, "Gee, she's not working again." I was caught in that failure syndrome of believing that I couldn't cope and was responsible for everything that happened to me—it was all my fault.

I understand these reactions better now that I'm starting to get more involved with Chicanas, because I am a Chicana, with the gay movement, because I am gay, and with the Women's Movement. I have experienced discrimination at work for being gay, though not for being a Chicana—I think because I'm pretty anglicized.

When I came out, I was naive enough to think that whatever I said was just going to be, and that was all there was to it. One of the men I worked with claimed he could spot a homosexual in a minute.

"Wow, that's pretty good," I said. "Would you think I am?" He said, "No."

"Well, you're wrong, because I'm gay." I told him.

That was at five o'clock that night, and the next day two of the women I worked with very closely wouldn't talk to me any more. When I walked through, they jumped about three feet. Oh, God, that was just awful. God. I've never been terminated from a job for being gay, but I think it contributed. It was certainly in their consciousness because there was no way that they could avoid it.

"All in all I can't get over the feeling that I'm leeching, even though I know that sometimes this happens to people."

The women's movement has helped me a lot in learning how to handle my anger. I've finally learned how to get the anger out. Now it's a matter of learning to channel it so that I don't cut my neck off on the job market.

I'm looking for something to do that will be better than what I've done in the past twelve years. I'm coming to terms with myself, feeling that I want to and can do better. I have two more years until I get my B.A., then I plan to get a Ph.D. in clinical psychology or go to medical school.

Right now I'm not doing well financially, but I'll be able to make it with part-time work if I can get some student grants. Because I am living with my sister, I don't have to worry about paying for an apartment or food. I do have to worry about gas, and I'm not going out very much because it is very hard for me to allow someone else to pay for me. All in all I can't get over the feeling that I'm leeching, even though I know that sometimes this happens to people. Most of the time I feel as if I am living off of someone else.

In some ways I feel it's almost selfish of me to be going to school at thirty years of age, and not working. Part of me felt and still does feel a little guilty, like something inside of me wanted to quit. I have mixed feelings about having such a very, very bad work record and one part of me is ashamed about it. I guess it's that Christian or Puritan work ethic that if you don't work, you're a failure.

The job market can be gruesome, absolutely humiliating. It can completely wreck you. The tremendous amount of pain that comes from being terminated is a horrible feeling. Though things are getting better, there are still some really unfair job practices. This society has not yet gotten to the point where every job is respected and where people can take pride in what they do. We all, myself included, complain that nobody does anything right any more. But how much respect do we give to street cleaners or janitors or clerks or typists? We expect those people to be so proud about what they do, but they don't have a lot of reason to be proud. We complain about taxes, but we don't give those people a very fair wage.

I want to work because I find satisfaction in working and in contributing, and because I feel that there is a stigma to not working, even to the idea of the idle rich. I don't think I could be one of them. It would be a luxury not to have to depend on the money that you got from working, but it must also be some terrific kind of luxury to get paid a living wage, not a scraping wage, and be able to do something that you enjoy doing.

That's why I'm going to school. I want a salary that will let me plan a vacation and actually have the money to take it. I want a salary that will let me go out occasionally to the theater or a movie, or buy a gift or an antique. Most people are not fortunate enough to have that kind of money and to also like doing what they are doing, but I'm optimistic. I have a thing inside of me, and I do not know whence it came, but like the sun is going to shine tomorrow, I just know that I'm going to get through school and have these things.

Elena stayed in school, determined to keep her dream alive.

Lem   Red Hill Community, Alabama

Arriving home a bit late, Lem made his way through the papers and clothing that were strewn about the front room of the crowded trailer to the kitchen where cans, tools and children's games overflowed in great disarray from the shelves. Thirty-nine years old, he had light brown hair and a quiet manner. He pointed to his paunch—the result, he said, of idleness during the six months since he had quit his job as a crane operator. Three or four children ran noisily in and out of the cramped space as we spoke. He chastised them gently.

I'm raised down here, way 'round on this mountain, back across that river, and I was born back over there in Wildcat Hollow near where I was raised. I ain't been out of Alabama but one time in my life when me and my brother went up to Indiana. He said we could get us a job up there. We got up there, looked around and left to go back.

My people are all around here. All told I have fifteen brothers and sisters—five half brothers and sisters from daddy's first wife and ten of us by his last wife. I'm thirty-nine and me and my old lady we got six kids. Two of them are not with us.

I have fifth grade schooling. If I had a chance to go to school I sure would. They give trucking lessons around here, but I know how to drive a truck. I'm sure going to try and make sure my kids get to school if there's any way possible. I know what I missed and I don't want them to miss it.

I worked for one company goin' on nine years loading and unloading trucks and running a crane. I quit about six months ago. I didn't like the way they was treating me down there. They promoted me and then they put me back down. I never did ask them why—I was sayin' "howdy." I know if I started asking them, everything would get worse than what it is, so I decided to quit.

I figured I could get a job right after that, but I didn't. I started waiting around the strip pits, trying to get me a job in there. Strip pits is where they shovel off the top floor of soil so they can get down where they can get the coal out. But there's a strike going on now. I put my application in and I've talked to the boss man. He told me he would think about me when he started back.

I always made my own way. I ain't never had no help with food or money. I would take if I needed to, but I don't like to impose on nobody.

"Pretty days I try to get out and fiddle around a little."

But I ain't hungry. We get food stamps, except you can't buy the same things with food stamps you can with money. We get Social Security for the two older kids living with us. The four older kids ain't mine. They're from my old lady's first husband. He died.

I get bored being around the house since the bad weather. Pretty days I try to get out and fiddle around a little. I piddle around; I been riding from there yonder helping my family get wood and things. I got two pickup trucks and a car.

This morning I wouldn't have went nowhere, but my brother came up asking would I help him get wood. We got over there and his brother-in-law wanted to go fishing, so I just let the wood go and went fishing (*chuckles*). I don't care too much about fishin' except I just wanted to be up there.

I get bored piddling around. I'm getting bigger in size. I don't eat much; it's because I'm not getting enough exercise. Laying around makes you feel different, worser. Makes you feel like not doing nothing.

I was happier working than I am now. But I'm not sorry I left my job, 'cause if I'd stayed I probably would have wound up in some trouble and I didn't want to do that.

Doreen   New Orleans, Louisiana

Fired from her job as a bookkeeper in a chain store for women's clothing, Doreen was in her early twenties. She was very neatly dressed and spoke in a quiet, rather timid voice as though she were at a job interview.

I used to pass the unemployment office when I was working. I'd look at the lines and lines of people, but I never thought that I'd be among them.

I was fired from my job seven months ago. I was a bookkeeper for a chain store of women's clothing—a bookkeeper, cashier and saleslady.

I worked there for five years under eight or nine different managers. Some were all right, but it was pretty hectic working under the last two or three.

The last one, well, he had it "in" for me. I could see that things had really gotten rock bottom. And the morale of the whole staff was low. I tried to approach him and ask if there was a problem. We had one word after another and I was fired. Of course he's the manager and I'm not, so I was fired in such a way that it looked like he was right.

I was fired because I didn't follow company policy—a policy that went into effect about a week before I was fired. I needed two signatures on a deposit slip I turned in at the end of the day—and I only had my signature on it. I did give it to another cashier to OK, but I left before she checked it. That's all it was.

They said I couldn't get unemployment because I should have known the new policy. I went to one unemployment review board and to another, but they said no. I've filed a complaint in a federal agency also, because I felt I had been mistreated on the job.

It's ridiculous the things people have to go through to get unemployment. People standing in line for hours. And sometimes you have to come back the next week maybe to get your last name right or your social security number straight.

When I wanted to see the review board, they had about seven or eight people with me at the same time. The lady said, "Oh, well, it's going to take a while." I saw what she meant; that "while" for me was from September till November.

In the meantime, what are people supposed to do that have housenotes and stuff like that? Some people stand in line there for maybe only twenty or thirty dollars. I guess every bit helps, but I think it's ridiculous.

Luckily I have some money saved on the side, and a friend is helping me so I can pay the rent. I try to use my money wisely. I put myself on a budget and watch every penny.

113

I notice that I need less. When I was working, I'd splurge and buy stuff I didn't even need or use. You'd say to yourself, "I need this; I have to have it." I don't seem to do that now.

When I lost the job it bothered me in a sense because I liked what I was doing and I was good at it. I even did work for them when they were in a bind and I was sick in the hospital. They depended on me. Nobody could do what I did. But I wasn't all that broken up about leaving because I didn't get along with the manager.

The first few weeks I wasn't working were fine, but after a while it was boring because I missed having a goal. And I missed having my own money. In the last month staying home has started getting on my nerves.

"It's funny; when I fill out applications for a job, I remember what it was like sitting on the other side of the desk when people came in looking for a job."

I go on a lot of job interviews. It's funny; when I fill out applications for a job, I remember what it was like sitting on the other side of the desk when people came in looking for a job. I used to see all the different reasons a manager wouldn't hire someone—either not enough experience, or they'd talked too much, or they didn't like the way they looked. Or people got hired because they did like the way they looked and talked.

I remembered those people. They always used to stay in the back of my mind, but I wouldn't pay too much attention to them because I was working. Now I know how I seem to the people who are interviewing me.

ANGUISH AND DOUBTS

Ted   New York, New York

*Slender, thirty years old, his light brown hair appealingly
tousled, he bade a warm welcome to his book and record-lined
apartment. His greeting had the eagerness of a person who
had been isolated far too long. Ted expressed his feelings
easily and freely admitted how lonely he had been since he had
lost his college teaching job. Though he had been out of work
for months, his emotions still had a frantic edge.*

From the age of five, when my mother took me to kindergarten,
until the beginning of last school year, my entire year had
always been planned out in advance. I never had to make any
decision about what was going to happen next.

After I got a Ph.D. in chemistry I sent letters out to about
forty colleges in the metropolitan area. The small Catholic
college that took me was the only one that answered. The nun I
was to replace had gone on leave to get her doctorate and it was
made clear to me that I would only be a one year appointment.
Being a college teacher was the culmination of my existence,
so I reconciled myself to the one year appointment. I couldn't
wait to get into it, so I wasn't going to shop around, especially
considering they were the only ones who replied. I was like a
thirsty man in the desert.

I had wanted to stay in the city to hang around the publishing houses because I had written a book on rock music in the fifties.

As it turned out, the book never got published and I taught for three years. I had wondered how this woman I was replacing would get a Ph.D. in one year, especially when it took me five, and I had a little more upstairs than she had. And, indeed, came the end of the year—surprise—she didn't have it. So she asked for another year and got it, and then it went on for a third year.

I began to get very comfortable and started doing all these things which have long-range implications. I really broke my ass doing my job, and I did it quite well. I made friends with the people I saw every day for three years. In retrospect it was foolish of me to think the job was mine, but it really becomes a part of you and you begin to take it for granted.

Then, because the college had a rule that you can't have more than three years leave, the woman I replaced was going to come back, though she didn't even have her degree. I felt very bitter, and when it was time to go I didn't want to. Maybe I was scared because I was going into the unknown, but I believed I had more of a right to keep that job than she did.

My salary stretched out some six weeks after the semester ended, so I went to England, very conscious of the fact that when my vacation was over it was open-ended as to what I would be doing. For the first time nothing was required of me in September.

"I think the hardest thing to do on unemployment is to keep telling yourself that you're right and that all those other people are fools."

It was as if I never had any free will until last September, when it finally dawned on me that if I'm going to do anything with my life, I had to do it then. It was very scary and I felt like the plane ride coming back was going to bring me into the hardest time in my life.

As it turns out, this year has been THE most anxiety-ridden time I've ever had. I mean, I have suffered from depression. I constantly have to keep bolstering myself up and reaffirming my own worth because I've had enough rejections, enough slights, and enough neglect this last year to last anyone a lifetime.

I think the hardest thing to do on unemployment is to keep telling yourself that you're right and that all these other people are fools. When you're not working, you somehow have this feeling that the world has made a decision that you're not as good as the people out there who are pulling in great salaries. You have to keep telling yourself that 90 percent of them are incompetent and that the other 10 percent got theirs by being at the right place at the right time, by dint of having a friend, or by just a series of circumstances. Doing that has really been the hardest thing of all.

Sometimes you get into irrational thinking, like "Gee, they fired me because I wasn't as good as they are." Of course, all I have to do is realize who all the people are that I left behind me, and Jesus Christ, there's no comparison. But it takes time to refocus your mind and get back in there, and sometimes it plays games with you when you're just sitting around, not doing anything. And in the last few months I haven't been doing much because I've been waiting on calls here and calls there which never come.

I feel a real bitterness towards the college. They think they're hot shit and better than me, and I'm so much better than those people. Sometimes I think of bombing that place, I hate them so much. As non-violent as I am, when I think of that dean I could really almost be kicking that woman in the face, wrestling around on the concrete. I get so angry when I think of those people that I'm writing a fifty page story about that school, which is a rip-off from the word go—a racket, a fraud—just to fill the time. Yet, because I'm not doing anything, I wish I was back there. It would fill up my day.

I am obsessed with filling up my time. Instead of preparing dinner in forty-five minutes, I'll invite people over and take two hours to prepare a feast. I feel I must do something constructive. It's hard for me to read a book; I keep thinking I should be out improving myself. When I'm doing something frivolous, I feel that I'm throwing my time away. I never felt like that when I was working.

I don't feel mentally unhealthy; I accept it and I can bounce out. Despite the many disappointments, I figure it has just been a knockdown and you've got to pick yourself up and get back in there. I feel freer now than ever. It's almost like I feel free to be depressed and that I have every fucking right to be depressed if I want to.

What I want to get into is rock and roll. I sat with records even when I was six and seven and it has been kind of a relaxing pursuit to me, like a drug that you could always turn on. It brings me a lot of pleasure and I care for it a lot.

So I've decided to try to get into the record business, in an executive capacity, something leading up to A and R—Artists and Records—which is signing new acts, planning their itineraries and promotion campaigns, and getting them started.

I want to work with talent I believe in because I want to share whatever goodness they could bring to people's lives. Even within the crappy capitalist set-up of record companies, I think that goodness can still prevail in the right hands and that I could make a contribution. And I kind of like the whole environment—you get free records and free shows—so it's extending my adolescence in that way.

I write very long, involved, I like to think witty, funny letters to the record company presidents. Of course, they're usually intrigued by this guy with a Ph.D. and invariably they call me for an interview. I follow it up; finally they forget.

I hear about these high salaries in the record business and it's like "Let's Make a Deal." I just pick right, behind Door Number Two, and get all this money. What the hell do I need all this fucking money for? Certainly I'd like to have a little more than what I get on unemployment so I could piss it away without thinking about it, but I was never in want of money when I was working. If people want to give it to me, that's fine, but I'm really comfortable here in my little world.

When I went to England, I had ninety pages done on a novel about rock and roll. It has wound up being five hundred pages and is now being read by a publisher. It might be my only bread and butter, because I certainly am resigned to not teaching any more.

Writing the book was a major effort because I didn't know what was going to lie at the end of the rainbow. I was absorbed, yet I was afraid to do the book because I kept saying,

"I may not get a cent, and if nothing happens, this is really a waste of time. What's going to happen when the money I've saved has run out?"

I haven't wanted to let myself fall into an unemployed lifestyle, thinking about whether somebody would ask, "Why don't you get on food stamps?" I have to carry myself in a way that says I am still Numero Uno. Now, I have an all-leather briefcase that cost about ninety dollars. I didn't pay ninety dollars for it—I got it wholesale—but it wasn't what I paid for it that matters; it looks like a distinguished piece of luggage and it makes me feel better. I didn't carry it around when I was working, but sometimes when I go to the unemployment office now, I use the briefcase. And when I go to an interview, I carry the briefcase around with my resume and a few pencils and my date book—which is around 365 pages blank. It makes me feel like I am working towards something where I will be more productive instead of carrying myself like a schlump.

With not having a job and working on a book, which is a very lonely experience, there have been times when I absolutely craved people. In fact, I looked forward to this interview because it gives me a chance to just talk. When I was working I had enough of talking and I would take the receiver off the hook when I came home. Now I'm always looking for people. I keep barging in on people, seeking them out much more because I really need the company. When I just sit around, irrational thoughts come to me, like "How come I'm not working—thirty years old."

Sometimes I get angry about my social life. Since I taught in an all girls' school there was always a woman around when I needed it for any purpose, whether it was purely sex or just for company. Since I've left the school I think I've met only one new woman.

And relationships with women have been affected. I feel now that I come first until I get into something from which I have an income. If I get into the record business, it's as if it's trivial to go out with women now. I don't place going out high on my priority list. The only reason why I would want to would be strictly because I was horny.

Sometimes a nurse I'm seeing will call me up and tell me about how terrible a night she had at work. And I feel like saying, "What the fuck are you telling me all this for? I don't even have a fucking job. At least you're making your $15,000—I'm making shit. What am I supposed to do, feel sorry for you? No one asked you to become a nurse." I really am very intolerant of listening to people talk and talk about their line of work.

I believe that I can always get a job just to make money, even if it's doing something I hate. I think of myself now as a worker and I think it's because that's always hanging over my head. Yet I always think of a worker as a guy coming away from the factory. I cannot imagine enjoying watching the car come down the assembly line and putting a body and hood on it. To me that is inherently unfulfilling and I think we should address ourselves to the quality of life.

I have an opportunity and can parlay what I have not to have to do that. I guess I am lucky to even be able to say something like that. I have a certain vision of what quality means to me, and certainly it does not mean taking any job that comes along.

People on unemployment were laid off from their last job and goddammit, they're entitled to do any fucking thing they want to do. I don't think they're goldbricking—unemployment is not an unlimited subsidy. I don't feel that I'm taking anything for nothing. When I go to the unemployment office, I feel I'm getting my due; in fact, I feel that even more because my former employer had to pay into that fund. I hope it's like automobile insurance: if they have enough accidents, they'll keep raising the premium. I hope the college is paying through the nose.

Ted made it in rock and roll.

Judy   New York, New York

A woman of rare beauty, but without the confidence one expects most beautiful women to have and with almost palpable anxiety, Judy seemed extremely fragile. She had sublet her artist's loft, leaving easels and paints behind, and was looking for clerical work as a way of staying afloat. In her boyfriend's tiny apartment she seemed to suffer from being cooped up, but her alert intelligence and ready humor revealed inner strengths.

I got out of art school with an M.A., and I was very depressed because I hadn't prepared myself for a job. I freelanced doing maps and charts, but the more I tried, the more of a downhill effort it became because I wasn't able to channel whatever talents I have into the right fields, and my portfolio was never strong enough for the commercial world. I always had the impression that I wasn't pursuing the right avenues.

For about five years I was living on a little stock I had and was partially supported by a man. I started to become more depressed and afraid of all kinds of things—afraid of being raped, afraid to go out in the street. I actually had a mild nervous breakdown. My relationship broke up, my inheritance was completely spent, and I managed to get myself $4000 into debt.

I went onto a Social Welfare program and started receiving disability because I was in no condition to find work. My art portfolio looked like that of a beginner and I didn't have a lot of confidence in myself or my work, so they told me to get some typing skills. I just hate to type and in two years of sporadic efforts of boning up on it, I haven't gotten any better at it. I don't know what I was doing wrong, but I simply could not find a job anywhere, doing anything. One seemingly sure thing after another, things I desperately needed and desperately wanted, fell through. I couldn't even get a job in a department store.

Finally I did get a job, my first real job. The monotony was almost unbearable, but it was the only job I could find and I needed the money. Eventually even my boss could tell that I was bored and he encouraged me to go out on interviews. I did and got what I considered to be the ideal job, at Columbia University—from which I was fired after one month.

That was crushing. There were weeks when I woke up completely filled with remorse that I was fired, going hopelessly over it and over it. At Columbia I had felt connected with the intellectual world and I felt like a human being with prospects. Over the past three months, since I lost that job, I've lost all my sense of self-worth.

I've thought of calling them and of going back up there because I don't think I should have been fired and I'm angry about it. There was supposed to be a two-month probationary period, but they only gave me a month. They could have at least warned me and said they were not too sure about how I was performing. I should have protested about it but it's long past the time now. I just tell myself it's water under the bridge. Lots of people are fired.

The first three months that I was unemployed I just went crazy. I went to place after place and interview after interview. Jobhunting was all I thought about from the minute I got up in the morning. I would systematically call every single possible number in the *Village Voice* and even the *Times*. I went to employment agencies and temporary agencies. I would answer ads like "Nice company, good benefits, call us now," where they wouldn't even say who they were or what kind of job it was.

"I'm only good for one interview a day, really, because it's frazzling to walk around the city and meet these people."

Keeping myself together for interviews was another problem. I'm only good for one interview a day, really, because it's frazzling to walk about the city and meet these people. Some days I just couldn't get myself to get out of bed and go to some strange part of town when everybody in the streets was running to their own job. They all seem to know what they are doing and I feel like an outcast in the street.

Despite my fears I had a lot of confidence when I first started out and now I don't have any. Finally, last week, my counselor at the Employment Center told me that I looked too bad even to send on an interview and that I should try to get a hold of myself.

Right now I've decided to sort of give up on getting a job and that has calmed me down quite a bit. I just can't hack jobhunting any more because everything depends on having typing ability; it seems incredible, but that's the way it is. If only I could type eighty words a minute then I feel like I would solve all my problems.

I'm trying to get enough money together to take a long view of getting employment. I'm still on disability. My unemployment is going to run out in about two months. I'm living in my boyfriend's apartment now, so I can rent my apartment out to somebody else and make a little extra that way.

These days I'm learning to live on very little money and to pass time at an incredibly slow rate. The hours weigh on me. I don't have to do anything—to keep things clean or to keep myself up. I haven't exercised. It's almost a mental problem at this point. I'm just depressed.

In the morning I'm just crazy when I wake up. I jump out of bed and smoke cigarettes. I know I should relax, have a cup of tea and listen to the radio, but I can't. I try to sleep until noon, if possible, because then the mornings are out of the way and most of the day is gone. If necessary, I sleep in the afternoon. We watch a little bit of television and I have to worry about what to cook for dinner, then we go to bed early.

"If only I could type eighty words a minute then I feel like I would solve all my problems."

There's nothing to do here. I brought my pencils and my pens to this little apartment because I decided to start drawing, even if it's only drawing circles to improve my mechanical skills. But this is really a crowded apartment. There just isn't any place to spread out and make it seem like a home. We don't even have enough space to hang our clothes up.

I realize that I don't like to do anything and that most of the time I don't like what I'm doing. I've lost all interest in the fashion magazines, which I used to pore over constantly. I don't like it when I'm on the bus. I don't like it when I'm washing the dishes. The only time that I like is when we're out visiting people and talking. But I don't get out enough. Most of my friends work and I can't get myself to visit because I always think I have to have a purpose when I do it.

Instead of worrying about how vapid—if that's the word—it is to live this way, I've just gotten into it. Otherwise I go through this litany, "I'm coming home from Columbia. I typed all day," going through all the things that would have been the substitute for my glorious day. And I think, "Well, I didn't lose that much."

My relationship with Ron is the most important thing to me right now. If it should fall apart, then I would consider relocating to the coast. Both my sisters are there, and I'd have them for solace. I think I might even be happier out there. We're really stuck here in this garret, living on nothing, and it makes me wonder what I am doing with my life.

My main problem is wondering what direction my life is going in. Here I am, thirty, and in debt. The other day I was thinking how miserably I've sunk into doing nothing. We had someone over for dinner last night who was on welfare and it really shook me up, because I may be going in that direction myself.

The money problem is very real, though renting my apartment is going to help quite a bit. I have the debt to take care of and with the interest it will be $5000 by the time I finish paying it off. As soon as I get a job they have the legal right to garnishee my salary and I'm trying to keep it from degenerating to that level. They want twenty dollars a month, so I'm trying to get the money together to give to them. I would really feel good if I could start paying them back.

My parents are my only recourse and they have absolutely refused to help me. They've told me I'm thirty and I should be self-supporting. They always put down my efforts at art, and then, when I had a breakdown, they told me that all I could do was art and I should try to get back into it.

The only other alternative is to deal, do something illegal. I don't have the strength or the intelligence or the talent to set up my own business, like knitting or cleaning people's houses. And I can't waitress. Something just hits me every time I'm about to do something; I think I can't do it or I just despair.

Welfare means waitressing off the books and trying to deal a little bit. It almost excites me—I'd sort of like to do it. But for me dealing and waitressing is like giving up and moving to the country. It's so counter-culture. I just can't picture myself doing it. I'm still hanging on to some sense of professionalism and trying to get a job.

I definitely want to work, but I want to work at something that's pleasing to me, because otherwise it's torture. Maybe I just wasn't cut out for typing and if I developed my art skill to a level comparable to that of a secretary, I might even be happier in the long run. I'm supposed to take a typing course through the Office of Vocational Rehabilitation, but I'm considering asking them to send me to an art school instead. That's my latest dilemma. What's keeping me back is that I've had all this typing drilled into my head and I'm not sure that it isn't the answer. You can get a job just about anywhere, it seems, if you can type well. I've learned to look at secretaries as some kind of miracle women who can do anything and at the art world as just nothing.

I shouldn't put art down so much. I'd like to be an artist, but I gave up my studio in order to rent it and I'd need money to support myself as an artist. I don't know where that would come from, so I can't even complete the fantasy.

"But I've taken note of the fact that I'm unhappy most of the time."

I haven't even thought about self-expression except when I started to consider going back to commercial art work. Even doing mechanicals, which is simple work, might be a boost to my ego. It also might give me a sense of direction, even though it's not considered fine art. In a way I've soured a lot on the whole art world scene. I think it's a lot of hokum. Put one of Ron's pictures in a laundromat and nobody would look at it twice. Put it in a high-priced gallery and it's exquisite. It's all context.

Painting is personal—you do it for joy. You do it because you like it and you do it when you like it. Before I met Ron I was painting sort of steadily, planning on putting a group of work together, taking it around and seeing what would happen. But now there's no place to paint and no time to paint and I really don't feel a loss because I don't think my work was that important—it was a time filler.

I'm attracted to all these books about "How to use your time," and "This is it," and "Change your life." I read a page or two and it sort of helps me. I'm living day by day and it's just a matter of adjusting.

But I've taken note of the fact that I'm unhappy most of the time. Not terribly unhappy—I would say I measure unhappiness in terms of nerve endings at this point, and if I'm calm, I consider myself happy. But I don't think that's a way to live. I would like to feel free to go out and exercise in the morning and paint a little in the afternoon, and I don't have that sense of freedom. I feel that I have to lie around until I get an idea about my next job application.

MAKING THE MOST
OF NOT WORKING

THERE'S ALWAYS SOMETHING I LIKE TO DO

Frank   Seattle, Washington

So relaxed and friendly, he seemed to be a genuinely happy person. Paper-folding was such an important part of his life that with energy belying his sixty-seven years he interrupted his story to show all the beautiful and inventive origami that decorated each room of his big, old house.

Six and half years ago I left Boeing Aircraft during one of the big layoffs. They had to cut costs in my department and they decided that at sixty-one my capability for improvement was rather limited. I was a little shocked when they told me that they were dropping me, there was no question about that. They offered me another job, but it was in a totally different field, it involved working on a third shift, and it looked as though I would have to spend two years at it before I could do any creative work, so I rejected that.

I wasn't too unhappy to leave. I was a peacenik and I'd always felt slightly embarrassed about working for Boeing, but at the time it seemed to me that raising a family was more important than fighting for your beliefs. I looked upon the work I did as purely a defense mechanism, no good as an attack mechanism. The Minuteman was an attack mechanism and I refused to work on that. Three years before I was laid off I refused to go down to Nevada to participate in those underground tests, so I recognized that I was a natural candidate to be dropped when the layoff came.

I was very outspoken. They took it from me because when I went to work there three of us electronics and engineering technicians were busy keeping this big beast of an analog computer in operation. After perhaps two months I found out the one thing that was wrong and fixed it.

From then on it required only one person to keep it running, so for about five years I was the one person. That took about half my time. I spent part of the rest of the time inventing things, like a new way of handling an oscilloscope, a screen testing method of flying Beaumark missiles. I even got to be Man of the Year one time.

The remainder of the time I argued politics with the engineers. I was always sort of a radical. I spoke loudly against Joe McCarthy and McCarthyism and I was one of the ones who felt that communism wasn't the threat to the United States that fascism was. This was not in keeping with the thinking of most Boeing engineers, who are very conservative. I think I actually converted some of them, but it wasn't easy.

But they laid me off, then offered me early retirement, which I accepted. I was rather happy to get out of there. Boeing is a kind of curious company. We think of it as a great, big company, but really, it's a lot of little organizations beveled together. You establish friends in a group and you establish people you can go to and who come to you for information. There was a definite social value in that, but I found that I had no desire to go back and look the people up after the thing was over. I've never been back since and I worked there eighteen and a half years.

I'm sure I can go back to work today if I want to. I never had any trouble getting a job. Almost all the jobs I've ever had, I enjoyed. There has always been something that you could add to them or take out of them. You could invent things or you could dream up new ideas.

But I love not working. I never felt embarrassed about it. I grew up during the depression years and we would work a few months, then be laid off for a while, then work another three, four months and be laid off for another while.

I don't think there was any adjustment to retirement. I was just happy to change from doing things for them to doing things for myself. To my family it looked like there was a serious adjustment, but I think the hardest decision I made was not to go back to work again.

I worried some when I stopped working; I suppose it's a matter of conscience. I worried about whether a person is free to enjoy himself or not. It's something of a protestant ethic, I suppose. Not being protestant, I wasn't quite as afflicted with it as some people and I worked that out after a few months.

I've always been able to occupy myself with something. I ride a bicycle a great deal—take two or three laps around the lake then stop and have a few beers at a tavern where people know me. I'm sort of a sage there.

For a while I was interested in politics, but I gave that up; I'm no longer a precinct committeeman. I am a member of a local political group and I assist in getting out their newsletter, oh, I suppose, five or six times a year, but that's about it. I got tired of the politicians and the constant splitting. We've got this split between the Democrats, the Republicans, the Conservatives, and the Liberals, between the smokers and the non-smokers. They keep chopping down into smaller and smaller groups and it's a little discouraging.

A year ago I got quite interested in a Senior Citizens Center that they were setting up, but the complexity of various interest groups was a little too much to cope with, so I dropped out of that. The people who were in the position to make decisions were all unemployed and looking for jobs, so there was a little pressure on them.

I've spent a lot of time on origami, paper-folding. It takes up about three hours a day during the week. I invent things—I'm a creative paperfolder. I've gone beyond the conventional origami and occasionally send things to the Origami Society, but I don't communicate as much as I once did.

I don't know how many things I've invented in origami, but I suppose if I counted them up I'd have at least sixty or eighty. You set yourself a problem, define it, and you sit down to solve it. My store of knowledge has never been very great, but my ability to figure things out has always been very high. That's what I've been doing all my life, whether it's a mechanical device or a relationship.

Having a wife makes a big difference. Widowers and widows have a much tougher case of it. My wife and I get into spells of backgammon like two idiots and stay up half the night in great contests. We're pretty close together, though I find myself watching the late, late movies on TV and she tends more toward reading. I'm sort of a movie freak and I can stay up to watch the old ones since I don't need as much sleep as I did when I was working. I used to sleep seven and a half, eight hours a night then; now it's five and a half, six hours.

I'm pretty content. I don't have any particular worries. I'm in reasonably good health, eating well, and my wife and I are quite compatible—we don't worry about many of the things that some people worry about. My wife works and she goes off, usually in the summertime, and takes a vacation trip somewhere. I don't go. I have no particular desire to go, though I might like to go to London or Japan some time. To look at Westminster Abbey and the Tower of London and those sorts of things doesn't seem too appealing, but there are a lot of paperfolders back there it would be fun to meet.

"I always looked forward to retirement, but it has no more turned out the way I thought it would be than the thoughts you have today are similar to the ones you had when you were in high school."

I always looked forward to retirement, but it has no more turned out the way I thought it would be than the thoughts you have today are similar to the ones you had when you were in high school. What you want at the age of fifty is quite different from what you want at the age of sixty-eight.

Stan   New York, New York

A laid-off sheet metal worker in his twenties, Stan had com-
muted from his New Jersey home to New York City, hoping to
find work where the construction trades were a little more
active. He had the broad shoulders and muscular build of a
person used to physical labor; under the shock of brown hair
his gaze was serious and thoughtful. His unusual self-
assurance was striking—it was the rare confidence of a person
who knows himself well.

When I started working at about nineteen it was a toss-up
between being a New York City policeman and being a sheet
metal worker. I had passed the Police Department tests, and I
was waiting to be called, but there was a long waiting list.

A friend of mine was a sheet metal worker and so were his
brother and father. At that time the thought of making $250 a
week was incredible, because nobody else was making that
kind of money. I was called by the union to take the physical.
They took me into the union, so I chose that.

I served a four year apprenticeship learning ventilation of
office and commercial buildings and high rise apartment
houses. As an apprentice you're guaranteed employment for
four years. Your salary is a lot lower than a journeyman's, so
the employer wants to keep you on. After about two years'
training you can do just about what a journeyman can do and
you're making half the salary that he's making. After graduation the policy is usually to lay the apprentices off immediately. I stayed on for about seven months because the shop
needed welders. Then they laid me off.

That was about four years ago. I had a couple of jobs, one
that lasted close to two years, then two years ago I was laid off
again and I haven't worked in my trade since then. There's no
work at all. Construction work seems to be the first industry to
be hit when the economy of the country starts to go.

It's frustrating to look for work because there are like a
hundred shops located all over New York City. You wind up
spending about thirty, forty dollars a week on traveling and
gas, and most of the time you're not hired. If you go to the
union, you have to go through the business agent, and friends

of the business agents get jobs before people they don't know. I could be out of work for a year and a friend of the business agent could be out of work a week, but he'll be put to work before me.

I'm so used to not working now it's like I never worked. I don't mind it but it's a hassle to worry about eating and how I am going to feed my family. I've taken jobs that I've disliked just to make the money, then I become miserable because I can't stand what I'm doing. The jobs are very constricting or confining—boring. Eight hours a day watching the clock. In a way I'm kind of in a trap. The field that I have the most experience in is mostly brawn. It requires some technical knowledge, but it's not what I like to do; I don't enjoy it. Not working, I can do the things I like, the things that make me happy. I'm going to college and I take karate lessons on the side. I'm with my two girls a lot more. I can get out; I can write if I feel like writing. I write mostly poetry. I used to write poems on the job—I'd get out a little book and a pencil and if I thought of a line I'd just jot it down.

I spent so many years forced into doing things that made me unhappy that now I feel productive because I'm doing things that I like to do.

"I'm so used to not working now it's like I never worked."

Not working makes me a much easier person to live with. When I'm working at something I don't like, I become irritable and grouchy and not at all a nice person. I don't like to be like that. If I could make enough money on the side to live on and just work when I wanted or needed to, I'd be very happy to keep on this way.

When I was working I was regimented. When you're on the job, you have to do what you're told to do. There's no room for imagination. Basically every day is the same, very mundane and boring.

You get up, you go to work, and you come home and forget about what you did. You fill in the time idly until you have to get up and go to work the next day. You live for the weekend and try to cram as much enjoyment as you can into two days because you know the next five are just a drag.

In a way I wonder, well, here I am twenty-eight now, I've been laid off and I don't really have any foundation. But I'd rather be living this way than buried in some type of job I didn't like. Other people my age started in a certain type of business and built themselves up to a higher level, but I'm still free to pick the field that I'd like to get into. I'm not looking for the goal of being Mr. Big Businessman or getting a lot of money; I'm not worrying about money and status—I just want to do something I enjoy doing.

I haven't failed. If I stayed at a job I disliked, that would be failure. If a person is afraid to leave a job they hate because they are secure and don't have to worry about being laid off, I think that's failing. You're not living up to your potential if you're afraid to try.

If you have a feeling that you want to do something, then evidently you haven't achieved what you're really looking for. Without being conceited, I know I can do anything that I really want to do. All I have to do is find it. And if you do what you want to do, you have to be good at it because you're enjoying it. And if you're good at something then you're a success. You don't have to excel above the others, you just have to do well.

"Money is no security; security is feeling comfortable with yourself."

I do have an aim. I was a medic in the Air Force Reserve and enjoyed it a lot, so I'm taking a two month course in a community college to get a state license as as emergency medical technician. New York City has a paramedic program where the ambulance can be patched right into the emergency room of a hospital by radio. They can transmit vital signs of the patient and the doctor tells them exactly what to do to sustain the patient. That's what I would like to do. That's a job that's doing something, helping people. Inanimate-type work like working with metal doesn't give me anything, whereas I think I would enjoy working with people.

I'm secure because I know what I want to do and I'm going towards it. I'm secure in the knowledge that eventually I'll be doing what I want to do. If I had a lot of money but I didn't enjoy what I was doing, I wouldn't be secure. Money is not security; security is feeling comfortable with yourself.

My wife considers me a little bit perplexing. She doesn't really understand me. I tell her I'm not happy in my job, and she says, "Well, maybe you won't be happy doing anything." When she sees me out of work maybe she's afraid that I won't be able to support the house and the responsibility of taking care of the kids.

I have money problems—that's the biggest problem I face every day. I worry about money, but worrying doesn't do any good. I guess everybody's deprived of certain things throughout their life. You have to be realistic. I know there are things that I can't have and things that I can have. And the things that I can't have due to my money situation, well, I figure when I get a job some day I'll be able to get some of them.

For emergencies I could borrow. If anything ever comes up, God forbid, where I'm really strapped, I know I can turn to either my aunt or my mother—they're wonderful. In a sense I'm not pressed because of that and it gives me more peace of mind, but I don't like to do it because it's not fair to them. They work hard for their money and I'm not comfortable asking them.

My expenses do run up. I still have to pay my union dues, even though I'm not working. If I miss three months as a member, I'm sent a letter—either you pay your dues or you'll be dropped. Now, you know, that doesn't give me much choice. The wages they're demanding are great for the unions, but what's it doing for the working man? If you're going to pay a plumber, a sheet-metal worker, fifteen dollars an hour, I can't possibly see how much work will be done, especially when there's a lot of non-union contractors that will do the work for half. There's something definitely wrong. I'm a union man, but evidently it's not doing me any good.

But I'm basically optimistic. I feel I can cope with whatever problems I might have. I've met so many already. I've been out of work before with no money in the bank at all, and I came back and got a job. Really it's nothing new to me; there's no more hard impact left on me. Getting laid off is just the same as getting a job; it's happened before and will possibly happen again.

After several jobs that didn't work out, Stan took a job as a prison guard. In a few months he had already convinced some of the prisoners to enroll in school.

Deborah   New York, New York

Deborah was volunteering at a community center for black youth—it was fun and she preferred doing something useful to frittering away the time until she could find another civil service job. Congenial surroundings attracted the vivacious, slender woman in her twenties as honey would draw a fly. Merry and talkative, she was far more interested in enjoying the moment and in laying out her strategy for finding a new job than in regretting the job she had lost.

At the time I was hired as a caseworker in the State Department of Mental Hygiene four years ago it was as a provisional worker. I knew that the job would be temporary, but I didn't take any other tests, because the state had a freeze. I tried to find something in private industry, but nothing came through.

When I was laid off six months ago, I said, "You know, this is the last time you'll be laid off for the rest of your life, so don't take it too hard." But I didn't handle it right. I thought a change of scenery would pick me up because I was rather depressed, so I decided to do some traveling. I went down to Atlanta for two weeks, then moved out to California.

In San Francisco, I was more or less content just waking up and doing nothing. I would get up at seven o'clock in the morning and go down to Montgomery Street, which is their Wall Street district, and watch the city come to life. I would walk back home, eat breakfast and relax, and go back out. I didn't do any jobhunting—I was just very relaxed and lazy.

But I missed New York and I knew I had to get back into the swim of things, so I came home. I think now that maybe I should have saved the money and got a little apartment here instead of moving out, because I was running away for a while.

Since I've been back, I've been doing a lot of things—going to all the cultural events that are free, jobhunting, just getting into New York all over again. There's so much to do in a day. I don't sit home and look at soaps. Today I haven't been to sleep at all; I like night life here and I was up all night. The night life has changed tremendously since I went away—all the new clubs have opened.

I have no problem whatsoever structuring my time. I get up very early in the morning, in time to see *"Good Morning America."* Stanley energizes me. I know he'll either make me angry or I'll feel real good, so I never leave the house before he goes off. He gives me that extra spunk I need to really wake up in the morning.

I'm not really career-oriented. If I'd felt like that, I would have bought another degree as soon as I got out of college. I think I'll go back to work for the state because I don't have a master's and that's limiting. I don't type and I really have no skills other than my work experience. And if you work for the government, as long as you save your time you can take a month off. I like having that time off because I love to travel and I want to go to London.

So I'm going to take a couple of state tests some time this month, one for Evaluation Specialist and the other for investigator for the Department of Social Services.

"I know I have to go back to school and buy myself another degree if I'm going to make any money."

I know I have to go back to school and buy myself another degree if I'm going to make any money. I'll never make $20,000 working for the state. After five years you get no more raises, just the standard increase.

I've been living with my sister and I just pay the phone bill. I have a couple of bills and I don't work the American Express card any more unless it's really necessary. I'm living off unemployment, so I just cut back. If I have $1000, I can spend it in five minutes, but if I have $3 and it has to go to the end of the week, I'll stretch it. I can steal the head off a nickel. I'll tell myself, "I'm overweight," and skip lunch. For two days last week I had no money to spend, no carfare, and I had to be staying in, reading. I adapt myself.

I try to be very nice to people when I have money. If somebody calls me and says they want me to do something, like babysit, I will. I ask nothing at the time because it comes back to you. Not working I go out a lot. Friends know I'm unemployed and they take me out. They say, "Oh, don't worry about it. You don't have the money now."

Basically I'm really happy with the world just as it is. I'm adventurous. I enjoy life. I try to do something worthwhile every day. I don't depend on a job to have feelings of self-worth. To be quite honest, the other day I was broke and I was sitting over at Roberto Clemente Park, looking out at the East River and reading a book, and I said to myself, "Gee, what's going to happen if you can't find a job, the job you want?" And then I said, "Well, I can get to understand suicide." But then I realized that there's always tomorrow—tomorrow's another day. I was depressed for that moment—sometimes you're really down and out—then the next day is a glorious day. It's so great to be here, and I'm so alive that you wonder how you could even let that thought run across your mind.

I can cope with it. Right now I'll just job hunt and send out my resumes and take the state test. When it comes time, I'm going to take an adult education course in typing. If there are no prospects, I'm going to get a job paying $100, $125, and type to make ends meet.

I would advise people who are not working to do what I did. Check out what is available like food stamps, and get your health insurance—get a Medicaid card—so you feel a little more secure. Then list your talents. See, I have no talents, so I just run over my job experience. Try to get a very good resume together, because you're selling yourself, and the more you can put into it, the better.

Get into different activities, into what's going on around town. You have to keep your head up, you know. Get into people—find something you like. If you like kids, volunteer—

there's nothing wrong with being a volunteer and it can turn you onto another job. You'll find something. Find something that you can groove on and get into it.

I've done all those things with my time but I'll never have this time off again because I never intend to be unemployed again for the rest of my life. I don't plan to marry, so I'm going to have to take care of myself till I finally retire. I know I can handle working full-time yet still have the freedom I thrive on. I manage to do it. Right now I can make it off unemployment, but when it runs out if I can't find anything, I'll even wash dishes in a hospital because I have to survive. I *have* to survive.

George   Omaha, Nebraska

The genial, relaxed man in his fifties seemed as comfortable in the union office as he might be in his own home. There had been no construction work all winter, but George was fit and trim, as though he were still getting a constant work-out. The hours he had been putting into union activities, politics and socializing seemed to be keeping him on the top of his form.

About three months ago I did some lather work—construction for new buildings and power plants. That was the last I've worked. Now it's March going into April and they haven't got anything; it's a late spring and building won't start till next month or maybe May. Then, when you start working again, you'll have to start saving, put some away each week from, say, May to October. After October it starts getting cold and they start cutting back. They can't pour concrete; they can't dig on account of the ground is hard—it's frozen.

I like my work. I'm fifty-two now and I've been doing it about nineteen years. I worked at Crawford Air Force Base underground, under the river, and on big buildings where you start below ground, come up to the top of the ground, and go up. A pretty big building kind of sways—sways all day long. When it's just a steel frame, you go back and forth. You get used to it. All buildings move. Sometimes they get creaky and people don't know what it is, but they're just moving.

If you get a good job, it will last through the winter; most of the time, though, you get laid off when the weather turns cold and it's kind of a hardship. What makes it so bad is the way they handle it at unemployment. At the ending of the year you got to wait two weeks before you can sign for your last check drawn in December. You cannot sign up for another month and that whole time you don't have nothing. Sometimes you've got some money saved to help you get by and sometimes you don't.

Sometimes you get other union work during the winter. I'm taking up architect and carpenter work at school now and that way I can do indoor work in the winters. I can work for the same amount of money I've been getting or up above it, but I cannot work for less. Those are the union rules.

I've worked in nuclear power plants and that's scary at times because of the way it affects you—it burns your cells up inside. They have to take inventory every day because one part of the room might be a hot spot today and tomorrow another corner might be. And you can't even see it; when you get in it, then it shows up on your badge. I know some workers who had to go out of the plant. When they're exposed so much, they can't go back for a certain length of time. One time there was an organization to stop building nuclear plants in the Omaha area, but I don't know—it's kind of hard to get along without it. You want to make sure there's no opportunity to get cold in the winter.

You take a risk working in a nuclear plant. You also take a risk working one hundred feet in the ground. A lot of people don't think water's running under at a hundred feet in the ground, but it is. They have air pressure in the underground room where you work to keep the river back. Being under is as dangerous as being up on a building when it's swaying.

When I'm not working, I feel that I should be working, but I try to make good use of the time while I'm off. I catch up on things that I didn't get done while I was working. I do quite a bit of helping different organizations.

I got into party politics from being in the union and I've been active in the Democratic Party for fifteen years. I've been the District Chairman and I've been on the County Central Committee and the State Central Committee. I've been elected Minority Chairman at the state level and I've been Minority Representative for the state and for the County Central Committee. I've also been active in the NAACP and in the A. Philip Randolph Association, which consists of all black union men in the state of Nebraska.

I'm always going somewhere; in politics there's a lot of emergencies. And we have meetings every month—every day when political time comes around and we're training people how to register and read the ballot. So whether or not I'm working, I'm busy with political affairs all the time and the satisfaction comes through.

I travel a lot for the different groups I'm active with. I was invited as a delegate to Washington for Carter's Inauguration Ball, but I didn't get to go. I couldn't afford it at the time, but from now on I will. You learn the ropes.

"...whether or not I'm working, I'm busy with political affairs all the time and the satisfaction comes through."

My wife belongs to a lot of organizations too. We had seven children, but only one is still at home, so we both have time now. Both of us being active in organizations definitely has been good for our marriage. We don't always see each other, but when we do, we sit down and discuss things that's going on and what we should do to help one another.

I couldn't quit work and do political work full-time. To do that you have to have some kind of income, and I only have what I earn. And I do like to work construction. I plan on doing it just as long as I can, till I'm sixty-five or maybe longer. My health is pretty good and I feel good. If I keep moving and keep myself busy, I feel more relaxed.

I think there should be a little more benefits during the winter months for construction workers though. Unemployment happens every year. For about six weeks to two months you can't collect the benefits and it's really bad. It's not on account of you, that you don't have enough hours in; it's a matter of the policies, that they cut off the extensions to the benefits each year.

It's a national issue. Even in Arizona or California they get rain during the winter and they're not working. I think the legislatures could grant extensions. I once had to have Home Relief, and I'll tell you, at that particular time I think something should definitely have been done about the unemployment benefits. If there were a little more political effort, I'd be pretty well content.

Mike   Omaha, Nebraska

A laid-off construction worker, and a widower raising three children, Mike was a rugged, cheerful, confident man who looked you straight in the eye. There was never a flicker of complaint in his voice about his situation.

I'm a Teamster; I drive a truck trailer. Construction pays well while it lasts, but I've been out of work six or seven months because the work is seasonal. I'm entitled to twenty-three weeks of unemployment which has run out. The government didn't extend benefits past that.

I think I have as much going for me as a lot of people do when they're unemployed. I handle my money well. A lot of the men in construction don't know how to handle their money. They make $500 a week and they're broke in the middle of the next week. But I'm a widower with three kids—a boy fourteen and two girls, twelve and eight. I save like hell—I really save my money.

When I go to the grocery store and I see a good deal on canned food, I'll buy a case—I don't fool around with two or three cans. I must have fifteen or sixteen cases in my basement. That'll last me six, seven months, maybe longer. And I have more time so I cook.

We eat out a couple of times a week—the kids like it. Also I like to travel with the kids. Every three years we take off. Two years ago it was Switzerland. This year I think we might go to Germany.

When I'm working a sitter takes care of the kids. I'm lucky; she's an older lady who is very good. But when I'm not working, I take care of them myself. I've done it for so many years, it's just part of my everyday life.

During the day when the kids are in school I'm usually racing around. I like the outdoors; I don't like working indoors. I go fishing and I also buy and sell rifles and firearms as my hobby.

I read a lot, about two hours an evening—novels and magazines and the *Wall Street Journal*. I like to know what's going on and what to invest in. I went to business school for a year and a half then worked at G.M., but I didn't last two months—I couldn't take it. They're stuffed shirts, bureaucrats who haven't earned a living like blue collar workers. In business, people will step on anybody to get a raise or a promotion. I'm a good union member and I go to most meetings. I've worked for all types of people and I'll work hard for anyone who is fair, but I'll slow down half speed if a guy gets on my back when I'm doing the best I can.

I go out with a few women and I think a lot about marrying, but I won't marry unless I love the woman. I think of it for the kids and for me also. I get awfully lonesome some nights.

Also, a woman adds love to a family. A man adds strength but it's better to have love than strength, because you can get the strength from other people within the family. Kids need to have constant love when they're growing up.

I've been asked so many times whether I'm more sympathetic to women raising kids and working because of my situation. I don't know; I don't have much use for anybody that leaves a family. When guys take off and leave women with the kids and the women have no choice, sure I'm sympathetic with them, but I think this women's lib is a bunch of bull. Suddenly women are taking off and leaving their families. But I've seen a lot of women leave the kids with the husband and it's harder for the man to raise the kids than it is for the women. When a man leaves a woman with the kids she can draw all the benefits, ADC and welfare, and I assume she can get support from him, which I agree she's entitled to. But a man, he's got to be the breadwinner. I certainly wouldn't go down to sign up for ADC and all that. It would step on my dignity.

I'm not interested in a career change. I have a goal set. I'd like to buy me a small resort in the Rockies. It will take me a few years to do that, but if I can get a good year in construction, I'll have enough for a down payment. I know I will get the resort, but I have to learn a lot about it before I do it.

"Sure, sometimes it's bad, but you don't show it. I don't let a lot of things bother me. I figure the hell with it."

I'm from a family of twelve and my father's philosophy was that if you've got a problem, don't let it out on others because you spoil it for everyone around you. We learned that if you don't keep smiling it's going to be hell. Sure, sometimes it's bad but you don't show it. I don't let a lot of things bother me. I figure the hell with it. I put the pros and cons together and the best always comes to the top.

AN ARTIST'S LIFE

Big Boy Medlin   Los Angeles, California

Each of us is all the sums he has not counted; subtract us into
nakedness and night again, and you shall see begin in Crete
four thousand years ago the love that ended yesterday in
Texas.

—Thomas Wolfe, *Look Homeward, Angel*

*"It looks like I'll be going to work Monday morning. Oh, I don't
know...," the long-legged man with the wavy, honey-colored
hair and a beard said glumly in a strong Texas accent. A
thirty-three year old writer, new to L.A., Big Boy was sharing
quarters with two other recently arrived Texans and a friendly, shaggy, amazingly smelly dog who found it comforting to
drape himself over the feet of guests. Shy at first, Big needed a
whole five minutes to get rolling. Humorous and witty, but
with his words carefully thought out, he was a natural
storyteller.*

Tomorrow I'm supposed to start a gig at *Hustler* magazine. I
didn't apply for it—some people there read my work and called
me—so I found that attractive. I don't like that magazine and I
don't want to work for Flynt, but Paul Krassner is the new
publisher, so there's a chance things might be changing
enough where I could do some real writing. I'm not super-

optimistic about it, but it pays good and all I've got to do is come in for three months. I'll be in pretty good financial shape then and I can take off.

This will be the first time that I've ever done what I consider I'm about, which is writing, as a job. I've never made much money at writing and I almost hate to call it work because so far it's been fun. I worry about it being a sell-out or a cop-out or something, but at the same time I'm so adverse to work that it could be virtually any job in the world and I'd be thinking of some reason why I didn't want to go do it Monday morning. I've never done something for money that I didn't really believe in. You don't want to work for the man and you don't want to create something that you don't approve of. But when you get right down to it, there's almost nothing you can do that meets your approval 100 percent, so...

What can you do if you don't work? You can write. But writing wasn't exactly that analytical with me; it just sort of evolved. In West Texas high schools they made everybody write two essays, one in support of the oil depletion allowance and the other on what you were going to be after you got through school. One reason I left West Texas was that everything out there is oil. The only possibilities you had were working in the oilfields or teaching school.

I had done scattered jobs in the oilfields, working on trucks, carrying drill pipe and that kind of thing. Oilfield-connected work was really lousy; the oil industry is probably the worst industry in the world—the most conservative, reactionary. Well, I made a very conscious decision I wasn't going to do *that* and went to the University of Texas in Austin.

Coming out of the desert, Austin was an oasis. It was there that I got interested in Thomas Wolfe and other writers. A Texan doesn't want to be thought of as intellectual, but there are a lot of intellectuals in Austin. It's a city where people with master's degrees drive taxi cabs and your bartender maybe dropped out of his Ph.D. program in philosophy. Still, there's a rough edge to it all and nobody feels that comfortable with it, which makes it even better.

I was delivering beer and saying I was a writer, but I wasn't doing much, just a few little articles here and there. When Jeff Nightbyrd started *The Austin Sun*, he and his partner wandered in and said they wanted a humorous sports story, so I wrote one. They liked it, so I wrote another one. It turned into a column and I did it for three and a half years.

It wasn't a living—*The Austin Sun* was a struggling paper and when I was doing the beer thing I didn't even take money for it. After the beer thing it was just barely enough to keep me in dope, probably not even enough.

Then last year Larry Flynt bought the *L.A. Free Press* and Jay Levin and Jeff Nightbyrd were running it. They called about working for them, so I came out a couple months ago to do my column here. One reason why I wanted to come was that I like to travel and their concept was that I would be on the road about half the time. The *Free Press* was supposed to go national and I was going to cruise around the country a lot and do big events.

But after I got out here the *Free Press* not only didn't go national, it ceased to exist. The first week Jay got fired, which was kind of bad. The second week they brought in this *Newsweek* bureau chief, who was sort of real straight, to run the paper. The third week was uneventful, the fourth week Flynt was shot, and the fifth week they suspended publication. So it was "Welcome to L.A."

I said, "Well, hell, I might as well head back to Texas." I could sit in Austin, maybe tend bar, and work for a couple years on a novel. Maybe it would be good and maybe I could publish it.

But I've decided I'm going to be a professional writer and I'm paying some dues right now. I think the next couple of years will be really important to me, so I'm looking at L.A. I can spend those two years here making contacts and learning how to write. I think I'm a pretty good writer, but there are a lot of things I don't know.

I think L.A. is not a good town to be out of work in, but there's so much money lying around here that I could see never having to really have a regular job, just getting by on freelancing. I'm no better writer here than I was in Austin, but just being here somehow increases your status. It's absurd, but it's true. So I can always crank something out and earn something writing, which is good and bad. It's bad that I would be grub-grinding that way.

I see myself doing some serious writing, but I've got to get a little bit more economic stability and discipline. I look at doing this gig at *Hustler* as kind of going through basic training. I'm very bad at structuring my time and I have to have deadlines imposed to get anything done. And I have to get back to living during the days, which I don't. They're very strict at *Hustler* about being there all day, five days a week. I've never done that; it's like being in school. An office is a real strange little discipline, all bureaucracy, which is why I compare it to the army.

I need discipline; still, if you think that you're an artist and you do something with your talent that you don't consider artistic, you're throwing away a little piece of your soul. This is the first time I ever really had to face that. And now, here it is—*Hustler*. My job will be in-house writer. I've got to write about women. I've never written very much about women. I've made some bad mistakes with women but never that I was using one of them for a story. I've never done erotic writing and I don't think anybody would find what I write erotic—wouldn't think so. I don't really know what my assignment will be, but—*(sighs)*—fear the worst.

"I need discipline; still, if you think that you're an artist and you do something with your talent that you don't consider artistic, you're throwing away a little piece of your soul."

There are, I guess, three things that are really offensive about going to work for *Hustler*: There's the nine to five discipline. There's not really any room to write—it's going to be all formula—I'll just be glib. And it's sexist.

In Austin there were militant women—militant feminists—which I thought was just kind of silly, but—you know, it does make you kind of think. I don't know how it happened exactly, but—why don't I use this story to clarify a little bit. When I was a kid I used to go rabbit hunting all the time and I'd shoot—God, this is going to sound real sexist—I'm comparing women to rabbits—but I went out and killed fifty-nine rabbits one afternoon. Just killed them—don't pick 'em up or anything—just shoot 'em, leave 'em there.

And the next day me and my partner wanted to break the record, so we shot sixty. We hit fifty-nine and we had one bullet left. We shot this rabbit and just hit it in the leg. It was running around wounded, and you don't want to leave an animal suffering, so we had to run it down across the prairie and beat it to death by hammer. And whenever a rabbit is wounded and dying, it makes a noise like a baby crying. It's really hideous.

I had a horrible nightmare the night after that. It never bothered me before, and suddenly I went, "Wow! All this killing of rabbits—it's not right." The lessons of my whole life came together in my mind to show that I was violating my fundamental beliefs in things.

And somehow that happened with women. The women in Austin started asserting themselves more, refusing to play traditional roles. I realized I—and everybody else—were very cavalier. I probably still am—I'm still a male chauvinist pig— but in my consciousness I'm trying to improve. And I have, certainly.

You see, I'm not really excited about this job. The right work is different from—the wrong work. I probably wouldn't feel the same way if the job I was going to Monday morning was loading trucks; any kind of physical labor I wouldn't be giving of myself. But writing is like selling what I value the most.

There's only so much writing you can do. I don't think I'd be able to sit there writing from nine to five, then do other writing at home at night. I don't see how you can have writers working from nine to five—period. How can you tell somebody this is the time that they're going to write? Ninety percent of the time I've had my best ideas either late at night or right when I get up in the morning. Then the rest of the day you don't have anything, but it's been a great day because you've got something really good to show for it.

I said to those people at *Hustler*, "What happens if I get through with all my work by noon?" and they acted like they never heard of that possibility. They said, "Well, there's always something to do, you know."

So it's going to be busy work, and I never have liked that. I think there could easily be some stuff I'd refuse to do. It sounds like I have a chip on my shoulder. Maybe I'm just feeling sorry for myself. Well, you know, I've never really been against work; I can sit and watch somebody work all day. If everybody will work or can send me money, it will be just fine.

I don't feel guilty when I'm having a good time. I feel guilty when I'm not doing anything and I'm having a bad time doing it. I spend my time best writing, of course, but that really is a small percentage. I'm a rock and roller—party, honkytonk. In Texas I got a stimulus from rhythm and blues. There are so many honkytonks, so many good pickers, it's sort of a lifestyle. A lot of people don't think it's very healthy, but to me it's energizing to be around music and people who appreciate it. I haven't gotten into it here because I haven't been too impressed by the music scene, but I'm enough into rock and roll that I was a roadie for a while. I toured up and down the East Coast with Doug Sahm and a band called The Texas Tornado.

I spend a lot of money on partying and going out places. I'm pretty gregarious, sort of a party organizer. Places where I've lived have always been sort of party houses, which makes living with me not too good if you're doing an eight to five gig, because a party might start at three o'clock in the morning— taking drugs and drinking a lot.

So I could use the discipline, but besides that, the only other good thing I can see about going to *Hustler* is that I don't have any money and I'd like to have some. Still, I've always been able to get money when I need it, so I don't worry about it too much. My house burned down a year and a half ago and I lost a lot of stuff, but it didn't really seem to matter. And, you know, I don't spend a lot of money on a wardrobe—I make all my own clothes—see this T-shirt? (*laughter*) Money takes care of itself. When you get right down to that last fifty bucks, then you go—oooh—but good times always happen and I'm an eternal optimist—things pop up.

One thing that's helped me out a lot in not working is that I got wounded in Vietnam and I get $240 a month. If you've got $240 it's a lot easier; you're that much more free than if you don't have anything. I'm 60 percent disabled according to the army. I got hit in the hand and I don't have much strength in it. When I bend my wrist, I can't straighten out all the fingers. For a long time my hand was just bent over and paralyzed and they said it wouldn't get any better, the nerve wouldn't grow back, but when I got out, it did.

I should have tried to get out when I got drafted, but I was too caught up in the Hemingway syndrome that you've got to experience everything before you write about anything. I really thought you had to go to war and be in life-death situations to understand life.

I knew about thirty seconds after I got to Nam that I'd made a big mistake. It was a little late then—saw them MIRVs in the 101st Airborne! At the time I didn't feel the way I felt even two years later, that it was more than a mistake, but was a real—I hate to say evil—but malicious intrusion.

I went through all that; still, I feel a little frustrated right now because I've got to go to work tomorrow. Work! You couldn't have picked a subject who disliked work any more, I must say. I'm all for people working, but—why me? I don't know why my life is so much tougher than anybody else's. Actually my life is probably a little bit more simple.

So I'm going to *Hustler* tomorrow. On Thursday they said, "This is the unofficial call. We all agree we want you to work for us and we've just got to get some things OK'd at Columbus, Ohio. We'll give you the official call tomorrow."

Well, I waited around here Friday till one o'clock, and then I went over to see the Dodgers play. I haven't heard from them, so I haven't ever had the official call. My original plan was to be there at nine o'clock, but now that I've gotten close to it, I've changed it to calling them at nine o'clock to say, "Hey, I haven't heard from you." That doesn't seem unreasonable, does it?

I wouldn't hustle like this for more than two years, but for that time I can deal with this other reality here in L.A. and make enough connections so that I can go back to Texas and do anything I want to from there—me and my pen and pad and the telephone. Some people would say I'm not hustling now, but for me I am—just being here is hustling for me. I'm real homesick. I still haven't found a groove.

I make too many generalizations, I know, and I've only been here two months, but this town—I don't know. I miss the loud, obnoxious people in Texas. Nobody here is loud or obnoxious because everybody's trying too hard to make an impression. I thrive on that bizarre, straight-ahead, hell-bent-for-leather energy that a lot of people have in Texas. I don't like the way people relate to each other here and I miss the loud, obnoxious people. I don't like being the only loud, obnoxious person.

It hurts me to say it, but I may be actually more goal-oriented at this point than a lot of the Texas-Bohemian-Beatnik people are because I know that I want to do certain things. One novel is pretty much outlined in my mind and I've got other creative projects that I want to do. Even having something you want to do is out of place around most of the laid-back Texas people who aren't working.

The little direction I have I feel comfortable with. I'm taking a chance, but I don't feel vulnerable; I'm pretty egocentric. I'm a writer, I've done some good work, and I think that when I get to the right point I'll do something much bigger. I have that confidence. I'm a storyteller. At thirty-three I've been through some things and times that not too many people have done: being from a Bircher family and growing up in Texas, the drug thing, anti-war politics, tribal war, being a roadie and a jock and a scholar. There are so many different combinations of things that I've got a lot of stories to tell in a longer way than I've done so far. I'm just now getting my style together.

Actually, I just made all this up. I'm not even from Texas— I'm from New Jersey. I wouldn't mind eating a nice cheeseburger now.

The official call from Hustler *never did come and Big Boy was spared having to go to an office and write from nine to five. Nor was Paul Krassner's free spirit contained in that office much longer; his free speech point of view did not suit* Hustler's *marketing goals and he was let go. Meanwhile, Jay Levin started the* L.A. Weekly, *and for a while Big Boy wrote a column for it. He then then wrote two screenplays with Michael Ventura, the second of which,* The Roadie, *was produced as a film.*

Camilla   New York, New York

In her stunningly cluttered apartment where pretty objects were piled atop each other in no apparent order, with indomitable spirit, delighted laughter and a talent for finding the

*funny side to any story, Camilla talked gaily on—dramatizing
every emotion with flair—at one point actually falling off her
chair. An actress making the rounds, over twenty-one and
under sixty-five by her own admission, Camilla brought
boundless enthusiasm to a consuming stream of activities.
She battled her landlord in court, bought and sold antique
clothing and jewelry, bicycled from acting to singing to
exercise class and always managed to show up for her work
shift at an organic food coop, all between roles.*

I'm a professional actress. I belong to three unions, but I'm not
paid up in any of them at the moment.

The first paying job I was offered in acting I grabbed. It was
with a children's theater. We went on the road, traveling on
what they call a bus and truck tour. I got paid $40 a week—
$38.20 take-home pay—and I had to cover my own hotel and
food. We were doing *Snow White and the Seven Dwarfs* and I
played five parts, including the off-stage voice of the mirror.

That job and another road show about three years later were
the only times I made a living completely from acting. I think I
got $125 for the other show—big money after $38.20. Each job
lasted about five months.

I started working on my nightclub act in '75 and the first job
I had doing it was on a cruise ship in '76. When you're
developing an act, you don't expect to make any money when
it's new, they tell me, but once I almost broke even.

I've had a lot of crazy jobs and they're all in my nightclub
act. Those terrible jobs I had made me physically sick. I guess
you'd call it psychosomatic. I'd get nauseous, have accidents,
and run high fevers. I even gouged the corner of my eye a
couple of times. I noticed that those things would happen
while I was under pressure.

To get acting jobs I had an agent—the dregs. I mentioned his
name to somebody once and they said, "Oh, is he out of jail?"
But he gave me my first singing job. He booked me into the
Times Square area and said, "You have to hustle drinks...but
it's very light hustling."

I didn't last but two minutes in that job. I got so frightened
my hands were frozen to the bar. I sang two songs and the
owner said, "Well, business is not too good. Take a taxi home."
I took the two bucks and ran. It was the first time I got paid for
singing—a dollar a song—looking on the bright side.

I worked at the Coliseum at those girly-girly jobs, dressed in black leotards and stage hose, walking around, giving out things for a company. I also did shoe modeling. It's not easy work. I was modeling a 4B shoe and I wore a five and a half.

I also did go-go dancing as a French dancer. I didn't know how to do the dancing—who knew from rock and roll? But I thought, *"Eef* I talk with a French accent, they can't help but love me. I'll be *sharming."* Well, I learned on the job. That whole scene was like a B movie.

After the job I went for unemployment, but the owner of the bar contested the claim. She said she didn't know who I was. Well, of course, I used my real name when I filed for unemployment and I no longer had "ze French accent." I won the hearing and I got the unemployment.

I had some more go-go dancing jobs in little crossroads barrooms in the coalmining area of Pennsylvania, which were *really* the dregs. One night I had to call out the state troopers to protect me. I needed unemployment credit for the two weeks I had worked down there, but everyone associated with the hearing was a bar owner, even my lawyer's mother, so I lost. The next step was to go to Albany to appeal and I said "Screw that. If they're going to make it so hard for me to make a living, let them support me. Nuts."

"The next step was to go to Albany to appeal and I said, 'Screw that. If they're going to make it so hard for me to make a living, let them support me. Nuts.' "

That led me to my current non-working status. I was knocking myself out with those dumb jobs just to stay alive and it was a constant problem every month worrying about how to keep a roof over my head. I was entitled to the unemployment and they had cheated me out of it. It was the last straw.

I had to fight to get on the welfare rolls and it took me about a year. I got letters from two doctors saying I could not work except as an actress or in related fields. But they really made it hard for me. I was white, I had a college degree—I had some nerve.

They said to me, "We don't like our jobs either. Why should you be any different?" They were encouraging me to be a caseworker—trying to force me, never mind encourage me. "You could sign yourself out in the field and still go to auditions," they said. They wanted me to cheat like they were doing.

They made me take the caseworker exam when I actually might have gotten a performing job. I had auditioned and had gotten a callback to audition again, but I couldn't go because welfare was making me take the exam or they were going to cut me off. I passed the exam because I couldn't cheat and fail. It was all I could do to get them to leave me alone after that. They were putting more and more pressure on me and I got colitis. They said if I didn't get a job, I wouldn't get welfare.

So I got another crummy go-go dancing job. I needed money for a costume, and it was probably the only time welfare ever paid for a go-go outfit. The hours were unheard of and not like the original agreement. When the guy told me I'd have to dance till 4:00 A.M. I said, "Oh, no," and he wouldn't give me my money. I had to threaten him with the Labor Deparment to get the check. I've had this constant fight to collect money. I can see why Sarah Bernhardt wanted to be paid in gold before every performance. She wasn't so dumb.

"I've had this constant fight to collect money. I can see why Sarah Bernhardt wanted to be paid in gold before every performance. She wasn't so dumb."

At one point there was a hearing because I wanted welfare to pay for my acting class. They did pay my answering service bill and my union dues, but they're supposed to pay for your training too. The welfare official told the judge that they would rather I didn't work. They judge couldn't believe it.

Welfare then transferred me from Home Relief to SSI and classified me as disabled because I could only work as an actress. SSI doesn't cover rent raises. If you're aged and poor, you get a rent exemption; if you're poor and disabled, they won't pay. It's fascinating—they discriminate against the disabled.

Well, I haven't paid my landlord the increase anyhow. I won a case against him. For years it has been a running battle between us. I've spent a lot of time in courtrooms over the last four years and I've learned a lot of law representing myself in court.

The income from SSI is not enough to get by on. I've been getting help from the Actors Fund to pay my phone and electric bills. To make ends meet I sell antique things that I buy in thrift shops and junk stores. In the beginning I just picked up attractive things very cheaply for myself, then I would discover that sometimes they had value. I bought a cigarette case for $3 and I sold it for $500, and a necklace for $10 and sold it for $300. But that doesn't happen every day.

I've always had a problem looking for work. Just looking for jobs becomes a career in itself and you forget what it is you're doing there. One actor I know used to say, "I was offered a job in a Broadway show last week, but I couldn't take it because it would interfere with making the rounds."

I think it would be nice to have a very active career, although I have mixed feelings. When I did my nightclub act it was successful. People laughed and enjoyed it. When I got through I was elated—there's no other feeling like it. But even though it was there in front of me, I felt like it was an accident and that it was not going to happen again. Now, I could understand why I would put off doing it again if it had been a failure, but it wasn't and I couldn't quite figure that out. My shrink tells me that I'm afraid of success. Who would ever believe it? Afraid of success!

I also feel that I would have missed something if I hadn't done the legal stuff. It has given me a whole other dimension, a feeling of worth—a different kind of worth than if I'd just been acting. People no longer talk to me in the way that they still talk to actors, as though they're doing you a favor to talk to you.

If people were allowed to do what they wanted to do instead of being pressured into doing things they don't want to do, society certainly would be much better for it. I guess that's anarchy—the good kind of anarchy. That's self-government, which we don't have. I think people act badly because they hate what they're doing. They're furious. I have had anger directed at me, especially by white middle class people, who have the attitude, "We hate what we do, we hate our life, and we hate our work. We have to do what we don't like—why don't you? Why should you be any different? Why shouldn't you have to get a crappy, dumb job and be miserable?"

I feel sympathy with people who are pressured to make a living by doing things they don't like up to a point, but I find myself saying, "If you don't like your job, then quit. You can go on welfare. Don't get mad at me because I did it rather than grouch or scream at somebody."

I'd like to be working in acting. When I'm working on my nightclub act, that's total concentration. I've never really been able to focus on it because I'm always having to take time to make a few bucks or work on the legal cases against the landlord. If my landlord were smart he'd get me hired in a Broadway show. That would take me out of court and he wouldn't have to be bothered.

I feel that if I don't act, the skills will atrophy. Sometimes when I get away from performing it feels like forever and I'm afraid I'm not going to get back into it. I keep thinking I have to do something. If you're an actor, you've got to perform. So many actors who are forced to take other jobs get sick like I did. If all the actors who couldn't stand doing crappy jobs went on welfare, we might get a federal theater, as they had in the thirties.

I think it's important for people to do what they have to do and want to do. I was going to start looking for an agent again. I feel this pull in the middle of the courtroom that I've got to get back in there and find some work.

I started to contact some agents and I could just see them saying they were going to send me up for an aspirin commercial. I could not do a commercial now, telling people to take some crap that I go around in private life telling them not to take. I would rather be on welfare.

I had an interesting dream a couple of months ago—that I had nothing to do. What a confusing feeling! It was so strange. I thought, "Gee, it might be nice not to have to worry about anything," but I'd probably be bored to tears. I'm always worrying about all this extra stuff—the pressure of doing a show—getting it together and having things work right—getting a pianist, getting the owner of the club to act like a human being. Then there's always this feeling that I haven't done something—finished a legal brief on one case or another. Now I'm ready to start developing new ones—I'm going to start suing this dry cleaner who ruined my drapes. I'll be right back where I started from.

Phillip   New York, New York

With finished canvases scattered about his huge loft and a new painting, resting interrupted on the easel, Phillip held court around a table ringed with friends and acquaintances. An energetic, compact man in his thirties, he distinctly enunciated pithy observations in a ringing voice. Telling stories, giving a haircut, he refreshed everybody with unusual new ideas and observations.

Eleven years ago I was pursuing my work to get a good gallery and establish myself and I reached a point of financial crisis. It was my normal periodic crisis when I run around like a madman, attack all my resources, and turn my life inside out.

Full of insecurities, expecting to be rejected, and under-pricing myself, I took a portfolio of my work up to a gallery in Provincetown. The owner looked at the drawings, and obviously very impressed, asked what I wanted for them.

I didn't know what I wanted for them. I wanted out of the hole.

"Do you want me to buy them? Do you want to leave them on consignment? What are you here for?" he asked. "I'm here to show you my drawings," I said, "Make me an offer."

He bought the entire portfolio for a couple of thousand dollars and I took that money, packed up the loft in Manhattan, and moved to a cheaper studio in Brooklyn. I thought that after I had paid off my debts, it might get me through six months, if I was really careful.

Then all of a sudden the air smelled incredibly filthy and the noise of the traffic, the incessant clatter of the telephone, the total input of this city overwhelmed me. In less than twenty-four hours I made the decision to split. I packed my life into one suitcase and took off, not knowing where I was going or how I was going to live.

I survived as an expatriate in Spain for ten years. I learned a couple of languages, a number of professions and I made some incredible friends who will be with me all the rest of my life.

When you're taken outside your normal social roles, nature sort of guides you to deal with things in a much more ingenious way. You learn not to be an opportunist exactly, but to know when your moment has arrived, to sharpen your wits and be ready to take a chance on yourself and risk all. Of course, if you're not holding much, it's not a big thing anyway.

This freedom I have is symmetrical with who I am. It's the way I live; it's a point of view. I would imagine I would have that freedom even if I were working in a factory.

Within that freedom I do what I consider to be work, which to me means engaging in something and effecting a change in it. I'm not sure whether I hold that the idea of effort is involved in work. If something requires effort, then it's labor—it isn't work. I might be using these words sloppily, but I find work to be directly related to how much I understand of something.

For instance, I picked up the guitar at age thirty. I didn't want my life to go by without being able to find out what music was all about from the inside. It doesn't bring me any financial reward, yet for me it's work. When I put the guitar down I have the satisfaction of having done something with it.

I've never been able to hold to the idea of a self-imposed discipline. As soon as I stipulate that I must work three hours minimum at my painting, I'll spend the day meeting with friends and getting high. If I get out of bed early in the morning and the work goes down with a certain amount of authority and clarity, then I'll do that for a couple of days until I hit two or three days in a row when it doesn't work. Then another system comes up. I don't take these systems of discipline very seriously.

I can easily sit and do nothing, just look at the wall for a long time. I have no trouble being alone. In Spain I lived alone in the countryside for years without going into town. People would come out to see me once in a while and there would be a couple of weeks in the summer when I'd get very social and run around and see everybody.

I'd fill the lamps at night, draw, read, build a fire, cook, clean up and feed the animals. When you're living that kind of life, you don't have free time. Your free time is late at night when it's dark out and cold in and out. You're sitting by the fire exhausted because all day has been a schlep to get the wood for the fire, the water up out of the well, and the food made and cleaned up while it was still light and you could see what you were doing. By about 8:30, when that's all over, what free time do you have? You're dead.

During one period I moved back to town because I was preparing for a show. I would get up in the morning, go to the studio, and start to work. I'd have lunch sent up from the bar downstairs and work right on until 8:30, 9:00 at night, then break and go to dinner. Sometimes I'd go back to the studio for a while, otherwise I'd just go to the apartment, play the guitar a little, and go to sleep. Then I'd get up and go to work.

It was a divine time for me. It was like a perfect life. I didn't have to worry about where the money was coming from because I had a thousand dollars to get my material together and cover the rent. I had the freedom of letting myself fall all the way in and I loved it.

At the end of two months of preparing for that show I was so high on my work and on working, I didn't want to stop. The idea that I had to go pack it up and show it almost killed me. I was a maniac that night; it was frightening. I fell apart because I felt I was at a consummate point of beginning. I had achieved a new clarity and managed to move up to a new level in myself.

I like being very conscious. That's the most fun, the most natural. I envision some point where things function very clearly, but guess I don't believe it exists.

To me making it means being able to reach a certain point in my work when the feedback I'm getting from my own experience is complete and consistent. There are moments when you feel you're doing things with clarity and other moments when you don't feel so clear about what you're doing, so I worry that I'm not going to succeed.

I've had some brushes with fame already. Something in the nature of my life has made me into a minor celebrity figure and sure, I like it, though it seems a bit silly. You cannot judge your value by your fame; you have only your own dreams for judging it.

But I think I'd like being a celebrity in the sense that I might be able to do financial things. I'm a little older now—I'm thirty-seven. If I work as an artist, where am I going to get my materials and how am I going to be able to afford to do my work?

I know how I spend my money, but I'm not always sure where it all comes from. At one point or another, though not always consistently, what I do brings me money. I've been an architectural consultant, have sold a few paintings, and done an occasional poster since I've been back in New York. I give haircuts—that forms a substantial part of my living. I was an astrologer and I've done commercial art and some graphics for a couple of movies. I like to cook and a person I know who has a restaurant said, "Come and cook. It will be your special night and I'll give you some bread." It's hustling, a kind of madness.

The money comes from somewhere, but conversely, if I have a $100 in my pocket and I know I'm going to need $150 to pay the phone bill or cover the rest of the rent, I go out and blow the $100. I'll take a taxi instead of the subway because it's too cold and I want to be home—I'm not going to wait for a train. I'll say, "Where would I like to have dinner? I have a hundred dollars; I can have dinner anywhere I want." I guess I really like it when it gets crazy because I created the situation.

"I know how I spend my money, but I'm not always sure where it all comes from."

I've taken the point of view that everything I've experienced has been of my design. Because I created the situation, if there is deprivation within it, I created that too, so that's a kind of fulfillment to me.

I can handle my life. I chose it and I'm enjoying it, although there are times when it has been incredibly difficult emotionally. But everybody has a center in their being to retreat into. Because you're creating it all, you're also creating what you would be resisting, so your strength is infinite.

I know that I elected to live like this and I know the point at which I made the decision. When I was around seven or eight years old my mother and father were trying to instill in me the value of saving. "See, if you just give up that candy bar and put the money in your piggybank...." I was supposed to learn the lesson that when that fucking plastic pig was full of pennies, I would have enough.

I heard a tinkle one night and went downstairs. They were in a financial crisis and they were trying to get the pig open to get my bread. It had accidentally broken. They were freaked out and I was completely mindblown, I was so outraged. It was like everything they'd told me had been bullshit. At that moment I burned a hole in my pocket and developed a burning itch in my palm to get rid of money.

That's the way my head works. Of course I don't like to have debts and I don't like to buy things unless I have enough money to pay for them. I can't, anyway, who'd give me credit? Oh, I can save money—I do it for at least two or three weeks. If I have a lot of money, I can budget, but if I don't, I don't see the purpose.

"If I die tomorrow, what difference does it make if I die with debts?"

I don't anticipate ever being able to change because who knows if we're going to be here tomorrow? If I die tomorrow, what difference does it make if I die with debts? When I'm dead that's it, babe, that's the end of the problem.

Gene   **Washington, D.C.**

He was a writer in his early forties whose milky soft skin made it clear that physical labor was not his calling. His eyes were somewhat sad and lonely but reflected the determination with which he pursued his writing whether he was paid for it or not.

161

We sat in the dimly-lit kitchen two steps from the typewriter and writing corner he had created in the room.

I drifted into the newspaper world and was in Memphis when the *National Observer* was started by Dow Jones, the year that James Meredith enrolled in the University of Mississippi. A managing editor told me later that I had gotten so much stuff in the paper on the Meredith thing that he figured it would be cheaper to bring me up to D.C. as staff than to pay me at a correspondent's space rates. I was with the *National Observer* for thirteen years.

I went to Vietnam the first time in 1965 when it was a very small war and nobody hated it. I did other stories in Asia, I was in the Middle East for a while, and I was in London and Northern Ireland.

Then things changed at the *Observer*. It became a kind of how-to-cope-with-life magazine—*New York* magazine without *New York* magazine style. The new editor and I never really got on very well. Their complaint was that I sometimes took liberties with the facts. I saw it coming and I got canned.

"I came as close to tears as I think a man is allowed to get."

I came as close to tears as I think a man is allowed to get. There was this great feeling of "this doesn't happen to me." Age twenty-eight to forty is a hell of a good chunk of a man's most productive years and I felt like I'd been betrayed. It was a newspaper that I loved. When the paper folded a year later I felt like a father whose runaway daughter had been found dead in a whorehouse fire. I was very sad.

The night I went to clean up my desk I saw the editor had put some kind of horseshit, evasive note up on the bulletin board about why I was no longer there. He never used the word "fired." So I sat down and wrote a three page valedictory to the *National Observer* and pasted it up right under his. I got a lot of reaction from the people at the office who told me it had great impact. That helped a lot.

There was a great sense of humiliation. The psychological thing was the most important. For a few days it really drove me crazy—spending thirteen years with a paper and then to be told you're not good enough to work there... I took being fired as a personal affront, though not as a personal failure. I could see the paper was going down, but I would have liked to have stayed with it to the end.

But I felt, okay, the decision has been made for me. I felt a great, great sense of relief because I had been unhappy with the paper's new emphasis and when the new editor came I could see it was not going to be for me. I was going to take my profit share which with careful husbanding was enough for, I guess, five years, and go off to London or get a little mud house in the isles off the coast of Scotland and write a book.

I had great ambitions. I was going to write one book in the morning, a novel, and one in the afternoon, a non-fiction book about Little Rock twenty years after the Civil Rights business.

The novel is partly based on Vietnam and Washington. It has been great fun because I've been able to take my time and write the way I want to: a comic story about a president who has to deal with all the fatuousness of bureaucratic Washington. I took the non-fiction book idea to an editor I knew who said, "Well, it's fine, but civil rights books traditionally sell nineteen copies, so we're not really interested." So I've had to fall back on the novel. I still think the Little Rock book is good and I might do it. It could be made readable, not academic: a personal rendition of what it was like for black and white.

I had a great advantage in not working in not having a family, I've only got me, my rent and my groceries. I also have friends who invite me over to dinner which I appreciate, not because I need the grub, but because it makes a change from hot tamales out of cans.

My friends are fairly unconventional people, so it wasn't too hard explaining to them what happened. And the women I'm attracted to don't really seem to care about it and it certainly hasn't affected my masculinity. I have a very strong sense of who I am and my masculinity was not defined by Dow Jones and Company, Incorporated.

The thing I miss most—and this has to do with two years of working on the novel—is bouncing ideas or finished work off other people. I think what I'm doing is pretty good stuff, then I'll go back a few months or a year later and think, "Well, I don't know." But I have shown some of it to a woman friend who I have a great respect for and she likes it. In fact, if it hadn't been for her, I might not have stayed with it.

I have a newspaper job open any time I want it. There are times when I wish for the discipline of a job. It doesn't have anything to do with the money, it just has to do with thinking, "My God, here I am almost two years and I'm still working on this fucking book. It's time to be done with it." I'm turning into the kind of person I've always had contempt for, somebody who makes a big deal over something. "Just do it" is my kind of philosophy.

I think sloth and lassitude exact a great toll on us if we don't work. I don't think everyone should necessarily have to work the same way or the same hours, or go into an office, but I would feel like I was getting a free ride if I didn't work.

When I was fired I was eligible for $8000 or $9000 worth of unemployment compensation. I went down once but I didn't want to wait in line so I said to hell with it. The truth of the matter is I didn't want to take it. I know this is not right, but to me, emotionally, it's a hand-out from the government. I've got no criticism of people who do take it, and I'm not anti-welfare; I know my feeling comes from being a preacher's son.

I remember once being with my father when he was going on a train journey. He had a card that entitled him to a 10 percent discount—you know, the sort of thing airlines give old people— good for the sixth Thursday of the thirteenth month. I'll never forget how humiliated my father was. I'll never accept anything from anybody, never.

Freddie   Nashville, Tennessee

It was late at night and the honkytonk where we had arranged to meet was so loud with the music that is Nashville's heartbeat that we couldn't hear ourselves talk. So Freddie led the way to a quiet bar nearby. He was nice-looking—light brown hair grown long and falling over his forehead, a slim athletic-looking twenty-four. He began speaking about himself with easy assurance, but there was little expression in his face, as though he were holding something back. Then somebody made a gesture that struck his fancy and he broke into a beautiful, warm smile.

I'd had a bummer night at the club in Missouri one Saturday night and I said, "Susan, we're going to pack tomorrow." It was the middle of January, snow on the ground and I got a U-Haul trailer and moved, just that fast. Two days later we were in Nashville. It was a snap judgment and I was a little scared of what was going to go down, but I knew I would get by. I'm glad I did it.

I'm a musician. I play steel guitar and I also write songs. I'm trying to throw as many irons into the fire as I can to be successful. In the two and a half years since I've been here there's been times when I haven't worked much, but I guess I'm doing pretty good compared to most people who try cracking into the music business in Nashville. In terms of age, at twenty-four I'm probably farther than most people, though there are people a lot younger than me who have gone to the top. I feel pretty lucky with what I've done so far.

"I'm all the time encountering people who say I should get out because only one in ten thousand is successful and becomes a star, all that baloney. But I don't look at it like that. I can sit down and write, then pitch the tunes and make enough money to get by."

I'm all the time encountering people who say I should get out because only one in ten thousand is successful and becomes a star, all that baloney. But I don't look at it like that. I can sit down and write, then pitch the tunes and make enough money to get by. One of my songs was already published and I think today another one probably got accepted. And if it happens that I get some kind of record deal, that's fine. If not, that's fine too.

It has been a little slow lately. Sometimes the music business is kind of funny. You'll have strong periods and then you'll slack off and the work won't be there for a while. I'd rather be working full-time, but when that's going on, I don't waste my time—I use it well by writing.

When things get slow, I don't really care because my wife has got an income and I've got an income from what I can do part-time. I'll go through the ads and buy instruments, then turn around and sell them for a profit. Sometimes I work on people's cars. I'm kind of a natural at making a buck when I have to, and so far we've been getting by comfortably. We've got what we need, we eat good and we just bought a good tape recorder.

I don't drive myself too hard. I do practice a lot, but I'm not a fanatic. I've worried about why they didn't call me to a recording studio or to a gig, but as far as worrying about being good enough, I'm not worried about that. I know where my talents are and what I can do.

The music business in Nashville is kind of a game. Sometimes you have to socialize even when you don't feel like it just to deal in the business. The game is a pain in the ass. Some guy might play really good, but his personality didn't fit in or he wasn't in everybody else's clique so therefore he's out the door.

I would like to be working more now, but I don't really hang out to help myself at the bar or the Pickin' Parlor where all of them hang out just to be around the rest of the musicians. Not playing that game probably isn't good for me, but then again, it's good for my head.

In Missouri I was a big duck in a little pond. Down here I'm a little duck in an ocean, but being here definitely is an advantage. It's good to hear musicians who are good and it's a challenge to be able to do what they're doing in your own way. When they're playing these licks on their guitars that I don't even know where they're coming from, it inspires me. I start thinking, "Wow, will I ever be that good?" Then I stop and realize how long they've been playing and how long I've been playing. Some day I'll be able to do that, so I'll just keep truckin' until I do.

THE WHITE ROLLS ROYCE

Rick   Fire Island, New York

*On this island with no motor vehicles permitted, there were no
exotic cars for Rick to buy and resell, and he was reveling in
every sybaritic moment of his brief vacation. Happily he
described the delicious dinner he has just indulged in and
displayed the art objects he had bought at a bargained-down
price. Slender, his deep tan set off by his white silk shirt and
gold neck chain, proudly holding his favorite woman on his
arm, he was the picture of "success" and "the good life."*

I need a comfortable amount of money for my lifestyle. I got
into fast living through rock and roll. I went for the older
British rock and roll and I wanted my own American Rolling
Stones-Yardbirds type of group, so when I was eighteen years
old, I started a band in my father's basement. I broke my foot
putting it in a few doors, and when the time was ripe we went
on some professional tours. The band started getting a name
for itself, but a lack of discipline and bad drug abuse caused us
to get thrown off one or two tours. I was living a fairly
glamorous lifestyle—traveling, limousines, dollars, new Pors-
ches, flying here and there for custom clothes—but I never
thought the band would go any further because of the antics
and the lack of professionalism, so I left. I took cash in my
pocket, was replaced and they went on tour again.

Ha, ha. What can I say? Less than two years later they became the biggest damn thing you can imagine. I think at present they have six gold albums. I don't keep up because that's a dark period of my life. Every one of them is worth $4 million today. That's OK, because I sold them their Ferraris.

I still played music and I had a new band. I had handpicked the members, gotten financing and worked out a contract for them to open for Santana. We were starting from the middle and working our way up. But my guitar player decided he didn't like the singer and refused to do the two opening gigs I had listed.

From then on I decided that I didn't want any more bands because I'd gotten slighted by them all the time. I did a little bit of studio work and a brief stint with Patti LaBelle, which was nice, but that is all.

I had made pretty good money in the exotic car business and figured perhaps I should turn a profit in it for myself instead of somebody else. And so I did.

I buy and restore cars. I take commissions to purchase Aston-Martins, Rolls Royces, Shelbys, Bugattis and Ferraris. If I see a beautiful Porsche sitting in the street, I'll leave a note on the windshield and it's just a question of salesmanship and what I can purchase it for.

My marketing skills have always been pretty good. I write an ad and if a person is looking for anything that even resembles the car, he just can't be without it. I usually never advertise any of my cars more than once.

Someone can have a car as is, or if he would like the car restored, I've got people who can do that. All I do is push a pen, writing in a healthy profit at the end. I've found that one good score can net me up to three or four thousand dollars.

And that's why I don't need to work seventy hours a week. I've found that I can support my lifestyle with maybe twenty hours of work a month. These crazy toys are a good investment. If the time comes when the cash flow becomes tight, you can bail out because they're so beautiful there will always be somebody who is going to want them.

I've moved into a building where the rent is a bit high, but it affords me everything I want for the lifestyle I lead: platform tennis on the roof, indoor-outdoor swimming pool, work-out room, sauna, weight room and whirlpool. I am always doing something. If I'm not working on my tan in Cancún, then I'm parasailing here, playing backgammon there or car racing. If I ever get bored, I pick up my guitar and write a beautiful song which I can usually turn into a lot of cash. If someone were to hand me a $60,000 a year nine to five job tomorrow, I don't know where I'd find the time to fit it in.

As of late I am with people a lot and I'm finding little or no time to myself, which I feel bad about. Within the last six months I've acquired a small but rapidly growing entourage. I like hanging in fast crowds with friends who can appreciate the things I've done. I like living fast—leather bars, movie stars, exotic cars.

People are very jealous of me. They say, "He's got this, he's got that, and he never works." I do work; I just feel I'm smarter than they are. I think money and power are virtually synonymous: money is power; power is money. You are always going to meet people that have more and people that have less. I would like more. I would not like to have less.

My lifestyle has come to dictate a certain amount of cash flow, so I'm almost forced into making a lot of money, but I still have to be happy in what I'm doing or I'm not going to do it well.

"I thought my white Rolls Royce was power: it was absolute shit."

But of recent I've been thinking of just becoming happy and I've had to reorganize my goals. I worked a beautiful deal one time where I wound up with a stunning white Rolls Royce that was restored in England. I thought my white Rolls Royce was power: it was absolute shit. I thought it would become a thing I would work all my life to get. Once I had it, it was simply there and it just dictated a different kind of lifestyle. It did not become what I was living for because it was an acquisition. I thought my white Rolls Royce was happiness. I thought the world's best rock and roll band was happiness. I thought a penthouse with a beautiful view of New York was happiness. Gee, I had some pretty warped ideas of happiness. They all seem to be attached to dollar signs.

If I enjoy what I'm doing, I could probably do it for close to nothing, but I like to know, of course, that my rent is paid. For the first time in a few years now, I'm trying to set some goals, to decide how many condominiums I want to own by the time I'm thirty-five—back to the dollar thing again. I'm going to get some of the things I want by busting my ass, or using my head or maybe both.

I seem to bounce from one profession to another, which is good because I never really get bored, but I never take each thing to its max and I'm not developing my full potential in any one field. Shit, I'm not thirty years old yet—I think I've still got a good chance. It's going to take more self-discipline and a good, strong woman in back of me to push me—someone who believes in me. I think I've got what it takes, but I'll probably need a bomb under my ass to have it brought out.

Damn it, I've gone around once and I want to try and live every day now as best I can, like it's my last. I live dangerously. Three weeks ago I was chasing barracuda in Cancún. I almost had him before he turned on me and bit my leg. I was foolish enough to wear gold into the water and that's what they go for.

A lot of people are afraid to grow old; I'm afraid to die. I guess that's why I parachute or parasail or go 200 miles an hour on a motorcycle. I'm so afraid to die that I live close to it.

But I think I'm more afraid to fail than to die. What have I made of myself? I've been here twenty-seven years and I've lived a damn lie. I feel guilty for having lived as well as I have and for cramming it into the years I have.

I seem to have a lack of—what's the word I'm looking for? Security. I live too damn well and sometimes it scares me, and I'm a Virgo and Virgos are chronic worriers. I've had an ulcer since I was twenty-one. I would probably feel more secure in a business of my own. As I find myself maturing, I want security because I've found a woman that I would like to share part or most of the rest of my life with. I would like for her to be secure, for her not to have to work, for her to have a maid.

I'm looking to make a million dollars. I've got one or two damn million-dollar ideas—I know it. I'm keeping them under wraps because I've been burned in the past. Having a million to start them would expedite matters and I'd be able to pay it back pretty fast. I play to win and I'd say that 85 percent of the time I'm a winner. That's not bad. How can a winner be afraid to take chances? Insecurities.

If I'm feeling insecure, taking my Porsche over 100 miles an hour calms me out. By nature, I am not a calm individual. I don't think anything really calms me out except turning a quick deal—making somebody else's two month salary in three or four hours. That green has an amazing calming effect on me.

I'm the kind of guy that's always going to have money. If the time comes when I'm without it—see this book of matches on the table? I'll convince you how much you need it and I'll get top dollar for it. I've made my living with my tongue and I have a good, keen eye, good sense and, most of the time, both feet on the ground.

"I'm not opposed to working; I'm opposed to working and making money for someone else when I'm damn smart enough to be making it for myself."

Would the day ever come, God forbid, that I was down to my last thousand dollars and I really needed to, I could go wash dishes. I'm not opposed to working; I'm opposed to working and making money for someone else when I'm damn smart enough to be making it for myself.

SELF STARTERS

Liz   New York, New York

At ease in her small rent-controlled apartment, Liz, a slender,
dark-haired woman in her thirties, sat surrounded by beauti-
ful objects that she had creatively put together as an expres-
sion of herself. She had recently been laid off from a publish-
ing job as editor of a small newspaper for a New York
publishing company, and was at the point of feeling both
angry about how she has been treated and excited about some
new opportunities. She was open and articulate and very
pleased to have the occasion to talk about herself.

I started working in publishing eleven years ago and became a
production editor. As time went on I became a bit sour on big
companies and about four years ago I started working for a
mail order book packager. The guy had five women working
for him, like a harem. He said women tend to detail better than
men and besides, he could get us for less money. He was a real
bullshitter, but he was an exciting guy and as long as he
wasn't bullshitting me, I didn't mind.

This man really knew how to get the most out of the people.
He divided the work so that we each had all the responsibilities
for a project—production, design, and editorial. It was a great
learning experience, but it was really a baptism by fire, and I
wound up with colitis. I was on a baby food diet for seven
months.

My boss wanted to be everything—father, brother, lover and confessor. When I became involved with somebody, he grew to resent the involvement because he wanted all his women to be available to fly to Milan to pick up film or go to a printer in D.C. for three days and, if necessary, wind up staying nine. He took care of us very well. One year he paid all our medical bills, and at that point mine were very high, mostly because of him. But he didn't want us to have any ties other than to the company.

I was going out with a man who had started an incredible process of awakening in me. He was a kind of Svengali—he just had this thing. At that point, personally and professionally, I was ready to totally fall apart or bring it all together, and he turned out to be the catalyst to bring it all together. My father had just died and I spent the entire following year with that man. I left the job; I don't think I worked a day that year in the sense of earning money or going out to an office. But I never worked harder; I worked on my head. I'd say it was the best relationship and the most productive year I have ever had.

I had gotten together the concept and a presentation for a cookbook and I was writing it, or trying to write it. I'm not sure I had the confidence to do it because I might have had to call myself a writer and I didn't know if I really wanted to do that. Then I happened to have lunch with someone who thought I was terrific and offered me a job, so I started working three days a week. The balance was still good—four days not working, three days working. I hesitate to say "not working," because the connotation is that you are not doing anything. In our society working means going someplace, doing some labor and getting paid for it, but from our talking at home I used to feel as if someone was inside my head ticking from the inside out.

They were paying me $900 a month for twelve days work. I think they just liked the way I looked. I came to think that they were paying me too much and they could get someone for a lot less money who didn't mind tying up the loose ends I was doing for them. It's not that they were menial tasks; it's that I had grown so used to using my mind that I couldn't stand not using it.

That was when they offered to let me put out a paper for them by myself. I agreed to do it and the relationship with my boyfriend started to fall apart. He took a job which took him out of town for five days a week and I felt abandoned. I would work five days and take care of the house and the dogs. When he returned on Friday night everything had to be perfect—everything. I couldn't have a headache and there was no sense that I had worked all week as well.

Our thing didn't hold up outside in the real world. It doesn't mean that it wasn't valid; I just think we took it as far as it could go. There were moments, very short moments, when I felt I might have given up the relationship for the job, but I don't think that we would have gone out and gotten the jobs if we hadn't felt that some movement was necessary. The piggy banks were empty—eventually something would have brought us out of it.

When I started the new job with John as my boss, I had no intention of getting involved with anyone. But when John and I started working together both of us were unhappy at home, and that was one of the reasons we enjoyed working together so much and staying late. The atmosphere at work was better than at both our homes. He separated from his wife, my boyfriend went out on his travels, and I got involved with John.

"I wasn't the kind of person who would say the emperor had clothes on when he didn't."

Then the newspaper I edited for the company failed. I had no real control over its fate. They made all the marketing decisions and they made the wrong ones. They were paying me a fair amount and when the paper folded they couldn't find anything else for me to do. They were scaling down the whole operation, so they let me go. They pressured John about me. I can remember quite well when he told me; it was in a movie theater. I said, "Will you tell me what is going on?" He said, "OK. They have done everything but say to me, 'get rid of her.' " I was quite hurt.

I think they pressured him into getting rid of me because they thought I was insolent. I wasn't the kind of person who would say the emperor had clothes on when he didn't. I wasn't insecure and I wasn't particularly anxious to start work to begin with. I was the only woman executive at the top, but I was making the lowest amount of money. They treated all the women the same. I think the fact that we were having a relationship may have been a reason for them letting me go as well.

When John fired me we went through a very rough time, needless to say! He was very self-conscious about even giving me a watch when I left. Then two months later they fired him and he really was under a great deal of pressure—he had no money. They really put it to him and he didn't have much choice.

After finishing the job I worked on getting out another newspaper for John, a one-shot deal. I worked very hard on it and I earned a $100. It sold 50,000 copies. I don't know exactly how much he will have made on it, but it will be a great deal more than $100.

It was then that I decided that I was not going to be shortsighted any longer. I would forego getting $100 in my pocket the day after I finished work for a piece of the action. So now I own part of at least two of the things we're involved in together. For the first time in my life I'm investing money in my talent. I'm putting my money on the line as well as my talent. I'm not making any money from these ventures yet, but I'm willing to take these risks.

We're going to do a monthly newspaper together and if we make a profit I will get 49 percent. John wants to retain control of the paper. That doesn't really bother me that much. This is my first leap into that kind of thing, so I'll settle for 49 percent. At first I got my back up, but then I realized that I didn't care. The success of the paper is what matters; the 1 percent is not going to make a big difference in the money. He will not treat me any differently; I can guarantee that. It's all going to be drawn up legally so that the money that I've invested will be returned to me even if it fails, so I'm not really worried about it; I'm excited about it. Our relationship actually benefits when we're working on the stuff together.

It has been ten months since my last full-time job and I've become absolutely terrified at the thought of going back to work for a company. You get terrifically caught up in the con. It's like walking on the side of the street where everybody's coming in the other direction and you have to move over, otherwise you're going to be mowed down.

When I started that job I was just going along, tranquil and cool, singing my song, and somehow found myself changing. It's not a conscious thing. You fight it, then one day you realize that you're worried about being late to the office. It's not because you're worried about losing your job; somehow you get conditioned to feel these things, so you get caught up into it, even though you don't want to.

I don't want the claustrophobia, the insecurity, and the dependency that working for a company fosters. The only way a company can work is to put you in a cubby hole, put a label on you, and put a number on your personnel file. I don't want that; I want to grow.

Even though I'm leading a relatively insecure life, living on my savings, and I should have those pains I had in my side when I was working, I don't have colitis any more. Frustrating situations used to give me that kind of thing and frustrating situations come out of not being in control. Most people opt not to be in control—maybe not consciously—and they turn over the control of their lives to someone else. To me that is scary.

I remember those times when I'd walk into work at nine and suddenly it would be five and I didn't know where the day went. I don't believe in another life, so this is it. I want to be involved in it and I want to watch it go by. I don't want to have it go by without knowing where it went, so I'm willing to take these risks.

After telling us her story Liz thought further about her partnership and renegotiated it to be fifty-fifty. She then published a successful book without her partner, followed by three others not long afterward. Her colitis returned, then left again.

Marianne   New York, New York

A short, delicately-boned woman in her twenties, Marianne knew how to command attention through her assertive bearing. After a frustrating start trying to vault to the top in fashion merchandising and TV sales, a successful stint of nude modeling had introduced her to the rewards of freelance enterprise and now she was sold on it. Excited and confident, she had already begun packaging herself: though the apartment was not hers, the walls were hung with photos capturing her in a variety of moods and poses and even our interview was destined for use—she had hooked up her own tape recorder and had tailored a presentation in advance. But she responded with interest to the spontaneous questions, eager to give a full portrait of herself.

When I graduated college I said, "OK, my husband's not moving to New York? Fine, but I am." So I fixed him up with another woman and got divorced.

When I first came to New York from Detroit I worked as a buyer at Macy's because I wanted to be a businesswoman and I love fashion. Then I found out there's a lot of money in TV sales, so I decided to start in it as a buyer and make my connections. The job I got was boring and they wanted me to type, which I sort of resented. I was starting to feel like a secretary and I'm more special than that.

I started interviewing for sales in every agency in town and after six months there wasn't anyone in the industry I didn't know and anyone who didn't know me. I had steam behind me and sometimes I'd have eight appointments a day. There are very few women in the field and I was a little freaky—my hair, my lack of experience—but soon I tried out for a training program. I was the only woman who did.

I made big posters and I was there at eight in the morning putting little gimmicks on each guy's desk. I concentrated on the guy who was head of the whole thing and finally changed him from thinking of me as "this little pipsqueak" to believing I'd be the best out there on the street. Then somebody else got his job. I didn't have a good relationship with his replacement because he'd crack sexual jokes and I'd top them. He'd get all frustrated because women weren't supposed to do that—they were supposed to blush. He didn't like my hair and I didn't agree with his opinions.

I knew I didn't have a chance but still I didn't give up. When it came right down to it I didn't get the job, but my philosophy is that I didn't get it for a reason. It didn't affect me in any emotional or physical way and I figured I could go on.

I went on unemployment. I didn't have my buyer's job any more because they had found out that I was hustling to get a job in sales all day long. Then Mardi Gras came and I had to get away.

In New Orleans I met Lauren and she asked me to model nude. Neither one of us had ever done it before but it was fun. We were both women and we weren't intimidated by each other.

We went out in a forest, got ourselves high, and took a very beautiful set, which we sold. So far we've sold five sets to a men's magazine. They have scummy-looking girls, but our photos aren't scummy. They're cute, they're funny, and they have a sense of humor because we have personality. Girlie shots are the most fun to do of everything. You can be as crazy and freaky as you want. I was never intimidated sexually. Even at thirteen I was very, very sexual, wearing skin-tight shorts and tight tops.

We're like the virgins of the industry because we don't mess around with anybody. They think we're crazy because very seldom does a model come in with the photographer to show pictures, but I'm Lauren's business partner, so I do. We intimidate them and with both of us there they don't dare fool around. We frustrate them and they don't know how to handle us. At times they don't like us because we want our money when it's due. I wouldn't *dare* let them owe us money—I'd haunt them.

I'm sold on Lauren. She has been very good for me because she has pushed me into things and shown me that I can do them. She's strong. "We're never going to do movies because that's really disgusting and you're not going to sell yourself cheap," she told me. Sometimes she stops me short because I can get carried away. She's like my mother looking after me.

Lauren is positive for me because it's a real emotional relationship, not a sexual one. We don't compete with each other and we each see the talent in the other. We're working together to push each other. We really make an impression, a hit, and together we knock people out.

We're invited to celebrity things and we go to a lot of discos. We wear really bizarre looking costumes. I'm very competitive and my costume has to be the best. At Studio 54 I'm sort of the star. At these places we look very weird, very hot, but we're very professional. We take people's pictures and people put their arms around us, but I never left a disco with anyone. You have to keep it very professional or else you become a cheap joke in their eyes.

Next month I want to start promoting myself with these pictures we've been doing. I'm going to go out and knock them out. I'm sure I'm going to be rejected, but I don't give up because I'm so sold on myself.

In a year I'd like to go to California and do something in films. Plays would bore me a little bit because you do the same thing over and over every day. I think I'd be good in films and I'd rather see myself on the screen.

"It's like breaking an egg—I broke into something else that I never knew existed."

Now I'm running to get my portfolio together. I want to push myself as a new look. There's been every kind of model but a short model, and I'm going to promote short people the way they promoted thin people through Twiggy. It doesn't matter what you look like as long as you can push yourself. I don't want to be a beautiful exotic model; I have a variety of looks and I want to show my pictures to ad agencies and say, "Look, I can look cute or I can look sexy or I can look like a teenager or a housewife." I want to show that I can do everything. I'm an excellent saleswoman and it's just a matter of having confidence.

I'm extremely organized. You see, I even made a chart for what I'll be doing every hour from eleven to three. I have two blank books for appointments and when the portfolio is done, I want to set up appointments.

179

I know what I want to do and what I don't want to do. When I started doing the girlie pictures I still wanted to work in a structured thing, but now I could never work a nine to five job and I could never work for someone else. It's like breaking an egg—I broke into something else that I never knew existed.

I'm twenty-six now and I'm able to function for myself. For a long time I only understood a structured role. A lot of people who aren't working are confused about what they want to do and usually I don't relate to people like that. To me they seem lazy. I like people who have a goal in mind and if they aren't working it's because they can't put up with something and have to do exactly what they want to do.

Everyone I came across who was very creative was lazy and had no ambition. I had ambition, but I didn't have talent. Now I realize that there are things I can do and I want to promote myself.

I know myself and want to take a chance on myself. When you put your cards on somebody else, you can't always count on them. I wouldn't let somebody else get the recognition for my work like when a chemist makes up something for a plant and the owner of the plant gets all the recognition. I want to live my life pushing myself, never shortchanging myself, never being cheap.

I want to realize my worth and find someone equal to me who can really appreciate me. I was a virgin until I was twenty and I want to go back to being like I was when I was a virgin. I feel very cheap going out with different people all the time. I want to go out with people who respect me and like me, and I don't want to just hop in bed with them. They don't have to be rich, but they should be able to afford me and buy me things, be good to me. I think I deserve it because I'm really terrific.

I never thought this way of myself before. I was very stupid when it came to men and paid their way into the show. I always had the money because I always worked and had a decent job.

Now my unemployment is running out and I need money. It's very hard when I don't have money; I get very depressed. I'm very expensive—I'm the model and I spend money on clothes and on myself—my hair, my nails. Keeping myself up is the most important thing for me.

I'm doing a lot of things I shouldn't be doing, like shoplifting. I've done it for ten years and I'm very good at it. I'll steal food and maybe clothing, because I need clothing, but I don't become greedy. Once you become greedy you're going to get caught. You're going to get nervous and overdo it. I could go out and shoplift all day long, but I don't. I don't want to get caught and I don't want to become obsessed with it. I want it to be like 1 percent of my life until I can make my own money.

I'm selling grass, but that's not anything because we're not able to sell it. I don't want to sell to kids on the street; I'd just feel guilty and I wouldn't want to deal with that. It would be fine if I had a decent clientele, maybe ten people a week that I could sell cocaine to. I'd rather deal to your middle class society that can afford a $100 a week for cocaine. But I'd never let it become part of my life because it's so nothing. I want to really be proud of myself. I just need money to get by.

I've considered everything, even being a prostitute maybe twice a week. I did it once, but I was so bored with it. I'll probably never do it again.

I could see myself as a prostitute if I was ever attracted to somebody with a lot of money, but I would never want to be a mistress because my time is very limited. They couldn't have me that much—once or twice a week and that's it. To have me they're going to have to be very special because I'm starting to think very highly of myself. In fact, after this boyfriend, I'm not even going out on a date unless they're buying me something or taking care of me.

I'll probably never get married again or really commit myself to anyone until I make it myself because I don't want anything stopping me or holding me back. I don't want to marry somebody rich to make myself rich. I would never be happy with somebody else's money; I want to make it on my own. Relationships affect my working and my pushing myself because sometimes I get emotionally involved. I won't let anything stand in my way. It's got to work and I'm willing to work at it. If I'm held back, it would only be because of me.

If I didn't make it on my own, I would feel that I failed. If I don't make it, I'd rather be poor. I don't want to be middle class because I would worry continuously about money and my job. I would be pretty bored and not really happy most of the time.

181

I have doubts at times. I'm terrified of success and I can't stand rejection. I'm afraid that maybe I won't be able to handle success the right way, but I know I will once I get it. I'm bringing people around me. I want advice from my entour... age—whatever you call it. I'm a very generous person and if I make it I'll have everybody else there. If I have a big house, everybody will be with me one day.

The thing is, I have to listen more to people instead of saying I know all the answers. I have to get ideas from people and use them to my own advantage. I get lazy and spiteful and chop off my own nose, but I'm trying to be more mature now. I'm very superstitious and I guess I'm very religious, because I'm afraid of karma coming to get me. I don't want to be bad to people because I know it's going to turn around and knock me out.

"I want advice from my entour...age—whatever you call it."

If I get it all together, get the opportunities, and push myself hard enough, I'll be very successful. It's just a matter of being very stubborn. I would like to meet a man who could promote my work, someone who would have a lot of confidence in me or the money or the connections to push my ideas. The best people are friends because there's no sexual contact. If I met a man like that and he just saturated New York with short women posters, I think that could make it. I would put the work into making it work because it's also promoting me—I'm short. It sounds very selfish saying if you have blue eyes you should push blue eyes because that's what's going to make you real popular, but I sincerely feel it's time for short people to make it and that's why I'm doing it—for selfish reasons.

FROM DIFFERENT PERSPECTIVES
DIFFERENT VIEWS

Margo St. James   San Francisco, California

Margo St. James is the head of the prostitutes' union called COYOTE—an acronym for "Call Off Your Old Tired Ethics." The purpose of the organization is to decriminalize prostitution within the United States. Margo formed the organization in 1973 and has been its spokesperson since. She has mounted her campaign in the press, in the schools, in legislatures and in the courts, usually with a sense of humor and a sense of the outrageous. Although the laws haven't changed much, she has cleared the way for change by bringing the discussion out into the open. She is not paid for her efforts, so Margo "hustles" to survive—without turning a trick.

I got political five years ago and started pushing for the decriminalization of prostitution. I created the job and it became my campaign, although I'm still a volunteer and never have gotten wages out of it. I've built a huge information center of everybody's research all over the world and try to get it around as much as we're able. I publish a little newspaper four times a year, if we have the money. Of course, it really doesn't pay for itself, so I have to do speaking engagements at women's conferences and on campuses to subsidize the operation.

183

I try to stick to women's issues—rape and violence and things like that. I work with people doing diversion projects in the criminal justice system, trying to find alternatives to prostitution for these women. I've pumped my name up in the media to the point where I can use it to earn money and get votes. I was talking and running around convincing people that we were doing the right thing, and the straight people in the community tended to be supportive, so about '74 I started organizing Hookers Balls around Halloween. I started out fairly small, maybe 2000 or 3000 people, and now about 12,000 to 15,000 people come.

When I was twenty-five I was arrested as a hooker, and that was the turning point in my life. I was a loose woman and always had people hanging out and smoking dope and partying. I was surrounded by dopesmokers and artists and poets who were just hanging out. My place was a crash pad, a crossroads for people of all classes and races.

The cop on the beat had a brother on the vice squad and he must have told his brother that I had people going in and out all the time. They assumed that I must be charging and the vice squad came and solicited me in my own home. I didn't even say yes and they dragged me off!

The judge found me guilty because I said, "Your Honor, I've never turned a trick in my life." He said, "Anybody that knows that language is obviously a professional." In 1962 women weren't supposed to know what a trick was. That's all part and parcel of being intimidated by sex. We're not supposed to know, and if anybody mentions it, we're supposed to look down at the floor and blush. Hookers don't do that, they look you right in the eye and talk about it nitty-gritty, matter of fact, just like men.

I was labeled a whore as soon as I was arrested. I had been working as a cocktail waitress and the cops paid a visit to the bar and made sure that my cocktail job was out the window. I filed an appeal and after two years the appellate court found me innocent, but that doesn't make any difference in my job status; fifteen years later I'm still unemployable. No one has ever offered me a job. People won't hire a hooker even if she's an ex-hooker. They think you're going to start doing it on the table or something, so they won't trust you with their kids or anything like that.

A year after the arrest I did become a hooker. I was working for the bondsman for free to work off my bail and paying off the lawyers by serving summonses for them. Then my car got swiped. The judges and D.A.'s and what-have-you still kept hitting on me and finally I just started saying yes because I needed the money. I was a hooker for three or four years, until I was twenty-eight. I would just do enough to pay the rent and stuff; I was never in it for the usual reason which is to make lots of fast money. I was probably the first socialist hooker—I started the thing of not charging for passing on a customer. It had always been 40 percent no matter what. In the late sixties it caught on that women were not to be so competitive, but to work more together in a collective.

I was going to law school to learn enough to file my own appeal and I met this guy there who worked at a cosmetics company. I got him to set me up as a company whore. Then this old guy who imagined I was Isadora Duncan reincarnated kept me for a couple of years. After that I moved in with this guy who was a compulsive worker and tried to become respectable. I fit right in, thanks to my father, who was a compulsive worker and worked me like a dog on the farm when I was a child.

"I also found that if you're interesting and you have a good rap, people are willing to take you to dinner."

For five years I worked as a maid, a domestic, a housekeeper in Marin County, a rich suburb outside San Francisco. It was a three buck an hour job, three or four days a week, and included babysitting, gardening, and carpentry. I usually made $120 to $150 a month and I had food stamps once or twice during that period till they got hard to get. I didn't like the humiliation trip they started laying on people like me who were trying to get them and I decided I'd rather go hungry than do that. I also found that if you're interesting and you have a good rap, people are willing to take you to dinner.

When I was in law school the dean agreed with me that the prostitution laws are discriminatory and unconstitutional, but he thought that nobody would help me then. He told me to wait ten years, and I did. Now I've got the ACLU, the American Bar Association, over a hundred women's organizations, and all the criminal justice organizations except the Catholic Church to support the decriminalization of prostitution.

I was driven. That arrest was like watching your relatives burn in the ovens. It's something you don't get over; you stay mad. I'm still mad. The cops take it personally sometimes, but it's not a personal thing. I don't hate men; I hate the system and I'm out to change it and put women into decision-making positions so these kinds of things stop happening. I'm the kind of person who has nothing to lose. They can't do anything else to me; they've done everything that they could except murder me. Once they take away your reputation, you're dead. But I turned it around on them. I capitalized on the notoriety and made it pay, though it doesn't pay too well.

"Being very poor is like being very rich; you never have to make decisions about money."

But I don't worry about money, because I've never had any. Being very poor is like being very rich; you never have to make decisions about money. I have an affinity with many rich people, but they never think of giving me money because they really don't think about money. And I rarely ask them for money because I'm not thinking about getting money; I'm thinking about doing things. Usually I rush out and hustle up money after my project is already under way. I ask somebody for money, teach a sexuality class or a dance class, put on some bizarre flea market—any kind of hustle like that works to get a little cash flow. And, of course, radio and TV stations and networks are willing to pay you for being on. They pay a lot of the transportation costs, so I've been able to travel around the country. My mobility is pretty high for someone earning $4000 a year, and the more contacts one makes, the more likely it is that you'll be able to generate more cash.

I came from five years of being a real recluse doing housework to running around, talking on the phone twenty hours a week, and working about eighty hours a week—living in the office, because on $4000 I can't really afford an apartment or a car. I ride a three speed bicycle. I don't have facilities in the office to cook or shower. I joined the YMCA, so I can go there at midnight and shower any time I want. I like going to my lover's apartment at night. There's no phone there so I can't do any work and I'm forced to take a vacation. When I was living in the office all the time, I tended to work all the time and I had a hard time maintaining my sense of humor—just too strung out. A lot of friends have given me keys to their apartments, which I can use if I have a hot date and they're out of town, or if I need a shower. I clean the tub and stuff, but I'm not responsible for paying the bills for the hot water and I don't have to pay rent. I see myself as living free.

Although my time is my own and I don't like to be committed to anything or make appointments, I'm actually very ritual-istic. I get up early, usually about 6:30 or 7:30 A.M. Sometimes I go jogging, but lately I've been going right to my favorite cafe. I have two or three cappuccinos, read the newspaper and go through my mail, then I head for the office. I answer the mail and I start making my schedule for the day. I like to leave it loose so that I can deal with stuff and emergencies as they come in. That way I don't have to say, "I'm sorry, I can't help you right now; I've got something else to do."

I got my private eye license three years ago and I do a lot of investigation for women who are raped, robbed or whatever. I found this was absolutely necessary if we were going to win anything in the courts. If a prostitute is attacked, she finds it hard to get the police to do anything about whoever attacked her. The D.A. is reluctant to act, too, so we start collecting the hard evidence and building the cases so that they can't refuse to take cases and still be within civil rights laws. Men in the system are just unconsciously sexist and prejudiced against prostitutes. They don't do the legwork necessary to get a good case and win. We've been doing it ourselves and forcing them to do their work. So I like to be free to deal with emergencies as they arise.

I think people need free time to themselves, maybe 40 percent of the time, so they can think and read and organize their minds. My coffee time and an hour when I lie in the sun or take a jog are that for me. My freedom is important to me, more important than anything else. I was married at seventeen and I had a child, but even before then I knew I didn't want to be married. I left my husband and kid because I was having fantasies of murdering them and I recognized I had to get out of there or else I was going to do something bad. Years later I figured out I was pre-orgasmic. They just didn't talk about stuff like that twenty years ago. Maybe the lack of sex education is why I became preoccupied with sex.

Men are intimidated by me. They know that prostitutes know all about men, so they're not about to try to pull something on me and they leave me pretty much alone. Just recently, though, young men are beginning to get on me, men maybe ten or twelve years younger than I. I like that. If they're willing to do the housework and stuff, they can move in, and if they've got a car that's even better. If they play tennis or jog or something, I'm willing to participate, but my time is strictly self-centered. My work is my center, not the relationship. This is not true of most women, who are into making the relationship the center of the universe.

When a man wants to snag a woman he makes the relationship number one, then as soon as he gets her, it's back to work and she feels duped. I've experienced that, and I wouldn't want to do that to anyone, so I'm upfront about the fact that the campaign is all-important and time consuming, and if it means I'm getting phone calls in the middle of the night from some hysterical hooker who is in trouble, don't bitch at me because the phone rang at three in the morning.

I think hookers become selective about their lovers because sex is work and with a lover you have to want to do it. I would never fake it with a lover; that's work. And I would never have a relationship with someone where I had to pretend that he was better than he is. I found that as a hooker I enjoyed equality with men—not in public, but in private—because they were looking to me for advice as an expert in sex.

Seeing sex as work was a good experience for me. The whole purpose of my campaign is to get the public and government to recognize that sex for hire is work and to treat it as such rather than as a crime. In Israel, prostitutes have been put under the National Health Insurance Plan along with all other professions, because they recognize it as work. That's what I'd like to see happen in this country.

I think one of the things that has kept me working for myself is that I've never learned to conform. Once I was labeled as a hooker I was outside of society, and I found that it was really free out there. I didn't have to dress in any certain way and I could be as outrageous as I wanted to. I actually liked that. Plus how many offices can you get naked in, if it's hot, and smoke pot any time you feel like it and not give a darn who walks in?

"I like living in the cracks."

I like living in the cracks. I've lived a very loose life for the last fifteen years and I doubt very much if I could really fit into the employment market today. I work very hard. I laughed when an interviewer asked about my personal life. "I don't have any personal life to talk about," was my answer.

Joshua   New York, New York

The victory of freedom is possible only if democracy develops into a society in which the individual, his growth and happiness, is the aim and purpose of culture, in which life does not need any justification in success or anything else, and in which the individual is not subordinated to or manipulated by any power outside of himself, be it the State or the economic machine; finally, a society in which his conscience and ideals are not the internalization of external demands, but are really *his* and express the aims that result from the peculiarity of his self.
—Erich Fromm, *Escape From Freedom*

Books lining shelves in every room and stacked in piles on the floors, papers in the typewriter and spread out over every flat surface of the study testified that while thirty-eight year old Joshua might have been denied tenure and was no longer teaching anthropology in a university, he was still leading an active life as a scholar. Curled up in the corner of a worn couch, he confidently described how it felt being out of the system. His words rang with commitment and intensity, but the way he used his hands to illustrate his points echoed the great gentleness in his soft brown eyes.

It has been approximately two years since I've had a job. I had been teaching anthropology for nine years and I was denied tenure, which means I couldn't have continued teaching at that university if I had wanted to.

"I tested the system to determine whether I could get a just evaluation, and the end result was that the system rejected me and I rejected the system."

But the actual fact is that I wouldn't have continued teaching there in any case. I tested the system to determine whether I could get a just evaluation, and the end result was that the system rejected me and I rejected the system. Now one could look at that as sour grapes, but I believe that a fair evaluation of my dossier would show that all the university's criteria were more than met by my achievements and competence.

I had been politically active on campus and off in the late sixties and early seventies. As an anthropologist studying my own culture, I taught classes resulting in cultural consciousness raising which was both highly academic and very radical. I was using sophisticated anthropological knowledge about cultural revolutions to explain to my students why their culture was turning upside down. My obvious success with students—majors in anthropology increased over tenfold after my first two years in residence—made the administration and some of my colleagues very nervous. They tried to get rid of me every year.

In a curious way I found myself developing a reputation as a hot-headed rabblerouser who would leap upon any opportunity to foment violence and destroy the university. In fact, just the opposite was true. For example, in spring of 1969 a band of black "outside agitators" rampaged through the school cafeteria, breaking up furniture and threatening students. Simultaneously, a leaflet attacking black students as complacent and gutless was distributed.

When I arrived at the cafeteria black and white students were on the verge of a race riot. I sat down between the two sides and one of my students, a physically imposing but sensitive "jock" whose father had been a hero in Iwo Jima, but whose brother had recently died in Vietnam, came over. "We don't want to fight," he said. "Well, let's talk," I answered.

I pointed out that when something like this happens, you have to ask the question, "Who is going to benefit?" Obviously neither the black nor the white students would benefit from a race riot. Only an authoritarian power, the administration or a government agency, would come out the winner. I explained that this was a tactic for destroying the student movement.

Meanwhile a trusted and committed colleague was talking to black students of his on the other side. Before long we were meeting together in a jubilant and relieved reunion. Black and white students issued a joint statement of solidarity and a warning to those who were attempting to divide them.

Subsequent analysis by the administration turned up evidence that the disruptive leaflet had been typed on our department's typewriter. Someone had wanted to set us up, but it had backfired.

Since the Freedom of Information Act was passed, we have learned that such incidents were part of a massive, illegal government conspiracy to destroy the legitimate political movement against the Vietnam War by causing disruption and discrediting those the FBI called "Key Activists." I was in the unusual position of protecting my students from the government's domestic counter-insurgency program, COIN-TELPRO, while at the same time being its probable target. In that climate, where university administrations actively cooperated with government counter-insurgency activity, my success as a peacemaker was an unexpected and unwelcome event.

I should add, though, that I was always ambivalent about teaching in the university. I believed that I was lending credence to a system that really did not deserve my support or the support of the students. I found it hard to identify with the role of the university as a factory—an assembly line—producing uniform products for the larger, post-university institutions of the society.

After I left the university I went on doing what I had been doing on the side all the while, writing. I probably spend more time working now than I did when I was teaching. I do get up in the morning and work. I don't feel that I have to do it; I want to do it.

The writing is a comprehensive representation of my thinking over the years. It's not fragmented but very wholistic. I will probably want to continue on it so long as my ideas continue to grow and develop. I feel productive. I would probably feel more productive if the work were further along in the process of publication—seeing it in print or getting paid. But as it progresses, slow as it is, I do feel more and more productive about it.

I work when I feel most productive—two or three hours in the mornings, usually during the mid to late afternoons, and sometimes in the evenings. While I don't feel bound to work only five days a week, I frequently do.

As a person aware of cultural differences in the perception of time, I've tried to experiment with the traditional weekly and monthly structure of time. But it's very hard not to follow the time cycles of one's own culture. There are many subtle cues which tune you into its rhythms. Despite the fact that we live in a basically secular society, there's still a quietness in the air on weekends which gives you a sense of the sabbath, of nonwork. As a result you feel you deserve to have the time off.

Of course, we're conditioned to that from going to school the five days in childhood. Our sense of the cyclical pattern of work is continuous with our childhood experience. Being free to play on the weekends is very deeply ingrained.

From time to time I feel locked into my own personal work ethic in a way which doesn't permit me to waste time enough. Sometimes I feel I should take a vacation from my work ethic even though from the outside it might appear that I'm on a continuous vacation. I've been working hard for a long time; it might be a good idea to just go somewhere and do something totally different that would take me away from the more or less continuous thinking aspect of my work.

Still, I do feel free. Nothing would stop me from doing whatever I wanted to do. There is obviously a question of economic survival, which is something that I imagine impinges upon a person's sense of total freedom, but if something different from what I'm doing today came up tomorrow, nothing would stop me from following my instincts and doing it.

An inherent aspect of my sense of freedom is to be able to organize my own time. Perhaps that's something of the artist in me. So I don't think I'd ever want a nine-to-five job.

When you're not working the possibility exists of becoming isolated and of living with your own ideas, thoughts and observations. Sometimes I feel like I'm neglecting friends, luxuriating in my situation by not taking the initiative and reaching out the way you do when you're working. Working, you feel that your free time is more valuable, so you probably make a more conscious effort to see people you are not able to see while you're at work. When you're not working, you feel you have all the time that you want for having social relationships, yet you don't do it. Because your time is more free, you do your own thing more.

My family's response is interesting. I sometimes have a very strong feeling—a sad feeling—when I talk to older relatives that people feel sorry for me because I'm not working. Many people in my parents' generation define a person on the basis of his work—my son the doctor, my son the lawyer. So if someone's son is not doing anything in those terms, it almost makes the person non-existent.

While my parents' generation sees a person defined by the work that he does, I'm probably on the other extreme. I feel that my work is important, yes. I have observations and analyses to share with other people, and to the extent that sharing this work can contribute to a better world, that's important. But beyond that I don't define my sense of self or self-worth or self-esteem on the basis of my work.

I imagine that certain people that have some general idea of what I can do would like to have a concrete expression of what I'm doing. And I would like to have that for them, too. But I have higher expectations of myself than other people have of me, so that doesn't concern me.

I ask a great deal of myself and because of that I don't permit myself to produce in the way of people in the university world who are caught up in the publish or perish syndrome, producing for the sake of producing to get promotions or jobs or whatever. I feel that I'm in the process of self-realization, of self-actualization, and I certainly don't believe that I'm not achieving my goals.

I don't worry about money. I do dislike having to pay so much money for health insurance. I would like to see national health insurance that would not make a person feel that to be healthy, you have to work. I think that's awful.

But generally I feel secure because I'm confident that what I'm doing is significant and ultimately will permit me to have some economic survival from it. Also, I feel that in doing it, I've sharpened myself as a scholar in the field, so that I will be capable of making money whenever I need it.

My wife and I have recently dipped into savings somewhat. No huge amount. I never really knew what I was saving for anyway, so I don't feel tremendously attached to savings. The kind of savings we have are relatively small amounts that can be accumulated rapidly, if you want to. In America, if you set your mind to it, it's not too hard to do.

Maybe it's the way I grew up, but I never really felt that money was a problem. I imagine that if we had children, my feelings about jobs would probably be affected by that. Not having children makes it a lot easier to live in this kind of situation. There's much greater freedom.

I suppose that having credit also adds to my sense of security. I'm very privileged when it comes to deciding what to do to make money—I have choices, I have options. There are millions of people who don't have that luxury—who have to worry about having a roof over their heads or don't know where their next meal is coming from. Their only option is a job and jobs are a scarce commodity these days. When people have that sense of desperation, any kind of job looks desirable. I'm very sympathetic to the people in that situation, but I don't look upon working that way.

You could probably say I don't believe in work. I consider work an artificial concept. People should not have to fight to do the kind of work that is done in factories. I don't think work like that corresponds with human dignity. As much as I identify with the need for workers to have better conditions, I feel that the problem is, rather, a much larger, complex, overall one of changing the whole productive system of the society and changing our idea of work.

Being an anthropologist I know that human beings can live a thousand times more simply in a material sense than they do in our culture. People that are living traditionally, close to the land, survive and reproduce very well, and they do it without factories. Factories are just an invention of the last two, three hundred years of western industrial culture.

"I don't believe that a society built around the Protestant work ethic is adaptive to our current technological capacities. The work ethic produces too many workers who have to do too much work to satisfy that ethic."

I don't believe that a society built around the Protestant work ethic is adaptive to our current technological capacities. The work ethic produces too many workers who have to do too much work to satisfy that ethic. Modern automated technology can produce much more than workers can, more goods than society needs. So we have an excess of workers, an excess of work ethic, an excess of material goods and a discontinuity in the society. The technology has outrun the value system.

The answer is to change the value of work and reorganize the society so that people don't feel that they have to work so much and so that their identities are not oriented around work. The myths that people live by which make them obsessed with work and competition and threatened by cooperation and communication have to be dissolved and replaced. We have to rid ourselves of myths of work, myths of profit, myths of nation, and myths of competition. Then we can begin to restructure a society on the basis of the actualities of the human condition rather than on the myths which currently support the crumbling system.

I don't think that the current system, which has corporations and the big multinationals in control, would permit the necessary changes to be made, although there does appear to be evolving a certain recognition of these problems in the most progressive societies, such as Sweden. But I believe the corporations will probably be removed from control in the future.

The technologies, however, will continue to be important. They will be differently organized, more in tune with the larger interests of the larger mass of the human population.

I'm optimistic because I believe that the upcoming generations are freer from the old myths and more open to the creative use of new technologies than the older generation. In the long term I think there is hope for radical change. I just hope that at thirty-eight I'm not too old for the new generations. I feel like I'm a strong survivor. I guess my strength comes from the integrity of my own ideas and actions.

I feel fulfilled up to this point. The things that I've done and the ideas that I've developed have tested out fairly well and have a genuine validity. That gives me comfort and confidence.

However, I think that one can be over-confident. One can be arrogant, too, particularly in the field that I'm in. The role of scientific observer can produce a kind of tunnel vision which sometimes functions to shut out information you get from participation. Being an intellectual elitist is a danger, and that also relates to being isolated in your writing. I might be learning a lot more if I were out interacting with the world instead of writing about it.

I feel that I have to have a balance between the things that are going on in my head and the things that are coming into my head from the outside world. I just want to sustain an openness to input which would enable me to be creative and responsible to the current world and also to contribute to it.

Tony   Brooklyn, New York

In his modest little apartment in a working class neighborhood, the solid-looking man in his mid-thirties with a paunch

sat at the kitchen table. Tony exercised such impressive control over his facial expressions that he was a living illustration of what "poker-faced" means. Momentarily, when he began to tell how he felt having to leave the Yankees, the impassive mask broke. But he quickly resumed his expressionless look—the loss of his professional ball career was too painful to think about.

I was a professional baseball player for the New York Yankees. The first week I was out of the service I was signed as a pitcher and I played three years. Then I got hurt and called it quits.

I lived a wonderful life when I played. I traveled all over the country with the farm team and we really did all the best— Holiday Inns and whatnot in every town we went to. We got paid for everything. We got paid to have our clothes washed and to leave tips. All our hotel bills were paid plus we got paid a salary on top of it. And I was doing something I liked.

I haven't been to a ball game since I finished playing. I couldn't see paying them to go watch somebody else play ball, because I felt I was his equal. I watch the games at the bar or I listen to them on the radio. When I finished playing I was depressed for quite a while, a couple of years. It still bothers me now when I get into talking about it. Playing ball was my whole life since I was a kid. The only work I wanted to have for my career was professional baseball, and after that fell through, it didn't matter. I wasn't looking for a future of working in any capacity.

I had to find other means of supporting my family, so I became a gambler. I work as a dealer in poker games. It's a good living when you're working, but you get out of work because things close and you have to wait till one of the clubs opens again. You see, every game only can run for so long because of the police and because people will go broke. Naturally you lose those players and you don't have a game. That's when you go to another game, and when that game folds up you go to another one. There's always someplace where you can go.

I worked for the Mafia for fifteen months. The game went broke. They lost half a million dollars. I'd work for the Mafia again. I wouldn't get involved in anything more than the

197

game, but that's not hard to avoid. It's a matter of how far you want to go.

I can always get a job. I deal, I'd say, three nights a week, fifteen hours a night. I make anywhere from $100 to $200 a night, tax free. On a slow night I make eighty or ninety dollars. And that's the way I've been living a little better than eight years.

My family gets what they need and what they want every day. Two, three times a week I'll take home Chinese food or something where my wife don't have to cook. I like to have the best. I wouldn't let my wife buy a cheap steak or anything that's cheap. That's what I base my life on besides gambling— giving my family the best.

I feel comfortable and secure and I think my wife and the kids do, too. I make a lot of friends and I have a lot of leisure time. We go out and we have good times. We take the kids to Great Adventure and to carnivals and feasts. We live decently. To be 100 percent honest, if I told my wife I wanted to go to work and give her $100, $150 a week, she wouldn't accept it.

When I'm not gambling, most of the time I sleep. My wife says I sleep a lot, but sometimes I work for two full days and when I come home I need to sleep. In the afternoon I go to the club and kill a couple hours playing rummy and pinochle. When I play cards for leisure in the afternoon, I win 80 percent of the time.

I also go to the racetrack. There are times I come home without sleeping and go to the track. I feel it's my pleasure to do that. I'm not going to tell you I win all the time at the track, but I would say that when I win, I win much more than I lose. In other words, if I went to the track with $200 and lost it, I lost $200. But the next time I go, maybe I'd win a thousand or so. Makes up for five times I went and I lost.

I would say I'm a loser at the track, but I won't say I'm a loser at cards. Even if I lose after I'm through working I always bring my wife home something. I wouldn't come home penni- less. If it's not a whole pay, I'll bring her fifty dollars, enough to get by till I go to work the next time. The worst it can get is that she can't do a big shopping, but that's only once in a while. My wife gets nervous the day before a holiday because that's when she always buys everything, but she knows I'll come through with it. We've never had a bad holiday. She's not worried that I'll fail her.

Not everybody can do what I do. I think I'm smarter than 90 percent of the gamblers around. I play all the basic games and I win; everybody will tell you that. It's an art and I'm proud of it. A lot of places I go to nobody could play me. I've never been to Vegas and I'd like to play cards there. I could probably go to work in Vegas, Atlantic City, but I wouldn't because my wife doesn't want to go.

My life is pretty much cards, but I never think about it. It's an automatic thing. When I play, it's a pleasure, but I don't base my life on playing; I base my life on gambling. Any time I can, I gamble. I gamble for the money—I think every gambler does—I don't think any gambler could tell me different. Why would you gamble? My wife thinks it's like a circle—you win, you lose, you win, you lose—you don't get any further. But I don't think that it's a circle. Most of the time I win. When I go to work, it's not a question of winning or losing, it's just a question of how much I'm going to make.

I don't play things where I don't think I have a chance. I like to play fifty-fifty—me and you—and see who's better. How should I describe it—let's see—like when a cat is on the prowl. But I'm the same whether I win or lose. I have no feeling unless I win a large sum. Then we'll go partying—we'll go to the track and sit down in the dining areas and have filet mignon. Once I won $2000. We were having dinner at the track and I left a waitress a $120 tip. From there we went to Atlantic City and I lost $1000, then we came home.

We don't put money in the bank and we live more or less day to day. I would probably be a rich person now if I knew how to save money. My wife doesn't gamble, but she doesn't save money—she spends it on the house. She has no budget and I have no budget.

I've thought about how I'd feel if I had a million dollars. I'd probably be very unhappy because I wouldn't know what to do with myself. It would be stupid for me to gamble. If I had a million dollars, then what could I win at the racetrack, $100? $200? $1000?

I'd like to have some money, but I wouldn't like to have that much, maybe $50,000. With $50,000 we'd be more comfortable, but it would probably go. I'd give some to my wife and I wouldn't touch it, then I'd probably go to the track every day, every night. Also, with $50,000 I could get my dream car, a

Cadillac. A big one. I'd have to have the money to pay for it all at once. That's the only way I'd get it. I'm pretty optimistic I'll make it.

Nobody would ever tell me to my face, but I think people who work probably would look at me as a bum. It doesn't bother me. It doesn't stop me from making friends—I get along with most everybody. I don't have close friends, though. I live my own life. I don't want anybody to follow me and I don't want to follow nobody.

"Nobody would ever tell me to my face, but I think people who work probably would look at me as a bum."

Hundreds of times my mother has asked me why I don't get a job. I just won't tell her—I wouldn't feel comfortable working. I don't like being cooped up in one place a week at a time unless I really enjoy something. I don't like getting up at five o'clock in the morning in the cold weather and going to work, then coming home at nine o'clock at night. And I don't like to take orders from anybody. I worked hard a lot of the early part of my life and now that I'm thirty-six I don't choose to do it any more.

Life is pretty exciting—everybody looks for some kind of excitement in whatever they do. I like my life. I'm content. I don't go around asking anybody for anything. If I had it to do all over again, I would go the same way. I wouldn't trade places with anybody.

Roger   Chicago, Illinois

Je plains le temps de ma jeunesse,	I regret those days of youth
(Ouquel j'ay plus qu'autre gallé	(when, more than most, I had a life
Jusques a l'entrée de viellesse),	of joy until old age came on)
Qui son partement m'a celé.	which left me when my back was
Il ne s'en est a pié allé	turned.
N'a cheval: helas! comment don?	They didn't leave on foot, alas,
Soudainement s'en est vollé	or horseback. But how then?
Et ne m'a laissié quelque don.	Suddenly they stole away,
	and left me not a thing.

—François Villon, Verse XXII, "The Testament"

Dark blond, thin and attractive, with a swagger meant for the streets, twenty-six year old Roger was in his natural element in this rundown neighborhood where bar after bar dotted the street below the El station. Intolerant of the drudgery, tedium and exploitation of working for other people, he had chosen to survive on the fringes. Through the flowing poetry of his words, Roger fit his romantic visions and hard-cut realism into one grand perspective.

I came up in pretty much the heavy sixties, and I fell in with the South Side set, being a South Chicago boy. I quit working when I was a junior in high school and most of my activities were in dealing grass and soft drugs. I was making too much money to bother holding a fulltime job.

I got in a bunch of trouble with the police and my mother dumped me on my father in Guam for a year. They were divorced and he was an air traffic controller, so he was my ticket for traveling in Asia. We made off like bandits: all that shopping, the cheap Hong Kong suits. And Taiwan was a ball because it does have a real party section of town.

I've always been on and off working. I'd amass a small enough fortune then fall back for a while and drift. I just fall into things as I see them. For a while I had a term paper writing company. I made money hand over fist, then through marital squabbles I sold the business real quick, made a bunch of bucks, and went down to New Orleans.

Another time I did a short stint in a factory that was owned by a pretty sharp dude. He overpaid me too fast. I got about four or five hundred dollars in my pocket and split down to Texas.

I do like to travel, for sure. That keeps me steadily sold on this country. I was a traveling salesman for a while and I did really good, but a salesman's life is really a drag. You've got to wear zoot suits and wear your hair short and not be high when you talk to a buyer—all sorts of little raggly-taggly things.

I had really good products and I'm the type that feels if I've got something you need, you should want to buy it. I shouldn't have to go through all that song and dance. I lost interest in the job because of that. Then, the commission check wouldn't show up for two weeks because you had to wait for these clowns' credit to clear, so it wasn't regular money. I just gave it up.

I did a little time in prison for dealing grass and cocaine, and they taught me how to weld in there. Needless to say, I've never welded since then, except for stuff like a couple of my friends' motorcycles.

I exist here in the city without work. When it gets right down to it, I'd rather not work because it's productive for somebody else, not for me. I've never had a job that was productive for me. I'm opposed to some kinds of working; I'm sure dead set against me walking into one of those mills. I had a job in one for, I think, a month and a half when I was a kid. Too greasy, too dirty, too nasty. I'm not going to spend my time doing that. I'm lining up all my resources to go into school next year to pursue an acting career because I think I've got a little talent. I tried acting a couple times and I always had a good time.

I haven't been unemployed that long. I worked fourteen months prior to being laid off the last two months. I lived all the way till now with absolutely what they call no existing well of income. They gave me a big hassle about getting my unemployment compensation and it took them a good nine weeks to send me my first check. My nerves are really shot from the whole thing. They finally sent me a little dough the other day. It was really gracious of them to finally cut loose.

I'm always spending the same, whether I'm working or not. I'm a hand-to-mouth man. If I've got ten, I spend fifteen. I've got credit at the grocery, I've got credit at the bar, and I'm constantly borrowing from Peter to pay Paul, just juggling my accounts. I can get the money I need if I scuffle around. You get a few dollars in your pocket and you buy and you sell.

It's rarely anything illegal—well, sometimes it's an itty-bitty shady. You don't know for certain whether what you're doing is completely legal; it's just transfers of property.

You fall into things; you do it through your wits. It's kind of hard to explain and kind of hard to follow. You say, "Mm, there's an opportunity. It's there, it's takeable—I'll take it."

"You smile and razzle-dazzle them, show a little teeth, and you walk away with a little money. Survival."

When I need to get certain things taken care of right away, I basically fall back on the old carny tricks, if you want to get right down to it. You smile and razzle-dazzle them, show a little teeth, and you walk away with a little money. Survival.

It affects the way you act with people, with strangers, but it even affects friends more. Sometimes I feel a little guilty, and it probably explains why I drink a lot and why I get into my traveling.

I don't have what you'd call close friends, maybe one. To me the word "friend" has got a very reserved, special meaning. It's not something I bandy about—that's either "pal" or maybe "buddy." I've found that friends accumulated over the times and they're just not always there at the right time. The best advice I ever got was from a guy in the penitentiary who told me, "You're going to be able to count your friends in your lifetime on one hand. You're going to be able to count your acquaintances all day long."

"I entertain myself the way I figured young men did it in Paris back in the 1500s."

I spend my time doing what I want. I read a lot. Tinker around, run around the bars, scandalize ladies. At twenty-six

I'm turning into sort of a Chicago crazyman. Wherever I go, I make sure I have a good time. I entertain myself the way I figure young men did it in Paris back in the 1500s. I can just as well do it here.

If I get depressed, first thing I do is get out of the house. Sooner or later I'll break. I'll be headed up towards the clouds and eventually see the sunlight and go "whew."

I like to go out and booze it up in the bars. And that does cost, even if you're drinking in the cheap bars, if you really drink—and I drink pretty seriously. I get out there partying, man, and start throwing them beers down, dancing around, playing the jukebox and pinball and what-have-you. I usually do that two, three times a week for relaxation. It's like burning off steam.

Most of the time I'm one of those happy drunks who laughs a lot—dadadalada—everything's yuk-yuk. Sometimes, though, I get nervous when I'm drinking. I'll get aggravated and get into the fight trip. It's easy for me to get bothered. My drinking worries me once in a while. Drinking definitely interferes with your future. Kidney stones the size of a golf ball, what-have-you. I've thought about it.

I'm ordinarily pretty relaxed, though I can get very, very reflective. What do you say a person's mood is if they spend three or four days not speaking to anybody, not being unhappy, not hiding, but just reading all day long? I read novels all the time—gobble them up. Action novels and some sci-fi. Just the dreamer's world.

My plans for the future are so grandiose that they can't possibly come true. Within ten years I'd like to have a beautiful hacienda overlooking a waterfall down in South America somewhere, with a complete fort and armed minions, and run all the cocaine plantations for as far as I can see. That's the regular get-rich-quick scheme.

Because I'd never return to the fold. That's where I feel I differ from all the rest. When my parole officer said to me, "If you'd just come in two more times, I'll write a letter and get you cut loose," I said, "The hell with your two more times. I'll come in if I can make it. You'd have better luck if you want to meet me at the tavern for a couple beers."

He said, "OK, where is it?" and that's where he meets me for my parole. And I don't care if he writes a letter or not.

Those people locked me up like an animal for a year and a half and made me jump. Then do you know what they did to me, a nice, young, rehabilitated kid that had just gotten back in the streets? They put me in a junk program.

I'm no junkie. For a year and a half I had to go down there and pee into a little bottle every single week. Of course, I never came up dirty, never.

So I think of ideas for getting rich without going back into the fold. The idea that really gets me happened just after I got out of the joint. I had been reading about all the people down in jails in Mexico and I said to my pal, "Why don't we just hustle up some hardware and a van and go on down there. I could find out who these people are, then contact their families and see how much a head they'll pay to bring them home. And we'll go get them." I was sure that there was somebody down there whose parents would pay a thousand bucks to get their kid out of that jail. Two weeks later some Texas hillbilly and a couple of his pals did it.

"Work's got to be done, but if you're going to be stupid enough to do it for somebody else, at least it should be for a certain price."

That kind of way of making money really appeals to me. Work's got to be done, but if you're stupid enough to do it for somebody else, at least it should be for a certain price. I see a lot of people that do things for the wrong price. I saw a guy out in this winter weather welding. That's dangerous in this snow, even with rubber boots on. I couldn't believe those guys were doing it for $3.50 an hour.

The only way I could see working in a job would be if something were to happen to my ex-wife so that I would be raising my little girl myself. I'd hate to think that my own flesh and blood was getting raised by somebody else. I'd get a job then if I had to, though I'd try to figure out a better way and there might be a damn good chance that I could. But I'd take that responsibility, even if it meant breaking down and working.

Outside of that, I can't see what else would force me to work, unless I really wanted something really bad. The working situation is not like it used to be. I don't know what they've done with the money and I don't know if the government is making any attempts to bring the necessary pressures to bear on market pressure points.

The United States is a major producer of food and those other countries are major producers of oil, so why don't we stop selling our food so cheap? And why don't we do more exporting of food so farmers aren't killing thirty, forty cows and burning them in mass graves? Export the damn things if our economy can't bear it. Those people have to eat.

I don't know if anybody's thinking that far ahead or worried about things like that. The only thing I worry about is that American society exists as it is. There have got to be short-comings somewhere. Somehow or another we're getting beat.

That's why I got tired of working. If I'm working, how much money is going out of my check every day? I'm seeing nothing. As it is, I'm in the same house now as I was before, living just as good, and eating just as good, and I'm not working, so....

Robert   New York, New York

Unable to find another ad agency job for over two years, this mathematician in his early forties had created a satisfying, busy life, amusing himself most recently by writing plays. Everything about Robert was intense—the way he had burst into his friend's Greenwich Village loft announcing that he had probably scotched his chances of having one of his plays produced by meddling in theater politics, the way he brushed back the lock of straight black hair that kept falling over his forehead, the way his eyes darted behind his thick glasses and the way he played with his ideas as he spoke, turning them over and around to examine them from all sides.

I had been working in an ad agency, and as everyone knows, advertising is the first business to get hit by a recession and the last to recover. I worked in one of the glamour ends, operations research—the mathematical analysis of problems. They never listen to it anyway, so it's one of the first places where they cut.

My boss was supposed to retire and wanted to leave me his job, but couldn't unless I had a Ph.D. So I quit to work full-time on the degree. It was a gamble, and as it turned out, I lost. He became politically unsuccessful and his power base was cut out from under him. He ended up a title hanging in mid-air and I ended up on the street.

When the dust settled I had been out of the industry for close to two years. When I tried to get back in I discovered that I had violated a taboo. Employment agencies told me that the clients were specifying someone actively working in the field at the moment, not someone who had been out of work.

"No matter how well qualified you look on your resume, after your second year out of work they say, 'There must be something wrong with this person if he hasn't been able to get a job within this time. I don't know what it is and I don't want to take the trouble to find out, but obviously there must be alcohol or drugs or he hears little voices or something.'"

Now I won't try to argue for or against that, but I found that after a while this thing becomes self-perpetuating. No matter how well qualified you look on your resume, after your second year out of work they say, "There must be something wrong with this person if he hasn't been able to get a job within this time. I don't know what it is and I don't want to take the trouble to find out, but obviously there must be alcohol or drugs or he hears little voices or something."

For about three years I was underemployed, teaching mathematics in college at a salary about one-sixth what I was making in advertising, and for a year now I've been out of work. I tried to get full-time teaching, but *zonk*—that's very difficult. All the children who are going to be going to college within the next ten to twenty years have been born and counted and there aren't enough teaching jobs to go around. The few part-time jobs open are for people still working on their degrees. The only other jobs are in places like Brasilia. I'd relocate, but I didn't finish my degree and there's no market for anyone without a Ph.D.

"Finding a job if you are over forty is like child adoption—an infant is placed very easily, but it's almost impossible to get a ten year old child adopted."

I've looked into doing things like writing ad copy, but I don't seem to have any particular talent for that. I enjoy working with my hands and I'd be happy to be a carpenter or a welder, but I'm forty-two and apprentice programs don't take anybody above about twenty-seven. Occasionally there is a job on the Civil Service list with an age limit of forty-five, but they're awfully dull and I'm saving that for the last try. Finding a job if you are over forty is like child adoption—an infant is placed very easily, but it's almost impossible to get a ten-year old child adopted. It's not only that you're set in your ways, it's also because the company is not going to be able to make a profit out of your pension plan—things like that.

It would certainly be helpful if this society had a more realistic appraisal of the value of education. The main function of education is to lead people to expect a better deal than society has any intention of giving. When I was teaching remedial math, my students thought they were going to solve their problems by going into nursing or medical technology. From what I had heard, these fields were going to be very deep pools of unemployment by the early 1980s, so I would tell them they were knocking their brains out for nothing and that they should try something they didn't need mathematical ability for.

"Look," I would say, "the main function of the educational system is to keep you off the job market for a few years longer. The second function is to baffle you and exhaust you into harmlessness. Third is to convince you that you have a chance when you have none at all." But they didn't want to hear it.

Education is a snare and a delusion. It's not going to solve any problems—it's one more evasion. Whenever I was baffled and I would ask some professor I respected for his opinion, he couldn't suggest anything except that I go back to school. At each major crisis I've had no solution for life's problems except to go back to grad school for one more degree. That has always been a mistake.

"Instead of trying so hard for so long to be sensible, I should have started acting like a lunatic from the beginning. I couldn't have turned out a whole lot worse and at least I would have had more fun."

My education limited the possibilities I would consider. It never crossed my mind to do anything except as a salaried employee of some company, which is absurd. In good times running your own business is no more dangerous than working for a salary, and in bad times working for a salary is no safer than running your own business. I am generally pissed that I was trained, educated, and prepared for a society that no longer exists. What I should have done was to have had the courage of my insanity and gone off with some nice girl, or joined the Foreign Legion, or just written plays and not worried about the obligation of bourgeois respectability. Instead of trying so hard for so long to be sensible, I should have started acting like a lunatic from the beginning. I couldn't have turned out a whole lot worse and at least I would have had more fun.

By a series of immanent, irrational decisions, I have found myself in an absurd position. The trap was in keeping faith, ignoring the obvious, and trying to make up for it by looking for subtleties where they don't exist. It took me a long time to realize that the reason I have trouble finding the solution to the problem is that there isn't a real solution: the game is rigged against me. A few people can win, but if enough people do win, they'll change the rules again so it becomes harder.

Now my life is all recreation and leisure. I set myself little projects. I was really into model airplanes, model tanks, and painting toy soldiers for a while. I was third ranked on the east coast and among the top ten in the world. While it's an ancient and honorable art, nobody wants to hear the rap; besides, all my colleagues were eleven years old. More than that, there's absolutely nowhere to go with it except maybe California to try to get into the Special Effects Department of *Star Wars*.

Then a very good friend of a very good friend had a play produced Off-Off Broadway and all his friends and friends' friends and friends' friends' friends had to go, so I went. There wasn't much to it but somebody talking. I said, "Well, I can do that," so I did. I wrote about five plays in six months. I had a couple of readings; one tiny little theatre Off Broadway says they want to produce one, but I'll believe it when I see it.

Zonk. Writing plays and building model airplanes is pretty fulfilling. I have given up on the plays for a while because although they're pretty good, they all express the same view of life. All the major characters are waiting throughout for the outcome over which they have no control. There's something of the life I've been living in these plays and I think I'd better wait till I get a different point of view before I write any more.

I've been working my way through all of Shakespeare's plays, then getting into some of the late Elizabethan and early Jacobean era playwrights. I study karate with a genuine Korean lunatic and work out hard about three times a week. I read, argue with friends, and work as a volunteer in the Public Theater. I see a lot of plays, since I can see them for free, and I see a movie once in a while. I think about the theater and worry about obscure questions: In *Othello*, what is Iago's rank? No one knows and the explanations given are usually non-sensical. Obviously anyone who can get into worrying about things like that can keep himself busy forever.

Oh, *zonk*, I like to spend money in certain ways which I can't do any more. I have a small private income, so I've been surviving, but I haven't really been living within my means. Considering the size of my means, living within them would be too depressing to think about.

I tend to withdraw and also a bunch of things have been cut off from me. In some circles the first question out of a girl's mouth is "What do you do?" If that's her first question, you know what kind of sociological theory she's groping around with, so I avoided some ways of meeting people. I felt that it was ridiculous and that there must be a solution to it, but it seemed like a riddle I couldn't solve.

I went through all the usual emotions when I became unemployed—anger, surprise, puzzlement, bafflement, despair—all the things people go through, I suppose, when they're told they have cancer. I must be going through some sort of emotional regression—nothing drastic—but I can't think of any other explanation as to how I ended up building model airplanes.

"I went through all the usual emotions when I became unemployed—anger, surprise, puzzlement, bafflement, despair—all the things people go through, I suppose, when they're told they have cancer."

I have certain confused emotions. I have a real middle-class background and becoming unemployed was very painful for me. It was worse than committing murder because there might have been some provocation or excuse for that, but in my family, if someone was out of work he just wasn't talked about and was always under something of a cloud. So I have a vague sense of shame, but it can never get very big because I know how I lost my job and how good I was.

I did want to have children. I didn't get married because I would get to thinking that I could do better than the woman I was with. It's a common story, but I'm not young any more. If I'm going to do anything about a family, I ought to be doing it awfully soon, otherwise my children would grow up seeing their father pretty much as an old man. I certainly don't want my kids' earliest recollection of me as fifty-five or sixty — they'll grow up all out of shape. My situation has killed my plans for having a family.

Objectively I guess I seem very pessimistic, but I don't feel pessimistic. I think I'm a tougher, smarter, better person than when I was trying very hard to live up to all the things I thought I should live up to. I had severe doubts about myself when I was younger, but now I think I've got a pretty good estimate about my abilities and my limitations.

There were things I liked about working in advertising. There was always some crisis Monday morning which we had to solve or we would be out on the street by Friday. It was like the Nazi High Command late in 1944 with everyone running around. The first fourteen or fifteen coups d'état I survived were just exciting and I thought this was really living. After a while I discovered how gratuitous this excitement was, but the first couple years were just plain fun.

There was also a pleasure about making million dollar decisions—looking at those numbers with all the zeroes after them. Aside from that, there was the craftsmanship and more than that, the feeling, rightly or wrongly, that I was one of the best.

I suppose this is so emotionally loaded for me that I pour into clichés and use words like "craftsmanship" or "satisfaction." People use clichés because they're afraid of their emotions and try to get some distance from them by using somebody else's perception. But I would like to work again. I guess I want that feeling of life and surprise you get by working with other people. These days I'm pretty much thrown upon the resources of my own imagination. Though my resources are considerable, my imagination doesn't surprise me that much any more. I'm in a rut as far as writing goes and I need some new experience. I want to write. If you're past forty and you've blown it, there's nothing to do except start writing.

The funny thing is that it seems like I've finally got a job coming up in advertising. To clarify some obscure philosophical point I called up this industrial psychologist I had known back at the old ad agency. He's getting a job as department head in one of the best known ad agencies and wants to bring in his own men. There's a feudal system in these corporations and you bring in men who are personally loyal to you.

I told him, "You have mein complete loyalty, mein Führer," and he said, "Good." So it looks like I'm going to have a castle to defend me.

These things happen unpredictably when you don't know what the person on the other side needs. Once I interviewed for a job I was sure I couldn't possibly get. They said they were looking for a mathematician and I knew it was a mistake, but I had to check it out. I was at my absolute worst—I mean, my most bitter, my most cynical, my absolutely most contentious—and I got hired on the spot.

Six months later, when I knew those people a little bit better, I asked how I could possibly have gotten hired, the way I acted. And the guy said, "In advertising we like to get them a little bit bitter to begin with."

Albert   Washington, D.C.

Albert, a retired millionaire in his early fifties, had come from Paris to spend a few months in Washington to see his dentist. He carved out a few hours from his busy schedule of studying philosophy, physics and astrology to talk about his life. He did so eagerly if a bit painfully.

When I graduated college in 1947, I hadn't a clue, I just knew that I'd go out and get some fabulous job.

I was a bright, middle-class person, so an employment agency threw me into advertising. I was there for several months and along came a big reduction in the work force. I didn't know why I was hired and I didn't know why I was fired and I didn't really care. But I had learned one thing. I *never* wanted to get up and be somewhere at nine in the morning.

I got a thousand dollars together, formed a little company with a friend, and spent the next three years wandering around from London in summertime to Paris in springtime, to Vienna in ski time. We made about a hundred dollars a week; I took twenty dollars and he took eighty. That was fair because he had a wife and two kids and lived in America, I lived in Europe and couldn't really spend twenty dollars in a week. I'd buy drinks for everybody and it was a bit exotic because no one knew what I was doing, which is a very good way to live in Europe.

When the big pros started coming back into the business, the economics started to get a bit dicey. My idea of a job was just lollygagging around, so I stopped before it really got bad.

213

For a few months I sat around in a café, which is the "office" in Paris, wondering what to do next. I heard someone say "I've been offered $200 a week to go to Germany and sell encyclopedias, but I don't think I'm going to go because I've got a date this weekend." I said, "I don't have a date this weekend that's all that great, so I'll go." I went and I earned about $800 a week. I did it for several months and suddenly it dawned on me what I was doing. But I had about $10,000 in the bank. In 1954 you could retire on $10,000!

But after a few months of that I stopped and decided to get back to America and get a real job—do what the model says you should do, and probably earn $38.42 a week because what the hell, this was really nonsense. I sold my car, got rid of my flat, and while I was saying goodbye to everybody, someone said, "I've got to deliver some stuff to Errol Flynn in Spain." So I said, "I've never been there. It's on the way to New York from Paris, right?"

When we got to Spain, Errol was in Tangiers and that's on the way to New York too, right? By the time we got there, Flynn was in the hospital, so for three or four weeks we sat around on his yacht, the movie stars coming in and out, the scotch and sodas flowing. Suddenly a little voice said, "You know, Albert, there will be no movie stars' yachts when you go back," so I went back to Paris.

And two days later I ran into a very cool cat named Bernie Cornfeld, who was just starting out. I told him that I'd sold encyclopedias and he said. "No, no, investments. We're going to get the whole world rich." And he showed me how they worked. If the market goes down, the customer gets rich. If the market goes up, the customer gets rich. It was beautiful.

There were several million Americans living abroad earning high salaries, being paid bonuses by their companies. The stock market was getting ready to rise for fifteen years and there wasn't anybody to tell them what a mutual fund was.

I went home and did some calculations. I figured that in two years I could earn enough money to retire: $100,000 was my goal. I could live on $8000 or $9000 because, believe me in 1956, unless you had seventeen kids and four mistresses, you could not spend $10,000 a year in Europe.

So I went to work for the fastest rising company in the western world and after one year and eleven months I had reached my goal—I had $100,403. And I quit. This was 1959 and I was thirty-three years old.

I went to Geneva and Bernie was up to his eyeballs in business. Everything was exploding and he just couldn't handle it. So I said, "You've been nice to me, I'll be nice to you. I'll hang on—just pay my hotel bill."

I did it for about a year while the operation was being structured into a real company, then I worked until about 1965, right in the middle of it, on all those Boards of Directors. The company had been growing like a monster and my stock was worth over half a million dollars—I'd gone past my goal. Bernie wanted to earn all the money in the western world, but that was his dream; it wasn't mine. I'd arranged it so I could keep my stock in, so I said, "I think I'll just go and let you guys work your asses off. I really don't want to." My goal was to arrange not to work; I'd done that and here I was working when I should have been not working.

We were very proud of our little baby and people would say, "Albert, I don't understand it. There's nothing out there—this is the whole world." But I was living a left-bankish life in Paris, so I knew there was something out there even if those idiots didn't, so I said, "That's all right, I'll survive."

"So I was retired at age thirty-nine, living out of a nice little penthouse in Paris."

So I was retired at age thirty-nine, living out of a nice little penthouse in Paris. I didn't throw my money around, but I had a pleased air about me. I had beat the system and I was back at my favorite café table. There weren't many local boys who had made good quite like that.

When someone would ask, "What do you do?" my number was, "I am retired." "Oh, you're so young," they'd say. And I would smile because that won the game. "It's much better to retire when you're young and can enjoy it than when you're old and can't," I'd say, and everybody would smile wanly. I don't know what kind of aggression I was making toward their inner fantasies, but that was what I was doing.

I found myself producing films and some plays. I read a lot to keep up with cultural events and if you go to the openings and read the new books in two languages, well, you can put in a sixty hour week. There was never a time that I can remember that was boring, when I'd be saying, "Well, we're putting together this film," or "I'm flying off to Rome tomorrow"—all that European ship talk. With the foreigners in Europe, and now in America to some extent, travel takes the place of work. You just say, "I'm going off to Mexico City on Thursday," and people are satisfied. I look back on it now; I see that I deliberately went to Paris, which is a culturally acceptable place to not work or to have very bizarre work.

Then in 1969 our company went public. Millions of dollars floated in. Six months later the world came to an end. The stock started going down to zero and the hundreds of millions of dollars started flowing out. The twelve year cycle had just gone "pshuu."

We were into a competitive thing in IOS, but we were winners almost from the start—kind of like the Yankees winning pennant after pennant. It was as if you and your gang had won the Olympics and suddenly somebody came in and took away all your medals and said, "You're going to jail."

We didn't go to jail. I wasn't in the mess that was dragged up, and no one has ever accused me. In the books that were written about it later, I'm exonerated—I made sure the exoneration was out there. I organize a lot of energy in being right all the time and I spend a lot of time in not being wrong. I spent a certain amount of time, like I'm doing now, making myself right in that dubious situation.

That situation wasn't wrong, but it was dubious. I thought I was involved in it least of all because I am not into spending money—I had just gotten involved in a lot of things with the money that didn't interest me anyway.

But it was a big, big number, and it really blew my act. Psychically I was there; these were my buddies. It was like quitting Hitler in 1924, before anything had happened. As everything was falling apart, I spent two or three years trying to save enough out of it so I wouldn't have to start all this horseshit over again. I salvaged just enough so that at the moment I can pay my bills.

Two years later, I went to India and reevaluated my whole life. I had had an incredible trauma and very mysterious and magical things that I needed badly happened to me out there. I had been busy doing the western thing—getting ahead and accumulating—and it had knocked me ass over teakettle. I had to let it all wash over me.

India was my psychiatrist. I realized that competition, achievement, and accumulation—in fact the whole cosmos— are just a game. I needed to learn that very badly. I wouldn't want to compete again.

I realized that if I stayed in Paris I would just carry on this old out-of-date culture number. Paris was a marvelous, marvelous movie, but I'm somebody else now. Maybe life would be much more interesting if I could just start over again and create a new aura of activities that made sense. It took about three or four years to get out of all the things I had gotten myself into so I could clear the boards. I came to America because it's a place where I thought I would find some activities that are both work and groovy at the same time. My goal is to retire from retirement. I no longer get satisfaction out of having retired at thirty-nine. I'm very tired of beating the game. I'm trying to kill that whole persona that went through all that stuff and come up with something new. But I don't want to go down and get a job—it didn't appeal to me then and it doesn't appeal to me now at age fifty-one. It's kind of hard to get involved in all the nonsense that goes on with work when you don't have some economic motive and I don't really need to work. But work does have a role to play in your identity, in the way you relate to people. What the work is, is probably the problem for me. I think that going down and working from nine to five is only one of several definitions of work. I'm looking for a pattern, and part of the patterning I'm looking for is to find out if I was right in hanging loose.

I'm prepared for something different; I'm not totally clear that I'm willing to do it, however. I've not consciously set up any criteria. I'm going to try to be a little more aware of what I go through when I confront my next job experience than I was in the past.

I have a technique of having eight things to do in the next six hours which keeps me in a rush all the time. But it's not very satisfying; it's make-work, and at the end of the day I don't feel that my time was well-spent. It might mean that I need a structured job now to pull this all together. I've worked in my life in a very personalized way but what I really feel is a need for something that's perceived by other people as being work. I apparently need to get some feedback. I'm making no contribution to society, either that I can tell or that other people can tell, which is part of the definition, I suppose, of work.

One part of me says at least now, in the rest of my life, do something that has social approbation with the so-called ideals that you have. I'd always considered that the left wing were the good guys and the capitalists were the bad guys. But although I've read only left wing publications, my life has been out there where there was a lot of money. I thought I only wanted enough to retire on and that's more than any poor person from Alabama is going to see in his life. I'm a little wary now of saying what my sentiments are because I don't know what part of me is on the left and what part of me is on the right.

One reason I'm not helping the starving people of Alabama is because I don't even help the people around me. I find it hard to be generous. But the way I rationalize it is that poor people are living in a different universe from privileged people. I was born into the privileged class and I've taken advantage of it. If someone were to take away all those privileges tomorrow, I'd say, "Right on;" on the other hand, I'm not going to give it away.

"But I found that being a millionaire constipated me."

But I found that being a millionaire constipated me. I didn't realize at the time that having money created problems in my relationships with people, but when the whistle blew I suddenly realized to what extent it had been fucking up my life.

Money made me even more defensive than I normally am. Relationships are never easy and in some ways it's not quite fair to have money, because that game works best when everybody doesn't have very much. That's why millionaires only hang around with other millionaires. If you hang around ordinary people, there's no way out.

Now, I've got a double act I could pull so people feel sorry for me: "I've had more money than all you people," or "I've lost more money than all you people." But I want to stop making people uncomfortable. That was one of my Ph.D.'s in Paris.

I want a new life; I'm trying to get new content. Part of me says that another way of being on this planet Earth might bring some different satisfactions. I'm not sure what part of this challenge is in my mind and what part is in my gut. Everybody's life changes at every minute, yet our story often stays a bit static. My life has changed a lot and I'm trying to clean up my story to bring it into connection with what is happening. And I'm trying to clean up my happenings to get a better story. This double process is very confusing—and it's the adventure that I'm going through.

A SOCIETY IN TROUBLE

ON THE STREET

Paco   New York, New York

Soft-spoken, Paco spoke English with an accent but was fluent. At times his speech sounded like music; it was clear he had a sensitive ear for the spoken word. Tall and thin, in his late twenties or early thirties, he usually spent his days ranging from one streetcorner to another. This was his second day out of prison and, still somewhat disoriented, he clearly appreciated having somebody interested in hearing him tell what his life was like.

I stayed in Puerto Rico three years, then I came back here. I went to look for work, but I couldn't get a job. I didn't have nothing. So I started thinking, well, amigo, the only thing I have left is to get in a drug program to get welfare. They wouldn't give me welfare unless I was in a program. I wasn't using nothing at that time, and I didn't want to get on a methadone habit, but I had to so I could get welfare. There was no other way.

So I got into the habit of methadone. I was using heroin before, but I kicked it in jail. When I came out I didn't go back to it. They should have given me welfare without being on methadone, 'cause when I got busted again, to kick the methadone habit was forty times worse than kicking a dope habit.

What's happening now is the drinking habit. I used to drink every day. I started drinking just hanging out, 'cause there ain't nothing else to do. There ain't no work for me, so what am I going to do? I just come to the same corner, day every day, never miss a day, just to drink wine with the guys and get into trouble. It's been going on a year.

I've been busted thirty-seven times. I just came out of prison yesterday. They grabbed me on larceny. I was broke and I don't get the checks till the ten and the twenty-five, so I was busted. I was busted, I was hungry, and I was mad, so I went to steal. I stole a car. The owner of the car didn't want to press no charges, but I copped out before I knew that. They offered me sixty days, so I took it 'cause the car was worth $17,000. They would have took it to a grand jury and I didn't want it to go upstairs; I wanted it downstairs. I didn't want nothing published.

"I just come to the same corner, day every day, never miss a day, just to drink wine with the guys and get into trouble."

When I was in prison I had a friend of mine signing my welfare checks and paying the rent so they couldn't throw away my stuff. They throw everything away if I don't pay the rent—my mail, my clothes, my television, my radio—everything. The food money checks went for my friend, but at least he paid my rent and I didn't lose nothing.

Yesterday I got real drunk, first day out. Then I went home. That was it. I wake up early 'cause in jail they wake you at five o'clock. I look at the walls and think, "I got up early today." Nobody's around, but you know everybody's coming, some ten o'clock, some ten-thirty, eleven. Then you stand on the corner and talk. "Nyanh, nyanh," just "what's happening" talk, this and that. Since everybody is always getting busted, almost every day a new person comes that just got out.

If I don't want to be on the corner, I go home and look at television to stay out of trouble in the street, but that's boring, too. I like TV better than the movies if it's in color. The movies isn't together. It's too many weird things. I can see a movie right there, just standing on the corner, 'cause everybody's in drugs, in trouble there. You see action, you see everything.

I got piped, part of what I got from being on that corner, and they broke this thing in my neck. Forty-seven stitches in my head. I was in the hospital two days. It must be a nerve or something wrong with my neck 'cause I keep on twitchin'—twitchin' my neck. And that's why I always lay down my head on my shoulder, so I don't twitch.

When I got piped, that's part of what I got from being on the corner. I had an argument with a guy that messed up some kid. I stabbed him—when I stabbed him I looked at his face and I thought, "Wasn't that something?"—it was a friend of mine. Right guy, wrong friend. I hit him.

I went to the corner and told his friends what happened. This dude—it was a friend of mine—tells me that the guy I had stabbed was a friend of his, too. Later I was just sitting there drunk, drinking, and he came with a machete.

I was a sitting duck. I said, "You stab me with that and I'll kill you." So he put it down and I said, "Well, forget it," and we shook hands.

When I turned my back he took a meter pipe—*boom*. He kept hitting me and I couldn't get up. Every time I tried to get up he hit me again. The cops were coming, so I got up and walked to the hospital, all bloody all over. They told me, "What do you want to do?" I said, "Nothing. Forget about it."

I wouldn't do anything against him 'cause that's the rules the game gives. I'm not a man if I put him in the cross. I'm supposed to be a down dude. I ain't supposed to be afraid of nobody else. Now I've got to get even my own way. But when I get him, he's got to do the same thing for me—shut up and not say nothing. Nobody face no judge.

He's supposed to be a down dude. He did it wrong, anyway, because he hit me when I turned my back to walk away. But that ain't nothing. I'll wait. It's my turn. He's scared. That's why he tried to knife me behind my back.

He sees me. He knows I'm out. He stays away from me. They all know where I come from; I don't play. When I get mad, that's it. I think it's best, 'cause that day, on that corner, they ain't no friends. They ain't no friends, 'cause when I got piped a friend of mine had given him that pipe. And then the same guy went to the hospital to see where I was 'cause the guy that attacked me had said, "I'm gonna kill him 'cause when he comes out, he's gonna kill me." He was going to take out the lines—blood things they put in you—to take care of me. But he didn't find me 'cause I came out of the hospital too soon. And when I came out he was walking with a baseball bat. He thought that I was going to kill him.

After I got out of the hospital I went to the welfare and they told me, "Well, you can't work." So I said, "All right, I can't work," 'cause already I had got in the habit. I knew that all I had to do was turn in that form to get my forty-seven dollars and my rent paid. What was I going to get a job for? I already got hooked to be there on the corner anyway—"Hey, what's happening?"—so I think, well, I could live for free.

But there's nothing happening there because living for free you don't kill time. All you're going to do is just stand there and drink the same thing you drank the day before, and see the same faces, and tell the same person the same thing you told him yesterday, the day before—every other day. You get in trouble with the guys. Everybody drinks, and once they get a head, everybody wants to be tougher than the other guy, not just me.

If I did get a job one of these days, I got to do it someplace else, 'cause everybody that hangs around here knows me. They would hang around my job and they'd mess up my mind by drinking.

I'll work on a job, 'cause a job is better. I don't like to be standing on the corner. I'd like to work on something I like to do to kill time. I went to school for radio and television, but nowadays you can't even get a delivery job hardly.

Jobs I had I tried to keep, but after a while I lose them. I'd be absent and when I go back they say, "Well, we had to get somebody else." Being absent one day. If I like a job, then I won't have to put up with all kinds of "you got to do this, you got to do that." I like a job where I'll be my own boss.

What doesn't happen in the winter happens in the summer, 'cause all these kids come out of school and they take our jobs. They give them more chance than they give us. And nowadays, you get a job—you like the job?—they're going to fire you if you got a record. A lot of jobs call up—pampampam—and they find out you've been arrested, and that's it.

My wife doesn't work. We get along half and half. We ain't in that—that togetherness. Nothing. 'Cause I'm always busted and she don't know how to speak English. She don't know how to walk round here. She's mad that I keep her in the house instead of taking her out and teaching her.

That's another problem I've got, 'cause I'm the only one on welfare. She can't get welfare—she's not in the program—and I don't want her drinking that methadone, too.

I get forty-seven dollars every two weeks and seventy-five dollars to pay the rent for fifteen days. My forty-seven dollars got to get for me and my wife, 'cause I'm supposed to be alone and I'm not. Since I drink every day, I've got to waste on drinking and on eating. I can't get on forty-seven dollars—it don't even get me for two days, and it's going to get for me and her...? That's why I got uptight and I had to steal the car. They've got to give my wife welfare, 'cause that way I might last longer in the street. I won't have to steal.

I've got a lot of problems, 'cause I got kids from other women and I can't feed my kids. I don't see them much. The boy is in New Jersey. That's too far. I can't see the girl, either. They got an injunction.

"If I found a job, I don't think I'd steal....'Cause stolen money don't matter. 'Cause you got it fast, you spend it fast, not like if you get it out of sweating."

I miss my kids once in a while. I just lived with them a short period of time. I know what it is to live with the kids 'cause I've had dogs, so if you miss the dog when it's gone, you miss the kids, too.

I got to get money to see the kids or else they call the cops. The mother of the girl said that I said—which I did not say—that I was going to kill the girl and kill her. I didn't say that. I wasn't even around. I was in jail. I was supposed to go to court after I got a job so I could visit her and give them money, but I couldn't get a job.

When I get uptight, I steal. Doesn't have to be from stores, just—whatever's happening. It goes. Just about every day. It gives me a bother once in a while.

If I found a job, I don't think I'd steal. It would really have to be a dead case for me to steal. I do it 'cause I have to; I don't like to. To get it honestly, you work for it. But if you don't work for it, then you've got to steal for it. And stealing is—hard. Sometimes you steal fifty, sometimes you steal a hundred—and then what? It goes in a day or two. 'Cause stolen money don't matter. 'Cause you got it fast, you spend it fast, not like if you get it out of sweating.

Somebody, my countryman, he say, "Hey, give me five dollars." And if you have stolen money, you'll give him ten. "Oh, well, here, my friend," you'll say. Give him ten. But if you worked for that money, he'll say, "Give me five," and you say, "Well, here's two."

Money is survival, 'cause without money you can't live. Money talks. I wouldn't have been in jail if when I got busted this trip I would have had money. Money seems to be everything in the world. You can't rent the room if you don't got money. You go to a restaurant to eat and tell the guy you ain't got money, he's going to put you in jail.

Once you hang out on that corner, you can never plan for the future. When I find something to do, I can get away from that corner, but when there ain't nothing to do, I just stick to it. If I leave that corner, where am I going to go? To another corner? 'Cause I ain't got nothing to do. From corner to corner. I'm here or on that one or on the other one. That's three corners. I just stand on the corner. What else to do?

I don't think I got a good future. I can never think of the future. I think of right now. The future is too far away. You can't look forward. You just got to wait. Look, when I got busted, there was something I wanted to see on television, a cowboy movie, I think, and I didn't see it. And the time before that, there was a fight on TV and I wanted to see that. And, you know, I saw that—in the prison.

This last time I got busted, I could have told them, "Don't give me no sixty days, man," 'cause I was uptight—I didn't have no money, and I needed for food, and I had my woman to feed. I just figured, man, do something. The car was there, the keys were in the car. I went and got the car. The connection just looked at it, then he backed up. The cops came. That was the main mistake.

225

DISABLED

Darryl   Roanoke Rapids, North Carolina

He had felt strong enough to walk—slowly—downtown to the Carolina Brown Lung Association Office that day, to enjoy the sociable atmosphere and catch up on the latest news. Tall and thin, with warm, friendly eyes and a peaceful manner, he was obviously extremely frail. But he was determined to tell his story in complete detail and paced his breath carefully until all was told.

I worked in the textile mills from 1942 till 1977. I never had any extra time to do anything. I stopped on account of breathing dust in the mill—brown lung.

I was a doffer. I had to blow off the cotton dust. I blew down overhead frames and got them all cleaned up. It was nothin' but dust. Then they put air conditioning in and we'd keep the frames clean, blow 'em off, and keep the dust off them. The dust would get so thick on 'em we had to blow 'em off about three times a day.

I started to hurting—actually I started what you call shortness of breath—funny feelings in your lungs—somewhere back in '68. It didn't bother me enough to affect my work, but I could tell there was something wrong. The doctor sent me

226

for X-rays but kept treating me for a cold. I mailed him my checks, but he never said what it was.

I went to another doctor on emergency and he said, "You know you got a touch of emphysema?" I told my doctor and he told me, "Well, there's not much you can do about that."

I worked a lot of overtime and that was bringing the tightness on. All during '75 I was beginning to hurt real bad. When I'd get home I'd cough a whole lot. Sometimes my wife would sleep in the next room because I'd be coughing so bad. In the mill I'd walk around outside to get away from it, then I'd go back.

In '76 I had to go down under the mill to unjam a broken belt caught in the dust. There's not much circulation down there and something happened—my breath went completely away from me. Momentarily I blacked out. It scared me real bad and I didn't know what to do about it. And the same thing happened again under that mill a little later on.

"I told my wife I was going to ease up and I might just have to walk out, because if I'm going to die one day early, I was not going to die in there."

I connected it to the work but the trouble was nobody else would connect it. I told my wife I was going to ease up and I might just have to walk out, because if I'm going to die one day early, I was not going to die in there. I quit working overtime, then after some months I told my doctor, "I got to stop. I can't work no longer."

My doctor wouldn't recommend that I stop work. He didn't give me no paper or nothing and Social Security wouldn't put my case through for disability.

So I kept on trying to work, but I couldn't do much. Most of the time I'd sit around unhappy. I couldn't stand it no longer and finally the Duke University medical people sent a letter recommending that I stop work. I haven't worked for ten months now.

When I got out of the mill, got out of the dust, I began to breathe a little better. Before I got out, every time I'd walk a block I'd have to stop. After I got out I got to where I could walk a little farther, but I can't never walk fast. You never get to where you can do anything you used to do no more, because that's gone.

When you start doing anything, you're going to get out of breath before you get turned around. You learn to pace yourself. You learn what you can do and what you can't do. In the mornings I have to stop before I get through shaving. Taking a bath, the same way. You get tired. My manner of life is just coming around and setting, going up the street every day. I've got to have fresh air every morning. Long as you're getting around, taking it easy, you get along fair.

Five months ago they operated on me for an ulcer. I had it the whole time I was working, but the last two years, with the breathing and lung problems, it seemed to get worse. When I'd start to do something, I'd get to hassling for breath and then it would worsen and worsen till I just went blank. You talk about fear in somebody—that's real fear.

I hurt the whole summer from the ulcer because I didn't go see a doctor. I didn't have the money. When I did go, the doctor gave me an X-ray and soon as he seen it he told me to get to the hospital. When I came home from the hospital in October I weighed 127 pounds. They built me up a little bit. I lost down to 112 pounds in '68. After you go as long as I did, it don't never come back.

When I put in for disability and stopped working, I had to move. See, I lived in a company house—I had to work for the company fifteen years before I could stay in that house. I couldn't make it down in Rocky Mount, not with no money coming in, and I knew I was welcome to stay in my mother's house up here. She's gone a lot. I talked to my two brothers before I done it to make sure the thing was all right because I didn't want to just push in here.

I have no savings. I didn't make much. You have no insurance when you leave the company. My wife's been sick a long time, too, and I spent a lot of money on her and on me. She don't work because she has epileptic seizures.

I live from one month to the next. I have to borrow money on the next month ever since I got out and I still can't keep up. My disability came through a few months ago and now I get $293 a month. I didn't get but $118 a month Social Security. I still owe some doctors' bills and the hospital bill. I don't know where the money for medication is going to come from because I don't have it.

They were trying to tell me over in the Social Services that they would count me in my mother's household. I said, "Well, you don't expect my mother's going to take care of me. I'm fifty-three years old and I worked thirty-five years. She's seventy-two years old. There ain't no way you can work it like that."

My children can't help me, neither one of them. I don't ask them. It's not their place to take care of me. In other words, I'm making out best I can.

I'm just existing now, that's about all. My life is just a mess. You've got to have money coming in from somewhere. Just because you had stopped work, you don't lose your bills.

I found out that the Brown Lung Association would help you so I come around to talk to them and then I filed charges against the company. We're still waiting on the doctors' reports from Duke. I'm hoping they'll speed them up some so we can get some compensation and I can get all the bills paid off.

"I feel lost all the time. You got time and you can't do nothing, is what it is."

I'd rather be working and have my health than have this stuff, I'll tell you that. I like textile work. Ask the people working in the mill if they like it. They'd like to have a job where they could earn good pay and work dust-free, if they could get it. When you work thirty-five years in a mill you're used to working. You're lost when you're not working. I feel lost all the time. You got time and you can't do nothing, is what it is.

When I first came out I didn't think I'd live a year, to tell you the truth. Before I never worried about things—now you can worry before it starts. You know you're going to get down, but you try to keep that out of your mind. You got to live the best way you can, so that's the way I do.

That dust is terrible, you know. You can tell when it's getting you—the feelings in your lungs tell you. People have been knowing about it for years. So many people are coming out with it. Some of them are worse than me. They keep respirators in the house. You're liable to get dust anywhere in the mill, not only in the real heavy dusty places.

The way I look at it is if they put engineers in there who could figure out how to tie up all the pieces, they could put engineers in there who can figure out how to fix it. It would cost a lot of money, but what's a lot of money worth against some lives?

I'm hopeful that the Brown Lung Association will bring about some real changes here. As a matter of fact, I'm not even worried about it. We're still working at it and we're going to have to keep working at it. They're going to kick about it, but we're going to kick back.

Clear Water   Los Angeles, California

Her face, long straight hair and squash blossom necklaces are all vintage, yet her looks are remarkably timeless. An Indian dancer, her movements and presence do not betray the fact that she is quite ill, nor that she must be nearly sixty years old.

I had X-rays taken after a car accident because I wasn't getting any better. They discovered I have a growth in the middle of my chest. All they can do is drain it, and they're going in to remove what they can, next week or the week after, and then I'll know whether I'll ever be able to work again. I stopped working now two months. I hate it. I'm going absolutely crazy.

After I left high school I had a very, very difficult time trying to get work. I tried all over. They wouldn't hire me. You hear the word Indian, the average person even to this day thinks dumb, drunk and lazy.

I got very disgusted. For a year I bummed around riding freights, drinking and not caring. I had an aunt in Los Angeles who was a model, and I loved her dearly. She was going with an actor who was pretty famous at the time, and one day I showed up very, very drunk, and started cussing him out. He was the wrong person to do that to. He spanked me and for the next three months he and my aunt wouldn't let me drink, put me under a doctor's care and straightened me out. They taught me you don't give up, you just take your other foot and go forward and you try again. My aunt would not help me get a job, they told me that was something that I had to do.

It took about a year, maybe longer to get it into my head, then I never stopped. I started working and started dancing—I had been doing it ever since I was eighteen years old, Indian dancing, Hawaiian and Polynesian—and acting school. I learned to take any kind of job to keep going—digging post holes, driving a dump truck—anything, even welding. I painted sets for a radio and TV station and eventually did some newscasting. And for a while my two older boys and I had a business painting houses.

"They taught me you don't give up, you just take your other foot and go forward and you try again."

Between jobs I'd be out touring with Indian dance troupes around the West. By this time I had a husband and he would be dancing with us. He had a very, very rough time with a drinking problem. We were going to try and get things patched up, then he just fell apart in the middle of a tour.

I raised all fifteen children by myself. The police and welfare wanted to place my children in foster homes. I could sell my house, they said, and get a nice apartment and see two different children each weekend! My children heard all this and they have respected me ever since because I told those two women to clear out and if they ever come back I would shoot their tires.

In the next two years all my kids learned to stand on their own two feet, to work hard and honestly. I sold the house-painting business, but not completely—I still get for use of the name and that. I got into acting and dancing full-time after my last daughter was married. I bought a farm in Grand Falls, Washington, and started raising animals, breeding and selling. I'm building the farm up to where I won't have to go out and really work except for myself.

Now I rehearse Indian dancing for an hour, an hour and a half, then I rest my body. I'm putting three new audition parts together. One is about how it is for a woman to be alone. I would like to put it over how I miss a man, or what a man in the home is really like.

I am trying to put a book together on how the children and I made it through the sad times—how Indian people can make it. I was real fortunate. School was very important to my father, and schooling from old Indians was very important too. We kids went back to Arizona to learn Indian ways and then we were sent back to Washington state, where my mother and dad lived, to get schooling. I raised my children the same way, so they have both educations.

"You have to have the Indian culture very strong, yet you have to slide into a lot of the white man's way, especially when you have to go out to work with them or for them."

You need the Indian ways. You have to have the Indian culture very strong, yet you have to slide into a lot of the white man's way, especially when you have to go out to work with them or for them.

When you're raised on a reservation, if you want to sit all day and do bead work, you can. When Indians that come from the reservation arrive in L.A. it can be hard. There is no discipline. You've got to learn. I think that's where acting comes in a bit; you can bend the twig without breaking it.

Now is the first time I started thinking of myself and the future. I can't plan anything, but I will not go on welfare. If I have to I will do bead work; I can make necklaces, chokers, and these things. I'll survive by honest labor.

Clement   Birmingham, Alabama

Forty-four years old, Clement and his wife both looked closer to sixty. On the floor of their rundown house their son, a thin child who looked much younger than his four years, lay still on an air mattress, gazing at the ceiling. Clement had lost his security guard job and was applying for disability. Sitting gap-toothed, unshaven and unmoving in his big chair, he spoke loudly, his face set into a sour expression.

More than four months ago I was doing security guard work. Read them papers right there and you'll find out for yourself why I stopped without me telling you. I got disabled and I can't work anymore. My legs wouldn't hold up on me and I had shortness of breath. I could work on a sit-down job and not too much walking and standing, but, uh-uh, that's out. You've got to have a college education to have a sit-down job. I have a tenth grade education.

Now, I've got a badge, so I could work on holidays if they called me back. The man that I been working with called me after I left when he needed people to work. But now I found out he pulled a shift by hisself. He knows he could get me and he wouldn't call me.

Why do you think that is?

Your guess is as good as mine, lady. All's about it I say is he got an idea, probably, that he just don't want me to work. Why, I don't know and care less, between me and you.

As far as having anything to really get rid of me, he didn't have nothing down pat. I'm going to put it to you this way. I went and drawed my pennies and if they had right out fired me, there ain't no way in the world that I could draw my unemployment. They held it up at first, but I appealed it and beat it in court.

With me fixing to get this disability now, there ain't no way that I'll be able to work or draw my unemployment, either one. I went over to see about food stamps yesterday and they told me I had to go back to the unemployment office and see when the last time was when I drew my unemployment. I could have told her, but she wouldn't accept it. If I knew why she wouldn't, I could tell you why. I'm not being smart to you.

Friends has helped me out, my brother's helped us out, but no more, and the church has helped us out, but you can go in that kitchen right now and that refrigerator is as bare as that wall is. We got some eggs, we got some bacon, and I got the baby some milk and that's it.

That baby hasn't been hungry, but me and my wife has. As long as that next-door neighbor lives out there, I ain't worried about that baby. She'd help him. She'd give that baby anything he wants. She buys his shoes all the time and we don't like it.

"When your own people turn you down, it gets pretty close to your skin."

When your own people turn you down, it gets pretty close to your skin. I don't know if you've ever had it happen to you or not, but I've called my own brother, who's supposed to be a preacher, on that phone right there and asked him would he bring me some groceries up here. And he told me he's got to feed his family, not mine. And when I asked the man I was working for and told him that I was working only for him, he told me in so many words, "I don't have to feed you if I don't want to." When that happens to you, how would you feel?

Pretty bad.

You answered it.

You work for about twenty years at night shift and it's hard to get over. I watch television and mostly sleep the daytime, and night too, now. I don't drive, my wife don't drive, and she don't got no car. When I do get out, it's mostly downtown shopping or to go to the doctor; that's about it. When I was young I used to hunt and fish and all that, but since I ain't got no way of going and there ain't nobody to go with, what else can you do? My hands are tied.

I spend most of my time in the house. And I'll put it to you this way: my own people don't come to me, so I usually take it from there.

Do you feel bitter about that?

Doesn't bother me. I look at it this way—they know where I live and they know they're welcome anytime they want to come. I don't care whether they do or don't.

At some point when people can't get their groceries, some-times they think about breaking the law to feed themselves. Did you ever think of doing something against the law?

No, I'll back a policeman up anytime, anywhere I see him. When somebody tries to start talking about the policeman, you're getting under my skin too deep, now. I haven't come to the point of doing something against the law, but I'm going to tell you this: when I get to that point, I'll grab hold of a man and ask him can he get me something. And if he tells me he can't, he might as well watch out, because I'm liable to do it. But he can't say I didn't ask him first. I've got a pistol laying right in there I can take and blow my brains out more times than one, but that's the dirty way of getting out of it.

Well, do you want me to tell you what I would really love to get into?

Yes, I do.

Service station work. I did that for about seven years. If the man at the last station I worked at is living, and if they can get the books on it, they can back me up on what I'm fixing to say. When I took over the night shift at that station, it was probably fifty gallons a night. And when I left, it was getting much more, two truckloads every week. That's how much I pulled in. And that's not cars, that's truckdrivers.

"I'd rather work more than anything else in the world. But I just got to the point where I can't make it. I know I look like I'm in as good health as anybody, but the outside don't show what the inside is."

I'm not bragging at all, but if I didn't have a way with people, there ain't no way in the world I could have done that. Your truckdrivers are out there on the road all night, and when they come in to stop, they want somebody to go on at them.

That's what they love and that's what I did. And I had them coming in there.

Running a service station myself would really be what I would want. They've got these self-services in there now and I wouldn't have to do nothing but sit right there and handle money. If I could get one of these self-services, I could make it.

Now as far as really wanting to retire and get this disability, that'd be the last thing I'd want, because I'd rather go to work any day than be sitting around here at the house doing anything else. If I live another two months I'll be forty-five years old, and I'd rather work than anything else in the world. But I just got to the point where I can't make it. I know I look like I'm in as good health as anybody, but the outside don't show you what the inside is.

Anything else you want to say?

Nothing, really, I don't know what this is for besides the book. I know there's some catch to it besides that.

No, there isn't. That's it, no catch. Thank you very much.

THREE WELFARE MOTHERS

Estelle   Santa Fe, New Mexico

It was graduation day in the job-training program just off the Paseo de Peralta, the loop that surrounds historic Santa Fe. Unlike her fellow students, who were all celebrating happily, twenty-two year old Estelle seemed withdrawn. Uncomfortable in her pregnancy and reluctant to talk at first, with encouragement she revealed her anger at the program that had not taught her any job skills, her despair in being thrust back into seeking fast food and cashiering jobs, and her anxiety about ever finding her way out of her difficult situation.

I had been working in a restaurant and lost the job all of a sudden. I've done mostly cashiering and waitressing, fast food things, since I was fifteen. I'm twenty-two now. I've about had it in restaurants already. You get tired of picking up after people. Checking gets boring and just doing the same kind of thing for so long gets tiring.

I got into this job-training program six weeks ago. I was interested in a receptionist job or being a secretary or beautician, something like that, but I'm trained for none of these things. I took typing while I was in high school, but I haven't touched a typewriter since, so I don't think I could still type.

I thought this program was going to train me for something, but it's not what I thought it was. It's interviewing skills and resume writing and getting people their high school equivalency. But I graduated from high school. Most of the things we covered here I already knew. I asked the director several times, "What am I doing here?" I did pick up a few things, but I did lose a lot of time. What we covered really shouldn't have taken six weeks. Now I'm back where I started from.

I'm pregnant at the moment and I'm currently in the situation where I'm going to have to find a job quick or get some type of income. I guess I'm going to have to settle for something I really don't want. There are classes in town where they teach the skills I want to learn, but they're night classes and I can't go nights because of my three year old.

I applied for a grant for picking up training at the business college through this job-training program. It's more or less guaranteed. My intentions were getting into the business college right away, but it can't happen that way. I don't find out about it till next month. I'm afraid classes might start in three months, which is going to leave me in worse of a situation because the baby's due in six months and I know me; usually my health isn't so hot. So I've got to work right away, just in case.

I'm on welfare, which isn't much, not enough to pay my rent and food. I don't get any money for my daughter from her father. If I can't pay something on time, my father will do that for me, but I have to pay him back. I wouldn't ask him to give me something.

"I don't understand how they could have one set of guidelines when everybody's situation is different— everybody's got different bills and different problems."

I think I've about covered all the agencies here that are supposed to help people. What I find strange is that they don't sit down and listen to a person's situation. It's like they really don't care. They have their set of rules and if you don't qualify within those rules, it's too bad. I don't understand how they could have one set of guidelines when everybody's situation is

different—everybody's got different bills and different problems. It doesn't make any sense. And if you're on welfare,
most of the other agencies don't really do anything for you.
They refer you back to the same people, back to where you
started from. It kind of makes you wonder why they're there. I
wish I could get a job so I could just leave all this behind, but
they don't give you a chance to get ahead.

I spend most of my time alone. It's not really by choice. It's
not so hard meeting people, it's just I seem to run into the
wrong ones. So I end up letting them go on and I just go back to
where I started from. I've been running in circles.

I spend too much time worrying about where I'm headed, all
my problems. I try not to think about them, but I can't help it.
I've got a lot of bills I'm trying to figure out what to do about. I
worry about my health. I've been told constantly it's all in my
head, but to me it's there.

It gets lonely sometimes, but when I'm feeling depressed and
worried usually there's somebody I can talk to that helps. I'll
ask somebody to come over and talk to me, just to keep my
mind off things, just to have somebody to talk to. They really
can't do anything for me—it's up to me to do something—but I
don't like to be with myself when I'm worried. I may be making
somebody else miserable, but I don't trust myself when I'm
alone. I haven't done anything stupid recently, but I have done
a few things when I was younger and, I don't know—I don't
trust myself sometimes. Sometimes I feel life isn't worth living
and a long time ago I tried to end my life, but now I've got my
daughter to think about.

Right now what I really need is money. I have to do
something to find myself a better job, or I'll just keep on doing
the same thing. If I had my way, I wouldn't work, but it's
probably just that I have to work that I don't care for it. I just
want to get married and I don't want any problems. I think I
would like a part-time job if I got married because I get nervous
with myself staying at home.

I'm always thinking about leaving Santa Fe, but I can't just
get up and leave. I've never really been anywhere in the first
place; I wouldn't know where to go. All my family's here and I
keep in close touch with them.

I don't take trips. I like to stay in town. Maybe just go to a
park or something, just not do anything at all. I like to dance

and, I don't know, go out somewhere and not do anything. I read or watch TV a little bit once in a while. I don't have time. It's so hard for me to crawl out of bed in the morning, I just go to bed early. I figure this can't go on forever; it's got to change some time. It's probably just one of those things I've got to cross.

Alice   New York, New York

She was on her way to a job interview at Burger King and had stopped in at the neighborhood community center for some encouragement and moral support. Tall, well-groomed and graceful, Alice had the kind of physical appearance that could give her a decided edge in jobseeking. But she was so shy and uncomfortable speaking to strangers, one could easily understand her apprehension about having to face the fast food manager and tell him why she should be given the job.

Two years ago I was a nurse's aide. Then I had a problem with my leg and couldn't go to work, so I had to leave. When my leg got well I wanted to work again, but they didn't have no more jobs for me over there. I tried to get a job doing something, but jobs was hard to find. They say they'll call you and they never call you. You have to keep waiting and waiting. I don't have any training for any other kind of work. I know how to do little things, but not typing or nothing like that.

I have two kids but my mother takes care of one. My mother raised her up since she was a baby. I take care of my son. He's three. I want to put him in a day care center if I get a job. I'm tired of staying and doing nothing.

I get some money for the baby from welfare, but it ain't enough. It's enough just to pay rent and my food—that's it—but I want money to buy other things. I'm going to get off welfare as soon as I get me a good job because I want to work. When you're used to working and you stop working and can't do nothing with your time, it's boring. Just taking care of kids is boring. You'd do anything—volunteer work—but I would want to get money for work.

I'm not that happy, because I don't have nothing to spend my time with, just the baby. I don't associate with people that much. I stay around my house or go to my mother's house. I go to parties sometimes; I like active people.

I have some friends, but I don't go around them because most of them work. I feel a little left out. I'm the quiet type. I don't even hardly talk to them—just a couple of words. They ask me to go out sometimes with them and I always say no. Oh, I go sometimes, but....If I was working, I'd socialize with people. You meet people and get to know different people, not the same friends all the time.

"I feel like time is wasting. I'm getting older and ain't got no job, can't get no job, ain't doing nothing."

I feel like time is wasting. I'm getting older and ain't got no job, can't get no job, ain't doing nothing. I want to do something beneficial with my time like go back to night school or something. I went to the eleventh grade. I want to make something out of my life.

I can sing a little and I made a tape. There was this guy, he was a group singer, and he told me that he was going to give the tape to one of the bosses so I could sing with them. But I said no because they'd be on the road all the time traveling, and I don't want to leave my son. I like being around my son and I don't want to go nowhere far if he can't go.

I think the reason it's so hard for me to find work is because I haven't got a good education. But partly it's because work is hard to find. A lot of people don't have jobs. They be waiting in line all day long and when they get there they still don't have a job. Everybody can do something, right? The government could give out more jobs.

My biggest worry is financial-wise. I don't worry that much, though. I don't let myself think too hard about it—that I'm down and can't get work. Always I'm hoping I'll find a job.

If I had something to look up to, I'd feel pretty hopeful. I want a career. If you have that, you have something to look forward to. But if you don't have that, you'll be looking day after day, knowing that you might not get nothing. It's hard like that.

I hope the future will be better than this for my son. I'm going to encourage him to finish school, of course. He's only three, but I've been teaching him to read because I want him to be something in life. I think he's got a pretty good chance. He can talk good and he's pretty smart. To be three and reading already...

I love kids a lot—not just my own. I like taking care of them. I'd like to work in a day care center or go into nursing, working with children. It'll take a long time.

They probably won't give me back the job I had because when I went back after my leg got well there wasn't no more jobs there. If I get something I like better than that, I'll take it. I like to work. I don't like staying in one spot, just doing nothing. It makes you feel lonely or sad. I can't explain it, but I like to be active.

Rowena   New Orleans, Louisiana

She was a young woman whose huge eyes brimmed with tears and occasionally overflowed as she told her story. Rowena harbored the dream of becoming a journalist, though she had little formal education, had been a hooker and spent most of her time in a daily battle to keep herself and her children alive. Even though the office of the local community center where she sat was heated, she kept her overcoat clutched about her in an attempt to keep her malnourished body warm.

You really have to go through life scrounging and grabbing and begging, and this is just how it is. I'm twenty-six and have experience in a whole lot of things in life. I have been writing enough things to write my own book. I just hope the teachers at the Neighborhood Coalition have the sense to put me in the journalists' program. I've already written in their newspaper about what happened when I was thrown out of my house because I complained about rats biting me and my kids, and how people passing in the street took my furniture.

Surviving is my biggest worry, trying to survive just to the next day. I'm looking for a house now. This is something that the city let happen and I feel that the mayor is not going to do anything to put a stop to it. Our mayor and other city officials own a lot of the ghetto housing.

I never went back to my mother. She doesn't have her own self. I remember when I lost my home and stuff another time, I called my mother and she said, "Well, what can I do? I hardly have for myself."

I have worked the streets. I worked the French Quarter in the clubs as a waitress, and when someone there asks for me to go out and they'll give me such and such amount of money, I have accepted it. I never went on a street corner to solicit. I was only arrested once, but I never served any time. I never bring it up when I apply for a job because I don't think I done anything to be ashamed of.

When you deal around people like that you get introduced to drugs. They say this will ease the hurt. I did take some pills and a needle. It didn't help the hurt because I started using it as a crutch. In the morning I would feel that I would need it to try to look at the world at a different angle.

I get money from welfare, Social Security and food stamps. The biggest part of my money goes on my kids' education. I had to take them out of public schools because there were times when I couldn't get them there. They didn't have things to go to school in. I put them in this little parochial school where I have to pay them about eighty-five to ninety-five dollars a month to try and help get them the education I missed. At least they will be able to express themselves.

You can imagine how hard I have it—having three kids and trying to pay tuition for school and ten dollars a week for transportation to get 'em backwards and forwards. Times that we had to walk to school because I didn't have the bus fare. I have to beg or fret for people to take me places.

Times that I have my food stamps to go to the grocery, but I don't have a way to carry the food back, so I have to keep my stamps and wait and wait and wait, buying sardines and rice at the neighborhood store to last me. I pay a dollar and something to buy two pounds of rice in the nearby store when for another four dollars I can buy twenty-five pounds of rice at the big store that can last me a whole month. I can't economize because I don't have the transportation.

"Times that I have my food stamps to go to the grocery, but I don't have a way to carry the food back, so I have to keep my stamps and wait and wait and wait, buying sardines and rice at the neighborhood store to last me."

My kids have a father who don't help with the support. He wouldn't give them nothing because he feels anything he does, I would benefit from it. He would rather go be locked up than help with the support. He would rather go be locked up than help me because I wouldn't stay with him. He was shooting and hitting me down. We used to go to court every week. When we were together, it was poverty, but he worked two jobs and I had things. I even had a hair dryer. Now I walk around with my head wet and this is when I get colds. I'm always cold all the time, and the kids don't have warm things. It's disgusting.

He told me he would leave me if I wouldn't have another child. I felt that all my life I had been given ultimatums and I never had the chance to do anything I really wanted to, and I left. I had gotten to the point where I wanted this education more than anything. I have a friend who wants me to, too, and he's trying to throw me an anchor. But it hurts me to go to school and see how people have things. Like this coat, these shoes ain't even mine. You look at your TV and you get tired of it because it's the same thing—you see how people are moving theirself up in life.

People have given me gifts. My neighbor, she's an older woman, she had given me a lot of things. You just get tired of people giving you and you don't have nothing to give to nobody else. Twice I have tried to take my life.

I asked my daughters—they are nine and eleven—"What would you say if I remarried?" How would you feel if your daughters tell you they would leave the house to go live with their grandmother? I feel they should acknowledge the way I'm scuffling to try to make things easier. The little nice things we do have they break, and it's discouraging. It really hurts.

But you know, I think I'd rather go ahead on myself. Men are trying to make it really their own self, looking for the same thing I am. They take advantage of the kindness thinking it stupidity or weakness. A long time ago my boy's father and I lived in a house together. I put his name on the rent receipt and he got the law to throw me and my kids out of the house. And it was even my furniture.

Now I know something's going on different in my body, 'cause I have to draw myself out of bed—I don't have the strength. I'm drinking Geritol and I still haven't built myself up. I have a deficiency, and I don't have an appetite too much. You start worrying about different things, and you get sick. I get tired of crying. People just ask me how I feel and it just hurts.

"You get tired of people giving you and you don't have nothing to give nobody else."

I need dental work and I really need a check-up, but Medicare don't cover me enough. They told me I can only go to the doctor one visit without paying. I was having trouble with my stomach, and I really thought it might be ulcers because my stomach was feeling like I might have acid, like bubbles. But if all I'm allowed is one visit I want to save it for a time when I really need it. But this is why a whole lot of people in the world are walking around sick.

The only thing that keeps me going is I believe in God. My parents brought us up that way. My kids are baptized. I don't send them to church like I should 'cause I don't have the bus fare. My kids have to go to church in their school clothes 'cause they don't have dress-up clothes.

I keep thinking—they got people in worse fixes than me. I have a neighbor, a heavy-set woman, who was on the bus and fell. She twisted her ankle. She had a job and called them and told them what happened and they told her they'd have to give her job to someone else. And she has three kids. So I gave her thirty dollars worth of my food stamps until she can see her way. Well, she didn't have anything to eat and now she do, and I just hope the Lord will be able to keep her.

"There have been times when I've had to steal, to take, but it don't really pay, because if I do anything to hurt another person, it all come back bad to me after a time. So I try not to do it..."

There have been times when I've had to steal, to take, but it really don't pay, because if I do anything to hurt another person, it all come back bad to me after a time. So I try not to do it, because I feel that what I'm going through, I'm going through—so leave it.

To survive you got to have faith in youself and the Lord. These are the only two people that you should believe in—yourself and the Lord. Because the Lord gives with His life. I wouldn't be alive today if it weren't for the Lord. You got to be strong and if someone throws you an anchor, you take that anchor and carry it. It's like the Lord carry that cross. An anchor is just a little weight, carry it too.

AN ALCOHOLIC

Burt   Seattle, Washington

*He was a dark, long and lanky man in his late thirties who had
lost his job as a coach and business education teacher when a
school bond issue failed. Sitting in his parents' home, where he
had been forced to live until his financial situation improved,
he seemed to be making a strong effort to be on his best
behavior. His funereal tones matched his sad face.*

I lost my job a year and a half ago after teaching eleven or
twelve years. I'm a basketball coach and a business education
teacher in high school. My school had a levy failure—the
schools in Washington are subsidized by the community in
which they vote a bond, and if the bond fails, the first thing
that goes in the program are vocational subjects like business
courses, and extracurricular activities like I was teaching.
After the levy I applied for a job and never got one—so I started
fooling around for a while and drinking too much.

In fact, I drank rather heavily for the last year and was
picked up twice for drunk driving. I could have gotten ninety
days in jail, but luckily the judge gave me a suspended
sentence. I had to join AA and my driver's license was
suspended for a year. Fifty percent of the jobs I'm interested in
I don't interview for because it's a requirement to have a car.

247

The middle of the year is also a bad time for a teacher to look for work and substitute teaching is difficult to get in the Seattle area. There's such a surplus of teachers—and getting a job as a substitute goes on a seniority basis. I haven't taught in the district before so I may be twenty-fifth on the list even though I have so many more years of experience than the others. It's frustrating because all the women who don't want to teach—who want to stay at home and teach once or twice a week, *if* it doesn't interfere with the bridge club—they get the jobs substituting because they've been in the district longer.

All day I'm usually beatin' the streets, through the employment bureau and interviews. I may have as many as ten to fifteen interviews a week, primarily associated with the CETA program. Maybe I'm wasting my time and maybe I'm not. I've got to get a job sooner or later. It has been difficult for me because my confidence is down. I thought I had quite a bit of confidence. I never even had to ask for jobs—they always came to me. I was always comfortable speaking to groups—now all of a sudden when I have to speak to one person it's difficult.

I'd like to be working even if it's not in education, and I have tried hard for the last four months to change my profession, but all the jobs I apply for...I'm either overqualified or underqualified. I'd like something like bookkeeping, but they want engineers in the Seattle area and I'm not trained in that. On the CETA jobs I apply for, they think there's something definitely wrong if I'm willing to take a $600 a month job, when they know I've made $1400 a month as a teacher. They come out and tell me that they think I'll only stay for two or three days. I'd like to work as a janitor—but they look at it in the same way, too—this guy is a real dud and screwed up with prison, with courts or with drugs—something's really wrong with him. It's hard to convince them. I have even gone as far as being hired as a babysitter for young children at the daycare center. It's frustrating.

Also there are jobs that I'm qualified for, but they want women and minorities—blacks and Indians. They don't come out and tell you, but you know what's going on. I applied for a job with a credit bureau; the woman didn't tell me during the interview, but at the end she told me they wanted a woman. I'm not against women's lib or anything, but I think they've gone to the extreme. I'm not radical enough or I would go to the discrimination court.

I'm not happy and I think part of it is being unemployed. I'm living with my parents and have very guilty feelings about it. Here's a thirty-eight year old man with a fairly decent education who had things going pretty well for him in life, and all of a sudden he can't cope with a few problems.

My mother has been helping me financially—they've been fantastic parents all my life, but I feel pretty bad about it. I've gone through my savings. There were certain unemployment benefits I was entitled to for a while, but I didn't even know about them so I didn't apply in time.

My father is with the railroad and travels a lot and my mother is a very old woman who doesn't speak anymore, so it's important for me to get out evenings. I go to AA meetings every night—it gives me an opportunity to speak to people, although I'm very shy. I kind of fade into the wallpaper, but I enjoy it—it makes life worthwhile. But I do feel bad if I come home late, around midnight or so, because I wake up my parents or they hear me when I go to the bathroom. It's pretty bad.

"Also, I can't take a woman out because I don't have a driver's license. I do have the car ready, though, in case I get the opportunity to get some woman out—or in case I want to go out, get drunk and tell the whole world to get blasted."

I was married for three years but we've gone our our separate ways. A lot of my problems were drinking-related. I think we were getting along better when I was drinking because of my guilt. I'd do these extra things for her, call her "sweetheart" or "honey," and take out the garbage twice—even when it wasn't necessary. When I wasn't drinking I said, "Hell, let her take the garbage out. I'm being a good boy." Maybe I was too immature. I'm not sure.

I haven't been back in the area in a long time so I don't have many friends, and all the people I knew are married or leading heir own lives. The first time I went to a dance it was quite an

adjustment for me. It was probably the first dance since I'd
been to college. I kind of felt out of place. And I was sober
because I wasn't even allowed to have a beer. I didn't know
any of the people, the men or the women, so I couldn't ask a
man who some lady was. I guess I have to get more confidence
to just go up to someone and say, "You want to dance?" Also I
can't take a woman out because I don't have a driver's license.
I do have the car ready, though, in case I get the opportunity to
get some woman out—or in case I want to go out, get drunk,
drive and tell the whole world to get blasted!

---

*"I miss having a mission in life and even if I had a
million dollars I would still want to have a job."*

I miss having a mission in life and even if I had a million
dollars I would still want to have a job. I'd be beating the
streets every day, like I am now. But having a job would not be
enough for me to lick the drinking problem—I've got to want to
do it. I've got to picture myself doing it. If it will lead me to a
fulfilling life, I'll probably try to control it, but if it is just being
sober and not being happy—then I'll pull the plug out of the
jug again.

If I were to get a job, I wouldn't tell them about the drinking
or the arrests. It's none of their business—they're my debts
and I'm paying them. Maybe if I were hired by someone who is
in AA himself, or maybe after I'm working for a little while—
but not in the beginning.

Only 70 percent of the people in the program stay sober until
they die, and there are millions of people out there who have
drinking problems that don't know it. I lived for five years
before I thought I had become tight or anything. I go to
meetings and enjoy it—it makes my life worthwhile. If that's
going to be the factor in my fulfillment, I hope someday I can
choose it. But I'm not at that point yet and I never will be if the
world doesn't change. All of us need help, but I guess I don't
need a finger anymore—I need a hand.

STRUGGLING FOR JUSTICE

Connie Panzarino   Hempstead, New York

Ordinarily confined to a wheelchair because of her disability, Connie had broken her leg and was immensely frustrated at being restricted to bed. But, taking a steady stream of phone calls, sorting through her files for newspaper clippings, dramatizing her story with animation and conviction, this committed organizer and advocate of the rights of the disabled in her late twenties kept up a lively pace that would have exhausted any non-disabled person in good health.

I was born with a condition called amyotonia congenita, a neuromuscular disorder. It's sort of like muscular dystrophy, but I don't get progressively worse. I've never walked and I need total care—I need to be toileted, bathed, turned in bed, and so on. I can't do anything like that for myself.

When I graduated from college in 1969, it was very hard to find a job. People were worried about how I would go to the bathroom and things like that. Finally, after two years, I found a job as a caseworker in Medicaid with the Department of Social Services. I was overqualified for my job, which was a less challenging office job, because I didn't have a driver's license so I couldn't do field work, but I would have been eligible for a supervisor's position after a while. And even the caseworker job was hard enough to get to begin with.

I had applied to the Department of Social Services and had been turned down. I get really angry when I'm discriminated against because I've never swallowed the lie that disabled people are not equal to someone else or that they have to take a second-class position, so I went to the dean of my college and said, "Look, you're graduating disabled people like myself and there's no way for us to get jobs. All I'm asking for is a chance to try."

Both the dean and the president of the university had gone to school with the commissioner of Social Services, so he called the president and the president talked to the commissioner. The commissioner had no idea that I was being discriminated against and he blew his top to the personnel director. That led to their taking me on as a provisional.

I was only bringing home about a hundred dollars a week, but I moved close to my job and saved money on transportation. The transportation problem is part of why a lot of disabled people don't work. You can't take public transportation, and if you are unable to drive, the rates for special transportation are outrageous.

I shared an apartment with a woman who had the same disability as mine. She wasn't working, so she was collecting Social Security, Welfare, Medicaid, and was being provided with a full-time aide. I supplemented the aide's salary by paying her room and board and she took care of both of us.

Then about a year later my roommate wanted to move and live with someone else. We were going through a lot of aide changes and she felt it would be better if we lived separately. It was very hard for the aide to take care of two of us, anyway.

That left me without an attendant. Now, I had never been on medical assistance—Medicaid, Social Security, anything. My education had been funded by the State Vocational Rehabilitation Service, but that was the only assistance I had had. I was earning almost $10,000 and I was paying taxes, my own transportation expenses, my own medical expenses—everything—but I could not afford to pay an attendant to take care of me. I didn't get any extra exemptions and my salary just wasn't enough to cover rent and everything else.

So I applied in my own office for medical assistance. They said I was eligible financially because I didn't have enough income to pay an attendant, but by law, if I was working full-time, I was not disabled, so I was not eligible.

My office sent me to Social Security to apply for SSI, but Social Security said the same thing. Then I went to Welfare. They said, "If you're not disabled, then you're a worker whose income is not sufficient to meet her working expenses, which include the aide. But if one of your working costs is that you need an aide, then you're disabled by our standards and we no longer help the disabled." Welfare even told me that if I quit work, they still wouldn't help me because they knew I was able to work!

So here I was in a *Catch 22* situation. I was really frantic and started calling every politician I could think of. Every senator and every other politican that I called assured me that he was going to do something, then two or three hours later he'd phone me back and say, "You're right. There's nothing we can do. That is the law."

"They said I was eligible financially because I didn't have enough income to pay an attendant, but by law, if I was working full-time, I was not disabled, so I was not eligible...So here I was in a Catch 22 *situation."*

I was without an aide for the whole summer. I had tried giving room and board in exchange for care, but I couldn't get anyone reliable. All I got were people who were ineligible for welfare because they were alcoholics or had some other problem. The last two weeks I worked a blind friend of mine took care of me, but it was hard and she couldn't drive me anywhere. I fell one day. There were three nights when I didn't go to bed at all; I was in a chair all night then went to work the next day.

My health was giving way and I knew I was going to have to resign, but before doing that I was going to form an action and not leave work at the end of the day. I worked for Social Services and they were responsible for the dilemma I was in. If I had no aide at home, I was just going to dump it on them, get the media there, and say, "Well, I can't go home—there's no one home to take care of me."

The detective at Social Services said that if I did that, they would have to put me into a locked mental ward because only there could I get care. They were threatening me and I chickened out. Sometimes I regret it, but I didn't have the emotional stability at the time to put myself through that. I was so tired and run down.

After about a week and a half I became really ill and I had to stay home. The doctor went through the roof and said, "Look, your condition is worse because you haven't had adequate care." He wrote a statement that I was unable to work at that point and within twenty-four hours they had an aide in there, I was on Medicaid, I was on SSI and everything was just great. Within a week of having an attendant's care, I was fully capable of going back to work. But I wasn't allowed to work. If I did, I would lose my disability status and my attendant. And that's where it stands.

My problem has been going on now for three years and I am suing the federal government, New York State and Nassau County on the basis that the law violates constitutionality and due process. In other words, someone with the exact same physical disability would get benefits that I wouldn't get simply because I would be working. The problem is, Legal Aid is very understaffed and there's not enough money to fight the case, so it hasn't gotten into court yet.

I've also gone through the media. I called the newspapers and I've been on TV. Representative Mario Biaggi, who is not even my congressman, has drawn up a bill in Congress that would change the situation, but it has been held up in committee for two years. We went down to Washington this year to lobby and got about twenty-six sponsors, but the bill will probably remain in committee for another twenty years.

Some New York State legislators offered to sponsor a bill that would suspend the definition of disability for me alone so I could have my attendant paid by the state, but I refused. I just wasn't that selfish. I said, "My publicity has gone far enough that people know about the situation the disabled are in. I'm not going to take advantage of it and be allowed to work while nobody else is."

There are a lot of disabled people receiving disability benefits who can work. I know hundreds who can on Long Island alone. In my opinion, every disabled person can work some, and certainly all of us who have been rehabilitated can.

I don't think that the American public knows this, but the law affects literally millions of people. With me it's the attendant. Someone else may need a kidney machine two or three times a week, which costs $200 or $300 a treatment. The government will pay $500 or $600 a week for their life care and give them money for rent and food and everything else, but if they work and earn over a certain amount, everything gets cut off. It's the same for people with mental illness who have to see a psychiatrist, say, twice a week, which could cost over $100. The government will pay that if they don't work, but if they work full-time, they will not. It's really absurd. And disabled people find it hard to take a stand and say they can work, because if they do, the state has a legal right to cut off all their aid.

It keeps the disabled dependent. It's fulfilling society's old stereotype of the disabled as objects to be taken care of rather than as people. It's following the same reasoning society uses to tuck them away in institutions where they don't have equal status.

"The state has spent over $20,000 on my education through Vocational Rehabilitation and they're spending a hell of a lot more on me now than they would be if Congress would change the law and permit me to work."

But the sheer cost of keeping me dependent is absurd. The state has spent over $20,000 on my education through Vocational Rehabilitation and they're spending a hell of a lot more on me now than they would be if Congress would change the law and permit me to work.

They're paying for my attendant, my doctor bills, prescriptions, room and board and everything else. They would even pay $1400 to $1500 or more a month for me to live in a nursing home. A nursing home is bad enough for old people, but there

255

are a lot of younger disabled people who are intelligent and able to be responsible for themselves living in institutions. The government is spending twice as much if not more than they would be if they were giving me partial assistance by just paying for my attendant while I work. Why is it willing to spend twice or three times as much money as it needs to keep the disabled dependent?

And I want to make money because part of working is earning your keep and contributing towards your own care. I like to work. I really enjoy it and I have a lot to contribute. I need the contact with people and I need the productivity. I miss going to the office and I miss the people. To get my Medicaid I had to go to the same office I had worked in and it just tore me apart. Some of the workers there made a complete turnaround and were very cold to me. In their eyes what I did was wrong. Since I knew I wasn't eligible, why did I get all those newspapers to publicize my case? Why did I embarrass the whole town and everyone else? If they would put themselves in my situation, they would realize why, but that's too threatening to them. They don't ever want to be on the other side of the fence.

Then my family went through a whole thing too. They wanted to know why I was just sitting back and not working. It was like—"You're on welfare now? You quit your job?"

My parents raised me to have a normal person's expectations. And it is important to feel that you're responsible for yourself. If you don't feel that way and your parents reach a point where they can't take care of you when they're older, then what do you do?—you find an institution. It's much better to take care of yourself before that.

I said to them, "No, I didn't quit my job," but it was hard to explain. I wasn't a good model for my sister, who has the same disability. She is in college now and is going to have the same problem. My parents' reaction was wrong because I am fighting back, but it was hard for them to understand how I could go on welfare.

When I stopped working it was emotionally devastating. I had been in therapy for my own personal growth, and I was doing very well; I was nearing the end of the therapy process. But I was so upset by all that happened that I'm still in therapy and it still bothers me. It makes me very angry and very depressed at times. I have self-anger too, and once in a while that crops up.

For the first year after I stopped working I didn't know what to do with myself. I had no purpose. I was watching "The Late, Late, Late Show" which I had never done, because I was having trouble sleeping. Once I fell asleep, I didn't want to get up because there was nothing to get up for. So I started to work toward changing the law and I helped Ron Kovic with his book, *Born On The Fourth of July*.

I also became an activist in Long Island. I do have a lot of knowledge—I know how welfare and Medicaid work and how to deal with people. My phone rings all the time. I work with disabled organizations and with people who need information and are having trouble getting it, or who just need somebody to talk to. I give a lot of help because I've been hurt and there are many other disabled people who are in bad positions.

I moved to California a little while ago to try to find a job because California is the only state that has assumed financial responsibility for disabled people who are working. But I couldn't find a job and I couldn't get attendants who were qualified, so I moved back and started graduate school in art therapy. If I could do private therapy, I might be able to afford to pay the aides myself. That's what I'm aiming for, but I'm hoping that my case is won or the law is changed by the time I'm finished. Otherwise I'm going to be in the same position I'm in now, only with an advanced degree.

At least school provides some structure to my life and I'm with people. That's the biggest thing. It's hard to meet people. I found there's a lot more prejudice in the East than on the West Coast. In California, I was able to go to a bar where a band played and people asked me to dance. It was really great. Here people stare and feel uncomfortable. I go anyway, but it's not really a place to meet people. School opens up an opportunity for me, but I'm going to be thirty and I can't really have a close friendship with eighteen and nineteen year olds, so it's still difficult. I would much rather be working.

The whole experience has changed me. I think if I could work off the books, I would. I've never been a dishonest person in my life, but after all this, if I happened to get an extra check, I would never tell them. I'm living on a shoestring.

257

I think it's going to take a hell of a lot of work to get the law changed. People are going to have to get knocked over the head. There's more involved than just apathy. I don't think the congressmen and senators and all these other people have just forgotten about our situation; I think they're really freaked by what disability means. Look at how they treat disabled veterans, and there has been a lot of publicity about that. Some of the hospital conditions have improved as a result of the publicity, but not by too much.

I don't understand it. We've had a disabled president, but no one thinks about that. Anyone can become disabled, so it's a weird kind of prejudice. In the name of compassion they put you in this box and say, "Well, you're safer there so you have to stay there," rather than let you fulfill your potential and really contribute.

I feel that I have a lot of intelligence and creativity and that I'm a person. It happens that I'm physically dependent, but everybody is dependent to some degree. I've become a very angry person as a result of fighting the laws. I guess that part of my anger comes from the fact that my personal future is hinged on what society at large does. You can say your happiness is within you, but when you're oppressed, that's very difficult, and I do consider myself oppressed. I was very optimistic when I was fifteen years old and working for changes. Now I'm not really optimistic, but I'm not defeated, either; I'm determined.

Since Connie told her story the New York State law has been changed to allow attendant care for disabled, but only for the amount of time the attendant spends on the disabled person's job—not for the aide's services at night and at home. Local offices are not adept at administering the new law, however, and the disabled still find it difficult to work. Connie is planning to build a rural facility at which disabled people can learn to live autonomously.

Mafundi   Birmingham, Alabama

To set off the drama of his appearance—dark skin against his impeccably tailored white suit—Mafundi had great personal style and poise. Years in prison, the nature of the police in Birmingham and Mafundi's personal commitment to justice had thrust him into a position of public advocacy against abuses in the criminal justice system which, in turn, had led him into more trouble with the law. In the local television studio where he had agreed to meet for this story, he described how he had been harassed out of his business and, at age thirty-eight, was again facing charges for what he claimed was another set-up. Still, his faith in the ability of humans to create a better world remained steadfast.

During my senior year in high school I was sent to prison for, allegedly, robbery. I didn't do it, no way. Ever since I was a kid I had been having problems with the Birmingham Police Department. During the late fifties and early sixties there was a lot of racial strife and we were having problems here with the Ku Klux Klan. Unfortunately I was living in the community known as Dynamite Hill, where at least forty homes were dynamited. It was no secret that the Klan was involved in the Birmingham Police Department.

The police would call us kids to the car and say, "Stick your head in the car."

You'd put your head in the car and they'd ask you, "Do you like my wife?"

"No," you'd say.

He'd go to beat you and say, "Why you don't like my wife?"

You'd say, "Yeah, yeah, I like her."

He'd say, "What you doin' likin' my wife?"

This brutality and harassment by the police was just a way of life. I didn't like it and I don't like it and I always would speak out about it. I got the image or reputation of being "bad." To me "bad" implies that you don't stay in your place; you rock the boat; you don't quite conform to what you ought to.

The police began to focus attention on me and next thing I knew I was sentenced to prison for thirteen years for something I didn't do. In prison I never got into a fight, never had anything to do with drugs or contraband or homosexual activities, but I was never even given parole consideration because they said I didn't have the right attitude. I had to do the whole thirteen years.

When I came out at the age of thirty-three, just five years ago, I could have wanted to get some hand grenades and machine guns. It would have been easy for me to have been like one of those people who gets up there in the Howard Johnson and goes berserk and shoots people. If I had been freed after the first two or three years, I probably would have, too, because I was really bitter at that point. I had never stolen anything in my life—I had never even thought about doing it. I was in my prime, I had a lot of ambition, and I could have gone in any direction I wanted to. I could probably have made it at anything I chose away from Birmingham. And they took me and put me in prison because of my attitude. It was really vicious.

But while I was in prison, we began to organize about prisoners who beat other prisoners for the pleasure of the guards—like slaves whose slavemasters would be pitting one slave against another and taking bets on them—and about other things. We established educational classes and taught basic education—reading, writing, arithmetic and law—to black and white prisoners, both. Prisons try to prevent black-white solidarity and promote racism, and we tried to break through that.

I began to think about how I got to be where I was and I saw the need to try to keep what happened to me from happening to other youngsters. Looking at the cause, not the effect, I felt that maybe things happened the way they did because the public wasn't involved, and that a more informed public would try to provide some corrective measures.

When I came out of prison, I had scholarships and offers to go to law school. They told me that if I could pass the entrance exams, I could progress just as fast as I could consume information. But I'm not interested in individual achievement. As I look at it, you can't live apart in society; you can't deal only with individuals.

I saw the answer as being an educational process to involve the public in the issues, and my contribution as helping people alleviate the problems. It turned out to be a mission, or whatever you want to call it.

We had organized IFA. Inmates For Action, in prison, and when I came out we organized the African People's Survival Committee, the Committee for Prisoner Support in Birmingham and a defense committee for seven prisoners charged with murdering two prison guards, one of whom is on Death Row. The Committee for Prisoner Support and the defense committee were directed toward dealing with the problems of prisoners and their families, to help them with legal counseling and services, transportation back and forth to prisons, and collecting items to send to prisons.

Primarily these committees were to try to sensitize the families and the public to what actually happens in prison, because a lot of people don't understand the mentality that governs law enforcement agencies. It's so unbelievable that people tend to say, "No, these things couldn't happen." A lot of things have been revealed about how the FBI and the CIA work, though, and the Sheriff's Department, your neighborhood police—it's the same mechanism. The law enforcement mentality is the same wherever you go.

At an early age I had recognized that the problem of injustice is with the Police Department because they enforce the doctrine to keep blacks and other minorities oppressed in this country; they are the front line that sets the criminal justice system into motion. We began to document that initial contact. We interviewed people who had had contact with the police; I used to carry a camera to document police beating up on people. We would document corruption and graft and the ways used to defame people, and we discussed the issues at the City Council and at various public programs and forums.

Then we got a lot of flak. I had established my own gift shop after coming back out into society, and the police began to come around to the shop and harass people, harass me, and create an atmosphere where people didn't want to be. I had to close the shop.

We continued documenting their brutality and harassment, and they kept on giving us flak, until they framed me. History is repeating itself and a few weeks ago I was convicted of threatening police with a deadly weapon and of possession of marijuana.

Everybody knows I don't smoke, I don't drink, I don't even eat pork—I don't have any of the vices. I'm kidded by lots of my associates, who say I'm either a preacher or a Muslim, but it came from doing a self-analysis in prison. Since I didn't enjoy the habits I had picked up, I decided I shouldn't indulge in them.

At my trial three different police officers on three different occasions said that I pulled a loaded pistol and pointed it at them while they had a pistol in their hand—and neither of us fired a shot. Their story is that I just turned my back and ran from them and that they finally took the pistol out of my hand.

The evidence technician first testified the same thing in court that he had written in the field reports: that the pistol they had didn't have any fingerprints on it. When they saw how ridiculous it was to allegedly take a pistol out of a person's hand and find no fingerprints, they reversed themselves. The next day he testified that he didn't check it.

The judge said he was going to hold an investigation for probation, but I entered an appeal anyway. It was such a gross injustice. Funny thing about it is that the judge that tried me and I had been on a couple forums together.

Black and white police officers who respect me have said, "Mafundi, I know what's happening and I'm not part of it. Just because I'm on the force, it doesn't mean that I go along with it."

I tell them, "You're supposed to uphold the law and you're telling me this? You're telling the wrong people."

People in the Internal Affairs Department, which is supposed to regulate the police, have said they knew I was framed, but there is nothing to do about it because I just don't have the power of the police. One of them told me that he had investigated the case and that the police lied.

"You're in Internal Affairs," I said, "You're telling us we don't need civilian review, that the police can police their affairs. That's what your office is for—to investigate the police."

He said, "I know I should have taken a stand, but I just don't have the guts. I don't have the financial security to do it."

That hurt me. I really sympathized with that man—anybody that can stand in your face and without any shame tell you he doesn't have the guts to take a stand.

When people come to me in private and say things they won't say in their official position, where they have credibility and could probably bring about change, that tends to make me disrespect them. I can't really describe my feeling about people who will acknowledge that a great injustice is happening but are not moved to try to do anything about it.

That has been the history of this country. The silent majority doesn't exactly take an active part in the social injustice, and they use that to rationalize themselves by saying, "Well, I didn't do it." But I think that by being passive and silent, they're really condoning what is happening.

To a man everybody who has said anything about the Freedom Rides, about the bombing of the Birmingham Sixteenth Street Baptist Church, and about all the other bombings in Birmingham has always implicated the Birmingham Police Department. But when Chambliss was prosecuted for the church bombing, there was no mention of any police involvement. Just before going to bomb the Sixteenth Street Baptist Church, the Ku Klux Klan met at the house of a man who has always supported the police and is now sitting in the legislature. But they can't prosecute this man because they gained their information on him through illegal electronic devices.

"I can't really describe my feeling about people who will acknowledge that a great injustice is happening but are not moved to try to do anything about it."

When they bring somebody to court, the Birmingham Police Department is "clean," but things have been going on for years in the Police Department and the government, and the people involved just move up into the higher echelons. Even the FBI said that the reason they hadn't turned their files over to state officials was because the Klan was involved in the Birmingham Police Department.

Not that the FBI is so clean, either. Through the Freedom of Information Act I found a memo from the FBI asking the prosecutor to prosecute me. One D.A. wrote a memo to his supervisor asking if he could understand why the FBI would be interested in trying to tell him how to do his job; it wasn't a federal case.

I'm looking to speak about things like this all the time. I have drawn a lot of flak from the Police Department, and this is why I have not been working the last year or two. I have really just been trying to stay alive. I feel pretty strong in terms of having to accept what has to be accepted and deal with it accordingly. A lot of people support me—family, friends. Even if there was nobody, I kind of live within myself anyway, so that wouldn't cause great distress.

I don't believe in working for the sake of work, but I go all out at whatever I'm doing. If work is meaningful and you feel good about it, if you're not being kicked around or suffering a whole lot of indignities, then any type of work can be good, whether it's sweeping streets or pruning trees.

Even if a person was paying me $1 million, I don't think I could accept a job in which I couldn't have some input, where my ideas couldn't be respected. I couldn't stay on a do-nothing job. A lot of people have jobs where they don't have any duties, especially blacks. They're just there because you're supposed to have some blacks there. I don't see how people could live like that. I could not deal with it. That's crazy.

"Even if a person was paying me $1 million, I don't think I could accept a job in which I couldn't have some input, where my ideas couldn't be respected."

I do things as they happen and I don't structure my time in any organized way. I just can't. I find something mechanical about it when you can program your feelings a week in advance. That's what's involved, because anything I do, my feelings and emotions have to be involved in it.

When I first came home I applied to the telephone company for a job. I had fifty questions correct out of fifty-five on the test and the lady was very impressed. I had every indication that I was assured of a good position.

Then it got around to the question of black employment. She was trying to sell the company and said, "Don't you think South Central Bell is making a lot of progress with black employees?"

I said, "Well, no, if you've got 2500 people working and 25 of them are black in a city that is 52 percent black, that's not really my idea of progress." And I told her about the type of jobs the blacks had—as operators, secretaries, and things like that—not in higher management.

"Now, I knew when I was talking to her that what I said was going to deprive me of that job, but I have to live with myself."

She said, "Well, OK, we'll give you a call." It usually took three or four weeks before they'd send a letter, but in a couple of days they said they couldn't use me. Ha, ha.

Now, I knew when I was talking to her that what I said was going to deprive me of that job, but I have to live with myself. I feel that to lie takes something from me. If I can't express my true feelings and opinions about things, I don't feel that the job is worth it.

Bitterness and frustration come about when you feel powerless and when you feel that you have to accept whatever is being rained down on you. Once you determine that you can do something, then you expend your energies and efforts trying to do it, rather than wallowing in bitterness and frustration. That's why I wasn't bitter about the experience after I left prison. I came back to do what I had to do, even though I knew it could be dangerous.

I don't live in fear—not for myself and not for my wife and kids. You can't live like that. Physical harm is not the worst thing that could happen: the worst thing that could happen to my kids would be if they had to go through the same type of social injustice that my father and I have been going through. If something happened to them while they were doing something they felt was right, I don't think it would worry me as much as it would for them to live on to be two hundred years old and never do anything right.

It's just unfortunate that people have to suffer, go to prison, and get beat up to bring a small measure of conscience and enlightenment to others. I think it is grossly unfair and very vicious to punish someone for their ideas. That's the cornerstone of democracy and what this nation was founded on—the right to protest and petition the government. America is the one country that doesn't even recognize the fact that they have political prisoners; they deny it. You've got human rights to take care of right here in Birmingham and throughout the country.

People don't like to accept that race is still the Number One problem in this country. The issue of racism is not in vogue now; still, the police don't beat up or shoot anybody but blacks. The black people are scared and the white people just let the police go, so you don't get anything done.

You have the image of the New South and Birmingham designated an All-American city, but things are really worse than they were before. Being more subtle, they are really more vicious. The people talk about crime, but the problem isn't crime. Talking about it as though it were just takes your attention away from the real issue.

There is so much to do and so little time to do it in. I'm not trying to create better conditions for my children or their children; I feel things are supposed to change in my lifetime. I think things could change overnight. All people have to do is make up their minds and come up with the moral guts to effect the change. People can wake up any morning and say, "Things are bad and they can be changed," but I think they are saying, "Yeah, we know things are bad, but what can you do about it? It has always been this way, so we'll just let it go."

I have found that basically people are the same, it's just that they are pressure-molded into different morals and into role-playing. So I go on with what I have to do and just say it like it is and deal with it the way it is. I don't try to be popular, just to be correct. As long as I feel I'm in harmony with the truth, then I'm satisfied.

My future is tied up with the future of the people, not only in this country, but throughout the world. An individual is just as insignificant as a grain of sand on the desert. I've got a lot of faith in people and I think ultimately they are going to begin to act correctly and do right things. You can't keep a people forever under the boot. At one point in history people are going to stand up and demand a change and provide some corrective measures. It's one of the things that sustains me, because I have seen it work.

FINDING ONESELF

TRADITIONAL AND NOT SO TRADITIONAL PLAYERS OF TRADITIONAL ROLES

Jill   Brooklyn, New York

*The welcome was as warm as the loving banter Jill carried on
with her three-year-old son. A tall, sweet-smiling woman of
twenty-eight, Jill had willingly left her schoolteacher's job
when Eric was born, ready to give her all as a mother during
her child's early years. Adept at dividing her attention, she
was able to keep a watchful eye on Eric, answer all his questions patiently, while keeping a coherent train of thought
going in her description of what her life was like.*

I always pictured children in my life and figured that once I
did become a mother I would be home, certainly for a while. I
didn't have any great goals. I thought that being a mother was
more than any kind of goal career-wise. Since I've had Eric—
he's three now—I've considered going back to work part-time a
number of times, but I don't believe I would make enough
money to warrant my having a babysitter or full-time housekeeper for him. And I think my teaching licenses have expired.

"Look at this—hey."

Eric, be careful. It was never like Paul said, "You have to
work." And it was never a question of feeling that my money
contributed to the household was really a necessity. Not that

267

Paul makes a fortune working for the city, but his job has periodic increases and lots of benefits. Financially we're doing fine. We've always managed OK and we don't deny ourselves that much.

I can't envision not working for the rest of my life, but I might not go back to work for another four or five years. We're starting to think about having another child, so if I start the whole cycle again, then I would want to be home. And I tell you, I really enjoy being with Eric.

I might have dreams or fantasies about being a lawyer. I've even thought about possibly starting a daycare center or forming a play group with a few other mothers for young children, three to four year olds because they're so cute at that age. I used to talk about that with a friend, but we've lost contact.

"Mommy, I have this now."

He's chewing on the thing from the teabag. I do things now just for enjoyment. I learned how to do pottery on the wheel. I joined the Y and took modern dance and slimnastics. I took stained glass and made a window. I put Eric in a creative movement class for kids that met at the same time as my own class. They taught them coordination and balance. It was nice.

Going to the Y was a concrete thing to do for a few hours a day, two days a week. Knowing I had a place to be at a certain time gave me a sense of structure in terms of filling up time. Then I started going only one day a week because I joined a mothers' discussion group, a rap group that was very good. This past session I haven't been going to the Y at all.

It's never been that I didn't have enough to do. When Eric's not in nursery school, I go places with him or go over to somebody's house. It sounds dull, but it's really not. I see a lot of a friend who just had a baby. There are some days when I don't do anything more exciting than walk on Flatbush Avenue and look in store windows, but I really don't feel discontent with my life.

There was a period of time when I didn't have too many friends to get together with, and during the winter, especially, you can feel very isolated and closed in if you don't have people to see. The days Eric goes to nursery school I'll go out for groceries or see a friend, but if I don't have any shopping or anything special to do in the house, I do need something to do for those couple of hours. I can sit down and read a book or watch TV, but I like being with people. To tell you the truth, I don't really have too many friends; I have a lot of acquaintances. Some of my friends have moved away from Brooklyn and I see them two or three times a year.

Sometimes I feel productive and sometimes I don't. Maybe I would feel more productive if I had a salary, but the things I'm doing for Eric are very valuable, and the things I do for the house, the basic necessities like laundry and cleaning up a little and shopping for food, are things that have to be done. If I don't do them, who else will? So it's productive in its own way.

"There are times when I get my full appreciation, but often I feel Paul doesn't realize what you have to go through being with a child all the time."

I think what I do is as valid as a regular job. It's not a pressure job—like right now I'm sitting and talking, and there are times when I just idle—sit down and watch a soap opera or something—but taking care of a child is a job. It's a job that takes patience and love and caring. I feel like I'm on duty.

There are times when I get my full appreciation, but often I feel Paul doesn't realize what you have to go through being with a child all the time. Eric is an easy child, basically, and 95 percent of the time he's good, but he can get cranky and bratty and occasionally I get annoyed and feel I could pull every hair out of my head.

"Mom, look the way that I did."

Very good. Paul comes home and if I didn't make him a good supper, or if he sees that the garbage wasn't taken out or that something else which is part of my household duties wasn't done he'll say, "Well, listen, I work from nine to five. What did you do all day?"

269

Maybe Paul thinks that it's very easy compared to what he does, but there are times when I feel I could be more appreciated for what I do do. Sometimes it seems like we fight every day, but there is fighting in every marriage and I think that if I were working, we'd just fight about other things. Fighting is healthy to a degree because you get out your frustrations.

Maybe we fight now partially because Paul sees the strength and confidence in me too much and he doesn't like it. I used to be much more of a clinging, possessive, insecure little girl and now he sees that I'm more of a woman who can stand on her own, fight back to a certain degree, and demand certain rights and freedoms. I'm not so sure he always likes that, but we have a good marriage and all in all, most of the time things are fine.

"Look at me."

I see. What kind of toy are you? A little doll. I think a lot about age, about getting older and what have I really accomplished in my twenty-eight years. I used to feel that I hadn't accomplished a heck of a lot. I wanted to go to Europe and to have...

"Mom, can I have this?"

We're talking, so you have to be quiet. My younger sister was always the more independent one and she's had, maybe, a more glamorous life. She's been to Europe a few times and right now she's working in Manhattan in this very fancy make-up place where Cher and all these movie stars come in. It may sound more prestigious, but I'm starting to learn that the basic thing is not so much outward appearances or status symbols as it is personal satisfaction and being content within yourself. I pretty much am, so I don't think that I'm really less accomplished than somebody else.

"There are times when I feel that the walls are caving in and when I wonder how I am going to make it through the day, but I do."

I feel much freer than I ever did before. I think I've matured a lot since I've had Eric. I get into moods once in a while where I can get kind of lonely or depressed, and when that happens I just wait. Think, ponder. Sometimes cry, sometimes yell. It comes and goes.

I think it's normal and that everybody should have those times because it makes you learn more about yourself, makes you analyze things and work them out in your own life. There are times when I feel that the walls are caving in and when I wonder how I am going to make it through the day, but I do. I've done it for twenty-eight years and I probably can do it for another twenty-eight years.

Larry   Seattle, Washington

In a friend's living room overlooking a beautiful garden, with a splendid view of Lake Washington and the mountains beyond, Larry relaxed and enjoyed the rare respite from his househusband and childtending chores. An extroverted, talkative man in his late thirties, with angular features and broad shoulders, he laughed and laughed at himself and at how he had gotten caught up in domestic routines. Yet underlying his good humor was tension. And he admitted that he was not going to be feeling entirely at ease about himself until he was established in the new government job in emergency planning he was relieved to have secured.

I'm nearly thirty-nine and I have a sixteen year old son and a nineteen month old daughter. As you can well imagine, the nineteen month old daughter was a pleasant surprise.

I had been a stockbroker, then I got out of that materialistic world. I could bring the business in and go out and sell the concepts, but I'm a very responsible type person and when people would invest their money in something on my advice and the stock would go down, even knowing that the advice I got was mostly from the company and people invest at their own risk didn't make me feel better. I felt like a darned hypocrite, so I decided that until I could get over that feeling, I would have to withdraw from the business.

I started getting involved in trying to help Asian-Americans. I was raised with the idea that you have to do twice as much as the white person because you're Chinese, so I had volunteered for Vietnam and volunteered for combat because I wanted to prove that I was an American. When I came back from Vietnam and couldn't buy a house in certain areas of Seattle, and couldn't get a job certain places because I was Chinese, that really ticked me off. I had bought it all for years then decided I would not be silent any more. But nobody was listening. They were cutting programs and removing all hope. So I became a campaign worker for Carter to get involved in the public sector and make them want to do things for people.

Now, my wife is one of the top administrators in the Seattle school district and she's also working on her doctorate. She's extremely competent and capable and was cruising along with her career when she became pregnant. I was undergoing this change from materialism and I freely admitted I was raised a sexist and a racist. I didn't know exactly what I wanted to do just then, so I figured, "Why take her out when I'm still in this mental state of flux? This is a great opportunity for me to withdraw and let her go for it because she is already on her way."

"You know, this househusband bit—it's all fine and it sounds good, but it's a bunch of crap."

So while my wife is pursuing her career, I'm staying at home to take care of Roseanne. This has been going on for almost two years now. I'm not working in the sense of drawing a salary from an employer, but I'm contributing to the family as far as cleaning the house, washing the dishes, cooking—in fact, I'm a better cook than my wife is.

I will be employed shortly in a government job doing planning for emergencies. I'm looking forward to it. You know, this househusband bit—it's all fine and it sounds good, but it's a bunch of crap. I can truly say that I know where women are coming from when they say they can't stand staying at home. Watching the child is crazy—it really is—because my schedule is conformed to hers.

I wake up at eight o'clock, feed her, then we run around or I might take her out for a walk. She goes to sleep at 10:30 and wakes up at 12:30. That 10:30 to 12:30 I sleep too, which is dumb—two hours of sleeping.

OK, so I sleep, then from 12:30 to 3:30 I've fed her and taken her out for another walk or wherever we're going, and at 3:30 she has to hit the rack again. And I sleep again from 3:30 to 5:30. Well, not really, because I'm preparing dinner by this time. At 5:30 everybody else comes home and they have her and they love her until about 8:30, 9:00, somewhere in there. Then she goes to sleep.

Now I'm sitting there watching TV because there's nothing else to do. Even when I don't have to watch Roseanne, I can't sleep. I watch TV till three or four o'clock in the morning then I go to sleep and wake up at eight to do this thing all over again. My hours are so weird, it's unbelievable.

Our agreement was that I would stay home for three years, because by that time Roseanne would be pre-nursery and she'd be having some concept of what Dad and Mom and brother are doing. Now I have the feeling that "Jeez, I'm deserting her by taking this job—I didn't fulfill my obligations."

I love Roseanne dearly and I spoil her and take her out for rides and everything else, but then I sit there and say to myself, "Am I competent?" I'm scared to death about this job. I do not know if I can handle it because I have started to have doubts about myself.

I think it's from having been out of the job market. I don't think I'll have a problem after I'm working; I have an uncertainty that has developed over these last twenty-two months. I'm sort of on shaky ground.

I'm convinced I wouldn't feel this way about the new job if I had been working all along because your momentum is gathered and all you're doing is moving from one area of interest to another at the same speed. This way, I'll be going at it from a dead start without any training, catching up with an accelerated program that's moving. It's like going out and running a marathon without doing any running for two years.

I'm concerned, but I can hide the feeling very well. They were all very pleased with me in the interview and they don't know I'm scared. I don't want them to know—they'll never know.

I have a mental need to be working now. When I talk to my liberal friends, they say, "Hey, Larry, you still taking care of your daughter? Gee, that's great." When I talk to my conservative friends, they ask, "Larry, what are you doing these days?" "Well, I'm staying home, taking care of my daughter." "Oh."

Now what do I say? Now what do they say?

I need a certain amount of support to be a househusband. I know where I can get my strokes and where I can't. I know when to tell people what I'm doing and when not to. It's a psychological thing that you have to be aware of.

I'm the type of person that needs limelight, anyway. Give me a compliment and I'm good for ten miles. So when I start running into mental blocks, I have to withdraw and sometimes it is very difficult. I just want to get in there and do a job, work hard, and forget about a lot of things.

My family has been raised to believe that work is the only thing that can get us ahead. Education and work—they're synonymous. Here I am, sitting at home, and I see my brothers working, my sister working—everybody working but me. I keep on saying I'm doing a very important function for my family, but nevertheless it's part of what makes me feel very uncomfortable.

My mother has never said anything. My sister has never said anything. But when you've been raised a certain way since you were knee high to a grasshopper and all of a sudden you ignore all these rules that you were raised with, it's got to wear at you.

In some ways though, this transition into a househusband was not really as hard for me as it would be for other people. The Chinese are very macho, but they also have a strong respect for the matriarch of the family. All the women in my family are very successful and there was no problem with me accepting that my wife is having a successful career, where I think that it would have a chafing effect upon a lot of males who are not brought up this way. When I say there was no problem, I don't want to say that I've never thought of it, because I have.

This time I've spent not working has succeeded in helping me get my mind together to a degree. I get on an idealistic horse and I start charging forward to try to save the world, if there is a cause. I don't know why I'm that way, but I do try to do as much good for people as I can. Now I've reached the point where, yes, I'll continue to do as much good for people as I can, but also remember that there's one other person that I'd better start doing something for—*ich*—me. I don't intend to be selfish about it, though I try to be. Still, I will always wind up helping somebody out.

Fay   New York, New York

In the large, comfortably furnished apartment she shared with her husband and children, Fay offered early morning coffee with the relaxed hospitality of a woman of leisure. But a briefcase stuffed with papers lay ready for the jampacked schedule of meetings in city government offices in store for this dynamic woman in her late forties, an active community affairs volunteer. Gesturing animatedly, dark hair framing features lighted by warm concern and enthusiasm, she chose anecdotes that would create a cohesive story and peppered them with humor. Not one for small talk, she kept her main focus in mind and drew a picture that had clear purpose.

Though I am not working at a job for pay, I spend most of my time at what I consider a full-time occupation. It may not be obvious, but it developed in a natural way from what I did when I had young children.

When my children were about three and four, I found that my time was directed toward everybody else's life. My day started out at six o'clock because somebody got up early, and somebody had breakfast, and somebody else had breakfast.

Then one went off to nursery school but the other one didn't. I picked up the first one for lunch and Robert would come home for lunch in order to spend a little time with them. So he would appear when one had to go back to school, and so it went.

Robert never got home before eight-thirty and the children were starved by six o'clock, so they would eat. By the time I was finished bathing and feeding the children, Robert was home for dinner and I would race in for that. Then the children would want some dessert because it's time to have Daddy home. I would divide up. I would have my meal with them because I felt that they were entitled to a family dinner. But then again, so was Robert. So my problem then became a weight problem as well, because I would sit down and have dinner with the children and then I would sit down and have dinner with Robert, the same way I had done it at lunch.

"Aren't you eating?" Robert would say.

"Well, I had some lunch with the kids."

"Aw, come on."

"Well, all right. I'll have a muffin with you."

Here I was doing this routine, and for part of my life I would be eternally fat because eating is such a social thing in my family. Not only was my time terrible, but when you look in the mirror and see your image ballooning out...! I gained about twenty-five pounds. I tried to figure out how I was ever going to control that and it was a laugh.

It was a most difficult adjustment period that lasted until both of the children had a full day in school. But maybe those years that were hardest for me in another way were for the best. I found I had to build a framework of my time and create a productive, separate life of my own. I followed my natural bent, let myself become actively involved in community issues, and through twenty years of volunteer commitment have helped develop the field of Community Affairs.

When I look back, I'm glad I did it the way I did it because it had a very good bonus effect on both of the children. They had to develop an understanding that I had to have a value placed upon my life and my time, that I couldn't be 100 percent available as I had been in the early years. The overstood child—"overstood" as opposed to "understood"—thinks, "My mother will do everything and anything for me. Her time is worthless. She does everything according to Daddy's time or my time." My activities were not an utter shock to my children because I had used free time to be independent and I hadn't always been home seven days a week. I didn't make a tremendous break, but I did make a conscious decision.

I didn't want to take a job because if you leave children with a maid or housekeeper, of necessity you have to set up guidelines and rules, and I didn't believe in structuring up heavy rules. We had our own structure, but we had a warm bill of rights relationship with the children and I wanted to be in a position to move around with the rules. Without a job and with a flexible schedule I was free to build my time into theirs when it was needed. There were moments when a child came home from school and I knew that by being there I had made a difference.

Robert was very supportive of my need to be involved outside the family. He is a doctor and the ultimate doctor—100 percent committed. There's no question that his commitment to his vocation spurred me to take on extensive outside activities. We toyed with the idea of my going to law school and he told me to do it if it was what I wanted. But had I set myself up in a profession, I would have been as committed as he was. And when he was free, I'd be working, when I was free, he would be working, and what-have-you. We wanted to at least travel together and be together when we could.

I started doing a fair amount of work trying to improve the public school system—not coming to school with cookies and going to PTA meetings, but going to Albany to see that schools were built in areas where they had not been built in many years, that facilities needed by the community were provided in new schools, and to see that special teachers were not moved from the elementary school system.

Then I began to participate in the Police Department's youth organization, holding meetings and reacting to whatever they initiated. When they established a Community Affairs Division, I was invited to talk to the new Commissioner and that began a long relationship with the Police Department.

I told them I would be happy to offer my honest opinion, but that I was not interested in telling them what they might want to hear. I've done a lot of speaking and forums for them and worked on many community-police problems. When it seemed that there might even be a possibility that my relationship would turn into some kind of a job, I made it clear that I couldn't be bought. How could I continue? If I were paid by them, I would then be co-opted. So I told the Police Department that I would continue to give them my opinion and they wouldn't be able to fire me because I wouldn't let them hire me.

The Police Department describes me as a longtime observer, sometimes as a consultant on community affairs. I have always made it clear that I'm not paid as a consultant. I don't hold a brief for the whole Police Department and I'm aware of the major problems that do exist. I cringe and cry when I see the police with their clubs and their night sticks hitting kids who have just run out onto the field at the end of the World Series and I know that we have a century to go before we're going to straighten out the problems. But if I've been productive at all and have helped in any catalytic manner, it has been somewhat rewarding for me.

About five years back I was appointed by the borough president to the community board. It was a sort of surprise because community boards are very political and that's a good little appointment to give to somebody who has carried a lot of petitions or done a lot of work for a candidate. The one thing I've avoided is belonging to any political clubs. I had never met the borough president, but I got the appointment because he had received a number of letters recommending me. I have labored long hours at that vineyard.

I have toyed with the idea of running for office and have had serious offers a number of times. I have made the decision that I would never run for anything because I find the whole process demeaning. I have seen very good people destroyed by the process—standing on street corners, begging for a vote, shaking hands, calling people and saying, "I've done a lot of good, won't you vote for me? I'm really a wonderful person," writing up brochures describing their accomplishments in which they were really stretching things, because no accomplishment is really individual.

I must admit, if there were a fusion ticket and in a Walter Mitty type of dream all the parties, knowing that I was the best candidate, would come together in a public mandate and say, "We want Fay because she'd really be terrific,"—I could get up there and do it. But by no means am I going to play the game.

When I was working crazy-busy on a problem helping starving kindergarten children living in welfare hotels, long after my own children were out of the public schools, some people said to me, "Why on earth are you so busy with all this? Your children will never be in that school." They were people who live in a "social world" and give much more to charity than I'll ever be able to afford to give—maybe a million dollars a year—and that takes care of their conscience. They could not understand why I couldn't send a contribution or write a letter—why I had to be seeing these things all the time.

I tried to explain that our children are going to inherit the problem. That five year old who is coming to kindergarten with eyes glazed from starvation is going to be what people describe as an animal, a savage, if we allow it to go on. When our children are grown up, it will be that child out there in the streets with a knife. Somewhere along the line it has to be visually seen to be corrected. You just can't be alienated from it and do it.

"I've always had the feeling that one person makes a difference, which I learned from the example my father set."

I've always had the feeling that one person makes a difference, which I learned from the example my father set. If you have that kind of background, you feel that way about yourself. I guess my philosophy is expressed by this little story.

A town in a very well-known Italian grape-growing area was being incorporated as a city and the president was coming. The people built a town hall and planned a big wine celebration for the day of the great event. For weeks all the famous families who had the famous vineyards would be bringing barrels of their wine and pouring them into a great big barrel set up in the middle of the town.

The members of one family said to each other, "It's such a good crop this year. We are going to make so much money. The barrel is so large, they will not know if we pour water in." So

279

they went to the big barrel late at night and poured water in. And nobody saw.

The day of the great event the president announced that the town had been established as a city of Italy. The townspeople said, "You will have the first glass of wine." They put the wine glass to the spigot, turned on the spigot, and water poured out. All the families had decided their contribution wouldn't make any difference at all, and all had poured in water. I always hope that wine will come out of the spigot when I do something.

The things I do are not so easy to explain and there are times when I feel very frustrated, but I figure in the long run if you produce something people understand, then you change their concept of what a gainful and productive person is. My family has a good sense of humor about what I do. And the best thing Robert said to me was on our twenty-third anniversary. "You know, I swear I have never been bored for a second," he said. "When I come home I never know whether you're going to tell me you were in a coal mine or in a sewer or out with the President. It's what I look forward to."

He's fully of the impression that if I wanted to be president of the United States, I'd do it. He's very supportive and he would never feel threatened about being second and that sort of thing because he has a tremendous amount of security in what he's doing.

The things I do led me into paths on which the horizons are unlimited. Still, people who feel that a woman must have a job and be economically independent from her husband do exert pressure on me, and yes, it gets to me every once in a while. One of my very closest friends is the senior executive vice-president of the largest public relations firm in the world and head of the Women's Forum this year. My other good friend is a senior partner in a major law firm. We love each other and adore each other. But I'm always hearing from my first friend, "Why can't you be gainfully employed so that you could participate in my Forum?" She was telling me that it would be very hard for her to bring me in because the other women would say, "Well, let's look at her curriculum vitae. I'm earning $150,000 a year and I don't want anybody who isn't my peer." The members worked very hard to reach that parity and that style. They're interested in knowing that you're earning a man's salary, as they put it.

My other very good friend and I had one little run-in, a social thing involving who was going to pick up a cake. "Look, you can't ask me to do it," she said, "my time is so much more valuable than yours."

I told her, "No person can ever say that to another person. My time is as valuable to me as your time is to you. Don't ever feel that way—not about me or about your maid or about the garbage collector. Five minutes in my life is worth ten hours of yours because I can't live ten hours of yours; I can only live five minutes of mine. If you're saying you get paid a greater hourly rate than someone else, that's true, but the value of your time is no greater than the value of mine."

I'm a firm believer in alternatives. You know, I see life from five feet five in the air and I can be walking next to someone who's five feet tall, and what we see in life is totally different. And I have no interest in changing that. I like my way, for me.

"You know, I see life from five feet five in the air and I can be walking next to someone who's five feet tall, and what we see in life is totally different."

And I'm a reassessor. I consciously trained myself to think in terms of how I will change—not just allow it to happen, but to think about it. I never look with fear toward the changes of the future—when a new phase is happening I always look at it as though it's going to have to be marvelous—that I'm going to love that next stage.

One more thing helps me to be anticipatory toward the future. Ten years ago I was very sick in the hospital for months. The different diagnoses they were considering were all very serious, some potentially fatal. I thought I might never see my children grow up and never have all the other things that I want. It looked as though it was really all over. It was a terrible problem, but I faced it in my head at the time.

Very few people get that kind of an opportunity; I call it an opportunity because I lived. It took a year out of my life and that year made a difference in my thinking. I just don't ever not appreciate everything that's happening and I always look forward to the future because I have the feeling that it could be cut off.

I don't yell in supermarket lines if someone gets ahead of me. If I don't get a seat in the bus, it really doesn't make that kind of a difference to me any more. That year gave me a lot of patience. And maybe that's what you need to do what I'm doing, because I suspect I need more patience than my friend with the terrific job who needs only to announce herself in order to get where she wants to go a lot faster than I can.

Richard   New Orleans, Louisiana

It had been almost a year since Richard had lost his teaching job. He had accompanied his lover to an out-of-town conference and not having a part to play in the professional activities had intensified his feelings of being isolated with nothing to do. Trim, twenty-nine and well-dressed he was ready for action, but with none coming his way, he was rather morose and tearful as he told his story.

I was an elementary school teacher until nine months ago and was laid off because of the declining student enrollment. They'd been closing schools in the past few years and laying off people according to reverse seniority, and I was at the bottom. In three years they've laid off about a hundred and fifty teachers.

It was my first and only job right out of college, so this is the first time I've ever really been unemployed. When I first found out that I was going to be laid off I had sort of mixed feelings about it. In the beginning I was happy because I was ready to do something else and it forced me to go find some other field. But I was also very scared because it was "a secure job." The salary was OK, I loved the vacations, and most of the time I liked the teaching too.

The first few months I didn't feel unemployed at all because my lover and I and another friend were talking about opening a restaurant. I was really excited about it, but after doing research on it—talking to contractors and people like that—we decided not to do it. An awful lot of money was involved and it was just too risky a proposition to go into.

After that I started thinking about what I wanted to do. I was really confused. I didn't know how to go out and look for a job; I didn't know how to go out and take an interview, really. The interview I had had for teaching was so long ago, when I was fresh out of college.

I even looked at some ads for some counseling agencies. I did subscribe to one and paid them $500. It turned out to be a waste of time and money, and I was kind of sorry about that. They said that I would meet with people from business and learn about different kinds of jobs, have mock interviews and be rated on them. They prepared my resume and told me they would send it out to whichever personnel departments they thought would be appropriate, but they never did it. I bugged the guy at the agency about it a few times and finally I just got very annoyed about it. But nothing happened.

"I sleep a lot, sometimes ten or eleven hours a day, not because I'm tired or anything, just to pass the time."

Then I started to read classified ads and learn as much as I could about getting a job. I applied to companies, banks and corporations. It's pretty haphazard. I spend maybe three or four days, depending on how I feel, going out, and filling out applications, leaving resumes, even going to agencies, though I get really tired of filling out their applications and hearing, "Oh, we don't have anything for someone with your background."

When I started looking I had certain standards set. Of course, now I've lowered them. I've considered driving a cab, because I can drive, so at least it's something people couldn't tell me I don't have experience for. Even lowering my standards considerably, I'm still having difficulty getting a job. It has gotten really depressing and lately I just started crying like a baby; I didn't know what to do. Nothing has come out of anything I have done so far.

When I'm not looking for a job, I just try to pass the time as best I can. I'd like to sleep later, but I don't really stay up that late, so I'm usually up around nine o'clock. I sleep a lot, sometimes ten or twelve hours a day, not because I'm tired or anything, just to pass the time.

I don't do much with my time because I don't want to spend money. I go to museums and things like that, and I've been spending a lot of time at the library. With more money I'm sure I'd be less bored.

I like to smoke dope for relaxation—it makes me feel less depressed—but it's forty or fifty dollars an ounce now, so I don't do that too often. My lover and I go out dancing once a month or so, and I watch TV. I also go to the baths a lot just for company; we have free passes.

My unemployment is $115 a week; my savings are gone. When we moved into our co-op, we needed money for the down payment and I contributed to that. Anything I had went—an annuity is gone, my life insurance policy is all cashed in and I owe lots of money. My credit is up to its limit right now.

"I feel less equal in my relationship with my lover now because I can't contribute anything."

I feel less equal in my relationship with my lover now because I can't contribute anything. When we first started living together it was the reverse. We depended a lot upon my income because he was just starting up his practice.

If I was a woman, my lover and I would probably be married. Even if we were just living together, it wouldn't be such a terrible thing for a woman not to work. It's interesting, but because I'm a man I feel like I have to be able to support myself and aside from that, contribute to the apartment. But sometimes I wouldn't mind just staying home, taking care of the house, and doing things that I like to do.

I feel unproductive and useless. For sure, that affects how I come across on the few interviews that I have. My lover has really helped me; he has been very supportive. I don't think I could survive this emotionally if I didn't have his financial and emotional support. My family has been terrific too. They never yell at me, they try to make helpful suggestions and although they are not rich, they slip me twenty-five or thirty dollars whenever they see me.

I always thought being unemployed was something that happened to someone else, that it was someone else's problem. Now when I hear the term hard-core unemployed, I identify very much. I know I shouldn't, but I do. I think something needs to be done about the way people seek employment in this country. It's just a demoralizing system. Being unemployed is much worse than I thought it would be.

The relationship broke up and Richard moved to another city.

Rachel   Brooklyn, New York

A retired schoolteacher, she was alert, physically fit and looked younger than her years. Her house was sunny, neat and spare. She told her story articulately and one could not help noticing the contrast between her cool tone and what she was saying.

The idea of going back to work does not appeal to me, but neither does anything else. I feel depressed. I don't want any burdens; I don't want any responsibilities. And yet maybe I'd be happier—I don't know. But right now I don't want to know about anything that would aggravate me. The trouble is, I have no hobbies or talents. I can't draw, I can't play music, I can't sew, I can't...I don't know what else I can do. I just worked like most of the people in my generation.

It has been four years since I retired. I was teaching on and off for about thirty-five years in the New York school system. I felt I had to get out because of what had happened to the system. The children weren't as responsive as they used to be and it was more difficult keeping them working. The attitude of the children, the parents and the community changed. Education somehow seemed to be a battle with the children and the parents on one side, and the teachers on the other. And always the teachers were to blame.

I really got tired of this. It became just a matter of keeping my wits about me and going through a day without anything traumatic happening. I had three more months to go until my pension, but I got out at Christmas. I had had it.

I was so relieved, so happy. I had no plans. The freedom of not having to get up and go into a classroom to start the games every day was such a relief. Then my son needed my help and I started working for his business. I went in hesitatingly, then it became a way of life. Even though I was not paid, I went into work with my husband every morning—he and my son work together. I did the best I could. We came home at night—there was shopping and cooking—and before I knew it I was glad just to get into bed and watch television.

I only did clerical work, and it was wonderful just to do the work and not have the page talk back to you, "I don't know that," or "Take your hands off me." And I felt I was doing something to help my son. That lasted for two years.

Now times have changed, and I can't even enjoy my retirement. I'm closed in in four walls because I'm afraid to walk in the street, afraid to take the train. When I go out I can't take too much money, because at my age I'm the first one they should attack. Maybe I don't look like an old lady or dress like an old lady or kvetch like an old lady, but they can tell, so I'm afraid to go places. If I have to go to the city I take the bus, but I don't do that often.

I'm not interested in lectures; I'm not interested in museums. I went to plenty in my life with the schoolchildren, and I hate them. I'm not interested in the theater. I can't get excited about anything.

I'm a very private person, and I cannot stand outside and talk to people about my life, my bank account, my children...I'll talk about politics, but most women that I know are not interested, so I get very bored.

I'm lost.

I get up in the morning, usually earlier than I should. I do the chores fixing up the house, which takes about fifteen minutes, and make lunch for my husband, have coffee, and watch the people outside going to work. At eight o'clock I put on the news until nine o'clock, then I shut the TV and try to think of what I am going to do until eleven. Maybe wash something, iron something or mend something. Then I watch a game program from eleven to eleven-thirty, and shut the television. I can't stand soap operas; they get on my nerves. I eat my lunch, then I go shopping. With that finished, I play solitaire for about twenty minutes, a half hour at most. It relaxes me just a little. I wait until two when I have another game show and when I get through with that I just start supper. Sometimes I don't prepare supper because I cooked the day before. I read the papers and then if nothing else I look out the window and try to relax until my husband comes home about six o'clock.

My not working affects him. When he comes home, I'm not that happy; I'm short-tempered, which I don't think I used to be. I don't want to do things, I don't want to go places, I don't want to see people. I feel depressed—I suppose because I have nothing to fill my time with. I feel guilty because my husband wants to do things, to travel, to go to a movie. I can't even enjoy myself in a movie—I don't even feel safe there. If you go in the middle of the week there is nobody there, and if you go on the weekend, there are too many kids there. My husband sometimes goes without me. He feels there's something the matter with me, but his loyalty doesn't change. But he's got another life; he's still working, of which I'm very thankful for his sake.

My children are all leading their own fruitful lives which I'm happy about. I don't question them too much about their lives. I try not to meddle and in return they don't meddle in mine. But still I would like to see them more often than I do. I speak to two of them once a week, and the other one practically every day because he and my husband work together.

I have only one grandson. But I have a feeling that even if I had more I wouldn't have the patience. I don't think I could be a dedicated grandmother who's there all the time. I don't consider grandchildren a burden or a blessing. If they're there, I love them dearly. If they're not there I have no one to love and I don't miss it.

I do have a group of friends who have been playing cards together once a week for about thirty years. They're all nice people and I'm very much at ease with them. Otherwise everybody else that I've been friendly with in my married life has sort of disappeared.

I have some friends who go to meetings, to lectures, every week. I may go too, not because I'm so thrilled with it but it's something to do. I find it harder to make friends now because everybody is set in their ways, especially me, and in order to be friends you have to do the things they want and discuss the things they want, which I am not anxious to do. I feel more anger and less patience, but I still control it. I won't tell them what's wrong with me. I won't admit it—pride.

I live in a very cloistered world. There are a lot of very fine people in it, people with morals, who I feel are good. The women may not have a college education, but they seem to know what's cooking, as they say. But I don't get intellectual stimulation from them or from my relatives, and I do miss that.

I thought about a Senior Citizen Center, but something suddenly changed my mind. About two years ago, I was on a bus with senior citizens who were going to the center and they acted in such childish ways. Many of them were screaming on top of their lungs and laughing and talking in such an idiotic way that I thought to myself, that's not the answer.

What would I do with senior citizens even if they were more my type? I cannot talk about my private life. I'd feel degraded if I went to a center. The idea of even walking in is degrading.

I feel left out of things, but I feel it's my fault. I have a guilty feeling about not reaching out, and about not wanting to do things. I never liked to travel. I like familiar things. I get used to something, even furniture. I've had that attitude through my life—not wanting change, wanting everything to stand in its place. But I can't change my nature, that's me. It's not my age or being retired or fear of change; it's partially all three.

There's another thing, I'm not healthy, which I feel may have been brought about by depression. I don't know what it is, exactly. I went for a check-up and the doctor thinks everything is all right. I went to him about two years ago and the look he gave me then was that all my symptoms and complaints were caused by nerves. But I've never thought of going to a psychiatrist or psychologist to talk about it. What could they tell me to do? Go to work, help in a hospital? I've heard all that, but I don't want to. I know why I'm like this; it's because I never wanted to go out, because I never wanted to change. I'm not going to change now, even if a psychiatrist tells me why I am like this. And after I talk about it to other people I feel worse than I did before. It doesn't relieve me.

But I'm going to lectures now; I'm making little steps. I know what I have to do and I have to work on it and try and find a solution.

"I don't feel I'm less worthy because I'm not working, but I feel it's my fault I'm not living up to what I should do."

I don't feel I'm less worthy because I'm not working, but I feel it's my fault I'm not living up to what I should. I feel that I've done my share in life, and I'm proud of what I did. I raised a family and I worked. I seem to have accomplished many things, but I know that what's happening to me now is caused by a drastic change in my everyday life.

I don't feel competent to cope with problems or challenges in the future. I don't feel competent at all. I don't know how to deal with it. I'm sixty-seven and it's like there's nothing else left. It's very depressing.

Vera   New York, New York

She was eighty-seven years old—a short gray-haired woman, who firmly engaged your attention with her lively blue eyes— and she stood taller, walked more briskly, and spoke more clearly than any number of people half her age. A former opera singer, Vera had vivid memories of earlier years and re- counted them with great gusto. Her spirit was inspiring, her humor infectious—she just loved to laugh.

I was the first one born here after my family came from Europe. That was eighty-seven years ago. I went to college then studied singing and sang with the Chicago Opera Company.

Mary Garden, from Scotland, was the head there when I went for my audition. The first thing they did in those days was ask you your religion, no matter where you went, even when you went to get a job. My teacher had said to me, "Look, don't ever tell them you're Jewish or you won't have a chance."

I thought to myself, "What can I say?" My brother's wife had turned Christian Science, so I said, "Christian Science. I'm Christian Science."

When I told my mother I got the role as Lucchina, the gypsy in *Il Trovatore,* she said, "Well, let's hear it," and when I finished she said, "Kind, du stehst wie ein Stück. Zigeuner geht so." We spoke German at home and that meant I was standing like a stick.

In those days nobody ever acted—they just stood and sang. But my mother got up and started to swing from the waist, then she said, "You start to shake a little bit from the shoulders," and she showed me how to act.

On opening night when I had to come across and strut, walk the way my mother showed me—acting—I looked in the corner and saw the manager, and boy, she was frothing at the mouth. When I got through it was so quiet. Nobody moved because they were all surprised. It was the first time anybody ever acted. I took the manager's hand and brought her out, thinking, "I'll give her the *Ehre"*—the honor.

Well, the ovation was so big that she couldn't be angry with me. "What made you act?" she asked. I explained what my mother had taught me.

"What made you point to me as though it was my idea?" she asked.

"Otherwise you would have killed me," I answered. "I want to tell you something. I'm Jewish. I'm of Hungarian background."

"You're what?"

"My mother always taught me that it doesn't make any difference where you come from," I said, "But they told me if I said I was Jewish, I'd never have gotten a chance. That's why I said I was Christian Science. I don't care now. If you don't want me, I can go to any opera company now."

"Oh, no, you'll stay here," she said. "All right, so you're Jewish."

In your contract it said you couldn't get married. You could have as many boyfriends as you wanted, but they believed it would spoil your voice if you had a child. I sang with the Chicago Opera for seven years and then I was thirty years old and I wanted to get married and have a family. So I stopped working and came to New York. I sang in the temple in Brooklyn and I got to sing in the Christian Science Church through my sister-in-law.

"I never went back to the opera because I wanted to have a family, and the chutzpah of it was that I didn't get pregnant until three years after I was out."

I never went back to the opera because I wanted to have a family, and the chutzpah of it was that I didn't get pregnant until three years after I was out. I just couldn't. Eventually I did and I had two girls, then afterwards I learned to use the ...(*laughs*). But the things we used to do in those days—we did the darndest things. Nowadays they use watchamacallits. They didn't have those in my day, fifty-four years ago.

I was busy all over and on the boards of organizations. I'm only on one now, the Crippled Children and Retarded Children. I still go when somebody can take me out there in a car.

I don't go out at night any more. The children said, "Mother, don't you think it's time to stop going out at night?" Now I go to concerts on Friday afternoon. I like to go to the Philharmonic.

Outside of that, I have two card games, one on Tuesdays and every other week I play bridge, and that's all. Sometimes I go to the grandchildren, if they call for me. One of them lives in Washington and the other one's over here in Jersey. I have two grandchildren in California and I don't know when I'll see them.

I'm not sorry I gave up my opera singing. This modern generation doesn't want all the old operas. They want the modern operas too, so you have to mix them in because you've got to please the people, you know, the younger generation. I can't stand the modern operas and I wouldn't have wanted to sing them.

Your life is written in the palm of your hand, some of it, and some of the gypsies, the old-fashioned ones, could see it. They never went to school, but they did have that natural knowledge that they inherited from generations and it was right.

The only thing I know of it is that I have a long lifeline. And these little cracks? That's your troubles. You get sorrow—my granddaughter died when she was ready to graduate. My husband died.

"What you do learn will never go to waste. You never know when it's going to come in handy."

In my life I've learned and I've sung, I wanted a family and I had it. What you do learn will never go to waste. You never know when it's going to come in handy.

IN TRANSITION

Carol   Queens, New York

One of the first women to receive a degree in engineering from the prestigious Ivy League university she had attended, Carol had never had a job in her field. Now, in her early thirties, with her daughter in school all day, she had enrolled in a special degree program designed to improve the employment prospects for women in science. With her small frame, bright eyes, light brown hair in a casual cut and ready laugh, she looked delightfully elfin. But her careful, deliberate manner of thinking things over revealed the alert intelligence of a woman who was altogether serious about making something of her abilities and her identity.

I received a bachelor's degree in chemical engineering in 1965 and I was unable to get a job in my field. The companies didn't know that they were supposed to hire women and there were still men available because it was before the big push in Vietnam. I went through the whole employment rejection thing and ended up as a blood chemist in a hospital. I took a civil service test to improve my salary and was offered a job with the Social Security Administration. I worked there for five years and when my daughter was born seven years ago I stopped working. I thought that the best place I could be was at home with the child. I didn't really think that I was going to be a housewife; I thought of myself as going to be a mommy and I did not see past the first few months.

"Nobody knows how boring it is to sit home with a crawling-around child until they've actually done it."

My daughter kept me fully occupied for about a year and a half and then I began to go absolutely crazy in the apartment with virtually no adult stimulation and almost no one to talk to but her. Nobody knows how boring it is to sit home with a crawling-around child until they've actually done it. You really suffer for it. My vocabulary markedly decreased. I couldn't think of words that I needed, and if I was reading something, I'd say, "Gee, that's a word I haven't heard in a long time." If I did talk to someone, I couldn't express myself as well as I had been able to. Not that I was ever a great scholar of the English language, but when I found myself searching for words, I knew that my mind was missing something.

I was getting lonesome and very frustrated. My husband, who works for the Welfare Department, was very active and would go to a lot of meetings. When he came home he would find me with bad headaches, very ill-tempered, and feeling lousy. I may not have been clinically depressed, but I was just feeling awful.

We had a big argument. He told me it was my fault I wasn't feeling good about myself and that I should go back to school, get involved in things—go do something.

I decided to try. I was elected co-chair of the co-op apartment building we were living in and got involved in fighting rent increases. I became the editor of the co-op newspaper and found a lot of responsibility and quite a lot of satisfaction in working on that. I even ran for public office. I had to get along with people and I made myself get along with people.

My activities certainly brought me out of my depression. With no time to sit home and be bored, I was no longer bored.

Interchanging with new people somewhat alleviated my need for adult conversation. Gary and I began seeing people we met through my community activities and I no longer felt isolated at all.

About that same time I started reading in the Women's Movement. When I was stuck in the house and feeling rather trod upon, I developed a sense of sisterhood with the rest of womankind which I had not previously had. I had felt alien from the problems in the traditional roles of housewife and mother before because I had felt I was beyond all that, but there I was, in the same situation. It was very helpful to me to share feelings and experiences with other women who were alone and isolated. Just expressing ourselves and getting feedback often alleviated our problems.

And now I'm going to school again. I'm in a one-year graduate school program funded by the National Science Foundation which is intended to reach women who got their bachelor's degrees in chemistry and allied fields between 1960 and 1974 and to train them in polymeric research and engineering. The program is funded to serve women who want to update their education and improve their employment situation.

Since I've been in school this last year my self-esteem has improved. I feel that I have direction and it gives me a feeling of optimism about where my life is going. My degree was lying fallow for so many years it was as though I had wasted my education. I needed something to occupy my energy and my intellect. I knew I could do better with my life. All of my life I've had the feeling that I was capable of more and that I should be doing more with my head. This last year I'm getting a sense that maybe I'll come a little closer to what I'm capable of.

"My daughter once said, 'Mommy, it would be nice if you could grow up to be a scientist.'"

My daughter once said, "Mommy, it would be nice if you could grow up to be a scientist." Now I've grown up and it would be nice if I can actually be a scientist. That I may actually be able to get a job and use my education makes me feel good, like the circle is complete. I expect to be working in about two years. There's some anticipation, some fear. The idea of looking for a job is frightening at this point, but once I get my skills up, I think I'm going to feel pretty confident.

It's important to me to be able to say, "I'm a chemical engineer," or whatever other kind of scientist I become. Once a doctor asked me, "What do you do?"

"What do you mean, what do I do?" I asked.

"Do you work?"

"Well, I'm a housewife," I started, and he stopped me. I thought maybe he was interested in how I spent my time and I was going to tell him about my community involvement, but hearing I was a housewife was enough for him.

Just being home and doing nothing else doesn't have a very high value in this society, and I don't really hold it in very high value myself. When I was growing up I had a rather bad opinion of women in general and I thought that being a housewife and just staying at home was not a very respectable thing to do. Now I feel that being a housewife is very important: somebody has to take care of the home and raise the children in the right way. But people should be encouraged to do things that they feel are of value—to use their talents, to express themselves, and to give to their community. If I were still sitting home uninvolved, I would feel that I was doing less than I should for the world, for my family, and for myself.

When I started becoming active, I had fights with my daughter about it. She was little and I must have felt some guilt about leaving her with a babysitter, but the problem was mostly her feeling that she should be spoiled and should have me all the time rather than just most of the time.

I was certainly entitled to some time without her, and while it's not necessarily better for me to be out of the house a lot, it's much better for her to have a mother who does things. In the last few years I think she's had a pretty good example from me as to what mommies do and she has an idea that Mommy is somebody who does something other than wash dishes and clean clothes. I don't think she would suffer needlessly if I was away for the late afternoon. She doesn't really need my attention as much as she did when I was little—when *she* was little. (*Laughing*)

Right now my time is free, but I don't really feel free. I would feel freer if we had more financial security. I would rather have a job and money than the free time. My husband would also like to see more money coming in. If I could make enough money to support us, then he could leave his job and go to school, too, if he wanted to. I'd like to be able to do that for him.

We're not managing very well financially now—we've had a lot of expenses this year. We don't have a lot of luxuries and we hardly ever go out. Still, we don't deprive ourselves and we sometimes take trips. We have some savings and we have family to fall back on in case of emergency. But I'd like to see us break even and I feel I ought to be saving money.

Gary and I don't talk about our financial situation very much; I just handle it. I don't want to bother him with it because he tends to get depressed and upset about things. He has enough to think about, so as long as I can handle the news, I'll just go on handling it.

My biggest worry is that Gary will get laid off before I can earn money and that we'll lose the house. A lot of people with our education have been laid off capriciously or through the current state of the economy, and I feel that that could happen to us any time. It's a shame people are laid off, but it's not a stigma any more. Some workers are laid off or are less well off than others, and, as they say, there but for the grace of God go I. I don't like thinking that it will happen to Gary, and he has enough seniority in the job so that it shouldn't, but with the way politics are in the city, it's depressing to plan. It puts a cloud on everybody's future.

Our financial situation bothers me because it gives me a feeling of uncertainty and I would rather be sure about what's going on. I may be worrying about finances a bit needlessly, but a little worry is never misplaced, I don't think.

Things should even out financially for us, but of course, if we were at the point where we needed help, even public assistance, then chances are we'd take advantage of it. As a Social Service worker Gary is pretty well aware of what services people are entitled to. Some people who are eligible for assistance don't take advantage of it because they're too proud. We don't think that's necessary. People are entitled to what's provided by law.

I believe that most people, given the opportunity, want a productive, fulfilling job and that it is possible for jobs to be made available to everybody. I don't believe that people are inherently lazy. This whole unemployment situation is politically created; it isn't natural.

"I hate corporations and big business. I may end up working for one one day, but working for one is different from liking them."

I hate large corporations and big business. I may end up working for one one day, but working for one is different from liking them. The big companies are making money hand over fist, laughing all the way to the bank—and some of them literally are the bank. They're greedy. Sometimes they invest the money out of the country to exploit workers from other countries, and I have a very negative feeling about that. Gary and I don't consider ourselves middle class in the political sense. We have to work to make a living, so we identify with workers. The corporate structure is designed to make people feel defeated and fight each other for a smaller and smaller share of the shrinking pie.

A lot of people I know don't feel the present political system can serve the people's needs, but I'm still holding out a little bit of hope for the capitalist system. As I see the way things are going, though, I tend to lose that optimism. The system, for example, is now designed not to educate working people and their children. It's not providing day care and it's not providing jobs. It's purposely raising a generation of people who don't have basic job skills. There must be a reason for it and I don't think it reflects a just society. Eventually the people will get fed up with it and maybe have a revolution, peaceful or otherwise.

I'm fairly pessimistic about the long-term future for this country, but I encourage in myself an optimistic personal outlook. I would like to be happily working at a productive job in a couple of years. I feel fairly strong, fairly competent. I don't feel that I can handle everything, but I can handle most things that will happen. I have faith in human nature and a faith in people. I have a faith in myself as a woman—I feel women are very strong.

So I have a basic optimism that the world will survive—not a religious feeling, nothing that comes from any political theory, but a kind of amalgam of my experience. I know that it's very important not to give up.

Carol went through the program and was awarded a fellowship so that she could go on for her Ph.D.

Milagros   Long Island, New York

Thirty-two year old Milagros was graceful and self-possessed and it was easy to think of her as successful at whatever she might attempt. Unhappy cooped up in her new suburban home, and worried that her marriage might be breaking up, she wanted a job for both gratification and economic independence. But with a retarded child who needed constant attention, she was reluctant to commit herself to anything that would take her out of the house. In the spotless kitchen her son played merrily and noisily with friends, frequently coming over to his mother for a hug and reassurance, while she described her dilemma, undaunted by the pain of the emotions that rose to the surface.

I worked as a legal secretary, then after I got married and had children I worked part-time for a temporary agency. My mother was living with me, so she was watching my older son. Then she passed away and I stopped working till both kids were in school. I worked as a typesetter for a newspaper for a year, then a year ago we moved to the suburbs and I haven't worked since then. Now I want to go back to work.

We moved to the suburbs because of the schools. Our younger son was attending a special school for retarded children in Brooklyn and we got a letter saying the city would no longer be funding special schools. We were going to have to send him to a special private school, which would have cost $4800. And my older son was going to a private school, also.

I was driving the younger one back and forth and I started to get very down. I wanted to live someplace where the kids could go to schools nearby and you didn't have to pay. I heard that there were excellent specialized schools that come out of your taxes in this district, so I came to visit a few and liked what I saw. Instead of putting the money towards private schools, we bought a house and made the move.

But personally it has not been a good move for me. I feel very, very trapped and I feel like I have to get out of here. I really have the need to get out and work. I always was very negative about the suburbs and saw the people who live in them as very bigoted and afraid of the big city. The worst thing you could say was, "Oh, you're a suburbanite"; it was like a slap in the face.

I've met people here, but there's not the warmth, the same atmosphere I felt in Brooklyn. It's a ride to go anyplace and I don't have a regular sitter. It isn't like living in a big building where there are people I can depend on. I don't have anybody to talk to and I miss the excitement of being with other adults.

Ideally I would like to work from ten to two at a super-great job and be home when the kids get home. I have a thing about that, probably because my mother was always home. I'm Puerto Rican and my mother was pretty traditional. She always put my brother and me first. She never left us with a babysitter and she never went out. So I feel guilty about leaving the kids with a babysitter because my mother hadn't done it.

If I can't work out that ideal schedule, there's a woman who has babysat for me that I'd trust. She's good, kind of a mother type, and she'd be able to stay till six o'clock two or three afternoons a week. I wouldn't feel as bad about not being home if it were her.

I enjoy work. I like the excitement of every day going someplace, of even just getting dressed to go someplace other than the house. And I would like it if somebody would say, "This was a good job," or "You really figured this out well." I like appreciation for my efforts and I don't find in the home that I get that same type of appreciation.

I also want to work again because I think my marriage is getting weak. It's not at the breaking point, but I feel that when it breaks I'm going to be up shit's creek because I can't really be self-supporting. If I started working part-time now and got some current experience, then if the day came when I had to support myself, I would at least have an in or something to go back to.

When I got married I had the idea that I would just have children and stay at home with the children. My husband had the idea that my place was in the home. I liked being a mother and I prided myself on being a great mother—not even good—great. And I think I was pretty happy when the kids were younger. I always felt I'd be taken care of. I didn't have time to wonder what I could do in the future, outside in the world.

Somewhere along the line I felt it just wasn't enough to be home. Women's liberation had a lot to do with making me aware of a lot of things. Little things, like why should I have to do all the childcaring, and why should I have to do all the clean-up? That caused a lot of problems because the more I read feminist-type articles, the more I said, "Gee, that's right. Why should I?" The things that I thought were part of my job as the wife and mother all of a sudden seemed not just my responsibility, but something for both of us. But my husband was not willing to change.

My husband doesn't see any reason why I would be unhappy about anything or have anything to complain about. He claims he would be very happy to be home and taken care of. I've offered to work and let him stay home, but he doesn't want that. He provides pretty well financially, and he thinks that I should be perfectly happy for all the things that he has provided and that I'm ungrateful if I'm not. And I am grateful. But he doesn't understand or won't understand the things I need.

When I was working, he was against it. He didn't even know where I worked. He didn't say I couldn't work—he couldn't stop me if that was what I really wanted to do—but he wouldn't even ask where I worked, or how did it go, or what did

I do. He wasn't available to watch the kids because he says I belong in the home and it's not his responsibility. He doesn't feel responsibility for the kids other than to pay the bills.

Whatever I do, he'll accept, but he would not help me toward that goal. He doesn't even want me to go to school. I told him I want to go to college and he said, "How are you going to pay for it?" He pays for the Adult Ed classes I've taken at the high school because they're during the day and they're not expensive, but he doesn't intend to pay for other things.

We have talked, sort of, about separating and he said, "Well, I'm not supporting you. I'll support the kids, but I'm not going to support you." And I thought, "Shit, what am I going to do?" I went into a panic and even got a twitch in my eye. So now I have to find a way to support myself.

Since that discussion we haven't talked any more about separating, but I know there's that possibility. My twitch hasn't gone away. I don't want to go into such a nervous state again. I'd rather know that I could get a job. I'm at the stage where I want to do it.

"I don't feel the way I did ten years ago when I could walk into any place and say, 'Boy, are you lucky I came here.' "

I feel like I have to be self-supporting for my own peace of mind. Right now I have every confidence in the world that I can do it, but I still don't know how I'm going to meet a prospective employer. I'd be a nervous wreck. I don't feel the way I did ten years ago when I could walk into any place and say, "Boy, are you lucky I came here." I'd be sitting there twitching and everything else.

I don't really know what kind of work to look for. I would like to be a writer and work at some sort of publishing place, at a magazine, for instance. But there aren't many places around here that need help, and I don't have the confidence, the experience, or the education to go in some place and write. In fact, I once did terribly in a creative writing class and I feel bad about that. But if I was a dynamite secretary in a publishing place, once I'd established my work in the office I could say, "I'd like to try writing."

I like being a secretary, but when I told my husband I was going to get a part-time job, he said, "What are you going to do, be a secretary?" I felt he thought it wasn't good enough, so that put a downer on being a secretary that in the past I never thought there was anything wrong in being. My husband's opinion about what I do does affect my feelings, even though I go ahead and do as I like, whether he approves or not. Wanting his approval is a conflict for me.

I don't know what's going to happen with my marriage and I'm on the verge of panic. I don't want to cause any dramatic experiences for the children, or be responsible for them not growing up with a father, or feel guilty if they can't have things that they need. So I just don't talk about what I want to do or what I feel I have to do. I don't want to cause any argument. I'll go along with the way things are and just be prepared if something does happen.

Things aren't falling apart just now—they're OK, they're OK—but I know that it's because I'm afraid to make waves. My husband doesn't intend to change, so I have to do the changing or at least pretend that everything is OK. I feel like I'm living a lie. I'm never honest with him. I feel if I was honest, he would leave and then I would be in a panic.

It's very, very scary. I've never lived alone. I went from living with my mother to being married. I never had to handle the money, I never had to budget, and I'm afraid of all that. It seems like too much and I don't know if I'll be able to handle it. And there isn't anybody I could turn to for help, like if I needed a month's rent. That's scary, too. I'm very nervous about what I'm doing and I wonder whether it will just make the rift bigger if I get a job. Are the kids going to suffer for it? It's a risk and I'm afraid to take it.

I'm comfortable about my older son, but I worry about the younger boy. Taking care of his special needs takes a lot of effort and costs a lot. His testing is very, very expensive, and his tutor costs ten dollars an hour. I think one of the reasons he's able to stay in the special class in the public school is because he has the extra help, and I think it's better for him to be in a more normal environment. If I were alone, I would feel guilty if I couldn't have the tutor for him and all the other things that make a real difference.

I think about other people who have done it, but they don't have the same problem with their children. A normal kid could stay alone in the house for a few hours and call up its mother and say, "Ma, I'm home." I couldn't work at a job that required a lot of attention because I would be thinking of what would be happening at home.

I'm not sorry that I wasn't out working all this time. I love being with the kids and I like seeing them grow. But now I'm thirty-two and I wish that by this time in my life I would have accomplished something great. I don't know what I think I could have accomplished—probably working for a magazine and having things published.

"Someday, when the kids are older, I would love to have a career and be important, not just a person in the house."

Someday, when the kids are older, I would love to have a career and be important, not just a person in the house. Able to make decisions—right decisions—and sort of be successful in whatever I would like to do. But I don't even know at this point what I want to do. So what I want now is a good job—just a good-paying job would be enough.

Milagros stayed in her marriage and began a business of her own, working out of her house.

Charles   Los Angeles, California

Wearing a conservatively cut suit and a tie, Charles looked a good deal older than most of the other, more casually dressed students in the job-training program for Asian immigrants. Eleven months before, this tall, very thin man in his late forties had been a successful businessman in Hong Kong. Now he was mustering up all his resources to make a fresh start in a new country with a new language. Making light of his problems, he carefully avoided giving the impression that he was the least discomfited by his hardships. Yet his good cheer could not entirely mask his need to be finished with this difficult period of adjustment as quickly as possible.

I left China in 1946, more than thirty-one years ago, and went to Hong Kong. For twelve years I was a partner as well as managing director in an import-export business, mainly metal materials such as aluminum extrusions for windows and doors. I sold everything and came to the States eleven months ago, mainly for my children's education. I have two daughters and two sons, twenty-one, eighteen, seventeen and twelve. They are in school now and also work part-time.

I got a job in an office after a month. I worked about nine months and I resigned. The pay was not so good and still there was no increment on my salary. I don't think there's any future for me in case I worked there any longer and I think it's easy for me to look for a job if I am not working for somebody else.

I have never been out of work in the past time. This is the first time. Before I resigned I know I will try hard to get a job, but so far not even one. I have been to many firms looking for work during this couple of weeks and I found the examination is rather difficult for me, especially for the vocabulary, because I only speak a simple English.

I need to find work soon because I have a little savings, but not enough, and I got to pay the house I bought.

Food is simple. It won't cost me that much because we are Chinese and we are not very particular on food. It's very minimal. But I got to pay the car, the organ for my daughter, accordion for my son—everything. It totals about $700, all the installments, every month. Sometimes something is less expensive than Hong Kong, but most of the items is more expensive, especially the labor. Everything costs money. Jesus. Is many, many more times than Hong Kong.

I'm looking for any kind of work that's my ability to fit. I cannot say, "Oh, I must get this job—I won't do any other job except this." I know before I came here to the States I wouldn't earn as much as I did before. I just want to get a permanent job, steady. I'm forty-seven and I'm not like a teen-ager. They like to go from one place to another. If I got a nice job, I can continue working in it.

I never have such a hard time before in Hong Kong. This is the first time I encountered it. I'm not so optimistic all the time. Sometimes I feel sad when I'm thinking something else—just for a while. I never have any friends here except my sister. I'm not quite social. It's a little bit hard for me. I'm not quite popular.

When I stay at home I really do not know what to do. It makes me feel lonesome and—I don't know what to do— standing, walking....Sometimes I feel discouraged, but my wife convinces me to continue, my kids also. Because they are growing up, I'm happy. I'm going to work again, maybe another fifteen years. I'm still healthy. I think I can do that.

I don't regret coming here. There's so many people in Hong Kong waiting anxiously to come over here, but unfortunately they cannot make it. A lot of relatives in my family have wished to come but they simply cannot get application.

My parents are here. My whole family in the States is in Los Angeles except for one family in San Francisco and another one in South Carolina. We got everybody in the same place, in my house, last Christmas. Altogether is thirty-one persons, seven families.

"It's fifty-fifty whether it's more exciting or more painful to change your life the way I have."

It's fifty-fifty whether it's more exciting or more painful to change your life the way I have. But I will continue looking for work; I'll try hard to get a job. I'm settled down here already. And what happens in my future, it depends.

Sherry   Seattle, Washington

Nineteen year old Sherry agilely led the way upstairs to a vacant room in the community center where we could talk in privacy. Her straight brown hair hung becomingly back from her face and from time to time a shy smile lit her face. Painfully self-conscious, she was concerned she wouldn't answer the questions "right."

I was a runaway. Two years ago I left L.A. and came up to Seattle. I lived with my mother's sister for six months and then moved out. My aunt's an alcoholic and so is my uncle, and they've got seven kids. They said, "You can make it on your own," and pushed me out the door.

I went and lived with a friend because he was going into a detox center and I would be able to have the place to myself. When he got out of detox I still lived there and so did a lot of other people. They were starting to use heroin, so I didn't want to stay there. I didn't do hard-core drugs or anything—maybe barbs.

When I got enough money together I moved out and lived in a rooming house for two months, but I didn't have enough money to manage that, so my friend has been letting me stay at his home again. We're not lovers anymore.

I asked my family for some help so I wouldn't have to move back to where I'm living now. My father said yes, but my mother said no. She feels that I'm never going to get anywhere if she helps me out. She wouldn't let me stay with her if I wanted to. I'd love to live with her if we could get along, but I don't feel like she can slap me around. I'm not going to stay with somebody when they're frustrated because I'm not doing things exactly the way they want.

People take care of me. If I'm really hungry and don't have any money, they'll get things for me and I will pay for it when I can. If they see that I need something, it will be offered.

I haven't worked at all the past three months. I've worked since I was fifteen, mostly at food places. I worked for a cleaners, I've been a nurse's aide and a maid. The longest I've worked at jobs has been a month.

I've always been hired. If I talk to whoever runs the place, I can get a job if I want it. I've never gotten fired; I just quit. I've either ended up not liking who I worked for and feeling they weren't treating me right, or just getting so bummed out at what I was doing that I left. I'm mostly unhappy with what I'm doing. See, I'm not proud to say I work at some taco joint. I think that's why I keep quitting my jobs.

"See, I'm not proud to say I work at some taco joint. I think that's why I keep quitting my jobs."

I dropped out of high school. I liked school for a while but I got to a point where I just didn't want to go. I thought traveling and partying with my friends was better, so that's what I did.

Now I'm nineteen and I want to go back to school and finish. Eventually I would like to work as a counselor in the juvenile department in the police station or something to that effect. I want to know about things and I'd like to learn more about the government—why things happen and what happened before that. I'm open to learning anything, if someone's willing to teach me, but I'm sometimes slow and I'll ask the same question twice. Some people get tired of explaining it if you ask the same thing over again.

I can probably get a grant to go to school because I'm an Indian—half Chippewa. Other people in my family have gotten grants, so I'm pretty sure I could get one too. But I'm afraid sometimes of going to college because when you get there you're supposed to pretty much know things. I've heard people in college say that if somebody asks a dumb question, they come down on this person. And I don't think I would want a person putting me down all the time. It's not that all my questions are dumb, but... I would be embarrassed if everybody around me thinks that I'm asking a stupid question. It makes me not want to ask questions.

It gets real boring doing nothing. I get lonely a lot. Sometimes I feel like I'm a real lonely person. I'm pretty down most of the time. For the past couple of months I've been sad because I've broken up with the man that I used to live with and I've been real bummed out about it. I'm not one for saying mother was always right, but my mother was always saying, "Stay away from older men," and that was true. He'll be twenty-seven soon. I've been depressed about that and about my not having a job. I felt like my world was broken apart.

For the past three months I've volunteered at the youth crisis clinic. I have a shift once a week, but lately I've been coming in every day. We talk on the phone to people who want to kill themselves and stuff like that.

You're probably wondering how this person can help other people and not help herself. That's the question in my mind— how am I helping these people? But they seem to go away happy and that's all that counts. I really like doing it, though often I feel like I work there because it makes me feel better.

I'd like to do counseling as a job. I've seen people that have their degrees and don't have a heart and I can't see anybody working with someone if they don't have feelings towards other people. I've felt sad and lonely too, so I hope I'll be able to do it.

Ruth   New York, New York

After the massive lay-off of New York City schoolteachers some years before, Ruth found a job and, she hoped, a new career in a design studio. Newly fired, here she was puzzling out how to move her life into the direction in which she wanted it to be going, taking advantage of the peaceful, calm environment she and her husband had created at home to think things through. A short woman in her mid-thirties, her voice low and well-articulated, her hair a mass of golden curls, Ruth was frustrated by her betwixt and between situation, but was not letting it interfere with her natural optimism.

I was unemployed a whole year after I lost my teaching job and as I had never been unemployed before, I didn't know what it was like to have unstructured time. At first I thought, "This is going to be great," because it felt like the continuation of the summer, which is not like being out of school but like catching your breath. Then I went through cycles of feeling very terrific about it—enjoying it, and feeling wasted—not accomplishing anything. I'd think, "Here I haven't been working for so many months, and I still haven't refinished those three chairs, or cleaned out the closets, or done a lot of sewing and crafts things I always thought I would get to." There were days when I just felt totally frustrated that I had nothing specific to do. I felt listless; I couldn't get myself going. But towards the end of the year I started getting into the rhythm of it and relaxing about not having a place to go in the morning.

There I was, one year out of teaching, and it seemed like a very good time to get pregnant. When I wasn't pregnant two months later I started to bite my nails and think, "OK, what am I going to do now, sit around and wait till I get pregnant?" You know, when you have no specific job you have a lot of time to dwell on problems. So I got a job in a design studio working on the drawing board. It was like I said, "I really should get a job," and the next day I had one. Maybe it dropped from heaven.

"It never occurred to me to quake in my shoes because I was five minutes late."

It was exactly the kind of job I was looking to do, because I could practice up and get real good, then freelance when I had the baby. I'd have my career, I'd have my baby—everything.

Well, a month ago I was fired from the studio. I annoyed the hell out of my former boss because I wasn't afraid of him. It never occurred to me to quake in my shoes because I was five minutes late. It was quite obvious that he thought of me as a secretary, even though he prided himself on not doing it and didn't refer to me as a secretary. We would both be working equally hard at drawing boards and he would say to me, "Call so-and-so to make reservations for lunch." That's a corporate mentality—it's a hierarchy. I dealt with large companies all the time and the females did the dirty work and the operational people who gave the orders were male. It's terribly sickening.

So now I don't have the job and I still don't have the baby, but I am in a position to freelance. I feel I have acquired a marketable skill, so I'm not quite so vulnerable or quite so nowhere as I felt at the end of teaching. I already went through a lot of the conflicting feelings about being unemployed, so it's not so new and strange and I don't have all those beginning emotions to go through.

But I still have some feelings of inadequacy. Here I am, unemployed again. And even though I have this skill that I can work at, I'm not really set up in it or professional yet, and I'm not convinced that this is what I want to do. I don't feel that this is my life's work, but that it is something that would allow me to have a child and work conveniently. And I do feel that I need a life's work; I need something important to me, something productive, of course. I want to save the world, I want to get very rich at it, I want to grow—and I want the summer off while I do it. (*Laughs*)

There's so much that needs to be done I can't believe that I'm just going to sit around and not get some of that. Get and give, because that's a very important feeling and I feel unfulfilled when I'm not giving. The one thing that teaching really gives you is that you're right in the middle of what needs to be done. Being a New York City teacher eventually you realize that you're really not doing it and that you have to get out of there, but you know that at least people need you.

In a way I'm disappointed that I'm not in an ongoing career, but my working life is separate from my sense of personal worth. I don't feel that I've failed. I don't feel that working or not working has any effect on the things I've worked out about my life. I have doubts about my productivity whether I'm working or not. I've never connected with work that's that meaningful and that rewarding.

I wonder if the biggest liability to someone who is unemployed is that you don't know how to structure time. I have a basic conflict about it. I don't want to develop a personality where I can't enjoy the freedom of unstructured time, the freedom of being able to connect with whatever happens to come up during the day and not feel rushed, but on the other hand, I don't want to squander. To me the best part of the freedom is being able to do certain concrete things I can't do when I'm working. For example, I wanted to do a lot of reading and get into Oriental philosophy. I haven't. Weeks go by and I think, "My God, what have I done in the four weeks since I've worked?" It bothers me and it doesn't bother me. Practically, I feel life is too short to be compulsive about doing things, but I guess emotionally I feel that I should be doing serious stuff and using my time very constructively.

I felt terribly, terribly pressured by working. I didn't have five minutes to catch my breath or to be with myself. It was very frustrating to be watching the clock, waiting for the bell to ring. It was just like high school. I was on a treadmill, but I also felt something comforting about that because at the end of the day you're exhausted and you feel, whew, you've really accomplished something. Now that, I think, is probably the biggest myth going—that because you're running, you've accomplished something.

After working full-time a certain amount of time is required just to shift gears. I probably still am in transition. I do have time, so now when I see a friend we can really connect. And it's wonderful. I have the leisure to shop and cook for friends and entertain in the evening that I didn't have before, and I actually do it.

I can't picture a time when there wouldn't be some meaningful paid work. The artificiality of some people going to work for eight, nine hours a day, five days a week, and some people not working at all really bothers me. In that kind of society I don't want to be the one that's lounging around, biting my nails—or polishing my nails.

I don't like the idea of my husband getting up at eight o'clock in the morning, going off to work for eight, nine, ten hours a day and of our having whole other lives. It smacks too much of housewife and hubby.

My husband and I have a place in the country, and if our lifestyle was to evolve to maybe living a much more relaxed life there, I think I would be very happy. If we both had leisure and both worked on similar schedules, that would be fine with me.

To me the ideal life would be working paid, structured work three or four, maybe five hours a day, four days a week. If I were to do freelance work with my husband, I'd have a lot more flexibility, but even so, when the work is there, you have to be able to do it. When you freelance, they want you there for the whole day for the life of the job, and that can be a three or four week period. After that you try to take a week or two off, but if you're in demand, it's sort of slitting your own throat to turn down work. You may not want to work as much as they call you, but you're afraid that if you don't you'll be left with nothing at all.

I always worry about money. We never have had enough money—all our money has been going into our country place, and then my husband pays alimony and child support. I don't feel like a junior member because I'm not bringing home a paycheck, but it does bother me that I've never gotten into the upper echelons of salary. My peak salary has never been more than half of what my husband's peak salary has been.

My husband is leaving work also, so we'll both be living on unemployment and whatever freelance work he can do. Sometimes I feel concerned, like how the hell did I get myself into this situation where I'm dependent upon what kind of arrangements he's going to make selling his business? Why is my life dependent on what kind of contract he's going to work out? It's his business, his partner, and I'm me.

I just try to live with it and say, well, when he first started, they weren't making money and my salary was sustaining us, so I have an investment there. But I am dependent, there's no doubt about it. I don't have pocket money, the bills are piling up, and it's very distressing, but because my husband is making money I don't feel compelled to get a job just for the reason that I am not independent.

One of my goals is to be financially independent. When I was working, I always made sure that I had my pocket money off the top. There's a tendency to pay all the bills and kind of squeak through with what's left over, but I really don't believe in living that way. One of the things I work for is to have that feeling that you have enough money in your pocket to go to the movies or out to dinner, or do whatever you feel like doing. It's the imbalance of his having money and my not, and my having to always ask, "Leave me twenty bucks," that I really hate. I hate feeling dependent.

The unemployment makes a big difference. If I were not going to be getting unemployment, I would be in a whole other bag. But ninety-five dollars a week—that's the pocket money. I won't have to go to my husband and say, "Give me twenty-five dollars because we're having company for dinner." We don't live very high on the horse, but you know, you have company, you want something for dessert. And that ninety-five dollars is the difference to me between being my own woman or not.

We don't have any savings and I guess it really doesn't bother either one of us. We laugh about money. I'm just as glad we don't have savings because I think probably it would bother me to watch a savings account dwindle away. Some people feel that they save to have money when they're not working, but I'd rather cut back on my lifestyle. We somehow manage to squeak through.

Last night, driving home from the country, I said, "How are we going to pay the rent this summer?" and, typical answer, my husband said, "We have to sit down and talk." I jokingly said while we planned, "What are we going to plan? Rob a bank? What are our options?" I just had these feelings—he's not going to have any income and I don't have any income. What are we going to do?

But we have gone through such dire financial times, we're both energetic, and my husband still has a very good reputation in his business, so I'm just not worried. What worries me more is being incapacitated. I'm able to work and it will happen, just like it's happened every other time.

Ruth and her husband adopted a child.

John   Big Bear, California

Big Bear is well over a mile high, but the fragrant tall trees surrounding the picture book serene house gave off ample oxygen to replace whatever might have been lost due to the altitude. John, a former nurse and hospital administrator, had

*chucked all at age forty in order to live free from the rat race in
an unpolluted environment. Dark eyes, dark hair, and trim of
build, he spoke quietly, in well thought-out terms. But later,
when he showed his paintings and talked about the new can-
vasses he was planning, you could see that his inner life was
filled with the excitement of art and adventure.*

When you're in dead-center, downtown L.A. with the smog and
all, working either for or against a bureaucracy, all you want
to do is get out the fastest way possible. Fortunately my wife
and I were making very good money, $2000 a month each, and
$4000 a month is a lot in anybody's language. We decided that
we should just sell up and leave.

Some friends owned a place up here in Big Bear and we
came up for the Fourth of July week-end. We looked around, we
thought it was great and thought we'd buy into some real
estate here. We quit our jobs and came up several months ago.

My wife decided to go into real estate, which has just
mushroomed here, so it's profitable. I approached the only
hospital on the hill for a job as a staff nurse and ran into a
problem. The director told me, "It would be to my detriment to
hire you because you should be doing my job."

I said, "Well, I don't want to do your job. I didn't come up
here to do your job."

She said, "I don't think an administrator can go backwards."

In some ways I had to agree with her. I had come to this
country eleven years before from a highly industrial area in
the northeast of England. After completing service in the British navy I found myself in the unhappy situation of working in
a coal mine. It was the last thing in the world I wanted to do,
but work was just not to be had. Then positions opened up in
the hospital field. I was doing first aid in the mines, so it
seemed like the ideal thing. Thirty per cent of all nursing in the
UK is done by males, as opposed to this country where it's one
per cent. It's quite a different picture.

I took the opportunity and found on graduation that there
were no nursing jobs. I found other work, but nearly three
years later business went into a recession in Britain and my
firm had to lay off 50 percent of their workers—the last in,
first out kind of routine. Next thing I knew I was emigrating to
the United States as fast as I could.

Initially I worked for the bureaucracy, for the L.A. County Sheriff's Department. They had a manpower problem so they tended to utilize the RN as a quasi-physician without ever telling anybody that this was what they were doing. You had maybe one hundred twenty guys who had been in the military, wearing white, looking very professional, practicing medicine without a license.

I started to ask questions and learned what I was doing was highly illegal, though I could never get them to admit that, so I went to work for the California Nurses' Association and represented the nurses who worked for the Sheriff's Department.

That way I was able to get something done. We took it all the way to Sacramento and the Attorney General came down on it. It was a positive move, though in some ways it was negative as far as my career was concerned. Once you have been in legal representation it tends to have negative connotations when it comes to moving back into the private sector. After the funding for my position with the Association ran out two years later, I could not get a job in a larger hospital. I was pretty well known by them and they were afraid. I ended up at a convalescent hospital and eventually they offered me the job of directing the place. I must have done a good job because I moved on to direct four or five hospitals.

I enjoyed it in a way, though it was kind of like being on a treadmill again, fighting the bureaucracy. It was an impossible job against impossible odds. The reimbursement rate for convalescent hospitals is $23 a day per patient, while in the acute hospital it runs about $150, $160 a day. It's just impossible to give the standard of care that you would like to see at that rate of reimbursement.

So again I became dissatisfied. We made the move up here, so now I haven't got anything, but I'm not in any hurry. I'm looking for something that will keep me occupied as opposed to working for someone. I'd sooner be working for myself. I'm still a young man—I'm forty. We're in a reversal of roles. Lee is the breadwinner and I do most of the work around the house and all of the cooking. I enjoy it.

I also like to paint. Oils and watercolors. I fish and I like to read. I've also taken up jogging. It never interested me, but now I do it, I think out of the need to be active. I chop logs too, backwoods stuff.

Quite often I get bored, but I get bored because I'm used to a lot of entertainment. We like the theater and a lot of activity and there's no entertainment up here. Yet we still have the best of both worlds. You just can't have it all the time.

It's taking me a long time to adjust. I had been in a very active management position and it's very difficult to take a subordinate position. I'm beginning to get the picture that I'm actually moving into a different strata or different level. It's really not important to be Mr. Macho, to be the boss, yet those things were very important to me at one time. At first I had a kind of left-out feeling and it took me a while to realize what my contribution was. My contribution is different from before, but I sincerely believe now that it is a worthwhile contribution and that I shouldn't worry that I am not in some kind of management role.

But I do enjoy working and being productive. Even in my leisure my mind right now is beginning to move back to painting. For some reason I quit and I didn't pick up a brush in some two years, but when I was painting there was nothing I enjoyed more. I could paint until three o'clock in the morning; I got a great deal of satisfaction. Now I'm beginning to get the feeling that I'm about ready to start again. I think it's because of all the leisure time that I've got.

I'm not saying that this kind of life is everybody's cup of tea—it isn't. Temporarily I guess it's mine, but it is not the type of life we would prefer to be in.

We're in a holding pattern—that's a nice phrase for a flyer, and I also do quite a bit of flying in my plane—but I have another goal, one that I certainly will reach. Four years from now we intend to buy a boat and sail around the world. We could have given up our former life and bought the boat instead of moving up here, but the time was not right to do that. We need Jill to finish high school and then we feel that we can move on. Plus we hope that all the investments will come to fruition in that time.

My wife is pretty level-headed, but I have the wanderlust and I like to dream a little. Reading has always been the fuel for my dreams; I've always wondered about the adventures of others. It seems pretty neat when people go off and magical things happen to them on those trips. I like to think they could happen to me, too. That sustains me. I count myself among the dreamers of the world, but I also feel you have to make things happen. Happily we're in the financial position right now where we can experiment.

"I count myself among the dreamers of the world, but I also feel you have to make things happen."

I would most certainly say to anyone interested in the kind of life I've chosen to follow your instincts and do it. Don't even think about it. If you've got to think about where your next dollar's going to come from, you'll go crazy and you'll never, ever do it. You'll end up like so many people who retire at sixty-five and drop dead at sixty-six. It's so useless.

I'm certainly happy with my life. If I were to characterize myself at all, I'd say I'm an absolute 9000 carat gold eternal optimist. I can see good in the worst situation. I always feel the bright side is going to come up and it does.

Eddie   Ashfield, Massachusetts

Eddie had just arrived home with two friends from a short trip riding the rails and was relaxing with a hot drink in the commune kitchen. Easily making ends meet on the unemployment he was collecting from a resort restaurant job that had ended with the ski season, he was taking the time he felt he needed to find the kind of job he wanted, something that would lead to a management position with real responsibility. From time to time, when something would strike him as serious, he would wrinkle his forehead and gaze intently with his wide-set eyes. Most of the time his fresh, youthful openness was apparent in his appealing grin.

Around the time I graduated from college, a little over a year ago, I found a job running a restaurant in the Massachusetts ski area. When the season ended I started collecting unemployment. So with a couple of brief exceptions, I've been unemployed for about six or seven months.

I was trying to get into market research and planning; I'm really not cut out for restaurant work, especially around a bar. But I'd moved in with a lady friend and I couldn't branch out too far from where we lived. I was sort of vacillating, thinking of carpentry work, landscaping, or things like that, and I did a short stint selling steel house siding. I liked my immediate supervisor but I found that in order to sell I had to push too hard and it wasn't something I felt good about. At the age of twenty-five I'm learning what kinds of work I *don't* like.

"At the age of twenty-five I'm learning what kinds of work I don't like."

Being on unemployment has allowed me to be a bit relaxed about the job search, a little pickier too. I know I could have had a job and made a good living, but I've chosen to stay on unemployment and keep searching for a better one. I have an idea what I'd like to do. I'm not quite sure it's realistic, but unemployment has given me the opportunity to keep playing with it.

I'm shooting for a management situation. I enjoy challenge, getting people to deal with their own jobs, planning and holding things together, trying for the best performance or making the most money. I enjoy the power and excitement and some of the pressure. I enjoy the responsibility, being in charge of things.

I worry though, about what I'm doing and what I should be doing. I worry more than I think I should. I feel guilty about collecting unemployment when I know I don't need to; at the same time, the money is too easy to just throw away. I get $108 a week and I'm spending it all. I've chosen to do some traveling and to go out, but I could easily live on half of what I get.

"I feel guilty about collecting unemployment when I know I don't need to; at the same time, the money is too easy to just throw away."

I'm not sure where all the money went that I made when I was working. I spent it for things I'd wanted for a long time—a tuner, a tape deck, a stereo, and a car— and I know part of it went to pay off bills. But my lifestyle hasn't changed, really, by not working.

The relationship I was in didn't work out and I'm living communally now. It has its advantages and disadvantages. I'm not so personally involved in sustaining myself without having to deal with the economy as some of the people I live with are. I'm not involved in performing my own services, like raising my own chickens. I have not come to the point where I have told myself that this is the way for me to live, but I think it's good for me to be around this kind of atmosphere.

Yet I feel that I should find some sort of a professional situation now instead of later. Somewhere, somehow, I should find a position in society that I feel good about where I can be productive.

Ideally I don't think it's necessary to have the structure of a job in order to be active and productive, but right now I need it. I need the impetus from outside. When I'm not working my energy wanes.

I do feel guilty about not being productive. It's something that's been ingrained in me. Sometimes I think it's silly to feel that I have to be working and productive all the time, but that's how I've been brought up and I can't really throw all that out the window. I have to live with it.

I'm more comfortable about being productive when I have the structure of a job, but at the same time I enjoy my own time. I just came back last night after traveling for over two weeks. When I travel I have energy experiencing new situations, new people, and new places. When I was working some of my personal interests suffered—my photography, reading, music.

I really appreciate my interests now. I'm taking more pictures now, listening to more music. I do a little more. How well it turns out depends on how involved I am. It's like a snowball—the more that I feel right about, the more I do.

So I think I'm gaining some benefit from not working, just getting to feel at ease with myself. Without the framework of a job I'm forced to spend time with myself, rely on myself a great deal more. I've had to deal with that and I feel good about it. I think I have the self-confidence to make whatever I want to happen, happen.

I'm more into trying the work situation and attempting success, but I don't have any plan for continuing that throughout my whole life. A good situation for me would be to work hard, save money, invest it, and perhaps find a situation where I wouldn't have to work, where I could maybe just work to sustain myself. But I'm ready to start looking for a job, more so than ever before in the last six months. I'm ready to go out and start pushing.

Jeanne   Boston, Massachusetts

Exuberant as an ingenue in a play, twenty-two year old Jeanne was full of enthusiasm about the new housecleaning business she hoped to start. A week before she had quit her job as assistant manager in a women's clothing store because her paychecks had been bouncing. Down to her last dollar, she ws more than a little nervous. Slender as a model, brown hair streaming down her back, she sat expectantly by the phone waiting for clients to call and, with high spirits and an infectious sense of humor, related her trials and hopes.

I was assistant manager in a women's clothing store, sort of a boutique, but not quite that exclusive. I did it for eleven months and I really liked it. It was fun.

I got raises occasionally, for what that was worth, because my checks would bounce. I left the job a week ago mainly because of bad paychecks. And my boss was supposed to be

321

sending me to school for retail. Naturally, they wrote the college a bad check, so I had to leave school. That was pretty depressing. I'm sorry to be out of work, but I'm not sorry to leave where I was.

I'm twenty-two and I've never been out of work until now. It's sort of a weird feeling. The first morning I walked around the apartment and didn't quite know what to do. I went up and down Boylston Street, all down Faneuil Hall, looking for other saleswork, figuring that at this time of year it would be fairly easy to find, but I was wrong. All the Christmas help had been hired. After the third day of pounding the streets and not finding work, I got bummed out.

I applied for unemployment and that was one of the weirdest things I've ever done—waiting in line with all these depressed-looking people—old men, young men—standing around looking really down. And these ladies at the counters badgering you with questions. I quit my job, which you're not supposed to do for unemployment, but I gave them the reasons why—bad paychecks. They told me I would possibly be eligible. I have to explain the whole story at an interview.

Right now I need immediate cash, so I put an ad in the paper with a friend who also quit the store, offering rapid house-cleaning for a price. We'll bring our own supplies and provide our own transportation, which is included in the cost. I imagine that we'll start next week.

It's kind of an experiment and that's what's fun about it. I've always wanted to open a business and when I was doing housecleaning on the Cape years ago someone said to me, "You should go into business—hire people, send out your little cleaning service in a little van, and run around with your mops."

These little cleaning lady services are quite the thing over the country because many women are working. They don't have time to spend cleaning and they don't really want to, anyway. This could be very good money.

I don't mind housework too much; in fact, I kind of like it. But the reason I like doing it as a business is that you can make your own schedule and it's great for vacations. All you do is call up all your ladies and say that you won't be in for a week.

For them it usually involves only one day a week, so it's no real problem. It will be a nice change to have a loose schedule after working forty hours a week selling clothes.

"I have so many bills—there are about five hanging up on the wall. They attack me every time I walk into the kitchen. They shine their little figures down."

I want to get back to work, mainly for money. It's a terrible time of year to be out of work. All of a sudden there are no paychecks coming in and it's Christmastime. I've sort of resigned myself that maybe I won't be able to do some things for Christmas that I really wanted to do. I have so many bills—there are about five hanging up on the wall. They attack me every time I walk into the kitchen. They shine their little figures down. The rent is due tomorrow and I have absolutely zero bank balance. I have nothing to fall back on and I'll do anything.

This big thing happened at the store the other day. They owed me thirty-five dollars and I had called the manager, who didn't like me that much and kind of had it planned for me to quit, and told her several times that I needed the money. She didn't give it to me, so I went into the store and took it from the cash register. That night I went out and got kind of smashed.

I guess I could be charged with petty larceny, from what they say. I don't think they'll prosecute, but if they do, I think I was justified. They had known for a week and that was time enough—besides, it's not like I was asking for $150.

Sometimes I do get discouraged. I'm sure if I really needed money, I could get it somewhere—go beg or something—but I've been thinking a lot about poverty and I think I understand what people who have absolutely no money must be going through. I can't take things for granted now that I've always taken for granted. Still, although this week has been kind of nervewracking and insecure, it's been a real learning thing, kind of exciting. It makes me nervous, but at the same time I seem to be energetic and very much out there, really out trying. Whereas in my little secure—or semi-secure—nine to five job I remember all the times it was boring and I really didn't want to be there.

It's nice, I guess, to be secure and to have some money, but at the same time the feeling of being secure can be dull unless you do things to make it exciting. I don't mind feeling insecure too much, not yet, but I haven't been out of work for that long. In a month from now, when people start getting on me for money, I might be saying something different.

Sometimes I make good use of my time and other times I sort of walk around here and don't even go outside. I like to be always doing something—reading, housecleaning, making Christmas presents; what it is doesn't really matter as long as I occupy myself and don't just waste time. I think that's sad.

I'd really like to just lay up and weave or do macramé. I like the whole idea of flea marketing, of hand-made goods and crafts. If I had no money worries, the craft thing might be easier for me then. I think it would be fun to open a little booth in the flea markets.

Being out of work is a little spooky, I guess. Looking for work and being turned down lowers your self-esteem a little bit, and as you go further down the street, you get a little lower. It does make you wonder if you're going to be able to do something. But people get you out of these bad times. My roommates are all patting me on the back, hoping the business goes; my boyfriend's putting an ad for me in the newspaper he works for. They come up with things and try to help you out, or take you out to dinner, or something like that. It makes you feel good and sort of takes away some of that lowness.

The only people who aren't offering that much support are my parents. They wanted me to do something heavy—career, finish school, all that kind of thing—but I just couldn't afford it any more. I kept building up loans and they were just skyrocketing; I still have to pay them off. Now that I'm out of work it's kind of like "I told you so" from my parents, but they'll get over it. They always do.

As far as my situation goes, I won't let myself starve. I have skills. I've been to school for medical technology—I was a medical lab specialist in the Air National Guard for three years—and I've been to school for retail, and I've been to school for liberal arts. I think there's a lot of potential for me in retail business, but I don't really think I'm cut out for the competition in the business world. Trying to get this housecleaning business together is probably the most aggressive thing I've done.

Someone told me six months ago that I should get out of that job. They told me that money didn't grow on trees and there would be hard times. I should have listened and taken that advice; they were right.

"If problems arise, I'm sure there's something that would come out from inside—a 'we shall overcome' attitude—I might develop some grit."

But I can't see myself as being beaten down by this. If problems arise, I'm sure there's something that would come out from inside—a "we shall overcome" attitude. I might develop some grit. When you put it all together, I guess the whole strength thing is the reason why I really don't mind being out of work right now.

KNOWING ONESELF

I'M MY OWN WOMAN

Linda   Birmingham, Alabama

We mistook the tall, graceful woman for the older sister of the energetic teenagers who had been running in and out of the room. But although she did not look her thirty-seven years at all, she was, indeed, Linda, their mother. A coal miner on strike, she was strongly opposed to having workers contribute to their own hospitalization and medical insurance and was ready to hold out for as long as it would take for the side benefits she believed were fair. Not working gave her needed time for meditation after a tragedy she had recently suffered.

One day, while I was working for the Alabama State Department, my girlfriend came by on her lunch hour. She had heard about women going into the mines and she said, "Just come with me to pass the time." She wanted the job. I wasn't particular about it at all, but they called and asked me if I was interested.

I thought they were kidding—me in a coal mine?! I couldn't imagine it in my wildest imagination. But it was quite a challenge and I like a challenge—so I went through the whole physical, the works. And I got the job.

326

I have been a coal miner now for eight months and we have been on strike for four months now. We knew this strike was going to come about but we didn't think it would last this long. It's the side benefits that are the issue, not the wages. I don't like the contract that they have now. We have to pay a portion of the liability hospitalization and medical and I don't think we should. Workers at the steel companies and the other big plants aren't paying and we're down underground. I don't think we should have to pay any of our medicals.

When I first started to work in the mines there were two black women and two white. One white girl—we are good friends—was wearing the loudest perfume—you could smell it all over the mine. Any time we'd go down in the mine the wind would blow the perfume back and the men would swoon.

At first the men didn't want us in there. And just the mere fact that they didn't want us made me determined to stay. The wives didn't want us there either, but after a while everybody started adjusting. The men really carried us through a whole lot to see if we were going to stick—curse, chew tobacco, dip snuff—I can't stand snuff—and they spit. When you just ignore it, they stop, or now, if they do it, they say they're sorry.

There are a few hard men though, who still want us to go. They say if you can't do the job, just go. We had to do work we weren't hired to do that they were tired of doing. But we can do it better. I'm capable of doing my share of work and so is the next woman.

So finally they offered us an easier job and now I trip-ride on the graveyard shift. I'm a switchman, like on a railroad. We pull sixteen tons of coal—sometimes eighteen—and I get off and switch tracks so we can carry it out or empty it or let people by or hook up the empties. What I got to do, I can do real quick. I switch tracks and then I hop back on, so we can continue moving to get more trips in.

I'm almost six feet tall, but certain places they run you through are four feet high. I stayed there like a punishment thing to show them I could do it and that I wouldn't refuse. Beforehand, I had claustrophobia. We got in these little things, about three on each side, and I felt real closed in, but I wouldn't give in. I just knew that it wouldn't last long and that I could adjust. At times fear would come over me that I couldn't breathe and I had to keep telling myself that this thing I was in wasn't that small and that I really could breathe. I also had to get used to the darkness, but once you do, you just go and you don't even think about what's out there in the darkness.

I like the mines but I'm not going to stay. I got a grant to study engineering. I've had it for the longest time. As long as I try to get into a school before May, I'll still be able to use it. I'm still going to be connected with the mine or the steel company.

I'm not going back into any of the regular run-of-the-mill women's jobs because I like the challenge of what I do now. Plus, it's more money and I'm head of the household. I figure then I should be making head of the household money and you make that in the fields where the men work.

It's not just the money though. It's a different thing working with a bunch of men than it is working with a bunch of women. I don't mind going to work now; it doesn't get boring. Not that you could tell too much in the mine, but you do go out of your way to do little extra things for yourself. With a bunch of women you don't do it because no matter what you do women don't look at you no kind of way. You get a better feeling being a couple of females around a bunch of men. It's a feeling of appreciation.

I still think women should be women, but I also want to be able to do whatever has to be done. If I was called to go to war, I wouldn't want my country to give in because I was incapable of going. I do believe, though, you can go out too far in a man's field and forget your way back. And if you try coming back, it won't be the same.

I've changed to a certain degree. All the women at work have. At the beginning four of us were divorced and four were married. And now, believe it or not, we are all divorced.

If I got married again, I know it wouldn't last because I'm so independent. I've gone through so much. I believe in being free. I've been divorced a long time, long before my ex-husband got killed. I don't have to ask a man for anything—I have my own credit, my own car and my own house. Even with the strike I'm not really having trouble making ends meet because two of my children are on Social Security. I don't get union benefits, but I got food stamps this month. I don't know what I could get from a man.

So much has happened since we've been on strike. About two and a half weeks after we came out my son was killed, and I've been really—well...I go into the Bible a lot, because I've been probing a lot of things I hadn't been able to understand, like death. I pray often, because I don't have strength by myself and I feel like I get it from the Almighty.

I don't value money as much as I did when I first went into the mines. My values have changed about a lot of things. I value humans more because we are down there. If one of them gets hurt, it's like a feeling of oneness. It's like when you hurt your hand, no matter which finger you hurt, it hurts your whole body. Down there a guy got his pelvis broke, and it was almost like you could feel it. In no time the whole mine knew that he got hurt, and they worked together, just like that.

"I value humans more because we are down there. If one of them gets hurt, it's like a feeling of oneness."

You're always aware that God is down there, right there with you all the time, taking care of you. Because no way in the world can you go that far down in the ground and be able to come out again every day without God.

Monica   Fire Island, New York

She was a sixty-six year old woman with a twinkle in her eye. She was between jobs as a private nurse to the elderly and she came to Fire Island for a holiday—to be waited upon, to be pampered and to have a breather—before she returned to the city to search for a job in which she would have to cater to others.

I have never felt I needed a man to complete my life. I married at age thirty-five and six years later, when my second child was a year old, he left. My husband was not a family man and did not want children. I was very happy with the children and, of course, I always had men friends.

329

In 1970 I started to go back and forth to Hungary every year. I had lived in Hungary until I was nineteen years old. My grandfather had been a prominent architect there and my uncle had been mayor of Budapest. There were a lot of ties and that was why I loved going back and forth.

But the Hungarians said that I should decide where I was going to live. Since my Social Security is only $219 and I had the opportunity to work in Hungary teaching English or synchronizing films or editing, I gave up my home in the States. My girls had become independent and I too, became an independent woman. I divided my things between my two daughters, sold my furniture and just pulled up roots.

I was there for only six weeks when the Social Security in America wrote to tell me I could only work one week a month. So if I worked in Hungary, I would not get my Social Security, and if I didn't work, $219 was not much to live on.

I had real problems getting out of Hungary and when I did finally leave I had to leave most of my things behind, lifetime beautiful things that I had inherited and that I had bought there. Anything above the value of thirty dollars you can't remove from the country.

But never mind; I am happy to be out. I had never felt the lack of freedom in Hungary before. I was a very honored tourist coming with dollars, but when I had only $219 a month, things were different. As a Hungarian citizen I wasn't entitled to live in hotels. They shifted me from guest house to guest house—harassment. And before I came back to the United States they forced me to relinquish my Hungarian citizenship and pay for an emigration visa. I had to fill out pages and pages.

On the first trip to Budapest I had looked after an old aunt. This was such a happy experience that when I came back to the States I decided to do private nursing. Of course, I didn't always get a job when I wanted one. Sometimes, also, the patient dies, sometimes they are unsatisfied with me, sometimes we just don't click or the job seems too difficult.

There are many jobs in this field and I have been with all classes—poor people with roaches covering them because they cannot move to get up, and very rich people who sometimes are sick and sometimes just senile. This last May I left the most ideal job: a Hungarian man who had Parkinson's disease and whose wife had just died. He lived in a beautiful apartment and I had a suite all to myself. Then five months later he married, so that job ended very abruptly.

I'm so glad I finally did this sort of work because I don't have the patience to sit in an office. At my age, sixty-six, this is an ideal way to make a living, so I'm really going to try to get back into it, even if at times it is not the most pleasant.

"I've treasured my freedom because I could pick up and do whatever I want. No husband would put up with this."

I haven't ruled out romance and I have very interesting relationships, mostly with younger men. It just happened that way. But I've treasured my freedom because I can pick up and do whatever I want. No husband would put up with this.

Elizabeth   Birmingham, Alabama

In a house that made modern art museums look tacky, light shone on smooth marble floors and the serene environment encouraged contemplation and quiet thought. Elizabeth was a tall, gracious dark-haired woman in her fifties, set apart from most other local women in her generation by her dedication to working for meaningful social change. Her impressive self-assurance and strong resolve were a traceable legacy of the lonely battle she had long been waging.

I was born into a very, very old patrician Birmingham family and I've lived most of my life in Birmingham. When I married my husband I knew I had to marry someone substantial who could take care of me well because I had no skills. I spent my free time doing the usual upwardly mobile things connected with the symphony and the art world that women do.

Then in 1956 Rosa Parks refused to get up and give her seat to a white man on that bus in Montgomery, Alabama. And the bus boycott which started the Civil Rights movement began.

I knew Rosa Parks. She was a seamstress at my house when I was a child; she came once a week to take up our hems. And I'd had a nurse, who was with me from the time I was a child until after I got married, whom I loved more than anything in the world. When Rosa Parks met with trouble, I felt that it could have been my nurse.

Since then I've been trying to bring about political change to improve the conditions of blacks and poor people. I felt that as a privileged white woman it was very important that I not just give my money, so I showed up with my body and began attending meetings of black organizations.

We tried to be the medium through which people could get help, but there were not many answers for the tragic questions that were being asked. What we were doing was putting band-aids on, not bringing about fundamental change. Everything led to City Hall, so I decided that my best bet would be to work politically and I became active in trying to open up the state's Democratic Party. I've been doing that ever since.

I have realized in the past few years that blacks have gotten political and that women have to do the same. When Gloria Steinem came to Alabama about 1971 to try to raise consciousness for a women's political caucus here, I knew it couldn't happen unless somebody with some clout helped it, so I did it. I testified for ERA in the Senate, and after the Houston meetings for the International Women's Year I started doing the nitty gritty of the organization.

I've never felt the need for a job, either to be occupied or to have credentials. I'm really sort of grateful that I don't have to work. If I did, it would be a disaster because I'm not equipped for it—I have no skills. I've never been forced out there.

People ask me why I don't run for office, but I'm really not interested. I feel that I can be much more important as a catalyst helping other people get into positions of power.

"I don't feel a sense of dependence at all and I don't give a damn what anybody thinks of me."

My husband holds positions of power on bank boards and corporate law firms and I know a lot of secrets. I can impart a lot of information to women. I feel that what I do is much more important than getting out there to work. I don't feel a sense of dependence at all and I don't give a damn what anybody thinks of me.

"Most of my peer group are drinking themselves to death."

I was raised to think I was a princess and I have never had any doubts that I was anything other than a good person. I was raised to be the person I looked to the world to be, even though I knew I didn't feel like what I looked to be. But it was not until I read *The Feminine Mystique* that I even knew I was a woman. I remember crying the whole time I was reading it. I went through an identity crisis from 1956 until I read that book; I had a very hard time and I had nobody in the world that I could talk to about it. I had a lot of trouble trying to express myself to my friends, particularly on the black question. Nice white southern ladies didn't do what I was doing. Women of my social and financial class were not interested in the women's movement either. I think some of them looked on me with envy, but they couldn't see that they could do anything themselves. Most of my peer group are drinking themselves to death.

My involvement with the Civil Rights and women's movements has been an extremely lonely battle, but my children have been very supportive of me and my family loved me. However, I had a terrible time maritally with the situation. We had had some really good years when I was being what my husband wanted me to be—an ornament. If I had lain on the chaise lounge all day being fanned by lackeys, and he'd have come home, spoken nonentities, and then been free to read his *New York Times* and his *Birmingham News* and go to bed, that would have suited him just fine. After all, I was supposed to stay home, to be his wife, and be the mother of his children.

I argued with him. I wanted to talk about things, but it made no difference. I got to feel like maybe I was going crazy.

I think I'm pretty much over that now, but it was awful and it has hurt my marriage. Though we get along fairly well, I can't tell my husband how I feel. He just doesn't understand.

However, the money I give away I get from my husband; I have none of my own. Many times my husband didn't know what he was giving to. He has given me—I hate to use the term—leeway, and has never said, "You can't do this," or "You can't do that." He was not at all of my persuasion and still is not, but he knows me and I think he realizes that I'm sincere.

I'm grateful because I can do as I please. He has been so generous. I can write a check for whatever I want, so I don't have a need to make money that is my very own. Now, I don't say that I wouldn't like to have some credibility or success in a creative way, but I don't necessarily feel that I have to make money to do it.

I do feel guilty about having so much money or I wouldn't spend so much time giving it away, I guess. But I'm not a totally serious person: I spend a lot of money too. I'm pretty frivolous in many ways. I love to travel and to have clothes and do things. I could have been a displaced homemaker right off the bat, so I do think that I'm just sheer lucky.

I get lonely, there's no question about that, but I am sustained in so many ways outside, and I have so much going for me, that I really can deal with that.

SEEING COMMITMENTS THROUGH

Hy   Miami Beach, Florida

As most people do, we dreaded going to a nursing home—the last residence of the aged and infirm who, for the most part, are left alone by those who had once known them so well.

Hy was a small, spunky man—Damon Runyon-style, New York tough and humorous—the rare, so very rare person who could not forget and abandon. Daily he came to the nursing home to care for Sarah, his wife.

After he told us his story, he invited us firmly to come upstairs and meet Sarah. There was no escaping our dread of the sights and smells of the corridors. Walking past the lame, the immobile and the babbling, we entered Sarah's room and were immediately set upon by her roommate, who kept up a relentless chant, crying for a corned beef sandwich.

Sarah looked up at Hy and, without a murmur, let him seat her in a wheelchair and place her feet on the footrests. Hy took the pad for incontinence on which she had been lying, and left the room to dispose of it; Sarah began agonizing sadly, "Babababababababa."

Her cry hushed as soon as he returned. He put his hand on her cheek and patted it. She lifted her hand and held it on his.

Watching, we felt an uncontrollable stream of tears flowing down our cheeks—tears for the love, the commitment, the patience—tears for the pain and the stupid, careless mistakes, tears for the shame, the ignorance and the known and unknown fears.

I always worked—made a dollar. Now I wouldn't say that at my age I wouldn't go to work. If my wife was all right, I'd still go to work because at sixty-nine I'm still a young man. But I feel my wife comes before anything else and that's why I'm here with her in the nursing home.

My wife had a hysterectomy; they gave her too much anesthesia and she had brain damage. That was about eleven years ago. I left my job in New York, then after about a year I figured the climate was not for my wife and myself, so I moved to Florida.

The first month we were here she was all right, then she went on me. It's five years now that she's in a nursing home and I take care of her every day. I stay here seven days a week from seven in the morning till five-thirty at night. I take her out of bed, I wash her and feed her, and take her down in the street about eight or eight-fifteen in the morning and keep her there until about ten. Then I bring her up again and take her to the bathroom. Sometimes I go shopping, but I come back and feed her lunch, then I go home at twelve-thirty and prepare my suppertime. I come back and feed her supper and leave at five. When I get through I go home, eat supper, turn on the television, and make a few calls locally. I go to bed about nine-thirty, ten and get up at five because I got to be here at seven. That's my regular routine.

If I were not here, the aides would take care of her, but not in the manner that I do. She's a very temperamental eater and you've got to use a pair of pliers to open her mouth, but there's ways of doing it. Sometimes when you get her in a good mood, she'll open her mouth. She weighed sixty-seven pounds when she came here and she weighs a hundred and fifteen now. She drinks two, four, six containers of milk a day and I arranged it with the administrator so that the food she eats will have a little milk in it to make it soft enough for her to eat. I don't think there's another nursing home that would let me come seven o'clock in the morning and feed and take care of her. They give me a little leeway here because they see what I do.

The main thing about my job, if you call it a job, is that when I get home at five-thirty, I know I'm content. I've done something. It could be for my wife, it could be for somebody else; it doesn't make a difference.

"The main thing about my job, if you call it a job, is that when I get home at five-thirty, I know I'm content."

She was a very good wife, very good. I can't explain it. And after so many years, forty-seven years of marriage, you don't leave someone flat. You've got to have a feeling for it. If you have no feeling for something, don't do it. I'm not looking for a bouquet of roses; that's the way I feel. If half the people felt what I do, it would be a different world entirely.

"If you have no feeling for something, don't do it."

I have two sons, one forty-five and the other forty-four, but there's a problem with them. Last year the forty-four year old took his mother-in-law home and she said, "Stop off at the grocery store and get a container of yogurt." There was a robbery in progress: the robber got $190 and he put five people in the back. As my son was coming in, the robber was coming out. The money fell on the floor. He took out a shotgun and killed my son.

The city of New York gave $10,000 or $20,000 to the widow. That's the way it worked: the Innocent Bystander law. The kids are too old, so my daughter-in-law can't get Social Security, so I try to whip out a little bit here and there, whatever I can, but it isn't enough. In other words, if you're a parent, you've got to have broad shoulders; you've got to carry everything.

It's very hard, very hard for me to get around. Unfortunately I spent over $63,000 on my wife, all the money I had. It's not a tragedy, it's just one of these things that happens, but it's very tough for me. I've got a nice apartment and I try to keep it that way. My wife's Social Security check goes to the nursing home and I get $297.50. My rent is $185, my electric is about $14, my gas is $4, and my telephone is about $20 on the average. It's really $13.85, but if you want to call your son or niece or nephew, the bill runs up to $20 a month. They don't take that into consideration.

So it's a little rough on me, but I'm not afraid to ask for help. I have a few people trying to see that I get subsidies for my apartment to help me along. I'm not looking for any charity, but I'm not too proud. If you haven't got any money, you go try to get some. You don't stick up anybody, but you try welfare, Medicaid—you try. When you're on the up and up, you're not afraid of anything—period. People respect me here and they respect me outside too.

"When you're on the up and up, you're not afraid of anything—period."

Since I've been tied up in the nursing home, I haven't gone anywhere, but I have a lot of friends. The laundryman came today and the barber came to give my wife and me a haircut. He was an old-time barber who retired and it keeps him occupied. Instead of getting $2.75, he takes $1.50 from me and $1.50 from my wife—that's $3.00. And I take him part of the way home.

There are doctors who have befriended me. It's easy to take out fifty dollars and give a doctor, and to repeat fifty dollars again and fifty dollars again, but there comes a time when you got to stop the fifty dollars. You got to ask them to take you on Medicare and they don't like the idea. But I got a very good doctor, a very good man. The first of the year I give him $120 and that covers my wife and myself for the whole year. This guy took a shine to me, so he comes here once a month.

I got a letter from Medicaid yesterday asking me questions about whether I've got a cemetery plot and a stone. I prepared all that years ago because I know we live today, we die tomorrow, and when you've got the money, you don't care. If you haven't got it, when you die and you haven't got a place to go, you go to Potter's Field.

Medicaid asked me some dumb questions and I felt terrible. I asked the interviewer, "Do you want to know if I have any sex?" I really did, she got me so darn mad. In fact, I wrote her a letter and told her, "You're really something." I didn't use no slang words, but I did use rough language.

I've been trying so darn hard to get along on the monies that I get and nobody—nobody—gives a darn. They push me from one to the other. Friday I went to see some man about a subsidy for my apartment and he said, "Forget it. You've got to wait eight months." Who the heck can wait eight months for a subsidy on an apartment?

In February they gave me food stamps, but in January they turned me down. Now, it's stupid—I had the same problem in January as I had in February. The whole set-up is full of bunk. I told them they sit on their fat can.

The administrator from the county came down to see me this Thursday at my home and saw three television sets. I brought two of them from New York—I have them eight, nine years— and one, a colored twenty-three inch, I paid twenty-five dollars for from a neighbor who was moving back to Minnesota or somewhere.

He says to me, "I would sell it." I says, "Oh, no, I'm not going to sell nothing." I got fifty dresses and a fur coat of my wife's that I won't sell. You can't stop me. As long as she's living I don't sell nothing, that's all. Sue me; do what you want—that's the way I am. It's a tough thing, but what can you do?

Bob Fass   New York, New York

The mellifluous voice was hauntingly familiar. If you closed your eyes, you could easily believe you had tuned in again to one of New York City's most popular and creative radio personalities. But here was Bob Fass in person—a tall, blonde, reserved man, attentive to every nuance of what he heard, responding to questions of what it was like not to work with fascinating originality. After a union-management clash, he had refused to sign an agreement which the radio station mangement had insisted all union members sign, on the grounds that it violated workers' rights and he lost his show. Now he was figuring out how to deal with one of the toughest adjustments in his life—the loss of his work and the loss of his source of support. With characteristic artistry, he was learning to live without being on the air and learning to live on air.

During the years that I was employed I would go to this church on the Upper West—Upper East Side of Manhattan—it's been so long since I've been there—let myself into the building, and walk across a big, open studio, go into a glass control room, sit down, play a few records, meet a few people, and the telephone would start ringing. I would put people on the air and I would talk to them and they would talk to me for five hours—from three to five nights a week.

I did a radio program on WBAI, one of the listener-supported Pacifica radio stations, a progam that was very community-oriented and very concerned with immediacy. The people who called with information about emergencies and about events and happenings in their communities had among their members a large number of activists, organizers, political people, artists, poets, actors, people who worked at night, and people who were out of work and were up at night, all mixed together.

I tried, as much as I could, to express the community's wishes through my program. Anyone who wanted to could get on the air, could say that they liked or didn't like the station, my program, and anything that was on it, at practically any time they wanted. There was no screening of telephone calls; there was no delay. The program was as free as I could make it.

Then there was a management coup at the station. Three new people joined the board and the day that they joined they voted to take the station off the air. The staff had gotten wind of some of the things that the board was going to change and had organized a union. The station manager went to the board and told them she thought the station was out of control. And they took it off the air.

The staff occupied the building in protest. Now the station is back on the air with much of the old staff. Certain of us were arrested when the building was taken back, and some of us, who were thought to be the organizers of the union, were told that we had to sign an agreement in which we promised that we were sorry and that we would never do anything like *that* again. The procedure, as outlined in the letter, was that you sign the letter, then you apply to the management for whatever job openings they may add. And, under certain conditions, you're asked back.

Eight people did sign the letter because they felt that they wanted to get back on the air. I refused to sign it, along with three others. I felt that a symbolic protest was more important for me than getting back on the air.

Would I want to go back? I would want to go back. I'd like to do that work again, yeah. It's also true that I'm forty-four years old and it's harder and harder to make it on that kind of a salary. The work that I did was not so remunerative and it was very rare that I would get my check during the week that I earned it. Sometimes we would be ten weeks, twenty weeks even, behind in our pay. When I did get paid, it was for months and months of work. Because the station was listener-supported, our cash flow was tied to fund drives, essentially, and it was a very badly under-capitalized operation.

I lived on the beneficence of friends and the grudging beneficence of my family. My friends, my family can't be depended upon forever and I need to make what's thought of as a living wage. I worked for a fraction of what people who do similar work in the media earn, and their work is less popular than what I did. I believe I had one of the most, if not the most, popular late-night radio programs in New York City. Certainly the most popular on FM.Things happened in those sixteen years on WBAI that were unique in broadcasting. And I think that I ought to be paid more money, that the people who work at the station ought to be paid more money, that less money should go into bricks and mortar.

I think the most central part of my program's success came from a respect for the audience and a willingness to listen, even at the expense of having people who'd been anesthetized by the rest of the media call and express their flatness of mind. To use radio as a kind of speeded-up Muzak—"And now here's the weather and now here's a driver report, and now, back to bababa—bababa," is a very narrow use of radio. I have miles and miles of tape with discussions and conversations that had real substance. Things happened in those sixteen years on WBAI that were unique in broadcasting.

When I had the show, my routines had to do with preparation for what I felt was a fairly rigorous five hours of very concentrated mental and physical work. I would get up late in the afternoon and start on newspapers, telephone calls, and television news. I would try to hear as many repetitions of the all-news radio stations as I could. I feel that there is a kind of community culture that's largely dominated by electronic media and, to a certain extent, by daily print media, and I would try to be up on those things.

I had a routine of physical exercises that I would do so that I would be able to handle the night. I still try to do my physical yoga to get myself into shape, keep myself physically fit. I have some very good friends who try to keep me on routines and try to keep me doing things.

I tend to keep to the old pattern of being awake nights, although perforce job appointments are usually very early in the day—or they seem to be early for me—so I've had to reorient my schedule. But even then it wasn't the pure nighttime schedule. I would be awake some mornings and some nights, and there appears to be a certain price that you pay changing bio-clocks so often. I guess I'm still paying it.

Sometimes there are things that I want to do that happen late at night. New York tends to be much more of a twenty-four hour city than most, and I keep my contacts up. When one of my musician friends is in town, I do my best to, if not see the performance, go and talk to him.

This life does have its good features. I have more time for relationships with people. I spend more time with my friends than I spent before. Then, my friends tended to be people who I worked with; now, my friends are people who are in their own work or their own unemployment. My friends who are artists—what's the work of an artist? Is an artist unemployed?

You need, you really need, in addition to food, clothing, and shelter, you need love and you need work in order to feel fulfilled. Now, work doesn't have to be wage-slavery employment, but you need work. I could find things to do that I would call work, but I need to pay rent and buy food. Clothing has to be bought and shelter, too, so you're faced with the necessity of combining your work with a job, and a job is not the same as a work. Most people don't even have the privilege of finding that out, but if you manage to find yourself some unalienated work, you can understand what I mean.

I believe I had work that I was less alienated from than most people can ever be. I loved doing it much of the time. I got to meet some of the most exciting people of this time, some of the most famous people, some of the most famous outlaws, some of the best poets, some of the greatest musicians. That's rare and a great gift.

What I tried to do was retain that one-to-one feeling while I was talking to a mass of people, or while a mass of people, as individuals maybe, were talking to me, or while individuals were talking to me in front of a mass of people. That became my work and I do miss that.

Not being able to do it must have affected me emotionally, though it's not as though it's been in my dreams for months. Only when the thing began and we were actively in the strike at the station did it get into my dreams. I think I have fewer moments now when the first thing that happens when I wake up in the morning—really, mostly in the afternoon—no, that's not true—I guess it's really the morning—I used to wake up in the afternoon—you know, when you're coming back into consciousness—there's a disoriented moment until I like pull myself back into where I'll be and what I'll do.

I imagine that—yeah, I guess I've been depressed. There have been times when I've felt depression, immobility. There's a kind of a nagging, inexplicable need to be in New York that I guess I can give rational reasons for. I could probably find an equal number of rational reasons to leave New York, but...

"If you go to a machine that produces something and you're the human part of that couple, you feed into the machine and, in a way, the machine keeps you doing only what the machine understands."

I've been thinking about the difference between how I use the time I have now and how I used to use my time. If you go to a machine that produces something and you're the human part of that couple, you feed into the machine and, in a way, the machine keeps you doing only what the machine understands. In other words, if you go into a structure, the structure has its effect on you.

Freed from the necessity to do what I do in front of a microphone with tape recorders and turntables, I'm still making things out of media. Now I make a movie. I record something on a tape recorder outside. I take a pen and I write something. I use the telephone. I don't know what this means, but someone called me one of the premier telephone artists of the time. I use a telephone differently from the way it's normally thought of. I use it more consciously. Even though I'm not in the studio now, I still use the telephone in the same way.

The movie I'm making is about the part of everyone's world that no one ever sees. If you eat meat and you don't know where meat comes from, you're only living a partly conscious life, I think. I went to a slaughterhouse with a Super-8 camera and I shot a color movie and interviewed a kosher butcher. That kosher butcher has an attitude toward his work, an attitude toward the inflicting of pain—even an attitude about the quality of food that he passes on to the consumer—that's totally different from the attitude of the people right next to him who are working on the meat assembly line. And it's a very interesting point of comparison—not to say that there's any less death, but—there's something to be understood about alienation at that point, because it's such an extreme example of it.

I've no way to measure the artistry or creativity of what I've done in this time. Sometimes I do crap—like if the machine had been there I would have been doing crap with the machine. Because if you're creative, your output is never steady productive. It's like you empty yourself and then you have to wait to be filled up. I don't know if I'm more creative now or less. I think some things I've done now are things I would never have thought of doing had I had the job.

But making the film is work; it's not a job. And there's no way to get money from it, or even for it—to do it. It doesn't stop you from doing it, but it slows you down.

Money. Well, I collect unemployment. I have some money that I get from my family. Every once in a while a friend buys me some groceries. I pile up debts of money and debts of love. My lights have been turned off. My upstairs neighbor helps me—he lends me electricity—there's an extension cord that runs out my rear window and up into his apartment.

It's one thing when your hot water heater breaks to be able to call Sears, Roebuck and order another to replace it. It's another thing—in a way—well, I don't know if it's more satisfying or not—but I went without a hot water heater, borrowing baths from friends, for almost a month till I got a telephone call from one of my friends who told me that a house on the Lower East Side had collapsed in the rain. I knew the people who had lived in the house—none of them had been hurt. The wall just crumbled and there were three hot water heaters hanging in the middle of the air in this house.

So my friend and I went to the house in his truck. He climbed up the side of the crumbling brick wall and we went in and unhooked a hot water heater, brought it here, and got it hooked up.

Has this led you into considering other economic shortcuts?

What do you mean?

Well, there are all kinds of illegal activities people do to bring money in. Some people deal dope. Some people shoplift. Kite checks. Rob banks, pimp—there's...

Wait a minute—I'm writing these down. You say there's money in these things? They sound like public services to me. I overpark...

No, as a matter of fact, when a friend says after a trip to the A & P, "Aah, I ripped them off this box of River Brand Brown Rice!" I always say, "Jesus, $.75, $.80 and you took a chance on..." I've got something of that bourgeois unbringing that makes it hard for me to think past "What if they caught me."

I collect unemployment and there's something dehumanizing about it, but I guess I manage with as little dehumanization as possible. I don't think I'm eligible for food stamps or any other state-run program. I have a source of income that I think other people don't have—from my parents—and it would make me feel sort of like I'd be, you know, taking something from somebody if I had income from a state-supported service, too.

If these programs were even doing a job taking care of really desperate people, people who are in real need, I might feel better about it, but they're not. I guess I could explore some of them, though there's something very dehumanizing about the way the food stamp program has been administered in the last couple of years. If these things could be handled humanely, oh, yeah, put my name on the list.

Still, all evidence to the contrary, I'm optimistic about this society. Allen Ginsberg says it looks like this is the last downward slide. John Lilly, the guy who talks to the porpoises, says that things are getting used up too fast. Timothy Leary says our only hope is to leave the planet. But somehow I don't feel there's any reason for pessimism. All you have to do is look around and see that the solution is here; there are better ways to handle the resources of the globe, there are better ways to do things than "crapitalism." That's not the same thing as capitalism—it's the artificial manipulation and creation of the desire for electric toothbrushes that's destroying us. It's unnecessary things that are being produced by all the production potential we have.

"All you have to do is look around and see that the solution is here; there are better ways to handle the resources of the globe, there are better ways to do things than 'crapitalism.' "

Still, I'd like to be able to afford to buy a Water-Pik. I gotta get a job—I think I've gotta get a job. I've got to get some place where I can do what I do.

Do you feel strong?

Mm hmm, I do.

Where do you draw your strength from?

Push-ups, brown rice, bean sprouts, fish. Oh, friends. Certain contraband—herbal sacraments.

Now, if I had an income sufficient to live on and buy materials to make things with—videotape, hardware—I think I'd probably create a structure of some kind that other people could work in, could do things in. "Time passes slowly up here in the mountains. We sit beside rivers and...Sit beside fountains?" Is that the kind of life I would live? Each man sitting under his vine?

Well, I've never had that situation exactly, although in a way I do, but...See, the thing I really haven't talked about is probably because I was lying when I said I felt strong. I feel strong sometimes and sometimes I feel very weak. The ego gratification that came with my work is not—I mean, I'm not—I miss it. It isn't there. And I have to find other things to feed my self-esteem with. There are times when my friends have to kid me along and push me to do things.

If you conceive of yourself as an artist, there are times when you feel empty and you're waiting for whatever the juices are that make you spew to fill up. During that time there's a kind of feeling that you'll never, you'll never be able to paint that next painting, or you'll never be able to put another note on paper, or word, or whatever it is that you do. And then friends help.

I'm not so sure that in that sense life with my job was all that different from not working, except that I don't have the constant stimulation of doing it every day. Your sense of yourself can be out of proportion to the actuality. A job, a paycheck, not having to stand on the unemployment line— those things contribute to self-esteem and the others diminish it. So you need friends more, and I have a few really good ones.

My situation is unique. I'm unemployed, but there are thousands of people maybe—a couple hundred, anyway—who are calling the radio station where I used to work and asking why I'm not there. So I get a certain amount of ego boost out of that that most people not working don't get. My situation is really one of the most fortunate of the unemployed, I think. Even fellow artists that I meet on the unemployment line who have unique situations don't have the kind of support and help that I get.

Every situation of finding yourself unemployed is different. I was fired from the station once before. It was within three months after I began to do my program, 1961 or '62, and it was devastating, devastating. When I was in the army, I was fired after two years, and that felt wonderful! When you're fired in a strike, it's another kind of emotional situation.

And I was fired in a way, many times, when I was in the theater. When a play closes, everyone's fired. If the play had any kind of a run, you had developed emotional and almost familial ties with anywhere from four to twenty other people and it's very poignant.

One time I was fired for a criminal act. I worked in a luncheonette and they caught me stealing coke. When a horse grinds grain, the biblical injunction is that the horse is allowed to eat anything he wants, but if you work in a restaurant and you take food....! That felt bad. I felt like I shouldn't have done it. It was pretty stupid.

I consider myself a worker, though I don't so much make personal identification, because I think everybody's life is unique. I have worked in a factory—in a very noisy and very alienated factory—so I know what I do and don't want and I know that there are other possibilities. I feel differently about what it's possible to get out of work. I don't identify with the alienation of someone for whom a job in an office working on a typewriter or sending out bills is their only work aspiration. But I identify with the oppression.

"I'm looking to make a compromise between the most remunerative and the least disgusting work that I can do."

I am looking for work. I'm looking to make a compromise between the most remunerative and the least disgusting work that I can do. I did hear about some work that I could have gotten that I didn't pursue. It was dubbing, doing a voice track, in a porn film. And, I don't know why, because I've got no objection to people going and watching porn films, but somehow I didn't want to do it. I never have done an analysis of it in my own head; I just knew it wouldn't jibe for me. The people who make porn or make money out of porn are not—there's something wrong with it somewhere. I think people who watch porn films are probably the only honest part of that production line.

I don't know where I heard this, but someone said it's like the American nightmare—forty and unemployed and with no money in the bank. Anyone thinking of changing jobs and not really ready to go work yet should make sure of having plenty of money in the bank. Ninety-five or a hundred dollars a week is not really enough for someone who's out of their twenties— or out of their teens, even—to live on.

I hear about people all the time who, to keep up appearances with their children, keep up appearances with their wife, get up and shave every morning and pretend to dress for work. And they go out—even if they don't look for work they go out as though they were. And I wonder whether that's a good thing to do or not. In a way it keeps them in the traces in a way that is bad for their ultimate re-entry into some other situation.

It's supposed to be a socially useful thing for people to change careers. They enrich the career that they go to and they make room for new people in their old jobs. I guess a good thing to do, if you have security and necessities, is maybe take a sabbatical. Everybody should have the right to take a sabbatical. You do the same work for a certain amount of time and it gets to be—well, if the human brain sees the same image over and over and over again, it stops seeing it—it doesn't detect the changes in it. There are enough images stored in the brain so that the brain says, "I've seen that one before." And I think that limits creativity and growth and change and thinking of ways out.

Maybe we're accustomed to thinking of the resources of this society in too limited a way. There is enough to provide for career change and for proper care of mothers and infants. There is enough to make sure that people have comfortable, warm old ages. Some people have much too much—too much is wasted on armaments—but there is certainly enough to redistribute and provide for these things. If military people, who tend to think in terms of aggression and hostility, had other orientations, I think maybe things would change.

Should we support sabbaticals for generals?

Well, no, maybe we could stop supporting generals. Then we could start supporting sabbaticals for everybody.

Without signing a loyalty oath, Bob went back on the air at WBAI.

Mark

Malibu, California

The contrast between Mark's no-nonsense style of a businessman accustomed to cutting hard deals and his profoundly calm underlying patience was startlingly novel. Here was a person who, in a most unusual way, had changed his concept of how a man should live and what a man should be and was living it out. The happy sounds of teen-aged boys in the next room were living proof of the success of his choice.

I was managing a band in the music biz. Over three years ago I made a record deal and made a lot of money. The band broke up before the record was released, so there was no continuation of income. I had to live off the money from the basic deal itself.

Everything about the record deal was wrong. The guys in the band were all wrong for each other. My partner and I were wrong for each other. The deal was wrong. But we forced it and made it happen. Then the group broke up anyway, so everything blew up in our faces and there were bad feelings all the way around. It was a good lesson.

All at the same time the woman I had been living with for three years and I broke up because everything just went stale, and my kids came out from New York for the summer, which they usually did, and decided they wanted to stay.

I got involved with my kids and decided not to force anything, just allow it to happen and sort of nudge it along. I decided I was not going to do anything I don't like doing and only do those things that flow easily without my having to break down walls to do them.

I flowed right into it. All I had to do was rearrange my life to do the things I found important to do. The other things—making money and building a career—became secondary, sort of an 80 percent/20 percent thing.

"Some of the greatest decisions that you ever make come out of trauma, out of terrible things."

It became the most dramatic change of my whole life. Some of the greatest decisions that you ever make come out of trauma, out of terrible things. You come out a totally new person. Since that time my outlook has been totally new.

My kids wanted me to coach the football team and I got involved in the Malibu Boys' Football Association, an organization that's plugged into the national Pop Warner football thing. I started by coaching the eleven and twelve year old kids, then the following year I coached the thirteen and fourteen year old group.

I spent every day working on it: practice five days a week, two hours a day, in addition to making up all my plays in the evenings. I loved it. It was something I had never felt before. Things relating to kids were coming out of me that I never knew were inside of me.

Then something happened that took me into a whole other life. One of the football players died from a drug-related thing: he took two Quaaludes, washed it down with some brandy and went swimming. I just stood there, then I turned around and said, "This kid didn't have to die. His friends all around him could have saved him. This is stupid. He died because of stupidity. He didn't know."

So I got involved in setting up a drug education project at the school. I'd always known that all opposition to drug education and sex education in schools is based on the assumption that knowledge is harmful and if we tell the kids about it, they're going to start doing it. Well, they're doing it. Whether we like it or not, they're doing it and we've got to teach them what they're doing.

When I first went to the school about the plan the principal said, "Just a few bad kids using drugs, so we don't really have a problem. The police can arrest them and take care of them."

"I told him, 'Before another kid dies, I will burn your school down.'"

But I'm a parent. My kid goes to that school, so I wouldn't accept what he was telling me. I told him, "Before another kid dies, I will burn your school down." He saw that I was serious and he got scared, so he let me in.

The program works real good. We have drug education in the junior high school and at an elementary school and we have a professional who is teaching information about drugs to the teachers. It's not just a little, local Malibu thing; we've been invited to speak and to teach drug education in other communities as well. The program is so large in scope and our plans are so big that people from Sacramento have come down to see what the hell we were doing.

I'm going to be one of those guys that's going to help change the laws and policies because they're stupid, but right now I want to protect the kids' lives, that's all. I want them to know that I'm there, that I'm their friend—I understand. I'm thirty-four and I used drugs recreationally myself, the way the kids are using drugs now, for fifteen years. I used everything in the world. I never was a junkie and I was never an alcoholic, so I'm not a fanatic. I don't have the urgency about me that if I shoot smack one more time then I'm right back into it—I don't have that shit.

My approach to kids using drugs is that I don't judge them and I don't moralize. I don't place a tremendous urgency on life or death because first of all, all kids are convinced they cannot die. A life and death urgency on a situation draws them toward it because it's exciting. I don't want to make it sound that dangerous because danger is exciting and drugs ain't that exciting, just a little bit.

I don't want to make heroes out of these kids, so I don't want to be arresting any of them. Arresting a kid, taking him to jail and keeping him there for three hours—the limit you can keep a minor—then having his parents pick him up and take him back home makes a hero out of him when he goes back to school. But these kids are not heroes. It's not acceptable to do drugs when you're thirteen years old.

So I don't want to make drugs romantic and exciting. I want to take the veil of mystery off it and let some fresh air blow through it, let it become just another thing that we live with, because that's what it is. The American drug culture is not such a big deal—it's like the American music culture and the American automobile culture and the American whatever. When you make it a big deal, people become afraid to look at it. Then the kids, who are naturally lured toward anything that you say "no" to are lured to it.

I want to take that lure away. I want the kids to be aware of the real dangers involved with drugs and to be aware of their own bodies, their own weaknesses, their own strengths. I want to raise the consciousness level so that they become aware of what motivates people to do things.

I don't want to scare them; I just want them to understand what drugs can do. Do the trip, go ahead; have a wonderful time. I hope it's a good trip. But just remember, if you're still tripping after three days, give me a call; I'll talk to you.

I think all adults should have the capacity to become fifteen again when they sit down to talk to a fifteen-year old person. They don't do it because they're afraid to say, "I don't know," when a kid asks a question, so they give them some cock-and-bull garbage.

Me, I tell them, "I don't know. Go find out for yourself, and when you find out I want you to tell me, so then I'll know." When you don't know things you become more human and you become closer to them.

I can't lie or not be totally honest and straight with a kid and I like that feeling. If I'm telling a story and there's a little lie in there, I make sure that kids know it's a lie and we laugh about it. There's enough lying and cheating and other bullshit going on so that I don't feel very pure in the work world, but I bring some of this attitude from working with kids into what I do in business. It helps me relate to the rest of the world.

I've been offered money to do this work and I won't take it. If I did take small amounts for speaking engagements, I would just kick it back into the project. I think it's important for everybody to know that so far I'm volunteering this service.

I'm living very poorly financially right now, but this is the richest time of my life in terms of people and community and my kids and recognition. Just the other night I got a community service award that's given to one person from the junior high school every year from the national PTA.

There's a directorship to the project that should pay about $32,000 a year. If there are ever monies to pay that slot and I am in it, then I will accept that kind of payment, drop anything else that I'm involved in, and do the work full-time, because I think it's important. That way I'll be able to sustain myself and do the job the way it's supposed to be done, not run around town trying to hustle up a publishing deal for somebody, then come home at six or seven o'clock and go to a drug seminar. Instead of living two or three different lives, I'd be able to live one life and be paid for it.

When I came out of the record deal, I had enough survival money so I could make it through however long I wanted to, living at different levels of comfort. I was about $16,000 in debt to all the plastic and all the banks, and in order to survive and take care of the food and rent and everything else, I had to put them on the secondary payment list.

Sometimes I had a flash or two on where I was going to get the rent money for the month, and somehow it came—a little shuffling here and there, a couple of phone calls, a couple of deals. I did some odd jobs, things I didn't really like to do like carpentry work—not really a job-job. Plus I was fortunate to be in a big enough house that I could rent out different units to cover my rent and a little bit more.

It works out; it comes together. It's all attitude. You can survive at any financial level as long as your attitude is straight and you don't consider yourself poor or destitute.

I have a couple close friends, people who care about me and that I care about. My relationships with women have become almost non-existent because the pressure and demands I've put on myself almost totally eliminate a real loving, caring, sharing relationship with a woman. Years ago I was able to go through a lot of women in a week or a month, but now that same energy is going in another direction.

Sometimes I hate it because I'm a normal, healthy guy, yet if it's a choice between being with my woman that night and going to the movies with fifteen kids, I take the kids. I don't want to subject a woman to that. Not only that, I'm not putting myself into an environment where I meet women, and those women that I do meet hanging around or something don't measure up.

After the band broke up, I didn't completely abandon the music industry that kept me alive for fifteen years. I have a lot of friends in good places and I work well with those people. If I have a tape of an artist, I can take it to a guy at Columbia Records—I can go to Casablanca Records—to different record companies. They will at least open the door and listen to it. If the music is right, they'll buy it. If I can help guide an artist's career along and make some money, I'll do it, but it doesn't take any tremendous ambition or aggression. I'm not that career-minded.

I'm working now with some artists in the studio and in live performances, and I'm trying to make a publishing deal. I'm writing a book on drug education. I'm doing research, talking to doctors, narcotics agents, and kids, mostly kids. And I draw from my own personal experiences about using drugs.

I find I'm very unhappy when I have to account for time, so I went in a direction where I'd be getting paid for however I felt I wanted to spend my time. I never went in a work direction. I work every day, I think, because I create things in my mind that eventually I put into practical application. Yet none of that is work.

I spend eighteen hours in a recording studio being with an artist because he needs me to be there. I don't do anything; I just sit there, but if I'm not there, he feels terribly uncomfortable and lost. And if I'm there, he feels very good and he creates more easily.

Eighteen hours of being someplace could be considered work, but it's not really work to me. I don't know what the hell it is, I just know that I have to be content doing things. If I'm not happy, then it's not going to last very long for me.

I only worry about one thing: that something will force me to move away from working with kids and being available to them, something economic or physical or medical. The kids are the most important thing to me.

The kids are the victims of a handful of powerful men who govern everything in this world. They elect presidents, they own countries; they *are* power. If they were really concerned about cutting off the drugs, the heroin would stop, the cocaine would stop, the pills would stop. The flow of drugs coming into this country could be cut off in a day if somebody really wanted to cut them off, but there's too much money and power involved.

There's insanity going on all around us that is too big for me to control, but I can control something here, so I'm concerned about my little thing right down here in Malibu. I don't want to lose another kid. And I would love to keep doing this for the rest of my life because it reminds me of the kind of person I could be, the kind of person that I am.

Stewart Mott   Washington, D.C.

At the age of forty, he had already established himself as a philanthropist of progressive political causes. He was forthright with us. As we sat talking in his Washington townhouse that doubled as home and office, it was clear from the efficient responses and the press clippings he showed us that he had been interviewed and had answered the same questions many times before.

I am an heir to the General Motors fortune and I was moved to work in philanthropy and politics by my education, by the fact of my inheritance and by the good example set by my father. I work full-time in public service. It's hard to define what a philanthropist is; most people go blank when I introduce myself as one. It's not like being a dentist; you know what a dentist does all day long. Those of us like John D. Rockefeller, myself, and a few others who don't get paid for it, you consider "not working," but I take it very seriously.

"It's hard to define what a philanthropist is; most people go blank when I introduce myself as one."

When I was a child I had the same childhood fantasies about being a fireman and all that nonsense as the other kids. As I moved into my teens I thought maybe I'd work for General Motors for a stretch of time. I did have some jobs and for a year I immersed myself as an executive trainee in the various companies that were wholly owned by the Mott Foundation, thinking I should prepare myself for a career in the Foundation, to help continue what my father had begun. He was already well into his nineties. But I found I wasn't exactly welcome at the Foundation, so I began developing my own priorities.

I realized that my home town of Flint, Michigan didn't have a family planning clinic so I became the founder, president and executive director of its first birth control clinic. It was a marvelous experience to come home and be in charge of such an operation. I continued to work on population control through Planned Parenthood when the government was doing virtually nothing about it. Now that the Federal Government is funding research and services, both domestically and internationally, I am working with the lobby here in Washington to urge additional funding, the likes of which I couldn't afford in the private sector.

At about age thirty I started to become active in politics. First I considered a political career of my own, then I decided to begin supporting candidates and work to reform the political and governmental systems. I worked closely with the leaders of the anti-Vietnam War Movement. My work now is a mix of population control and foreign affairs and military policy.

I suppose I began setting my money to work to alleviate social problems out of some sort of Puritan Ethic or guilt, but in a more affirmative way I think I realized that I had the income to permit me to do whatever I pleased. I found the people that I've worked with were extremely intelligent and enjoyable. It was fun to work with them and fun to develop the talents that were called for. I think my work has been the most successful aspect of my life. For ten years it has gone along smoothly and I feel that I'm doing many things for which I have a great facility. I'll probably wind up doing the same sort of thing for another decade or two.

My life is extremely unstructured, and since I work at home and allow part of my personal life to invade the working day, it's difficult to measure how much time I put in. I would guess it's about fifty to sixty hours a week now. I work evenings and weekends and a lot of my personal hours are work-related in some fashion.

I bought this house not just to have a Washington office, but also for the thirty to forty other people who maintain projects in the other rooms. The reception room is a nice place for me to entertain on occasion, but actually most of my entertaining is not personal but organizational receptions.

If I'm out late at night I don't hesitate to sleep until ten or eleven in the morning. But because my home is my office it's a bit embarrassing when my staff arrives at nine and sees my bedroom door closed. They have no idea what's going on in there.

My income this past year was about $2 million and a million of that will go into charitable activities. I realize that an income that large sets me apart from 99 percent of the American public, but I'm not very self-conscious about being wealthy because I spend most of my time with people who are not especially rich. Sometimes I feel as though people are treating me with kid gloves because I'm a major donor in an organization, but there are not that many differences between my friends and me in terms of what we like and the way we live. My closest men friends are people with whom I work. Most are middle income professionals thirty-five, forty, forty-five years old, in the $30,000 to $40,000 earning range. They're not poor.

I live a very informal life style, one which does not rely at all on butlers, chauffeurs, maids, limousines, yachts, and private planes, which often set apart the super-rich. In fact, there are a lot of people who have far less money than I do who indulge themselves far more in those luxuries. I ride my bicycle to get around New York for appointments and I wear jeans and denim suits. I have just not surrounded myself with the trappings of wealth. I think I use my resources wisely.

Money has played an unimportant role in the relationships I have with women. No woman who spends much time with me expects me to lavish gifts and gold. Sure, for a working woman who is supporting herself, perhaps the notion of living with Stewart Mott would relieve her of the necessity of having a nine to five job to earn $15,000 or $20,000 to get by. But the possibility of earning one's way is not eliminated, so in that sense I guess it's a plus for more militant feminists who want to go out to earn a living regardless of family wealth. Though I think it's a liberating thing to know that you don't have to plug away at a job you don't particularly enjoy. I think my personal life has been affected by my compulsive work style more than by my money—by the fact that I don't sit around home very much and watch television, read poetry, or cut the lawn, the sort of things a man does around the house.

Because of the number of news stories that have been written about me, it's rare to come across a new lady who has never heard of me. I'm bashful about introducing myself, so on occasion, when I have a blind date, I will send her a batch of interviews and articles about me ahead of time. It's my philosophy that if we each could have a little microfiche and feed into each other a basic set of data about where we were born and how many sisters and brothers we have and where we went to school, then we wouldn't have to go through all that basic data. Also, we could have all that on a little file card for later reference.

A week ago I did this in reverse when I had a date with Linda Ronstadt. She was just a name to me, since I'm not in that world at all, so I decided to research her. In the course of the evening we spent together, I presented her with a little slip of paper. On it were the names of the men and women in her life, her parents' and siblings' names and phone numbers, and all the albums and singles she's cut. I said, "This is your life." She looked at me and laughed and said, "Oh my God, it's like the CIA has a file on me."

But I think it's a courtesy to another person to give them some background about you for a meeting. I realize that researching a lady or a man before having a date sounds a little contrived, but normally, if a friend is introducing you, you would ask the friend to tell you something about him or her.

I'm well aware that the money I have available to spend and the power that I wield is small by comparison with the power that is controlled by the president of General Motors or the head of the AFL, or Billy Graham, even, or the president managing the U.S. budget. I have a $500,000 to $1,000,000 annual philanthropic budget, which in terms of what it buys in people's time and services is small compared to the more established power sources. But in my way I think I have bought a lot for my money and that I'm working on public policy here in Washington.

I don't respond as a philanthropist to requests for relief or for personal aid. I have to inure myself to that because I feel that the things I have decided to work on—trying to eliminate the threat of nuclear annihilation and limiting the world population—are vastly more important than helping an individual family meet its medical bills or getting an orphan adopted or sending food to Bangladesh. I've put on the blinders as far as working in fields not related to arms control and population control are concerned. I've felt as though I had to because of my limited resources and limited time.

I know that the other problems facing humanity are going to go on forever, but these are problems that have afflicted human beings for centuries. I'm just trying to get a handle on the couple of things that are so crucial to our survival in the latter part of the twentieth century.

Stewart has since married a sculptor and continues his work as a philanthropist.

Patrick   New York, New York

Patrick's energy was simply dazzling. Ordained as a Jesuit priest but dismissed by the order four years before, he was continuing his commitment to social change and ethical action. A tall, slender, dark-haired man of thirty-nine, dressed casually in sweater and slacks, he answered the constantly jangling phone, spoke to every one of the long stream of people who were popping into the church basement office that served as headquarters for a dozen social causes, fixed coffee and tea, and kept the continuity of his thought flowing in rapid-fire speech. Never pausing to catch his breath, he was as fresh when he finished as he had been when he began.

I was thrown out of the Jesuits in 1974 for baptizing a baby whose mother belived in free choice on abortion. In the search to make our personal lives tell at critical moments, we have to find some sort of clutchstick to get into a situation so that we can come out the other side with a sense of having done something. The Greek word for this is *kairos*. It means an opportune moment, a moment of truth. That's about all that's available to us.

Baptizing that baby was a classic opportune moment. The mother of the baby was the oldest of nine children born out of her mother's twenty-one pregnancies, and she thought that abortion was a valid, moral choice. A local parish had turned this family away; it is the Catholic doctrine to refuse a free-choice mother. But I can't see any reason any longer for a pastor to do that, so I came in and baptized the child.

I think I had been trying to take responsibility for my life for a long time and was ready to bring about my dismissal, to make it happen. But at the same time, it's very ambiguous and ambivalent in my mind because I had put a lot of time into the Jesuits; it takes thirteen years to become a Jesuit priest. And even though you may be at odds with a tradition like that, you're sort of more in it, as well.

I felt glad and sad. It was a real human act and I had human feelings about it. I stayed a little while in the community I lived with because they were protesting the decision about me, but then I left. They were chickenshit about taking effective action. Nothing reached the level of accuracy or truth there. It was no surprise, but it was disappointing. The community was quite real, though, and friendships remain strong.

I had had other moments of truth as a Jesuit. Going through the seminary in the sixties, being trained to be a professional moral theologian, I saw that there was no moral theologian. You could say some very fine things, but nobody could live consonant with his ideas at that time in history. It was almost impossible not to be a murderer.

Friends of mine and I engaged in direct action to disclose some of that immorality. Nine of us, mostly priests and nuns, went to the liaison office of Dow Chemical Company one Saturday in 1969. We put our own blood on the walls and on their maps and threw all their files with the Pentagon and State Department out in the street. And lots of friends picked them up and published them.

As a result, public awareness picked up on the corporate responsibility for the war. The newspapers said we were just protesting the manufacture of napalm and anti-personnel weapons, but the truth we were disclosing was not only that Dow made toxic nerve gas and that they have a long history of acting against national policy interests—for example, by giving over 90 percent of the world's supply of magnesium to I.G. Farben of Nazi Germany all through the thirties until they were caught in 1942. And it wasn't just that they have well over two hundred subsidiaries ripping off the resoures and labor of the Third World in many, mostly poor, countries around the world. It was also that multinational corporations simply are not interested in anything but their own development and profit. These systems are out of control. They're inhuman in a special sense, not by being angry, evil, Hitler-like instruments of decimation of the human will and body. Somehow the immorality and death just happen because these systems exist.

In civil disobedience you focus your action in such a way that the eyes that can see and the ears that can hear get a glimmer, a glimpse of what the truth of the matter is. Focused correctly, it has an enormous effect. Dow dropped the napalm contract shortly after we disrupted the place.

"The war was an obvious moral issue and here was Cardinal Cooke, the great sky-pilot, with his official title of Military Vicar and all his investments in war-related corporations, riding off to Vietnam, saying prayers over the dead."

Another moment of truth for me was my ordination as a priest with Cardinal Cooke officiating. The war was an obvious moral issue, and here was Cardinal Cooke, the great sky-pilot, with his official title of Military Vicar and all his investments in war-related corporations, riding off to Vietnam, saying prayers over the dead. We had extorted morality from the Jesuits, threatening public disclosure and scandal about where their investments were: the New York Province has about $20 million in five portfolios, all invested in the most outrageous things, and as soon as we disclosed that the consortium of banks that handled it invested in South Africa, the banks withdrew their loans.

Everybody I admired thought I was just wrong to go through with my ordination, that it was an immoral thing to do. But I had spent thirteen, fourteen years preparing to become a Jesuit priest and for me there was just no choice. If I didn't become a priest, I'd sort of be heading down my feelings that I was one and that I knew what it was about. So at the traditional ritual known as the Kiss of Peace I got up and said to Cardinal Cooke, "I find it difficult to kiss peace with war, and until you drop your title as Military Vicar and your war-related investments, I will find it difficult."

The Jesuits had originally caught my eye because I was looking for an institutional life that would have some movement and adventure, and that was the only institution I knew of that had a principled reform built into it—the modern notion of the *magis*—of doing not the best thing or trying to strive for perfection, but of doing the better thing. One of the big difficulties I had when I was dismissed was a kind of residual malaise because I didn't have any institution grating on me that I had to escape from.

It took me about six months to deal with the dismissal, and it was a big, funky time, but since then my priestly life has increased 100 percent and my capacity to be clear with friends about what I am doing has increased. Probably the only real effect of getting thrown out was that I lost my girlfriend.

It's been three years since I've been out. I sit on a lot of Boards of Directors of social change organizations—mostly abortion at the moment, though the Moratorium on Prison Construction occupied my time for a couple years. I priest a lot. I marry a few people. I chase moments that are full of future and teeming with possibility and new birth, like the public announcement of a love, a marriage. These things are most intriguing to me when they are under some threat of death.

I married one of the most famous lifers in the New York penal system at Sing Sing. There is no civil right of marriage for natural lifers in New York State. The system knew we were coming and did everything to try to keep us segregated. They tried to hide the inmate, then they tried to keep me away from the two of them. But human beings are stronger than those things. They were together for about four or five minutes and I recognized it. I had them put rings on each other and they were married.

"Disappointing the system is about the best we can do to prove that it can't totally conquer the human spirit and destroy human creativity and the will to work— the will to make meaning."

It sounds ridiculous, but the system just shook. Phones were ringing and everybody was going, "Oh, no. Oh, gee." It was another moment of truth. Disappointing the system is about the best we can do to prove that it can't totally conquer the human spirit and destroy human creativity and the will to work—the will to make meaning.

I feel it is probably better to do evil than to do nothing. It is probably better to keep getting into these systems—into the heart of the beast, into the whale's belly—than to stay around being alienated. That impetus is real strong on my mind now, so I would like a more direct relationship with the business community. I think that given the recovery of the outrageous profit structure in the United States, liberal politics is about to begin again, and I would like to be in on the interchange that has got to go on between business and the new styles of Socialist management. There is real potential for productivity in the conversation between the poor, with their new self-determination, and the rich, with their traditional styles of capitalism-socialism.

How to institutionalize and develop a morality of institutions is still a key motif to most of my life. This is a capitalist word, but I sort of like the idea of *imagineering*—of getting a good idea out there ahead of you, putting some flesh on it, and planting it so that it has the capacity to grow.

I don't imagineer my own economic survival very well, though. I have the worries everybody else has about security and finances. I've had to borrow money to get through December, and I find that sort of bad. For eight months we haven't gotten any money from the Moratorium on Prison Construction. The rise of right wing evangelicalism has had a real effect on the more mainstream churches and the money is going away. The foundations and church support are becoming more conservative. They're running scared, like Scaramouche up the stairs. I'm looking for a new means of support.

Sometimes nothing looks more appetizing than a little repression in which somebody would take the responsibility away. Of course, as soon as it happens, I completely go bananas. After you get an experience of freedom, it's hard to give it up.

After the action, when I was sitting in jail to be able to say I had survived with my integrity, man, you haven't ever seen anybody as happy—I got by—whew! I fuckin' got by! They didn't get my ass, no sir. To think that you have to struggle for yourself that way is outrageous.

It seems to me that the big tendency in my life for the next ten years will be the impulse to escape from freedom in the old ways. I mean, I am tired. I am upset. I have taken risks that have driven me crazy. It has taken me months to get myself back out of being hit over the head by the Jesuits.

Right now my life has very few satisfactions in the conventional sense and I'm sort of worried about that because some of them are pretty easy to get. I know a lot of other people do it, so I don't see why it isn't worth a try.

Still, I wish I had more money to have bought Christmas presents. That matters a lot. They're symbolic because I think you're really in bad shape when you don't have things to give. It doesn't have to be knitted hats and Saks Fifth Avenue coats and things. And when you care enough to make your own, that's good, too. But this year I didn't. I mean, there's something wrong. But I'm not quite where I would be and it probably has something to do with my relationship to the money world. That's why I'm very eager to get back into the beast in a different way from before.

Patrick worked out his wish and is busy consulting with businesses and institutions on the new forms of management.

AFFIRMING A NEW LIFE

Harry   Arcadia, California

In his house just a stone's throw away from Santa Anita, Harry was as convenient to the track as any horse trainer could wish. But his calm and discipline were light years removed from the turbulence of the grandstand and the tension of the paddock. A tall, powerfully built man in his late thirties, he expressed confidence that he had chosen right in this gamble with his career. The affection and gentleness with which he spoke of the horses showed that the choice he had made came straight from the heart.

I was always fascinated by horses because I was a coach, involved with athletics, and a horse is really an athlete. About nine years ago my brother and stepfather and I bought our first horse for $250 and won a race. When we finally sold her, we received about $1600. So we were on our way; we had our foot in the door.

I worked at the races in the summers during my teaching career, and any spare time I had spent doing breeding, racing and training. I worked for nothing at the fairs cleaning the stalls, walking the horses—just to be around the horses, acquiring the knowledge by listening, looking and learning.

The year we bought our first horse I worked for nothing for a trainer—an old-timer, real cranky and stubborn. He took care of my horse, but I was actually doing everything so I'd get the experience. I figured if I did anything wrong, I'd hurt my own horse, so it wouldn't hurt anybody.

Those years were the greatest time I had. I'd be coming back fresh to school from a whole new environment. Of course, the horse would still be racing somewhere and I'd have that in my mind while I was teaching. It was the ideal situation.

I had a winner back in Kentucky with my assistant trainer's license, then I came back out here, took the test, and got my trainer's license. And now I'm training thoroughbred race-horses.

I stopped teaching and took a year's leave of absence to protect my job in case I had to come back financially. But I don't have any aspirations to go back at this time. In fact, I'm going to apply for another year's leave of absence.

It was really a thrill for me to get a contract teaching when I came out of the army. For the first ten years it was just a beautiful experience working with kids. I taught physical education, health and history in junior high, a good combination. The kids were enthusiastic and mischievous, but not to the point where they'd be hardcore about it. I felt almost like a father to them.

Then about four years ago the situation really deteriorated. The school administration changed and there was a complete lack of leadership. The new principal really didn't care about the three R's—reading, 'riting and 'rithmetic—but was bent on pushing ethnic roots, having the kids shout about it in assembly. Gang violence was continuous, and I'd be out there in the middle of those fights without any support from the principal or from anyone else. Discipline was non-existent. Learning was non-existent. You were babysitting. Though there were still a lot of good people there. I couldn't relate like I had. I was spending 90 percent of my time with 10 percent of the incorrigibles, and it just drove me up the wall.

The teachers used to have social functions to bind the staff and the camaraderie was great. That deteriorated to nothing. The atmosphere was just negative, continually negative. Our lunch room turned into a Pershing Square kind of environment where everybody would spew their unhappiness.

There came a point when I dreaded going to school. I'd never felt like that before; in fact, I'd always been critical of the parasitic effect you can get with some teachers who have tenure—when they can't get you out. You get complacent, you don't do your job, you wait for your check, and you watch the clock. I found myself doing the same thing, so I said, "Well, that's it. I'm not accomplishing anything. There's not a feeling of worth anymore." It's a combination that builds up on you.

I still think of myself as a teacher and I didn't want to completely retire, so I took a year's leave of absence. The personnel manager has told me I can take one more leave if I want it, but the Board of Education has to OK it and they can deny it at their whim. They're a whimsical Board.

I can afford to train horses now because I have no financial obligations. I'll be forty in six months. I don't owe anything, I'm not married, I live in my parents' house; all I have is the horses. I can go on forever, if I keep in physical shape.

I want to get a stable that can compete in Southern California, which I think is the best in the United States. Santa Anita is probably the toughest place to race. There's a lot of competition because the weather is a lot better than in the East. And out here I can be around everybody I know— friends and fellow teachers.

The first two or three years are going to be tough. At the point I'm at now, I don't think someone living independently, who had to pay rent and everything, could do it. They'd have to have some source of income. It's not a living, no way.

Right now I'm barely making it. I had some savings, but I exhausted that fund and now I must work on what I'm getting monthly for training. I charge fifteen dollars a day for a horse, but all the money goes back into gear.

I have three horses up here at the auxiliary ranch at Pomona, racing at Santa Anita. I have to drive back and forth to Caliente, Mexico for one horse I have there, and it costs, even though I've been staying at one of the cheapest motels I could find down there. I'm hoping that these horses will develop into something, so I have to put up with this sort of thing to get them started.

If I could get stalls at Santa Anita, I could make more. They charge twenty-five dollars a day minimum and they run up to thirty-eight dollars. I could also make more money winning at Santa Anita. As the trainer, I get 10 percent of the purse. The horse I have in Caliente broke her maiden the other day—that's what they call it when you make your first win—but the purse was minimal—it was $1400, so I got $140. If I won with the same horse at Santa Anita, I could make $660: big difference. Of course, there is the competition and it depends on the caliber of the horse, but if you can win a big race at Santa Anita, you don't have to win as many. If I had enough pay horses—horses you train for another owner—maybe a half a dozen, and I could charge twenty-five dollars a day, I'd make money off a horse whether he wins or loses.

But I can't get in now at Santa Anita because there's a lack of stall space. There are many more horses than ever before. The best ones are supposed to get the stalls, but there's a kind of clique, too. If you have been there a while, you can get your stalls, but if you're new at the game, you have to come in the back door, so it's a little tough. I had a horse turned down while another horse which was inferior to mine was given a stall—why?—because the guy has been here twenty or thirty years. He's got about twenty horses, good horses, so he might get one in that's not as good as mine. If I apply for a stall, he says, "Well, Harry, you have to do a little better."

I'm my own boss now and I can do what I want to do, go where I want to go. On a typical day you do all your training from 6:00 a.m. to 10:00 a.m., then from 10:00 to 11:00 or 12:00 you do the horse up—put some type of liniment on him and rub him down. Then you come back and feed him in the afternoon. On raceday it's different. You have to be around just about all day watching the horse to make sure nothing happens. Every horse is like a student—different—different characteristics, different temperament. The two year olds even have the same child diseases, like babies, so you've got that headache.

I was streamlined in Mexico for a while, but I've lost some discipline since I've been splitting my time. I used to pop out of bed, but now I'm real sluggish at 5:30. Of course, it's so cold...

It's a pretty hard day if you put your time in on it and it's seven days a week. This morning I did a lot of paperwork; now I have to go pick up some food—and this is an off day for me. I should be down in Caliente, really, for that other horse, but today I put the groom in charge. Tomorrow I'll go down for sure.

You don't get any time off and that's why once in a while, if you feel you're getting sour, you just tell the groom or somebody else trustworthy, "I want this and this and this done. I won't be here Sunday." I hired a good groom in Mexico who comes from a horse family. To him the horse is his horse. He doesn't want anybody to touch it. I wish I could bring him here.

I'm going through a kind of trying time right now and it hasn't gotten to the point where I can really relax. This is a tough road and we've had a string of problems. One horse ran through a fence and killed herself. Another mare aborted and we had to sell her. Then I got into real bad luck with one horse that I bought as a baby. I had gotten him to the point where he was going to make money every time he ran. Then there was a sudden thing. I thought it was minor and I took him to the veterinary hospital. It was a cancerous growth on his lung and the guy said, "One in ten chance." I lost him. That's hard. You become attached to them like a pet, you lose them, and you break down a bit. Then you bounce back.

"I do it all because the dream is there and I have a chance for it. If you never give yourself a chance, then you're dead."

Eventually, though, I think it will get to where I can relax as I get all these horses started. I do it all because the dream is there and I have a chance for it. If you never give yourself a chance, then you're dead,

You always dream of having that quality type horse. The glory part is winning the race. The ultimate would be that you buy a mare in foal. She has her foal, her baby. You watch that baby grow for two or three years; he has a personality—you know him. Then you see him charging down the stretch. It brings change to you when you see that. That's your horse. That was our little baby. That's what overcomes you.

They'll tell you, "Don't ever get attached to your horse. It's bad for business. Just race him and don't worry about him." To me that's defeating the whole purpose of being in racing because I enjoy being around horses and seeing them grow.

When you're around them, you get to know them. You get to know their personalities. A horse without a personality to me is just a dud.

I don't care too much about the business part. I want to survive financially, sure, but being around the horses is the key to why I'm doing training. Plus the camaraderie. I have my brother, and my mother likes it too. Some day I hope to get the whole family in the Winner's Circle.

Then Monty, my partner, is so enthusiastic—Mr. Optimism. It's good that he's optimistic, even over-optimistic. I've never discouraged him, though the odds are fantastic against you even to get to the races when you breed your own mare. Fantastic odds, so you must enjoy doing it, and we do enjoy it. We had a New Year's Eve party at the ranch and at twelve o'clock we were outside singing "Happy Birthday" to the horses. On the first day of January they all become a year older.

"You get to know their personalities. A horse without a personality to me is just a dud."

So you have a relationship with your fellow man and with the horses. Most people that really like horses are kind people, gentle people. They're affectionate people. If you surround yourself with these good people, even with bad luck at the races it can be a very rewarding experience. I bet that it's as rewarding as it is for the teacher when you have a real close relationship with a child.

I try to disassociate with the gamblers. A gambler couldn't care less if the horse dropped dead as long as he cashes a ticket. If you gamble hard, you become hardcore and bitter, insensitive to everything. You lose perspective of life. The most hardcore gamblers crumble. They lose their sense and become mentally disturbed. The gambling aspect to racing is a loser's game. It must be there to support the system—without gambling you wouldn't have horse racing—but when you gamble, your personality changes. You're a Jekyll-Hyde.

I don't have many relationships with other trainers. They were raised in the game and they gamble and have the race track jargon, which I don't really condone. That's one of the bad points of being at the track—people start getting sour and start spewing the words out. A lot of people in the back side become alcoholics.

My morale does sag sometimes, not to the point where I've ever felt like giving up, though. You have your ups and downs. I'd quit if I got real sour, if I got to the point where I'd wake up in the morning feeling, "Oh, do I have to go there?" From time to time it gets to you, but there's nothing you can do about it, really. I eat and I can feel my weight. If you let yourself get out of shape, you get lazy and complacent. I've got to get myself in physical condition, otherwise I can't make it.

You've got to put your time in and you have to like it. I do like it. I just hope it can get to the point where it can be lucrative, at least to where I can support myself. I don't think I'll ever get rich at it. I haven't really won with it yet, but I do have one horse that's trained good now and the one Monty and I have in partnership looks like it has a lot of potential.

Training has its ups and downs. If you're a manic-depressive I don't believe you can make it, because the highs are really high and the lows are really low. I try to keep an even keel, but I get really high and then I get all excited.

What you learn is that you've got to keep perspective. If you treat people right and do good by them, that's the main thing. We're mortals and some day it's going to be all over, so you know there's more than just this. I don't see how anybody could survive without this belief. There's got to be something else—you can't just come and go and that's it. If you think you're going to die and that's it, then why do anything?

Harry is still training horses, hoping a big winner will come along.

Leah   Los Angeles, California

> The weak overcomes its
>   menace, the strong over-
>   comes itself. What is there
>
> like fortitude! What sap
>   went through that little thread
>   to make the cherry red!

—Marianne Moore, "Nevertheless"

Illness had prompted her retirement from secretarial work some years before, now orthopedic surgery at age sixty-five had laid her up again. But Leah was not willing to let her disability become a handicap. And though still recuperating, she wanted to sit up at the table to talk—she didn't like being in bed. Animated expressions on her face emphasized feelings recalled from the past and anticipation of the future. Open, forthright, playfully spirited and the kindest person you might hope to meet, she showed in all of her being what it means to be loving and life-loving.

I retired more than seven years ago. I had been a secretary at Lockheed Aircraft for twenty years, ever since we had moved to California from the midwest. I went to work because we needed the money. I felt guilty leaving a seven year old and a twelve year old home alone after school. I loved being with the children from the day each one was born—I think I am one of the very fortunate people in the world because I had so much enjoyment with my son and daughter. I was very, very happy when they were really young. That was a time of growth in my life as well as in theirs.

But we were in debt. We had to make payments to the loan company for the used furniture we had bought and we were still paying on the car. I think we had to miss a car payment or two, and that's the kind of thing people like us feel very guilty about.

So I figured that if I kept on working for a while, we could get on our feet and maybe even buy a house.

I suddenly discovered that I liked working because I was doing something again. I really knew my job. When I came down with arthritis, working became difficult because I was in a lot of pain—once I had to take a month off to rest in bed—but I kept on working. Part of the reason might have been because I had put in so many years and didn't want to gyp myself out of my retirement pay or lose the good fringe benefits, like hospital care. Also, the children were grown and I didn't have much else to do with my life, so I figured I might as well work.

Eventually I replaced a Contract Administrator who had been transferred to Washington. I did exactly the same work that he had done and got along better with everybody than he had, but I was still a secretary. When I asked for a change in job classification, they wouldn't make me a contract administrator because I was a woman.

And from that time on, although I liked what I was doing, I started getting pretty sour about working. I felt as though I had no place at Lockheed. I'd already had that feeling for a long time because other things were against me. First, I was Jewish, second, I was a Democrat, and third, I was liberal. The majority of management people were very conservative Republicans, and this was in the sixties when there was so much protesting in the universities. The Angela Davis affair had come up and my boss and some of the others were writing letters against her to congressmen and senators. I wouldn't type the letters for my boss because it was against my principles. He could write his protest letter by hand, if he wanted to. He wasn't going to get me to type it.

"I realized I was not young and flirtatious, but surely experience, good nature and willingness to work and learn should have had some importance."

When they closed down the Navy program I was working in, I was transferred. I had seniority over all the other secretaries in my new department, but I had only little nothing jobs to do.

Finally, exasperated, I asked my supervisor what was going to happen to me. He sort of shilly-shallied around and gave me the excuse that his secretary had been there a long time.

I interrupted and said, "I'm not asking for anybody's job. All I want to know is what are you going to do with me? Where am I going? What kind of work am I going to do? I'm not going to just sit here and do nothing."

It is frustrating to be doing such menial jobs that a kid out of school could do them, and it's especially frustrating when you have done administrative work. I realized I was not young and flirtatious, but surely experience, good nature, and willingness to work and learn should have had some importance.

The frustration ended, not because we resolved it, but because I got sick. I was in the hospital for three months with viral encephalitis, inflammation of the brain. I had a lot of disorder and disorientation; it was a full year before I could coordinate again. I took medication, but I think my recovery was sheer will power. I was determined not to stay sick and I forced myself to dress, eat, and get up and go. Slowly my mind started to function again.

We sold our house and moved to an apartment complex. That was good because I met new people and made friends. I played cards in the clubhouse. I swam and went to the Jacuzzi, the gym, the exercise room and the sauna. I walked. Finally it was good to be alive again.

And that was when I quit work. There was no question in my mind; I didn't want to work again, certainly not at my old job. I was completely dissatisfied with the airplane industry and with Lockheed in particular. Inwardly I was rebelling in the last four or five years when I was feeling unhappy at work. More than that, my mind was opening up and I was beginning to wake up to all kinds of things I had never thought about before. So when a nearby junior college offered a class for "mature women" who had not been in school for years, I enrolled.

But about a year after we moved my husband began having pains and after seven months the doctor diagnosed cancer. Two months after surgery he died. That was four years ago.

I knew I had to immerse myself in something I could be totally involved in so that I wouldn't just sit at home and cry and feel sorry for myself, so I continued with school. This year I got my A.A. I'm taking more classes, but I don't feel the need to get a Bachelor's degree. I don't want the stress that you have with a four year college. Also, I've become involved in other things that are imporant to me.

I'm active in the League of Women Voters and Common Cause. Through a class at the college I usher at the Dorothy Chandler and Ahmanson theaters. I can't afford to pay for the symphonies, ballets, and plays, and this way I'm able to see them. I have season tickets to the Mark Taper Forum, where they do new plays; they don't resurrect the same ones over and over and over and over again. I like being exposed to new thoughts.

Over the years I had learned not to assert myself if my views differed from my husband's. Mort was kind, loving, a good husband and father, and provided well for us, but he was positive about being the "head" of the family. My parents had an old-fashioned, European husband-wife relationship, and I fell right into that in my own marriage.

Since Mort died, I've changed. I've broadened my thinking. I go to discussion groups and I read the papers and periodicals with an open and questioning mind. I don't believe everything I read or hear in the media. Previously I voted the way Mort voted and seldom expressed an opinion. Now I feel free to express myself. The short way I've come these last few years is much better than the way I was before.

Right now I'm recuperating from orthopedic surgery. I haven't been very social for the last few months because of pain and difficulty in walking and using my hands. Now that the surgery is over, I'll be able to do more. I have a lot of friends. I've never had a problem making friends and I've always had friends from someplace in my past. We don't see each other all the time because everybody has their own lives to live, but when I was sick, I discovered that more people were concerned about me than I ever realized would be. It moved me tremendously.

Still, I'm lonely. All my friends are either married couples or women. I'd like to know men and go out to dinner or to a show—be friends with a man. I don't know that I would want to get married again, but I would like male companionship. I miss male talk. You can talk to men and get something from them as well as give them something from yourself.

I think I need more than just school now. I would like to travel—not a group tour of Europe—I've done that too many times. I would like to just go. I'm not afraid to go alone. I would go to France because I know a little French, take the train to small villages, and walk around the area to see what the country is like. I'd live with a family, if I could. What I want is the people themselves. I hear stories that French people are not too friendly, but I think that in small villages, if you're friendly and smiling and nice, then they'll be friendly and smiling and nice to you.

"As long as I feel young and think young and act spry enough and can get going, I shouldn't have any trouble."

Sometimes I'm concerned about doing the kind of traveling that interests me because of my physical condition and my age, but I don't think that being sixty-five should have anything to do with it. As long as I feel young and think young and act spry enough and can get going, I shouldn't have any trouble.

Leah is still feeling young, thinking young, acting spry, and going strong.

Tommy   New York, New York

A warm welcome, a proud display of new acquisitions— furniture, stereo, custom carpentry in process and an aquar- ium so new it hadn't even been unpacked—then, quickly down to how his new life came about. Tommy's description of his accident was starkly matter-of-fact. His short, thin body looked fit and muscular—the result of rigorous physical therapy—one could not have guessed what hell it had been through. He recounted the struggles of his thirty-four years with impassioned commitment to relegating them once and for all to the past.

I worked as a merchant seaman for twelve years. Nearly three years ago, on Friday the thirteenth, I was working as an Able Seaman—that's a skilled deckhand—on a modern container ship going from Manhattan down to Savannah, Georgia, having just completed a Mediterranean voyage. Off Cape Hatteras, where it often gets very rough. It started rolling back and forth. They called out the deck sailors to put extra lashings and turnbuckles on some of the cargo that was around the open hatch area. The ship took a heavy roll and I fell down two decks through the open hatch, into the hold of the ship, almost thirty feet, and landed on my torso. My back was broken, my right arm was broken in three places, I had six broken ribs and one of the broken ribs pierced both lung diaphragms. I'm lucky to be alive and walking around.

The company had absolutely no case. The hatch area should have been roped off. The cargo should have been lashed properly by longshoremen in port. Recently a lot of the shipping companies have been getting away with doing things at the last minute, even if they have to be done at the risk of life. It's cheaper if someone gets killed or sues them every once in a while than to pay longshoremen to do the job right, on a regular basis.

The word spread fast up and down and maritime lawyers were calling me in the hospital, hoping to get hold of my case. I waited a while and finally got a good lawyer, very competent. I ended up with payment for what would be my wages for the rest of my life. The total settlement was $585,000, out of which my lawyer automatically got one-third. I made a $100,000 donation to a left-wing political group I'm sympathetic towards, put a big chunk in a trust fund and a few grand in my bank account, fixed up the apartment, and have been traveling a bit.

The huge settlement is not only for wages you would make going to sea and for the pain and all you went through, but also because the percentages are very high in favor of various problems arising from the breaks I had. Although I'm in good health now and have had a good recovery, arthritis and

rebreaks and all sorts of other things can happen. You don't
know what the nature of your breaks is going to be, so you
shoot for the top.

When we settled, I had to sign about six documents stating
that this is the last time I'm ever going to get any money from
the shipping company on this claim, even if I have injuries in
the future that are worse than the ones I've had. A case like
this is like a game of chess. You're out to get what you can and
they're out to beat you.

Going to sea, there's always danger, especially when the
sea's a little bit rough, but I'd been worried more on other jobs,
like docking or working aloft on the mast, than I was on that
particular day and that particular job. Tying the ship up is
getting to be very dangerous with these new, bigger, modern
ships and fewer and fewer men. There's more strain on those
steel cables as these bigger ships are being pulled in. Sometimes the wires vibrate and every now and then they snap.
And every now and then when they snap, someone gets killed
or badly maimed.

Another reason working conditions are very dangerous is
because fewer men are doing more dangerous work as a result
of the unions kicking all the militants out and getting some
out-and-out finks to run the show. I'm very pro-union, and our
union was probably the most blatant, glaring example of what
happened when the left was shitcanned. For a long time
Curran was this stupid, grotesque president of the union. He
was groomed by the Communist Party and when things were
pretty shaky for the whole left, he jumped houses and ended up
redbaiting and kicking all the leftists out. He was a real
degenerate slob.

I'm still a member of the union and I possibly might ship out
again. I still pay my dues, I still go raise hell at union meetings
every once in a while, help leaflet and work out at the gym
occasionally with old shipmates.

If I do ship out, I'd just like to do it part-time. I don't want to
be dependent on going back to sea as a main thing. At a
maximum I'd do it about seventy-five days a year to keep my
union book up, but I would sort of like to keep a toehold there.

I'm clinging to the sea. I liked the ocean even as a kid. My
father was a fishing boat captain in Plymouth, Massachusetts. I have an early memory of being out in the fishing boat

at about age four and seeing something moving along the horizon. My father explained that it was a big freighter, probably from Japan or someplace far, far away. That image of bigger boats that went long distances planted something in my head.

Another reason I wanted to go to sea was that it seemed a bit romantic and I was the drifter type. I was a bit of a rebel and alienated, and by going to sea I wouldn't have to get caught up in a lot of imagery and role-playing and social institutions that most people in society get caught up in.

Plus, I realized very early that I liked to drink. Every week-end high school party I was smashed. Now that I'm more in touch with alcoholism, I know that even then I could see that this was a job where I'd be able to drink a lot. I was planning ahead with my drinking.

I loved to drink. I did a lot of drugs, too, mainly dope-smoking, but even needles off and on. Although I never had a junk habit, I screwed around with everything, very reckless. But booze was always my main thing, the one thing I was physically addicted to and had withdrawal from.

"A lot of my happy-go-lucky, tough seaman façade was pure bullshit."

I shipped all over the world and I'm glad I did. There was a lot of excitement and fun and I got to see a lot. But I also got into a lot of patterns I couldn't recognize at the time. I was cutting myself off from real human needs, not able to relate to other people or have close friendships. My experience with women was one-night stands, prostitutes, runaways in the park, and women drunk in bars. A lot of my happy-go-lucky, tough seaman facade was pure bullshit. Even though I convinced people of it to some degree, I was fooling myself.

Going to sea got to be pretty lonely and isolated. Although there's the romance of the foreign port and the sea, there's the other side where it's very much like a jailhouse existence. You're days, weeks at a time confined. Very rarely are there women on the ship and you get to be lonely and introverted. There's a lot of the isolation-type thinking and personality of people in jail. I know that movies often show seamen singing and drinking and all happy, but really, they're just pretty lonely drunks or getting into a few hours of compulsive instant gratification ashore, where they drown out all their problems.

In New York I would drink a lot and eventually run out of money. No woman would have anything to do with me and I'd think, "Oh, shit, I'm going to go out to sea and make a lot of money and start all over again. It's going to be all different." But it never really was very much different. That's been going on for millenia with seamen.

It really hit on me that I was caught in a trap when I started to go into the shakes and have convulsions. I started coming to AA four years ago, when I was thirty. With AA and by trying a little bit harder, I would go longer periods of time without drinking. At the time of the accident I hadn't had a drink for nine months.

An accident like that really does a number on your head, and they give you morphine, besides. I started thinking, "Here I haven't had a drink for a long period of time and I've had this worst disaster of my life," so between hospital stays for surgery I'd go out and drink. God, it was a horrible year—between that accident, and being in an arm cast and a body cast from my armpits to my hips, and the drinking. I was supposed to be lying in the apartment taking nourishment and watching television, and I was going around to bars drunk in a body cast, drinking till four o'clock in the morning and having blackouts. It was pure insanity.

Yet somehow I would still just drink a few days then dry out a few days, and even when I was drinking, somehow I had enough sense to keep in touch with the exercises I was supposed to be doing. Finally I started taking AA more seriously, got off the booze, and began exercising regularly.

For the year after I came out of the body cast I would sleep eleven, twelve hours a day plus take one or two hour naps. The doctor said this was normal and to keep pushing the therapy to get more and more strength back. I evolved from physical therapy to light calisthenics, higher calisthenics, then lifting weights.

It was close to two years before I was physically able to work, but though I've been able to this last year, my lawyer told me not to until the case was settled. Otherwise they'd say I was recuperated and a few months later I'd be having arthritic pains or some bad bone problem and wouldn't be able to do anything about it. My lawyer said they were just dying to get a picture of me doing even something like changing a car tire, anything really strenuous. In a huge case like mine it's common for the company to spend ten or fifteen grand having photographers follow the guy around.

So any heavy calisthenics I did at home, I would do with the shades down. I wouldn't carry shopping bags because I knew they were laying for me. I was determined not to let them get away with that.

I went to AA. I exercised. Although I never joined the party, I'd go to political meetings of the Spartacist League, who were very instrumental in building the Maritime Union Opposition Caucus.

After the case was settled I went to Puerto Rico and stayed in a real nice hotel for a few weeks. I kept aside a big chunk to buy a few new clothes with and fix up the apartment. I've been eating lots of steaks and lobster. I did go through a lot of crap with the accident and the past few weeks have been fun, but I don't want to do this forever. I want to get it out of my system rather than daydream about it.

Now I'm ready to get into something else. I feel more and more capable. I want to be productive. There's been a lot lacking in my life for me to develop, grow, and be happy. I want to make some headway in these areas and that would pretty much mean breaking from the sea.

"I see no reason to sit back and do nothing but consume if I'm capable of doing something productive with my life."

I plan—I hope—some day to be working again. I want to go back to school. Having been through a gory accident and being a bit of an exercise nut now, I've been thinking lately that I might be good at physical therapy. I'd feel productive, the pay's not too bad, and there are job opportunities.

I guess the reason I want to work is that I know I can work and I should if I can. I see no reason to sit back and do nothing but consume if I'm capable of doing something productive with my life.

At the same time, I have a fear about going back to work, and every now and then I get hit with anxiety about going back to school. I never was the greatest student. I've always had a lot of trouble with concentration. I have sat down and concentrated on political readings, but a lot of days I can't even read a newspaper article. Sometimes just trying to make up my mind can be a problem. Some people are like that—their mind's sort of like a wild horse.

I daydream a lot and I'm kind of disorganized. A lot of it has to do with all the liquor and dope. I took a lot of acid trips in the sixties and when you treat your brain like a basketball for twelve or thirteen years, that's bound to do something to your ability to concentrate.

I feel good about being me and enjoying myself, but I've been an insecure person—drinking testifies to that—so going into something new is a little bit scary. People in AA tell me it's common to have these polar opposite feelings when you've been out of work for a long time. You want to do something and you're scared of doing it. Sooner or later you just have to jump into that pool and start swimming.

Oh, every now and then I'm tempted not to take the plunge, sure. I remember lying in bed in the hospital after a morphine injection, thinking about what I was going to do when I got out and finally got a lot of money. I had this fantasy of buying a mansion down in the tropics, getting a lifetime supply of bourbon and opium, and getting six of the cutest teen-age maids to take care of me the rest of my life—and that's it.

But I've had enough experience to know that just having money is not the way. I want to do something productive, creative, fulfilling with my life and my being. That's the kind of person I am, and I think to some degree most people are, deep down inside. I would have thought it was corny to hear myself saying this years ago, but it's true.

I'm still kind of a loner. I'm working with my problems in AA and I've also seen a shrink a few times. I realize now that to overcome my problems it takes time and work and a little bit of patience. I used to fall into patterns where I believed that everything was hopeless or where everything was going to be great all of a sudden if I'd just stop drinking. Now I don't expect everything's going to change at once.

Still, I'm having trouble. Minute to minute, hour to hour, I feel kind of rocky and lacking. Sometimes I'll put on the stereo headphones and play music full blast. I have to work against this compulsive, escaping thing.

I want to do more than I'm doing. I almost get uncomfortable when people ask me what I do and I tell them that I go to AA, I ride a bike. I want to say I'm doing something—I'm a student—I'm productive. It'll feel good.

So I'm eager to start something new. Physical therapy is productive work and I've heard it's one of those jobs that's usually short-handed and pretty much in demand. And if working conditions don't suit you, you can get work someplace else. Hospital workers in New York have been one of the most militant sections of the New York League, so my political experience might apply there.

Part of the reason I'm clinging to the sea, too, is political. I'm still active in the union opposition caucus. The rank and file considers us too far left, but they like us and respect us. When you put that many years into building something up like that, you don't like to just shitcan it so quickly.

So I identify as a worker. I've been a producer and I'll probably be a producer again. This is not strictly worker chauvinism; I really believe in it. Even if I was in more middle class type work, I believe I'd still feel a part of the working class that is the vehicle for evolution and change and the very survival of the species.

It's strange the way things work out. Sometimes disasters are what it takes to propel a person forward. That's the kind of crap someone stubborn like me had to go through before I started taking the steps necessary to move toward something better than what I've got.

Astrid   Chicago, Illinois

Children and grandchildren had just left after a big midday meal in Astrid's cheerful little house. In the sunlit living room,

Astrid radiated contentment. Hardly moving at all in her big comfortable chair, she reserved her energy for vigorous communication. A volunteer community organizer for senior citizen issues, she brought enormous self-possession and a buoyant sense of humor to everything she did.

I've always loved being with people. For twenty-two years I had a very busy job as a sales manager and I enjoyed it very much. I'm just not afraid of strange people.

It never occurred to me that I'd retire. I was always so able and able to do so much. But I had diabetes and major surgery for cancer and then about twenty years ago I had four heart attacks. The doctor said no more working and told me I was going to be a cardiac cripple the rest of my life.

"I'd rather be mentally active and die with my boots on than sit around and wait for it to happen."

I was so angry at him for saying that to me that I changed doctors. You can plant a seed and a person will baby herself and become immobilized. I climbed the walls for about a year and it just got to me. I couldn't be inactive, yet I wasn't allowed to work. I'd rather be mentally active and die with my boots on than sit around and wait for it to happen.

Then I heard about an immigrant couple that was being pushed out of their home at the ages of eighty-six and eighty-four because of taxes. It had taken them a lifetime of low paying jobs to pay off this tiny, old cottage and little garden. I thought, "What a travesty of justice that taxes are so high that people are forced out of their homes. Everybody always says somebody ought to do something about it. I'm not going to be one of those people who says, 'Well, let George do it.'" And I took up the battle.

I began talking to civic organizations about a tax rebate system for poverty-level seniors. That was eight years ago and I was fifty-five at the time, but I posed as a senior and said I was sixty-six. The white hair helped a lot. I became active with the Citizens Action Program and we wrote up a bill, went down to Springfield, and got our representatives to back it in the House and Senate.

In big headlines the governor came out with his own tax relief bill for seniors, but it would have helped only half the seniors in Illinois and none on the poverty level, the ones we really needed to help. It wasn't adequate. He and his staff tried to get us to withdraw our bill, but we refused and our bill went through.

That's how I started. I became head of the tax coalition and next we went after the assessor. We exposed the terrible inequities of his office—how the airports, airlines and steel mills were underassessed 65 percent of their value, and how the poor were paying more taxes to make that up. It wasn't what you did or where you lived, it was who you knew that would get you a hardship break. We worked with black groups on the inequities in the South Shore neighborhood, a lovely area where taxes had been raised 100 percent, and got them reassessed. We did an awful lot.

Our photographer shot a poor senior's house and superimposed a tax bill onto the picture, then photographed the alderman's $50,000 home and superimposed his little-bitty tax bill on that. We filled the County Board with seniors. It was really fun. Each person had a picture of a senior's home and of the alderman's home in that area—it was very clever.

In becoming interested in the seniors' problems, I soon realized that many seniors were going without medication, the regular maintenance drugs they needed for diabetes and hypertension, circulation and heart problems. I, myself, spend $116 a month for medication, so I knew that it could run into quite a sum of money. Many seniors were making a three week supply of a diabetic drug last six weeks because they couldn't afford it, and that's like signing your death warrant. A parish priest had told me of a senior who had just gotten so sick of it all trying to make ends meet that he'd swallowed a bottle of Lysol. And the priest had gotten there too late.

I thought, "Oh, what a horrible thing that people have to choose between food and medicine," and I started campaigning for a bill for generic drugs.

The drug industry has so much money. They can spend so much paying lobbyists and buying off representatives that it's really very difficult to get a law like that through. Profit is the name of the game; to hell with healing. The pharmaceuticals spend $5000 on every practicing physician in Illinois to brainwash the doctors into using their drugs. We had former detail men testify that doctors were entitled to a fur coat or a color TV or a Caribbean cruise for writing out so many prescriptions of a medication.

We researched the costs of generic and brand-name drugs and showed preposterous differences in prices. Senator Kennedy heard about it and asked for the results of the survey and I went down to Washington. It took five years of going back and forth to Springfield and testifying before committees. The generic bill had big enemies, but it finally went through this year.

We've done a lot for our seniors. Our city government was sitting on a quarter of a million dollars sent here by the federal and state governments to erect bus shelters. I can understand that it's a temptation to draw interest on a quarter of a million dollars. For two years nothing was done about it and when we found out about it we said, "Wow, we're going to get those bus shelters."

We went down to City Hall on a beautiful, sunny day and demanded to see the mayor. All the TV stations were there and we were outside the mayor's office with umbrellas to illustrate that in bad weather this was the only shelter that a person had in Chicago. So we got our bus shelters. We've got 350 up already.

I know how to pace myself; that's how heart patients last a long time. They know not to overtax themselves. I don't push a broom or a vacuum, I don't hang clothes, I don't lift anything, and I try not to take too many stairs. I take a longer ride in the bus rather than take the El and try to get downtown in a hurry. I know my limits.

Being a volunteer I can call the office and say, "Look, I've got to lay low for a couple of weeks now. I just had a very bad spell." They might ask if I'm up to taping a radio show at home and will arrange for the station that way.

I've got a marvelous husband. He just does everything for me when I'm sick. That man can wash clothes, cook and bake when he wants a cake, and I don't feel up to it. We have a really nice family and we love our children and grandchildren. I have a very satisfactory life.

My husband is retired, too. He can find a million and one things to do around the house and he loves nothing better than puttering around and building things.

When he was working, he wouldn't go bowling or play cards with the fellows; he just wanted to get home and be with me. But I'm not that type of person. I couldn't stand twenty-four hour togetherness. I always tell him if something happens to me he's going to be a very lonesome person. If something happens to him, I have so many people I can lean on and so many interests, that that will help me to keep going.

I think twenty-four hour togetherness kills a marriage. You have to have separate interests so that it's refreshing when you come home. You each have something to talk about then, and it's not so humdrum and monotonous. I just turned sixty-three, but I'm working mainly with people in their twenties and that keeps me young too. I'll never stop being active. The Lord keeps me here because I've got so much work to do, and as long as I'm doing work that betters people's lives I feel He's going to keep me here for a while.

Many years ago a philosopher said that you should live your life so that when you're gone the world will have profited by your having lived. I try to do that.

PART III

PART II

A FUTURE THAT HAS BEGUN

Seventy-three stories about one experience, all very different from one another. But look at them as a whole and patterns emerge. If you trace the forms forward, some of the shape of the future can be seen in outline.

The stories exhibit how the quality of life without work hinges on how a person relates to time and money. The armies of working people who chant the popular litany, "If I didn't have to work, I would spend all my time skiing, sleeping or writing the great American novel" must believe that having hours of unstructured time at their disposal would be a blessing. However, a good number of the people we spoke to who did have the free time so many wage earners desire so felt that having days on end that were not programmed was more like a punishment.

Remember Judy's reaction to time without work:

> The hours weigh on me. I don't have to do anything—to keep things clean or keep myself up. I haven't exercised. It's almost a mental problem at this point. I'm just depressed...
>
> In the morning I'm just crazy when I wake up. I jump out of bed and smoke cigarettes. I know I should relax, have a cup of tea, and listen to the radio, but I can't. I try to sleep until noon, if possible, because then the mornings are out of the way and

> most of the day is gone. If necessary, I sleep in the afternoon. We watch a little bit of television and I have to worry about what to cook for dinner, then we go to bed early...
>
> I've taken note of the fact that I'm unhappy most of the time. Not terribly unhappy. I would say I measure unhappiness in terms of nerve endings at this point, and if I'm calm I consider myself happy. But I don't think that's a way to live. I would like to feel free to go out and exercise in the morning and paint a little in the afternoon, but I don't have that sense of freedom. I feel that I have to be around until I get an idea about my next job application.

Judy's quandary was very sad, but if ability to handle unstructured time is something one learns from experience, it is understandable. Hardly anybody has had much unstructured time. Our society is remarkably routinized, and regardless of whether people work or not, they tend to observe the conventional routines. Significantly, most of the divisions into which our lives are chopped are based largely around work. We go to school from nine to three, work from nine to five, and observe our holidays on Mondays, regardless of the date they commemorate, in order to have a three day week-end. We might feel sleepy at three-thirty in the afternoon, but do not lie down to rest until eleven-thirty at night. If "Happy Hour"— 5:00 to 7:00 p.m.—is any example, there is even an effort, no matter how tongue in cheek, to regulate emotions by the clock. On top of it all is the rigorous schedule television imposes— 7:00 p.m. news, Monday night football, "Let's see them another night—I want to watch the eight o'clock movie," "Please don't call from three to four—my favorite soap opera's on."

In structuring time so completely, this society cultivates a basically negative concept of free time by default, viewing it as time free from work. And work is so consuming and wearing, that most people's so-called "free" time is actually accounted for, assigned to keeping the body fit, the house together, and personal business afloat. Scattered hours left over are jealously kept empty for recuperation.

Inexperienced in structuring open-ended time on their own initiative, many people who are not working approach their situation with the same consciousness working people have, viewing their time as empty hours to be filled up with errands, personal obligations, and "fun." Overwhelming because there is so much of it, the unscheduled time of not working is seen not as something of value, but as a void—negative and unsettling.

Happily, no social conditioning is absolute. There are people who do view time as a precious resource and know how to use it in their own interests, people who can fully appreciate the hours not working puts at their disposal despite the hardships being jobless can bring.

Michael, for instance, really cherished his unstructured time. Although he was going through a personal crisis about not having a work-based identity and was frequently depressed by his situation, he had only positive, enthusiastic things to say about the time he had to call his own.

> I wake up pretty much when I like, I go to sleep when I like, I'm with my wife and my family most of the time. When I want to go out to play poker, I go. If I don't feel like going out on a particular night, I don't...

> Probably what I do most of the time when I'm not depressed is learn things, pretty much anything... Maybe I won't do anything for a week, but when I become interested in something it's nothing for six hours to go by like six minutes. I'm sure that the person who works on a regular basis doesn't get any more work done than I do...

> Gamblers recognize that the life of a person who works from nine to five is better materially than their own in some respects, but I find that most of them have a certain degree of contempt for the average working person, and I share it to a certain extent. The feeling comes mostly from recognizing that the nine to five situation is almost a form of slavery... The contempt has its source, I'm sure, in seeing people give up their freedom and autonomy, in losing their worth.

Others have come to the conclusion that to be free from the demands and routines of working is, in fact, essential to their well-being. A man we called Dennis who had made a decision not to hold a job had these very thoughtful observations.

> What happened to me released a lot of things in my head about the idea of living for a career. It was like a barrel wound up in a ball of yarn: each year in a career you put another strip around yourself. I didn't want to be a mummy.

393

The classic route of a job sets in motion something in your being, a way of responding to everything. It's got to be all superficial or you can't survive on a job. When you're working, it becomes a matter of habit that you always stay on skin surface with yourself; that's also how you start to relate to other people.

When you're doing something for twenty years and you don't know anything else, you get up every day and think, "Oh God, I know what's going to happen today. I'm going to do this and I have to do that."

I don't know if that's all that bad, but it ages you. Not only do you stay on the surface of yourself, but ice forms. The surface starts to freeze and each year decreases the possibility that you'll get back down into yourself. When you get up in the morning, you know the ice is there and that you're going to skate on the surface all day. Without an extreme effort you can't get back into yourself, so you don't even say, "What's going to happen today?"

If you spend twenty years just existing on the surface, which I think happens to men more than to women, and all of a sudden you're fired or have to retire, you're suddenly forced to look at yourself. God, I can imagine how frightening it would be to somebody who has been working in a factory for twenty years. Going back into yourself is like going into a mine—the coal is inside and you have to go inside to get it. By going in we somewhat satisfy ourselves, but we have to bring it out if we want to give to others. If we don't bring it out, we're incomplete.

Various factors contribute to the ability to structure time to suit one's own needs and desires. Privilege certainly can bring an enormous influence to bear. A person with money or a good education is equipped with powerful resources with which to use and enjoy free time. The sense of freedom that often accompanies exploration is enhanced when a person has an economic cushion or marketable skills to fall back on as security. People trapped in the ghetto or the barrio, poor people, workers with limited training and scant encouragement to do anything that might deviate from a conventional nine to five life have far fewer resources and social opportunities at their disposal.

But while such social structural factors do predispose people to respond in certain patterns, we found that personality and outlook were the key determinants of the ways in which people reacted to having free time. The people we met who were at ease and at peace with their free time were of varied backgrounds, ages, and occupational histories. What they shared in common was ripe curiosity, the willingness to test new ideas, and the belief that through their own acts they could influence their own lives.

As one might expect, most of the artists we interviewed were among this group. Painters, writers, musicians, and other creatively expressive people considered free time essential to their art and were frustrated if it was impinged upon, particularly if it had to be for alienated labor. But erstwhile office workers, factory workers, and technicians also knew how to savor their time. These people, who had things they wanted to do or who simply valued living the essence of the moment, did not view their time without work as empty hours. Rather, without external forces programming their lives into tidy segments, they were stimulated to turn their free time into a valuable part of their lives.

If the way in which these people dealt with unstructured time was an expression of personality, this does not imply that any particular person's style is fixed. The human species is very flexible. The freest of people can discipline themselves to accept scheduled lives; people dependent upon routines can break free from their programming.

Michael, for example, eventually did find a job in computer programming. He bluffed his way into a position that not only demanded advanced skills, but entailed supervising a good-sized work staff. With his own very flexible attitude toward time, he was delighted that the company he had joined was committed to the policy of flextime and had visions of arranging an unconventional schedule that would suit his personal style. Ironically, not one member of his staff had the slightest interest in flextime. They all adhered rigidly to a nine to five schedule, and in order to supervise them, he had to also.

Judy accumulated some work experience which helped her feel more secure about her ability to hold a job and be independent. When she found herself out of work again, even though the job market was twice as bad as it had been when she was first unemployed, her perspective had rotated 180 degrees. She left the house daily to work out at a health club, went on short trips out of town, and used her free time to relax and enjoy herself. She restricted her job-hunting to following up only those leads that seemed interesting and suited to her talents. Deciding she would prefer to have a whole summer free, she did not let herself become driven to find the "right" job. Halfway through her unemployment benefits she was still self-assured and confident that she could find something acceptable before her benefits would run out.

Money, money, money was the other part of the quality of life equation. Among most of the people we interviewed, finding a way to make ends meet was a very serious matter. For the group as a whole, unemployment compensation was the single most significant economic prop. It permitted people who had been working some time to make their way in a tight job market a chance to experiment with a new project or a new life direction, or an opportunity just to catch their breath. Most were aware that unemployment compensation is an insurance fund, neither charity nor a public dole. They generally felt entitled to draw all the money available to them for as long as they chose to or needed to, viewing it as they would any other insurance.

Because the middle class in this society has the ability to generate economic surplus, savings or the income from inheritances and investments provided many of the middle class people we spoke to with the means for maintaining a consistent and relatively comfortable lifestyle. It was the people who had to rely solely on publicly administered support who had serious problems in keeping their heads above water. Their income sources were simply not adequate for meeting the necessities of life. Welfare and SSI allocations just cannot be stretched to cover all a household's expenses, let alone allow for any extras. And Social Security is no livelihood. Retired people who could not supplement their monthly check with income from savings, investments, or a pension had to apply to welfare in order to get by.

Having a financial base without any elasticity often means spending more for what you buy. People who could not support a private car and had no money to spare for carfare or taxifare had no access to stores in other neighborhoods that advertised lower prices, so could not comparison-shop. Nor did they have the resources for economizing through buying large quantities or stocking up on sale items. People dependent upon the public support system needed considerable generosity of spirit to avoid the pettiness of mind which the necessity to be continually tallying one's assets tends to engender. The philosophical perspective many expressed was all the more admirable when you take into account the distressing and demeaning experiences they had to endure dealing with the bureaucracies that authorized their funds and services.

There was one critical issue which even the people who had the most casual attitude toward money considered a serious problem: the impossibly high cost of medical care for people who do not have employer-supported group health insurance. The message we heard was striking, consistent, and unequivocal. Over and again, people voiced their firm, clear belief that a national health plan that would cover everyone, both for the costs of ordinary medical care and for those of catastrophic illness or accident, should be a national priority. To avoid repetition, these comments were left out of many of the stories, but we were deeply impressed by the urgency of the concern.

Still, money pressures are no absolute barrier to using time without work productively and enjoyably. We found that people who seemed to be making the most of their experience not working had a transcendent attitude toward money: they were not obsessed by money and did not consider it of prime importance in their lives. Their point of view was rooted in a secure belief that things would fall into place one way or another—that one simply would not starve or go homeless or be obliged to become a different sort of person just because of a few dollars.

By no means were the people who had this attitude all financially secure. A good number who did not know where their next month's rent was coming from displayed not the least worry about money, while some people who were, in a word, rich, had great anxiety when we raised a merely hypothetical discussion about reduced income.

The people who had a transcendent attitude toward money had not buried their heads in the sand refusing to deal with money problems in a realistic way. They were not immune to worry when nothing but the lonely thud of a few copper pennies could be heard in the bottom of the piggy bank. Nor did their outlook doom them to a stark, spartan existence. In fact, many felt that good food well prepared, travel, and living in a comfortable, aesthetically pleasing environment were essential for feeding the spirit and they made it a lifestyle priority to have these things. The prime resource they had available was that they had rejected the prevailing social value of permitting one's life to be determined by economic considerations. The people with a transcendent attitude had a strong sense of who they were, what they believed in, and what they wanted to do, and did not permit money to interfere with their essential principles or goals.

Transcending money as the organizing principle in life can spur a wealth of creativity. A number of the people we met had turned activities they enjoyed doing, such as carpentry, or cooking gourmet meals, into sellable services that helped pay their expenses and left them free to continue doing the other things they wanted to do, such as paint, write, counsel young people, or just live without having to endure the routine of a job.

To succeed in this, sheer enthusiasm and the belief in their ability to conquer mountains were not enough, having regaled a dinner party for four with superb Crispy Fish Hunan Style, would not have been ample preparation for plunging into catering a Chinese dinner for fifty. They had to have enough talent and well-disciplined skill to provide a service that would measure up to professional standards and would not consume undue time.

They also needed the ability to make a good impression on others. Phillip, for example, had boundless interests and skills and a wide circle of friends and acquaintances who appreciated what a stimulating person he was. He could count on there always being people who would be delighted to spend time talking with him. And in the course of an afternoon of people dropping in and out, chances were somebody was going to want one of his meticulous, high-styled haircuts. Otherwise, something else would come along to pay his bills—it always did. People like Phillip, who succeeded in this ad hoc marketing of their talent, were known to be interesting people of character. This gave others a positive reason to seek and pay for their services, where they might have avoided the negative experience of dealing with somebody whose message came across as one of dire desperation.

Obviously, significant and adaptive as a transcendent attitude toward money and the ability to handle unstructured time may be, they are no solutions to mass unemployment. Only profound economic and political changes can solve this country's complex labor problems. Nonetheless, the fact remains that there are people who thrive on not working—people for whom the experience is fruitful and productive, even some for whom it is a watershed in their lives. With the number of people who do not work rising at an accelerated rate due to the governmental and corporate policy of reducing the work-force, the changes introduced by automation, and the trend toward having multiple careers separated by spells of time off, it is more than merely interesting—it is becoming truly essential to understand how people react to having time without work.

Some generalizations about the ways in which people respond to not working can be drawn from the material collected for this book which should contribute to such an understanding. In general, people's outlooks could be grouped into two distinct patterns associated with different styles of reacting to time without work. Those who reacted adaptively and productively to the experience held an affirmative view rooted in a strong independent identity that was not based upon work, and a healthy self-respect that was not dependent on a job for its fueling. That their self-esteem was not derived from work did not mean that they scorned work or rejected it, however; many liked to reminisce glowingly about past work they had done which had been gratifying, while others described work they were hoping to do with enthusiasm. It seemed that these were people who had experienced effectance in their lives—people who believed they could exercise their own capabilities, control their own destiny, and have an impact on the world. Thus, they were able to view the situation they were in as one that had its own integrity and were making the most of it.

The affirmative view was not necessarily fully developed when a person first began having time without work. Sometimes it grew slowly, as it did for John.

> It's taking me a long time to adjust. I had been in a very active management position, and it's very difficult to take a subordinate position. I'm beginning to get the picture that I'm actually moving into a different strata or different level. It's really not important to be Mr. Macho, to be the boss, yet those things were very important to me at one time. At first I had a kind of left-out feeling and it took me a while to realize what my contribution was. My contribution is different from before, but I sincerely believe now that it is a worthwhile contribution and that I shouldn't worry that I am not in some kind of management role.
>
> But I do enjoy working and being productive. Even in my leisure my mind right now is beginning to move back to painting. For some reason I quit and didn't pick up a brush in some two years, but when I was painting there was nothing I enjoyed more. I could paint until three o'clock in the morning; I got a great deal of satisfaction. Now I'm beginning to get the feeling that I'm about ready to start again. I think it's because of all the leisure time that I've got.
>
> I'm not saying that this kind of life is everybody's cup of tea—it isn't. Temporarily I guess it's mine.

In contrast, the people who appeared not to be benefiting from their time without work were noticeably resistant to the experience. What distinguished them most vividly was that their identity was based on work. And deprived of an external source of self-definition from a job, their self-esteem was weak or damaged.

A work-based identity did not necessarily mean that a person liked working, although some people did, especially people who had lost fulfilling, non-alienated work and were suffering from that deprivation. There were many, however, who were seeking to acquire or recapture a self-image they felt could be gained only by fulfilling the demands of the work ethic. Clinging to this belief, they suffered from both guilt and shame, and to make things harder, these responses compounded as time wore on, eroding what self-esteem they did have. As Elena put it, "I have mixed feelings about having such a very, very bad work record and one part of me is ashamed about it. I guess it's that Christian or Puritan work ethic that if you don't work, you're a failure."

Elena was intent on escaping her unhappy condition by earning a college degree, and as she progressed through school her self-esteem grew and the importance of work as the basis for her identity diminished. But for others, work remained central to the very core of their identity. These people found it virtually impossible to loose their creativity and explore the opportunities before them during their time without work.

If we look at the larger picture, the fact that the resistant view is as prevalent as it is means that new information and new resources are essential if we are to meet the demands in store for us individually and collectively. As this society continues to move forward into the post-industrial age at its accelerated pace, the economy will continue to go through major changes with more job displacement and more stress in the offing.

Theoretically, the potential for great progress in the future is prodigious. The new technology, managed wisely and humanely, could free an unprecedented amount of time for challenging pursuits; effective universal education could instill a belief in personal effectance throughout society on a mass level. The opportunities for enhancing freedom and encouraging creativity are greater than the world has ever known.

At the same time, the risk that the technological and cultural mechanisms that could free people might instead be used to subject them to oppression of a new order is serious, indeed. As we have seen, in certain industries the management practices for operating the advanced technological systems that are already in place can be as heartless and exploitative as the cruel practices of a feudal lord. The predominance of programs promoting narrow, self-advancing, self-oriented goals to the virtual abandonment of the principles of liberal education is already a dangerous trend in our educational system. The fear of deprivation—of being without money, without housing or fuel for heat or transportation, without an identity or deprived of self-esteem—has already been stimulated and is being pandered to shamelessly by those interests which stand to gain the most from it. If such fear, the classic mechanism by which exploitative control is emplaced, were to spread on a large social scale, it would make us alarmingly vulnerable to authoritarian control.

To avert being unwittingly coerced into a new post-industrial system every bit as binding as that of the industrial society and to realize the unprecedented opportunities before us will take awareness and conscious effort. The awareness must start with the recognition that those who are not working are the victims of our society's inadequacies, not culprits responsible for its problems. It is the failure of our system that we are undergoing massive unemployment, alienation and hardships in making the transition to post-industrialism, these serious problems can only be corrected by systemic changes.

Building a humanistic and progressive new system will be very difficult if the public does not have readily available to it information about both relevant and outmoded values concerning work and both adaptive and maladaptive reactions to not working. For only with such knowledge will large numbers of people come to believe that individuals can exercise control over their own lives.

One way such information can be acquired is by direct example which instructs and, in some cases, inspires. While there is no shortage of people who do not work to serve as examples, as we know, few of them talk freely about their feelings, and common respect precludes pumping them for information. Truly, we are indebted to the people who so generously shared their experiences and feelings in this book for providing a rare first-hand look at what people go through when they have time without work.

Another spur to understanding is through principles that organize individual facts that are amassed. To that end, the observations set forth in this chapter—that those who made the most of their time without work had an ability to deal with unstructured time and a transcendent attitude toward money, and that an affirmative or a resistant view toward not working, respectively, was associated with success or with great difficulty in using time without work—may be useful. Tested through appropriate research techniques, these observations may provide refined principles that will lend themselves to broad application.

In that regard, then, this book is but a beginning. But if, in addition to the revealing stories it offers readers, this book succeeds in outlining patterns that turn out to be fruitful dimensions when traced forward to the future, it will have served its purpose—twofold.